D1710235

Progressive Inequality

Progressive Inequality

RICH AND POOR IN NEW YORK, 1890–1920

David Huyssen

 Harvard University Press

Cambridge, Massachusetts · London, England
2014

Library of Congress Cataloging-in-Publication Data

Huyssen, David, 1979–
   Progressive inequality : rich and poor in New York, 1890–1920 /
David Huyssen.
        pages cm
   Includes bibliographical references and index.
   ISBN 978-0-674-28140-0 (hardcover : alk. paper)
   1. Rich people—New York (State)—New York—History.
2. Poor—New York (State)—New York—History.   3. Manhattan
(New York, N.Y.)—Economic conditions.   4. Manhattan (New
York, N.Y.)—Social conditions.   5. Income distribution—New
York (State)—New York—History.   6. Social classes—New York
(State)—New York—History.   I. Title.
   HC108.N7H89 2014
   305.509747′109041—dc23   2013030763

For Mary

We were very tired, we were very merry,
We had gone back and forth all night on the ferry.
We hailed, "Good morrow, mother!" to a shawlcovered head,
And bought a morning paper, which neither of us read;
And she wept, "God bless you!" for the apples and the pears,
And we gave her all our money but our subway fares.

—Edna St. Vincent Millay, 1919

Contents

Progressive Inequality

Fault Lines of Rich and Poor

> I think that to the extent that one perceives the drama of a thing
> one perceives the truth of it.
>
> —Louis Adamic

ON CHRISTMAS DAY 1899 poor New Yorkers shuffled into Madison Square Garden by the thousands for an evening feast, their breath made visible in the freezing air. Delights awaited inside, where the Salvation Army had promised roast suckling pig, tart cranberry relish, piping hot coffee, and warm companionship to all, as well as an entertainment program of optical displays and musical performances. Those who glanced up before passing through the cold marble archways would have beheld the statue of the goddess Diana high atop the Garden's tower, a vision of grace in the gloaming. The virgin huntress commanded the best view of Gotham, removed at the skyline's pinnacle from the earthly chaos in its streets, but with bow drawn and arrow nocked for some distant prey that never appeared, she kept her bronze eyes fixed on the horizon. Others, however, with all the ease of gods observing mortals, would watch in Diana's stead as hungry, motley denizens of Mulberry Row, the Tenderloin, Yorkville, and the Lower East Side entered that glistening temple of spectacular pleasure. For one dollar each, "thousands of well-fed and prosperous people, among them many women who had come in carriages and were gorgeously gowned and wore many diamonds" had gathered in the Garden's mezzanine to behold the poor consuming their Christmas meal.[1]

The Salvation Army's Christmas dinner was the largest of several such spectacles in New York that day. Other events included the annual dinner at Lyric Hall where "Frank Tilford, bank president and grocer caused 750 pounds of turkey to be stuffed into less than five hundred newsboys"; a dinner and gift distribution for hundreds at the Bowery Mission, organized by the publisher of the *Christian Herald*, Dr. Louis Klopsch; and an ice cream and cake party for a hundred and fifty waifs of the Avenue B Industrial School, sponsored by the Children's Aid Society and thrown in the Lexington Avenue home of a wealthy New York Society couple, Mr. and Mrs. Lewis Cass Ledyard.[2] Press accounts of these events usually included a chronological retelling of the festivities, a few heartwarming vignettes, the names of organizers and major donors, and some duly rendered effusions of gratitude from the recipients of largesse. In the case of the Salvation Army's dinner, *Leslie's Weekly* even printed a panoramic photograph of the event that depicts a serene, perfectly ordered image of charitable benevolence on an industrial scale. The dazzling spotlight casts a glossy glow over the poor individuals dining respectfully at long, parallel rows of tables on the arena floor. Merging the symmetry of the coming factory assembly line with the warmth (if not the intimacy) of Christ's Bethlehem manger, the image conveys a harmonious scene, heralding a renewal of social justice and brotherhood. Commander of the Salvation Army's American division, Frederick de Latour Booth-Tucker, gave voice to the hopeful vision when he declared, "Neither any Continental city nor even London has ever had to do anything approaching this in magnitude. It means the dawning of a new era, the bridging of the gulf between the rich and the poor."[3]

That gulf, it turned out, would not be so easily bridged. Despite three decades' worth of similarly hopeful, widely varied reformist activism and regulatory innovation, inequality between rich and poor became more, not less acute, all the way up to the stock market crash of 1929.[4] Historians of the United States have long referred to the period from roughly 1890 to 1920 as the Progressive Era. Materially speaking, however—and in important cultural ways as well—that era's conclusion saw inequality *progressing* down the same track it had been traveling at the period's advent.

Inequality, then, was both Progressive by virtue of its period label, and progressive by virtue of its increasing severity. This latter meaning complicates the already troubled notion of the Progressive Era as one of "progress,"

"The Salvation Army Feeding Two Thousand of New York's Poor, at Christmas, in Madison Square Garden," *Leslie's Weekly,* Jan. 6, 1900.

or improvement, from its much-maligned predecessor, the Gilded Age.[5] At the same time that working-class men, women, and people of color waged intense, often successful battles for greater political freedom and state protection from violence and discrimination, their material condition continued to lag ever further behind that of wealthy Americans.

This seems particularly worth interrogating, given that contemporary conditions of inequality in America have elicited prominent calls for a "new Progressive Era."[6] If the old Progressive Era did not actually redress inequality at the beginning of the twentieth century, what is missing from our understanding of its history that makes anyone think a new Progressive Era would do the trick at the start of the twenty-first? If Booth-Tucker's vision failed in 1899, why should our version of it succeed over a century later?

Writing sixteen years before the 1899 Christmas dinner at Madison Square Garden, the Yale College professor William Graham Sumner irritably declared, "It is commonly asserted that there are in the United States no classes, and any allusion to classes is resented. On the other hand, we constantly read and hear discussions of social topics in which the existence of social classes is assumed as a simple fact."[7] This observation reflected an American tendency to confuse political and socioeconomic notions of class, allowing for the otherwise contradictory position that while there were in the United States no class divisions (politically), there were certainly class divisions (socioeconomically).[8] Indeed, the beguiling faiths of individual liberty, republican citizenship, social mobility, equality of opportunity, and meritocracy have formed the foundation of claims to a classless society in America since the Revolution, despite the undeniable economic, social, and political divisions that define most lives in America.[9]

Few places or moments in history have belied the myth of the classless United States as did New York City when Sumner wrote his words. The economic collapse of 1873 had created mass unemployment and driven down wages in the city while encouraging swift corporate consolidation, feeding the growth of enormous personal fortunes in years to come.[10] African-American observers spoke openly of an ever-tightening caste system that was betraying the better angels of Civil War and Reconstruction.[11] Women's activism in both the workplace and public life drew greater attention to gender inequality in the social and political realms.[12] Increasingly visible collectives of militant workers and the poor inspired nightmarish visions of the Paris Commune on U.S. shores, eliciting explicit cries from the wealthy for class-based electoral reform. In 1877, New York's wealthiest citizens persuaded the state legislature, on xenophobic, taxpayer-rights grounds, to approve a constitutional amendment effectively stripping municipal suffrage from anyone with less than $500 in property.[13] The bill failed to fulfill procedural requirements, but its initial passage testified to its widespread and hearty endorsement.[14] Many of Sumner's privileged contemporaries not only recognized class divisions "as a simple fact," but advocated their legal codification as part of a social Darwinist vision for the future.[15]

In most contemporary narratives of the United States, the Progressive Era largely remedied such Gilded Age turmoil, ushering in the prototype of a regulatory state to tame the merciless beast of raw capitalism.[16] Muckraking journalists, municipal reformers, women's suffrage activists, agrarian populists, settlement-house workers, and other citizen-heroes are the protagonists in this story, succeeding through years of struggle in resetting the rigging on the ship of state, righting the course for a more classless, perhaps more democratic horizon.[17] Even histories that question this redemption narrative tend, more often than not, to demonstrate the power of working-class men, women, and people of color either driving reforms or protesting their regressive effects, thereby tightening the Progressive Era's grip on its public reputation as a moment of improvement for U.S. class relations and democracy as a whole.[18]

If the Progressive Era was a time of fundamental transformation for American class relations, then the evidence of change ought to appear most prominently in class encounters—moments that best represent what the immigrant worker and writer, Louis Adamic, called "the drama of things."[19] Indeed, dramatic encounters between rich and poor New Yorkers from 1890 to 1920 reveal telling transformations in the context of American class relations: among them, shifting philosophies of philanthropy and public welfare, changing public attitudes toward trade unionism, and a strengthening of the state's monopoly on legitimate violence.

Yet something else emerges from these encounters in which Columbia sociologists cross-examine tenement tenants, aid applicants confront charity volunteers, philanthropists react to begging letters, seamstresses march with Society ladies, businessmen beat strikers, and unionists sabotage company property. Even as they instigate change, each also reproduces enduring American assumptions that undergird inequality, assumptions about economic "natural law," appropriate social hierarchies, and personal morality. Collectively, they reflect certain sturdy cultural conceptions of class—ideas about what makes the poor poor, and the rich rich—that not only survived the Progressive Era but in many ways became further entrenched. The Progressive Era, in this analysis, did not redeem Gilded Age class divisions. Instead, its attempts to reform and transcend those divisions often underscored their ineluctability.

Histories of class in the Progressive Era have been shaped by an overriding concern with single classes or groups—the workers, the wealthy, the middle class, immigrants, women, and African Americans—and how their experience changed over time.[20] The focus on a particular side of the class (or race, or gender) equation and the historical impetus to explain change over time have produced narratives of bold transformation, often obscuring continuity.[21] If, instead of focusing on the contours of particular classes or groups themselves, we were to bring disparate cross-class encounters into comparative perspective, then the transformations that previously took center stage would give way to profound continuities. The logic that guided a bourgeois charity volunteer to deny a widow's request for aid in 1897 would look quite similar to that guiding a factory owner to hire detectives to beat striking teenage-girl workers in 1909.[22] The vision for America that an architectural genius imposed on a Lower-East-Side street corner in 1893 would resemble the vision that railway executives used to vilify union organizers in 1916.[23] Interweaving these seemingly unconnected stories and delving into the lives of all participants unearths deep continuities in class relations. Patterns begin to take shape, revealing fault lines that steadily extend themselves across an economic, social, and political landscape otherwise characterized by change.

Few epochs in U.S. history provide more compelling evidence of change than does the Progressive Era, a moment that in many ways defined the modern United States and reset the rules of American life.[24] The growing awareness of inequality and its dangers led to reforms that arguably saved capitalism, permanently empowered the bourgeoisie, gave birth to the regulatory state, inspired unprecedented collective movements and government reactions, and more. Yet it is precisely because it was a period of such momentous change that identifying class continuities within it enables us to perceive those continuities' long lineage and powerful durability. If cultural conceptions of class—such as notions of poverty's stemming from immorality or wealth's stemming from individual merit—both preceded and postdated Progressive-Era reconfigurations in American life, a case can be made that they constitute among the most stable elements in the chemistry of U.S. class relations.[25]

New York's relevance to understanding U.S. class relations and inequality during the Progressive Era is clear. The nation's urban population exploded in these years, and Gotham bestrode American life like no other city, financing its economic expansion and pushing the boundaries of its cultural development. Its thousands of poor and working-class residents lived cheek by jowl with more than a quarter of the country's millionaires in 1892, almost certainly producing the highest concentration and greatest variety of daily class encounters in the nation.[26]

New York at the end of the nineteenth century had already begun to replace the frontier as the apotheosis of the classless myth in America—a haven of opportunity and self-fashioning for poor immigrants or rural migrants—while paradoxically providing sanctuary for a burgeoning, wealthy elite. Its streets became the stage for all the acrimony, conflict, and occasional flashes of understanding between this elite and working people. In many ways, New York was, and remains, the urban paragon of American class relations. It may not be perfectly representative, but certainly no other city could hope to be more so.

Class and its contours are revealed most dynamically in moments and arenas of contact across class lines. Such class encounters also most profoundly inform what class means on a daily basis for individuals. In other words, people tend to experience class—or project it—most intensely when confronted with people who are different from themselves.[27]

Class is not a static, bounded condition describing a discrete relationship to the means of production, or a tightly defined political consciousness. Rather, it is what E. P. Thompson called "an historical phenomenon, unifying a number of disparate and seemingly unconnected events, both in the raw material of experience and in consciousness. . . . I do not see class as a 'structure', nor even as a 'category', but as something which in fact happens (and can be shown to have happened) in human relationships."[28] Accepting this understanding of class as something that "happens . . . in human relationships" impels a focus on those happenings—in this case, a number of dramatic encounters in one city over three decades—to locate those elements of class experience that survive or thrive over time.

"Class relations," then, becomes nothing more nor less than the contingent historical circumstances in which the rich engage with the poor, and the poor with the rich.[29] For the purposes of this argument, the rich or bourgeois are those men and women who do not perform manual labor for wages, and who enjoy income sufficiently exceeding subsistence levels to enable savings; that is, they are "capital-enhanced." The working class or poor are those whose income and employment fluctuate with seasonal or cyclical shifts in business, and whose resources rarely or barely provide more than the cost of living; that is, they are "labor-dependent."[30]

Rich, poor, and their various synonyms are not meant to convey a fixed or categorical truth here. Instead, they serve as expansive descriptors denoting the various congeries of economic, social, cultural, and political experience—and power—that individuals bring to particular encounters. They are words that encompass many who might elsewhere be called "middle class," a term practically designed—and extensively self-applied in the United States—to absolve people of their complicity or victimhood in the power relations of capitalism.[31] As Thompson pointed out, "The finest-meshed sociological net cannot give us a pure specimen of class, any more than it can give us one of deference or of love. The relationship must always be embodied in real people and in a real context."[32] Unless the understanding of class mirrors the endless malleability of "real people . . . in a real context," history will continue to make of that understanding a lens that obscures more than it reveals.

Malleability, however, does not decree shapelessness. Though the players may shift shape and assume new qualities, the stage has enduring, observable structures. American class relations since at least the mid-nineteenth century overwhelmingly fall within three broad fault lines of interaction:

prescription, cooperation, and conflict. These fault lines offer a comprehensive prism for approaching U.S. class relations—not in those relations' material or philosophical origins, but in their daily operations.

Prescriptive class relations occur when bourgeois individuals or groups attempt to prescribe or choreograph the behavior of the poor and working class with a minimum of violence, for instance, through certain legislation, work rules, poor-relief strictures, environmentalist reform of urban space, or targeted educational initiatives.[33] In specific instances, such prescriptive measures bear the marks of their historical contexts. Richard Watson Gilder's Tenement House Committee of 1894 and the building of Stanford White's Bowery Savings Bank demonstrate how the ideology and aesthetics of a new imperial progressivism inspired prescriptive class interaction to transform urban space in New York. Josephine Shaw Lowell's Charity Organization Society of New York (C.O.S.) and the 1899 Salvation Army Christmas dinner demonstrate how two charities, ostensibly divided by science and evangelicalism, both pinned the quest for class harmony on medieval Catholic philosophies of distinction between worthy and unworthy poor, while simultaneously molding themselves to the capitalist practices of marketing and publicity.

A more cooperative spirit of engagement also emerges, with capital-enhanced individuals occasionally listening to or allying themselves with labor-dependent citizens (or noncitizens) on collaborative terms. Sites of cooperative class relations at this time include certain settlements, cross-class participation in labor or community organizing initiatives, and religious, ethnic, gender, or racial solidarity groups. Begging letters, the philanthropy of Jacob Schiff, and Lillian Wald's Henry Street Settlement offer one type of contact undertaken in this more cooperative spirit in New York. The cross-class women's activism in garment industry labor fights offers another. The reforms enacted as a result of such cooperative activity were real, including those in housing, education, child labor, and public health.[34] Yet in all these endeavors, certain endemic realities—the lack of public funds, widespread anti-Semitism, competing notions of womanhood, or persistently unequal power relationships, for instance—hampered the cooperative spirit's potential.

Conflict and mutual antagonism roil the rich and poor as well, periodically exploding in violent confrontations.[35] These conflictual relations arose

most visibly in the Progressive Era through pitched labor battles, revolutionary political dissidence, mob violence, and the intervention of police or
militia forces to protect property against popular collectives. The Triangle
shirtwaist factory is a site synonymous with Progressive Era reform, yet the
abuses its owners perpetrated before the infamous fire also point to a pervasive culture of legitimized violence, both private and public, against the
poor and working class in America. As the New York transit strikes of 1916
demonstrate, worker violence against property disproportionately reflected
basic class conflicts and emerging corporate practices that survived the Progressive Era.

These three fault lines—prescription, cooperation, and conflict—expose
the classless myth by recognizing how material inequality determines different motivations and distinct levels of power in almost any class encounter. They avoid, however, the schematic and politically encumbered language of universal class war. In doing so, they make possible a more nuanced
conversation about class and inequality in the United States. These fault
lines are not absolute, but they do offer a comprehensive, critical framework
for exploring and discussing American class relations in a way that actually
reflects the lives of real people.

In the stories that follow, privileged and impoverished New Yorkers collide
with terrible momentum. Progressive-Era men and women threw themselves into the spaces of their social opposites with force and determination,
intending to remake the terms of class division and inequality in a radically
changing—and they hoped, improving—world. Their collisions produced
momentous changes for the century to come, yet they fell short of the desired transformation. On both sides of the "gulf between the rich and the
poor," even as they changed their world, these men and women tragically
reflected and reproduced earlier fault lines of class that had riven the nation
and would continue to do so for decades to come.

I

Invading the Tenements

> . . . dull grey smoke, faintly luminous in the night, writhed
> out from the tops of the second story windows, and from the
> basement there glared a deep and terrible hue of red, the color
> of satanic wrath, the color of murder.
>
> —Stephen Crane, "The Fire"

JUST BEFORE DAWN on May 31, 1894, Solomon Kleinrock's liquor store at
129 Suffolk Street exploded. The flames flew down the tenement hallways in
a deadly rush, climbing stairwells and dumbwaiters, writhing under doors
and licking at lintels. The blast had reverberated through the rickety old
house, startling Peter Rutz from sleep in his third-floor rear-apartment bed.
Rutz went to his door to find the source of the commotion. "The minute I
opened the door," he later recounted, "I was blinded with smoke and dirt
and blaze. I was chucked right clean back on the floor, and my wife commenced to holler, and the children came running out of the bed room."[1]
Rutz slammed the door shut, but the apartment was already filling with
smoke as the fire gathered strength. "I saw the flames bursting through the
floors," Rutz said. "I got them right in my face."[2] Rutz and his wife rushed
to save their sons, struggling past obstructions on the fire escape as they
frantically pushed the children out of the doomed tenement.[3]

Finally, Rutz turned back for his four-year-old niece, Lizzie Jaeger, still
in a side bedroom. "When I went to go in for her," he explained, "why the
flame was away over my head, already; couldn't get in any more."[4] Helpless

against the heat and choking on smoke, Rutz was forced to flee without the girl. The next time he saw his niece, "I saw her on the sidewalk, right after the firemen got her out; she was lying on a pillow; she was just like all swollen up. I looked at her; saw her face."[5] The firemen had been battling another blaze in Broome Street when the Suffolk Street alarm went out, fatally lengthening their response, and by the time they discovered Lizzie in Rutz's rooms, the girl was horribly burned. She died at Gouverneur Hospital shortly thereafter.[6] When her father, Charles Jaeger, came to see her body in the hospital the next day, he recalled, "I hardly knowed her."[7]

It is unlikely that Richard Watson Gilder—poet, club man, and editor of arguably the most influential English-language literary magazine of the day, the *Century*—would have taken notice of Lizzie's death under ordinary circumstances. Her demise by fire, after all, was only one among dozens that occurred each year in New York's tenements.[8] These fire victims were almost always from poor immigrant families, neither readers of nor contributors to the *Century*. Many lived not far physically from the editor's house just off Washington Square Park, but "The Studio," as Gilder's friends in New York's fashionable circles called his Clinton Place home, might as well have been in another galaxy for all it had in common with the tenements. Gilder's professional interests lay in expanding and championing American literature and in forging a distinctive national identity in the arts. Tenement reform was not an obvious priority for him.[9]

Only by seeming accident of fate did the worlds of the poor, doomed child and the successful, refined litterateur collide. A few weeks earlier, the New York state and city governments had initiated a program to reform the tenements, and Governor Roswell P. Flower had appointed Gilder to the Tenement House Committee of 1894. The Committee met on May 12, and appointed Gilder its chairman.[10] The group's mandate identified its first duty as making "a careful examination into the tenement-houses of the city of New York; their condition as to the construction, healthfulness, safety, rentals and the effect of tenement-house life on the health, education, savings and morals of those who live in such habitations."[11]

Gilder was a devout Christian, an obsessive worker, and a civil service reform advocate who abhorred corruption of any kind. He would not be derelict in his duties to the tenements. In the first of what would be several such investigations, he rushed to the scene of Lizzie's death as soon as he heard of the fire, anxious to play his role in bettering the lives of less eminent New Yorkers. The visit launched a cross-class reform project that would consume him for over a year and have him wading "heart-deep in misery all summer long."[12]

The same year Gilder waded in misery, his good friend Stanford White was overseeing a signature construction project in the same neighborhood. White, an interior designer, architect, and New York Society bon vivant, had recently enjoyed a triumph at the Chicago World's Fair of 1893. The Agricultural Building designed by his firm, McKim, Mead & White, had received prime placement in the Fair's "Court of Honor."[13] The building's neoclassical grandeur, sparkling white façade, and gorgeously sculpted pediments provided a consummate aesthetic symbol of America's industrial prowess and imperial ambition. As an article in *Scientific American* magazine gushed, "The glory of the Exposition is the Court of Honor, and the glory of the Court of Honor is the Agricultural Building."[14] The fairgrounds' layout reflected the reigning spirit of a powerful, expanding United States at the center of the world, surrounded by exhibits depicting exoticized visions of foreign cultures, all prostrate before America.[15]

It is no wonder that when the Bowery Savings Bank commissioned McKim, Mead & White that same year to design a structure stretching from Elizabeth Street to the Bowery across Grand Street, White's creative impulses returned to the themes of the Agricultural Building. It was the perfect vision to construct in more permanent form on the Lower East Side of New York: an emblem of American promise at the epicenter of poor, unassimilated foreigners, the literal crossroads of the Irish, Italian, German, and Russian immigrant communities.[16] Within limits determined by the constrained setting on the Bowery, White's design for the bank's exterior—particularly its Bowery and Grand Street façades—mirrored the Agricultural Building. He used many of the same artists, friends, and aesthetic collaborators for the stonework. Construction lasted from 1893 to 1895, and the result endures as a historic landmark today. That its marble magnificence sprang up surrounded by slums, in the midst of the worst economic calamity the United States had ever known, has been almost entirely forgotten.

Superficially, Lizzie Jaeger's death and the work of Gilder's Tenement House Committee bear no obvious relation to the building of White's Bowery

Savings Bank beyond a shared geography on New York's Lower East Side and a chronological coincidence in the 1890s. The Committee's work (and, to all appearances, Lizzie's death) grew out of an increasingly urgent crisis in tenement conditions, whose sensational exposure a few years earlier in Jacob Riis's *How the Other Half Lives* had helped stimulate a public, political response. Gilder's work would be handled through committee meetings, hearings with published minutes, consultation with every relevant municipal department, and exhaustive forays into the neighborhoods themselves by a team of investigators. The bank building, meanwhile, was a private business venture. The bank's trustees, designer, and developer, all of whom moved in a world of club lunches and European vacations, had largely unfettered control over a giant chunk of one city block.

Despite these differences, both Gilder's and White's projects illustrate a particular type of prescriptive class encounter endemic to the Progressive Era, in which private notions of taste and civilization entwined with public-spirited reformism, bringing the wealthy to the poor's doorstep with a spirit we might call imperial progressivism.[17] They were imperial in the same way that U.S. foreign policy was imperial in those years: affluent white Americans and their agents, armed with executive authority provided or endorsed by the state, inserted themselves into the spaces and lives of overwhelmingly poor and foreign-born populations. Once there, they asserted allegedly superior knowledge of politics, economics, science, and aesthetics to justify remolding those spaces and lives, maintaining or extending political and economic power over them.[18] In the case of White's bank design, those aesthetics were themselves imperial, derived explicitly from the idiom of the Roman Empire. The projects were also Progressive because the methods and motives fueling both were distinctive to the era. Employing empiricist investigation and environmentalist behavioral theory, Gilder and White pursued programs consisting variously of mugwump anticorruption, class reconciliation, and civic, social efficiency. The men leading each project believed not only in the justice of the power they wielded, but in the vision of a better, more harmonious city, a vision they aimed to realize.[19]

Both endeavors harnessed the privileges of wealth and power to reshape urban space, intending to improve the lives of poor New Yorkers such as Lizzie Jaeger. The Committee did so more directly, through investigation and analysis of tenement life by well-off, credentialed researchers aiming to produce an irrefutable, scientific argument to legislate tenements more strictly. The wealthy New Yorkers on the Committee and their state sponsors hoped to improve both the actual living quarters and "morals" of the poor.[20] The Bowery Savings Bank's approach was seemingly less invasive but even more abrupt, mobilizing resources and artistic talent possessed by the rich to transform the streetscape of a poor neighborhood. The bank's new home would be as stunning as one of the countless palaces for plutocrats being raised on the Upper East Side, but its doors would be open to the poorest of the city in their own world, on the Bowery. It intended to teach them the value of thrift and hard work in part by sheer physical symbolism, a marble and limestone allegory planted in their midst. It would also enable the expansion of mutual savings services to local depositors—services that the bank's founders in 1834 had already promoted as helping to assimilate immigrants to the American economic order.[21]

In their prescriptive intentions, both enterprises evoked America's imperial aspirations at the turn of the century. A renewed drive to create Thomas Jefferson's imagined "Empire of Liberty" had burst from the wreckage of the Civil War, spurring incursions of expropriation and occupation overseas throughout the Progressive Era—Hawaii in 1893, Cuba and the Philippines in 1898, Nicaragua in 1909, and Haiti in 1915.[22] Such foreign ventures aimed at opening new markets, directing economic policy, and promoting propertied American interests abroad, but they found public justification in potent domestic ideologies championing the economic, political, and racial superiority of "Anglo-Saxon civilization."[23]

These ideologies found various avenues for domestic expression: a movement to remake American cityscapes in the imperial aesthetic of ancient Rome; the fascination for evolutionary logic in emerging academic fields of social science that underwrote social Darwinism; and a post-Reconstruction revival of white supremacy in both South and North.[24] Such trends ensured that the corrective logic of spreading capitalism and civilization to benighted foreigners—logic that provided powerful rationalizations for conquest, occupation, and financial reorganization by U.S. elites abroad—would serve equally well in projects turning inward, toward spaces and persons of largely immigrant and nonwhite (or differently white) working poor within America's borders.[25]

To be clear, both the Tenement House Committee and the Bowery Savings Bank addressed serious problems on the Lower East Side. The squalor of New York tenements constituted an ongoing threat to public health in the 1890s, and working men and women absolutely needed a safe repository for their savings.[26] Neither project's participants were social-control fanatics, nor were they self-conscious domestic imperialists bent on exploiting the nonwhite working class. They understood themselves to be progressive men seeking solutions to the visible challenges of urban life, using the intellectual and material tools at their disposal.[27]

Yet the imperial flavor of these two projects, in approach and aesthetic, conveys an important aspect not only of Progressive Era class relations but also of the relationship between the progressivism and imperialism of the time. Among white Progressives in the 1890s, impulses toward social improvement through meticulous accumulation of data, scientific analysis, and reasoned regulation almost always existed in uneasy tension with racialized assumptions of civilizational superiority.[28] Such assumptions underwrote robust, often unilateral exercises of power not only overseas but on the domestic scene as well, exercises of power that seem to defy the ostensibly deliberate empirical methods synonymous with Progressive Era ideals. Imperial assumptions and Progressive Era ideals, however, could be made not only to coexist but to function in almost perfect symbiosis.[29]

Well-meaning, privileged New Yorkers such as Gilder and White saw themselves as avatars of a new American identity—progressive, efficient, optimistic, and grand—whose benefit they intended to bequeath to the poor. Both men pursued their projects with a prescriptive attitude toward the beneficiaries, a droit du seigneur reflective of the privileges they enjoyed as cultural leaders in a budding imperial power. Their pursuit of improvement on the Bowery had lasting effects on the class relations and urban space of New York, and ultimately of the nation. Whether they intended to achieve the effects they did—class alienation and physical dislocation of the poor, among others—is another question.[30]

Through Gilder and White, it becomes possible to see that the imperialist American vision of the Progressive moment was not simply an approach to foreign policy, not just a set of practices undertaken in the Caribbean, the Pacific, and Central America. It constituted an attitude and a set of structures for dealing with other people in any context, including U.S. class relations. Likewise, the Progressive movement's efforts at reforming domestic problems such as political corruption or urban blight did not function disconnected from an understanding of America's position in the world. American Progressivism and imperialism were deeply intertwined and informed much of the prescriptive class interaction during the period.

As for Lizzie Jaeger, the investigation into her death offers a haunting rebuke to Gilder and White's assumptions by exposing an uncomfortable truth: the goal of assimilating poor foreign communities to the structures and expectations of American "civilization" could backfire just as tragically at home as it usually did abroad. But that rebuke would not come until after Gilder and White had left their mark on Lizzie's neighborhood.

"When I was twelve years old and we were living in Flushing father took me to see the Mission at Five Points in New York," reminisced Gilder in 1901. "A door was opened and I saw in the half-darkness a huddle of human creatures. A woman with a blackened eye came to the door and begged the missionary to save her. She said, 'They are trying to kill me here.' We climbed down into a dreadful sub-cellar, and I saw a man apparently dying on a litter of straw. This was in 1856. There are no such slums in New York now."[31]

Gilder's recollection of the door opening for him onto the antebellum New York slums stands out in his memories of a childhood otherwise characterized by relative privilege, protection, and comfort. He was born in Bordentown, New Jersey, at Belle Vue, a sprawling colonial farmhouse his parents had inherited from his maternal grandfather.[32] His ancestors had been landowners and successful professionals: military doctors, measurers (a type of urban surveyor or assessor), and prosperous farmers in the northeastern states, descended themselves from British West Indian slave owners and French Huguenots. On the Gilder side, his grandfather's uncle had served with George Washington throughout the Revolution, and his maternal grandfather had been a major in the War of 1812.[33]

Gilder's father, William Henry Gilder, followed a peripatetic professional path. From a Methodist Episcopal ministry in Bordentown, William took on the directorship of Flushing Female College in Long Island (where Gilder attended school as the only boy), before moving on to ministries in Redding and Fair Haven, New Jersey, before the Civil War. Constant uprooting taught Gilder from a young age both how to make friends in new places and to develop a rich imaginative life. Many years later he recalled Fair Haven fondly, where he was given to "climbing into the unfloored loft of the parsonage, and there, away from the sight and sense of the busy world, writing yards and yards of extremely juvenile verse in the style of the 'Lady of the Lake.'"[34]

The Civil War left an indelible mark on Gilder's generation that young Richard did not escape. In 1864, his father died of smallpox in Brandy Station, Virginia, while ministering to the Fortieth Regiment of the Army of the Potomac, leaving Gilder responsible for his family's financial well-being and removing any possibility of a college education, a deprivation he deeply regretted.[35] Only a few years after hiding away in a parsonage loft to write "juvenile verse," Gilder struggled to earn money in several different, consecutive occupations: clerk and paymaster for a New Jersey railroad; freelance poetry editor and legislative reporter; and cofounder of the short-lived and unprofitable *Newark Morning Register.* He seemed bound for a life of ink-stained obscurity.

Then his luck turned. While editing the *Register,* Gilder took a second job editing *Hours at Home,* a monthly magazine published by Charles Scribner and Sons that became—as did Gilder—part of *Scribner's Monthly,* the predecessor to the *Century.* During these years, he also met and married Helena de Kay, an artist and daughter of an old Knickerbocker family, in whom he found both a kindred spirit and intellectual equal.[36]

With a revived career and marriage into a prominent New York family, Gilder had righted himself onto an enviable path, but misfortune touched him once more in 1877. His first daughter, Marion, whom he later described as "the most perfect and delightful being," died less than a year after being born.[37] He struggled with depression in the aftermath of her death, frustrated in his attempts to express the joy he and his wife had felt with their daughter, longing for the ability, somehow, to recapture it. "How barren every record like this is," he fumed. "There is no idea given here of the life we had some little time before Marion died. . . . We had an exquisite delight in her, a sort of passion for her." But that brief moment had vanished. A photograph of Gilder from this period conveys a hint of the trauma he suffered. He is standing slightly askew, knees buckled, steadying himself with his right hand gripping a chair back, and the left loosely in a trouser

Richard Watson Gilder. From Rosamond Gilder, ed., *Letters of Richard Watson Gilder* (Boston: Houghton Mifflin Company, 1916).

pocket. Dark shadows over his downcast eyes and a drooping mustache complete the picture of a young man made prematurely old by difficult years. Writing to a friend in the days after Marion's death, Gilder already recognized that he had crossed a Rubicon, entering a different realm of life entirely: "Certainly I did not know that the breaking off of so young a life could bring, as it were, a death to the living; or, what is the same thing, a birth into an utterly different state of existence."[38]

Over the next seventeen years, Gilder's approach to his work and life suggests what he may have meant by "an utterly different state of existence." He became embroiled in various efforts at reform and civic action, from pushing for international copyright law, to civil service reform—which, he wrote to a friend, "amounts almost to a revolution"—to presidential politics.[39] In his editorial work at the *Century,* he encouraged an ideal of postbellum sectional reconciliation, most notably by publishing the "War Series," accounts of the Civil War told by Confederate and Union veterans.[40] He joined or founded clubs that aimed at improving (and consolidating their members' positions in) American arts, including the Author's Club, the Society of American Artists, and the deeply influential Municipal Art Society.[41] In 1894, his years of activism in pursuit of progress on various fronts, local and national, brought him into tenement reform.

As a child and young man, Gilder had been an ingenuous dreamer, more suited to the Romantic age of the Transcendentalists than the Progressive Era of reformers. A dim reflection of this earlier self emerges in his recollection of the 1856 visit to the Five Points Mission—his phrases offer simple, vivid portraits of suffering men and women as seen through the eyes of a deeply empathetic child. As he grew older and in the wake of his daughter's death, his dreams shifted into the practical idealism of a reformer.[42] In the Tenement House Committee work, his attention fell less on suffering people than on the slums themselves, on a poisonous social condition requiring vigorous investigation and long-term political remedies. From a dreamer's youth had emerged a consummate Progressive, and a powerful, commanding figure in the cultural and political life of both the city and the nation.[43]

Only hours after crossing the smoldering threshold of 129 Suffolk Street to inspect the scene of Lizzie Jaeger's death, Gilder wrote to Edward Marshall, the Committee Secretary, enumerating three points of further inquiry: first, the "Origin of the fire (to determine whether the business conducted in the place of its origin was hazardous etc.)"; second, the tenement's "Construction, as to safety"; and finally, the "Number of occupants in each apartment." He described "going through the burnt building" in a letter to another Committee member, Roger Foster, two days later. "The origin of the fire is obscure,—with the suspicion of foul play," he wrote.[44] Gilder's sober, dispassionate approach to tenement reform reflected the scope of the Committee's mandate from the state. The primary goal was data collection on the houses, through which aspects of human behavior would be discovered and addressed. Phrases of Gilder's letter to Marshall describing his intentions for the investigation reflect this limitation, and actually repeat the state mandate—almost verbatim—from the act of legislature. He took his instructions seriously.[45]

Those instructions also reflected a long history of New York tenement house legislation in which the stated focus had always been on the buildings, not the inhabitants. After a decade of reports cataloguing physical inadequacies of tenements, the state had finally begun to legislate construction standards in the city in 1866. It took another year to pass a comprehensive housing law, the Tenement House Law of 1867, which defined tenements as a separate class of domicile for the first time.[46] The 1867 bill imposed basic standards for tenement houses, such as mandatory fire escapes. Yet another bill, the Tenement House Law of 1879, encouraged less congested streets by decreeing that new tenement construction could cover at most 65 percent of a 25 × 100-foot lot, as opposed to the pervasive 90 percent. The Tenement House Law of 1884, the most ambitious yet, required a host of physical improvements, including water supplies on every floor, direct light for all inner hallways and rooms, and electric street lights in the tenement districts. These successive legislative efforts shared two primary characteristics: the utter impossibility of enforcement through the regulatory structures tasked with their application, and an overwhelming focus on controlling physical space.[47]

Between Gilder's practical Progressivism, the state's mandate, and the historical context of tenement-house legislation in New York, the focus on physical, environmental data collection may have been overdetermined. Know space to control it, control space to control behavior: as the guiding principle of the investigations, this hardly differed from the city's previous tenement reform initiatives. What Gilder brought to the task was an exploratory zeal and a demand for data suggestive of both the particular spirit infusing American foreign policy and the Progressive obsession with the trappings of science. Through a months-long campaign to amass data on an unprecedented scale, his Committee would, for all intents and purposes, invade the tenements.[48]

Yet the interactions between investigators and tenement residents necessary to accumulate the desired quantity of evidence presented a set of problems—of personnel, time restrictions, and perspective—whose existence and potential to undermine the project's larger goal of improved social health seems to have escaped the Committee's notice. These problems leap from the Committee's final report, whose 649 pages of tightly fitted print and extensive collection of foldout, sometimes color-coded maps and diagrams offer an almost perfect expression of imperial progressivism. The report simultaneously betrays its well-heeled, native-born authors' assumption of the right to reorder tenement residents' lives, while also communicating a practically religious faith in the power of science and data analysis to resolve the problems of poverty.[49]

The Committee, and Gilder as its chairman, pursued many different avenues to accumulate material for the report, of which direct investigation of tenements was the most obvious. A challenge arose immediately, however, in finding qualified investigators. Because the state had imposed no criteria, Gilder tasked the Committee Secretary, Edward Marshall, with assembling a team as he saw fit. Marshall was a journalistic prodigy, the twenty-three-year-old editor of the Sunday *New York Press* who had made his name with exposés of tenement-house conditions.[50] Appointing investigators for a politically charged state committee was guaranteed to attract endless publicity. It was an enormous personal opportunity, but a perilous one as well.

Perhaps as a result, Marshall's selection of investigators reflected political caution. He based his choices on political sympathies (his own and those of the other Committee members) and expert credentials rather than on familiarity with the neighborhood or preexisting local relationships. As his description of the Committee's "Rank and File of the Workers" in his "Secretary's Report" explains, "There did not exist in New York . . . any large number of men having expert knowledge of such work, so it became my duty to select men of high intelligence to be trained in the task." Choices based on "high intelligence" not only overpopulated his team with the American-born and college educated, but also seemed to result in organizational connections or affiliations liable to produce a degree of distrust among the poor.[51] Specifically, he staffed the effort primarily with "the best of those who had been employed by the Church Temperance Society" (C.T.S.) and with "college men . . . willing to work through the summer vacation."[52] As an anti-liquor, anti-Tammany body, the C.T.S. would have appealed to the politics of Marshall's fellow Committee members, and the collegians to their Progressive desire for expertise.[53]

The C.T.S. missionaries' experience moving around the Lower East Side and the expertise of the college men, however, did not outweigh the fact that previous C.T.S. efforts to shutter saloons and beer gardens had antagonized tenement residents, and that few college men had prior contact with the poor and working class. Despite Marshall's insistence that "The selection was made most carefully and no similar work was ever executed with a higher average of intelligence," it was a selection based on political alignment and credentials from establishment institutions, with only superficial consideration of particular fitness for the task at hand. His choices, "progressive" in intent, had an imperial effect: they produced an investigative team marked by class and ethnicity that entered the Lower East Side as an invading force in a resistant space.[54]

If the selection of personnel reflected patronage and Progressive credential worship, the data-collection and confirmation processes were a model of both imperial execution and Progressive efficiency. Marshall documented that during the first phase, from June 3 to August 10, tenement investigators had to "report separately on the condition of . . . 15,726 families," in 2,425 houses, answering for the following information:

Date of visit.
Street and Number.
Number and size of rooms in this apartment.
Cleanliness of this apartment.
Location and amount of water supply.
Is there a bathroom in this apartment?
Number of families in this apartment.

Number of persons not boarders in this apartment.
Number of boarders age and sex.
Total number of persons over 16, male and (separate question) female.
Total number of persons under 16, male and (separate question) female.
Original nationality.
Weekly income per family.
Rent of this apartment.
Sanitary defects of this apartment.
Defects of lighting and ventilation.

Marshall insisted that "the greatest care was taken to insure accuracy," and that as a control measure "reinspection of houses selected at hap-hazard was constantly carried on."[55] Gilder was determined to make a scientific argument to the legislature, and in order to bolster that argument's validity, he had to demand strict precision of the investigators.

Yet the nature of the information Gilder charged the investigators with gathering—and the rush to gather it—aggravated the disadvantages of Marshall's personnel choices by encouraging abrupt encounters. Edward King, a tenement resident who gave testimony to the Committee several months later on related matters, alluded to the prevailing resentment toward inspectors within the tenements after Gilder had pressed him on a particular point. "Well, I tell you," averred King, "I don't put my nose into my neighbor's room in the manner in which the official inspectors do; I believe there is a delicacy even among the poor, and I simply know that there is going out and in certain rooms." Inspectors, King implied, had no feeling for such delicacy in their march through the tenements.[56]

It is not unreasonable to imagine that, even in the most leisurely circumstances, members of a working-class family might bristle at a well-dressed stranger's (or group of strangers') knocking on their door, declaring a need to investigate their private space, remarking on their "cleanliness," poking around to discover "defects," and asking a series of questions relating to age, nationality, and personal finances. King's indignation becomes all the more understandable when one considers that the inspection process did not proceed at a leisurely pace. Several inspectors claimed to have surveyed hundreds of houses, each house containing multiple family apartments, over a period of just a few months. One particularly industrious inspector estimated that he had been through "1,500 at least," a rate that would have been unlikely to encourage respecting "delicacy . . . among the poor."[57]

The report confirms King's implication of unpleasant undertones in these interactions, suggesting a combination of class condescension on the part of the inspectors and report authors for their subjects in the tenements, and distrust of the inspectors on the part of the residents. For example, Marshall reasoned that increased inspections were the only possible remedy for fire-escape obstructions because the tenants themselves "can not understand and *can not be made to understand* that they thus endanger their own lives and those of others."[58] Compounding these limits of understanding, he alleged, the tenants lied regularly: "Early in the work the inspectors informed me that they had little confidence" in the income statistics they gathered from tenement dwellers. "I am convinced," Marshall continues, "that inmates of tenement-houses are opposed to telling the amount of their income at all and, if pressed, will lie about it in nine cases out of ten."[59] He also suggests that proper hallway lighting would counteract tenants' tendencies toward "slovenliness" and "vile impulse[s]" in the dark, as inspectors had informed him that "tenants throw refuse of improper character— such as bedroom water and human excreta—into the sinks . . . more frequently than into sinks in well-lighted hallways."[60]

Marshall's generalizations about the tenants and his allusions to their irremediable ignorance, deceitfulness, and perverse habits lack consideration of possible mitigating factors (unavoidable overcrowding, fear of extortion, irregular pay, inadequate or nonexistent plumbing, etc.), but they seem restrained in comparison with the direct testimony of some of the investigators, reprinted in the report. Several of the Columbia University men engaged to explore educational opportunities for tenement-dwelling children generalized freely: "The Italians, as a rule," began one account, "I found to be dirty and regardless of sanitary laws." Another's assessment of the Italians contradicted the first, though in equally general terms: "They were much readier to give information and less suspicious than either the Germans or Irish who were in the district. They seem to be a much better class of people than the Canadians found in manufacturing places in Maine." Writing again about Italian Lower East Siders, one investigator observed, "Their personal appearance and also that of their children is slovenly. They are good-natured

and happy and do not seem to be deceitful. They are very curious, however, and easily excited."[61]

These characterizations, with their essentialization of ethnic and national
groups, not only invoked common tropes of condescension about native
populations abroad and racist stereotypes at home (inadequate hygiene,
childlike playfulness or curiosity, suggestions of sexual promiscuity in
phrases such as "easily excited" conveying the impossibility of such populations' self-government), they also demonstrated a broader tendency among
elites to assert power reflexively through declarations of knowledge. Committee investigators described poor immigrant New Yorkers in frankly
subjective terms, but that subjectivity appears within a web of meticulously
accumulated data, seemingly granting their opinions—of Lower East Siders as dirty children with no control over their emotions—the heft and
verity of science. The investigators' authority in this instance enjoyed the
further credibility of Columbia University's sociology department.

Such declarations of knowledge or superior intelligence formed the rhetorical basis of America's emerging policies overseas at this same historical
moment. Sometimes, in fact, they became more than mere rhetorical devices. The year before the Committee's investigations, Lorrin Thurston, the
central instigator of Hawaiian annexation, had impelled the overthrow of
Queen Liliuokalani and the imposition of U.S. rule in part by insisting on
the need for "the intelligent part of the community"—that is, the wealthy
white minority—to rule.[62] American power abroad would continue to assert
itself in the coming years at least as commonly through this kind of claim
to knowledge—not only of "civilized" forms of government, but crucially,
of the subject societies themselves—as through direct force.[63] The Committee's focus on acquiring knowledge of the tenements and their inhabitants through a Progressive, superficially scientific method was likewise a
project of acquiring or reinforcing power over them that would facilitate
their regulation.

Indeed, the Committee report—in addition to documenting the process
of investigation and interaction within the tenements, compiling data, and
providing a transcript of the hearings—would itself become a means of
rule. The report would be Gilder's key weapon when advocating all manner
of prescriptive regulations to the state legislature. It would provide the beginning, middle, and end of his arguments to impose stricter rules on tene-

ment space, and on the population within it. Any statesman favoring further regulation could point to the Committee's report for scientific support of his position; anyone opposing such regulation would have to contend with the same. Simultaneously, the report offered to the regulatory bodies in its wake a comprehensive guide to tenement neighborhoods, their inhabitants, and the spaces most likely to be in violation of law. It was not only a record of study, but an implement of power.[64]

Underscoring the rationale for such power's existence and vigorous exertion, the Committee's attention to poor hygiene and what it saw as deviant sexuality—as a result of the physical conditions in the buildings—appears everywhere in the report as evidence of broadly questionable morality in the tenements. The report's judgment that inadequate hallway lighting invited "vile impulse" noted illicit sexual behavior as well as hygienic neglect. Marshall decries the fact that "it is frequently true that young boys and girls receive first lessons in evil doings in dark hallways which they would entirely escape were their actions . . . open to the view of the other tenants in the house." He concludes that improved hallway lighting will better control the "evil doings" as well as the "slovenliness" of these populations.[65]

Marshall played to a receptive audience with this line of argument about the relationship between morals and space in the tenements. The public perception of the Lower East Side as a foreign geographical zone characterized by moral depravity had reached practically iconic cultural status by 1895.[66] The publication in 1890 of Riis's *How the Other Half Lives* and in 1893 of Stephen Crane's novella *Maggie, a Girl of the Streets* widely reinforced the received wisdom of decades: the area bounded by Broadway, Fourteenth Street, the Brooklyn Bridge, and the East River constituted an alien land on American soil in manners, morals, people, and politics. Periodic features in magazines such as *Harper's Weekly* and *Leslie's Monthly* solidified the notion as common knowledge.[67] For good or ill, some Lower East Siders had even learned to capitalize on their fellow New Yorkers' expectations, inviting tourists to visit opium dens and brothels, and otherwise publicizing the supposed moral decay in the neighborhood as a spectacle from which they might squeeze a profit. Steve Brodie, the Bowery man who made his name in a (disputed) leap from the Brooklyn Bridge and parlayed it to wealth as a saloonkeeper and stage actor, exemplified this entrepreneurial attitude by encouraging newspaper reporters, "Say I'm a crook, a faker, that

I never jumped off a curbstone; anything, so you print my name."[68] The Committee's tendency to describe the morals of tenement residents in more sinister terms than those generally used to depict the rest of the city matched the norm in literature, the press, and political rhetoric.

That tendency also underlined the Committee's interest in prescribing behavior for poor residential areas rather than extending prescriptive regulation to all areas in the city, as becomes clear in the report's analysis of tenement prostitution. "The tenements always have had, and probably always will have," Marshall concedes, "their share of immoral women—of a class peculiar to them and separate from the professional prostitutes driven of late into them, from houses of ill-fame." This "tenement class," he elaborates, "consists of women who have been abandoned by their husbands, and who, in order to support themselves and their legitimate children, are driven to depend to some extent upon evil sources of income." Otherwise respectable poor women, he reasons, "are surrounded by none of the glamour of the professional prostitute; do not ordinarily live or dress more elaborately than other inmates of the house in which they live, and are generally regarded with more pity than envy or resentment by their neighbors and their neighbors' children. Thus they are not so especially dangerous to the morals of the house."[69] The phenomenon of women being driven to prostitution by poverty and desperation was morally innocuous in Marshall's view because it was natural: a condition that poor spaces "always have had, and probably always will have."

On the other hand, Marshall thunders, those prostitutes organized in successful brothels who are "surrounded by comparative luxury and live lives of apparent ease, in the midst of a houseful of adults and children whose frugal, honest living is obtained only by the hardest of work and the most rigid economy, can scarcely be less dangerous to the moral health of the house than an apartment full of cholera-infected persons would be to its physical welfare." Taking this reasoning to its logical conclusion, the Committee recommended, "That a law be passed making the offenses of soliciting and the maintenance of houses of prostitution in tenement-houses *punishable with greater severity than when they are committed elsewhere.*"[70] In other words, the report proposed discriminatory legislation in which the same crime committed in differently classed urban spaces would receive differently calibrated punishment. Prostitution in itself did not pose an inherent threat to morality, only successful prostitution in working-class neighborhoods did.

Even more remarkable in marrying Progressive science to imperial prescription in class terms are Marshall's musings on how to implement a bathing solution for the tenement population. As Gilder relates, "out of a total population of 255,033 covered by the committee's inspection, only 306 persons have access to bath-rooms in the houses in which they live."[71] Marshall notes that "the first inspection alone" uncovered 11,627 people "who have no regard for personal cleanliness, and who permit themselves to fall into such a condition of bodily filth as to become traveling menaces to the health and comfort of the public at large." How the Committee measured "regard for personal cleanliness" in these 11,627 individuals remains unclear, but extrapolating from this data, Marshall considers "the advisability of empowering the board of health to force such persons to bathe and renovate their clothing." While he admits that "This seems like a long step away from the theory of personal liberty," he cites successful implementation of such policies abroad. "In one European city it is the practice of the health authorities," he relates, "when a house inhabited by persistently dirty people is found, to order them all to a public bathhouse, force them to remove their clothing, and then turn the hose on them."[72]

Gilder ultimately refrained from making this specific policy recommendation to the legislature, but its serious consideration in the report exemplifies the Committee's inclination to allow "data" to dictate exceptionally prescriptive behavioral regulations. That such regulations would apply only to the tenements and bodies of the poor could have gone without saying. The fact that it did not indicates a sense of entitlement on the part of the Committee members to impose a regime of control over a population they perceived as incapable of self-government.

As the Committee moved from the inspection and data-gathering stage into their public hearings, another project with imperial undertones was moving toward completion on the Lower East Side: the building of the new Bowery Savings Bank, designed by Stanford White.

2

Bank on the Bowery

> He was a personality of enormous power, a man of phenomenal force. . . . I always think of him as the embodiment of a particular period in New York life—perhaps in American life—a period of effervescence and of the sudden coming of elements that had long lain in solution and came together with a certain emotional violence.
>
> —John Jay Chapman

"ROME IS A WONDERFUL PLACE," wrote the twenty-five-year-old Stanford White to his mother on June 11, 1879.[1] In a letter otherwise devoted to describing his harried schedule, precarious health, and guilt over not having written sooner, the easy serenity of White's admiration for the Imperial City reflected the impact it had on him: not immediately explosive, but deep and lasting.

The Reverend Calvin White might have shared his great-grandson Stanford's appreciation for cultural manifestations of imperial power, particularly in Rome. Born before the Revolutionary War in Upper Middletown, Connecticut, Calvin had graduated from Yale in 1786 to become a Presbyterian minister, but he died in 1853 as a Roman Catholic, bitterly unreconciled to Jacksonian democracy in America and always feeling himself to be "a displaced Englishman."[2] Calvin's son, Richard Mansfield White, seemed at first better suited to succeed in a new nation of rough edges: he built a fortune in shipping that he supplemented as the secretary and financial manager of a New Jersey ironworks. He spoiled his five children during those flush years, and his eldest, Richard Grant White, gravitated toward cultural criticism in arts and letters. Richard Grant White found much to criticize in the land of his birth, declaring in a commencement address to his own graduating class at the University of the City of New York that the American cultural scene was largely barren.[3] Like his grandfather Calvin, Richard fancied himself a displaced Englishman, expressing cultural affinity for the Old World and regarding the American rabble from the comfortable perch of advanced education and wealth.[4]

In the mid-1840s, however, Richard's father lost the fortune he had spent a lifetime building, watching helplessly as steam power condemned his clipper ship fleet to obsolescence.[5] The sudden loss of the family fortune defined Richard Grant White's life, imbuing him with deep financial and class insecurity. The unfortunate combination of a rich man's tastes and a (relatively) poor man's bank account meant he could never afford to live on a writer's income. An avid book collector, he repeatedly auctioned precious tomes to pay debts. Of economic necessity, he took a position as a clerk in the U.S. Customs House, a job he loathed, but held for seventeen years. As if overcompensating for his fall from pecuniary grace, he developed in his writing and relationships a façade whose principal traits were vanity, arrogance, and condescension. An 1846 profile in the *New-York Tribune* cast him as having "an attitude of listless self-complacency . . . prejudice, vanity, obstinacy and all," while still recognizing him, almost begrudgingly, as "a remarkable young man."[6] He projected an image of himself as a "natural aristocrat" whom people of the lower orders "liked to serve."[7] Privately, insecurity racked him, probably exacerbated by the fact that many of the New York Society folk whom he believed to be the closest thing to his natural peers regarded him askance or, in diarist George Templeton Strong's pointed words, as "a second-rate fellow."[8]

To his younger son, Stanford, Richard Grant White offered great devotion but a mixed legacy. The boy exhibited a marked facility for drawing, and Richard encouraged it by exposing him early and often to music and painting, cultivating Stanford's discerning aesthetic instincts. At the same time, Richard modeled for Stanford a fascination almost to the point of fixation with the pleasures of wealth and power. The son inherited his father's snobbery, insatiable acquisitiveness, and obsession with beauty, particularly European beauty. Yet because he had not suffered Richard's traumatic experience of economic and social diminution, he showed none of the bitterness or insecurity that hampered his father.[9] Whereas Richard paired his yearning for the trappings of wealth with resentment at having lost them, Stanford matched his own ambition with boundless self-confidence, inexhaustible energy, tremendous charm, and an endearing sense of humor about himself. Not having suffered the pain of loss as his father had, he could live as if he had nothing to lose.[10]

And he did. One of Stanford White's first biographers captures the comet-like intensity and joy he brought to life and his desire to share it with others by quoting certain phrases he had almost personalized through constant use: "'You haven't seen it?' he would say. 'Why it's the finest thing of its kind in America! It's bully! It's wonderful . . . gorgeous!' To him everything in life—the paintings of Holbein, the cathedral at Laon, the shoulder muscles of Sharkey, Blanche Ring's singing, the wine at Martin's, the gilding on an old frame, salmon fishing, the cornice of the Maison Carrée, the voice of Emma Eames, the coffee at Delmonico's—everything was bully, wonderful, gorgeous."[11] White possessed a voracious appetite for the world and everything in it. His demonstrable pleasure in living, channeled through a conspicuous six-foot two-inch frame and wildly spiky red hair that invited comparisons to a porcupine, rendered him instantly recognizable on the streets of New York. When, years later, a curious woman on the corner of Fifth Avenue and Twenty-Second Street asked a young draftsman from McKim, Mead & White, "What sort of person is this Stanford White of yours?" he surveyed the block and replied, "I'll tell you. . . . See that tall, red-haired man hurrying up the street? Well, that's Stanford White. He's ubiquitous."[12]

Ubiquity will only get you so far, however; his father's connections—in particular, Richard's acquaintance with Central Park designer and writer Frederick Law Olmsted—proved critical to Stanford's success. After meeting Stanford in 1870, Olmsted introduced the sixteen-year-old to the budding architect Henry Hobson Richardson, who hired him immediately as a junior draftsman. White flourished in Richardson's office, providing significant work on some of the firm's signature projects, most notably Trinity Church in Boston. Trinity stands as a premiere example of Richardson's idiosyncratic and particularly American style, which is distinguishable most visibly in the dark, rough-hewn exterior stone from native quarries that lends imposing ballast to his work. When a more senior draftsman, Charles

Follen McKim, left the firm to start his own office just as the Trinity project got under way, White, at only eighteen years old, took principal charge of the drawings.[13]

In hindsight, the most astounding aspect of White's influence in the construction of Trinity Church is not his youth or relative inexperience, but the fact that he played such a central role in realizing the quintessential example of Richardson's *American* aesthetic, which came to be known as the Romanesque Revival.[14] Though White later took pride in having "made every drawing for Trinity Church, Boston, with my own hands," he became far better known, perhaps unfairly, for his ingenious (or, as some would argue, rapacious and derivative) transplantations of European styles and materials to the American scene than for an expression of true American originality.[15] With Richardson, White proved an ability to adapt his own tastes to those of his employer, a skill he would retain with clients throughout his professional career.

In those early years, the fact that White did not share Richardson's tastes manifested less in questions of aesthetic preference and more in the way Richardson conducted both his firm and himself. White complained to his mother from a business trip in February 1873 that "thanks to Richardson and his committees I feel as if I had been standing on my head all the week."[16] Writing the following year from Brookline, where he was living with Richardson while working on Trinity, White wrote similarly: "We've been a whole week preparing for work—'organizing' Mr. R. calls it—and nothing done. Heighho!"[17] Richardson's use of discussion and consensus within the firm clearly struck White as excessive and inefficient.

Despite his enormous personal affection for Richardson, White also found him boorish. Assuring his mother that she should not worry about his being "in my right mind," he continued, "How Richardson can be, I can't tell for, setting aside all brandies, gins, wines and cigars, it seems to me he chiefly subsists on boiled tripe, which he still insists on calling the 'entrails of a cow.' How's that?"[18] Traces of his father's snobbery and a desire for more refinement in life began to emerge more prominently in Stanford just as he was accumulating the purse to indulge them. Soon he would share his father's love affair with the Old World as well. When he left Richardson's office after eight years, it was to discover Europe for himself.

By the time White departed for France on July 3, 1878, he had made a name for himself in New York artistic circles, not only as a young architect and decorator of great promise, but perhaps more crucially as a delightful companion at ease among the wealthy and well mannered. Of the influential New Yorkers White had impressed in those early years, Richard Watson and Helena de Kay Gilder were destined to be lifelong friends. Just before White embarked for Europe, Helena called him to the Gilder home and entrusted him with a photograph bound for their mutual Parisian friend, the sculptor Augustus Saint-Gaudens. It was a portrait of the Gilders' new baby, Rodman, who was born in 1877, the same year that their eldest child Marion had died.[19] For Richard Watson Gilder, Marion's death had "ushered in an utterly different state of existence," subduing the romance of his youthful character. For White, his trip to Europe would have a similarly life-altering though opposite effect, expanding his creative imagination and offering him a grander vision of architecture than he had previously possessed. It was as if the photograph of Rodman Gilder were a talisman, the boy's new life transferring to White the sense of unbounded possibility that Gilder had lost when Marion died.

Writing to his mother, who was his constant correspondent, at the end of August, White described the initial tour of France as one might a military campaign, reveling in "taking each town without opposition," including, "Paris, Fontainebleau, Moret, Sens, Dijon, Beaune, Lyons, Lyons down the Rhône to Avignon, Arles, St. Gilles, Tarascon, Nîmes, Langogne across the mountains by diligence to, Le Puy, Issoire, Clermont, Riom, Moulins, Bourges, Tours, Blois, and back to Paris by way of Orleans."[20] Of the Hotel Dieu in Beaune, he wrote, "Indeed one would almost wish to fall sick, to get in such a hospital."[21] At St. Gilles, he found "the triple marble porch of the church" to be "the best piece of architecture in France."[22] At Nîmes and Arles, he swooned over "all manner of old Roman theatres, amphitheatres, baths, etc." He described how he and his travel companions McKim and Saint-Gaudens had "sat on the top row of seats and imagined ourselves ancient Romans" in the Nîmes amphitheater. Showing off for his older friends, White "rushed madly into the arena, struck an attitude, and commenced declaiming . . . I stabbed five or six gladiators and rushed out with the guardian in hot pursuit."[23] A few months later, White traveled through Italy to Rome itself, and later to London, where the pleasure of inspecting Greek and Assyrian art at the British Museum made his "hair alternately stand up and flatten down."[24] His letters expressed both youthful intoxication with new experiences, and a maturing seriousness about his own art—he may have been jocular, acting the fool with his friends, but his eyes remained open and sharp.

What he saw began a gradual transformation in his designs, inspiring a fondness for European styles that grew more pronounced over the course of the next decade, moving him away from Richardson's aesthetic. Professional colleagues at McKim, Mead & White, the firm to which White attached his name and himself upon returning to the United States, encouraged his Europhilia, no one more so than Joseph Morrill Wells. Wells was a passionate advocate for reintroducing principles of the Italian Renaissance to American architecture, and as another of the firm's employees later recalled, he served "by White's side, the helpful colleague as well as the beloved friend."[25] Over the next fifteen years, an ever-greater degree of Renaissance neoclassicism would infuse White's designs. He began the 1880s designing Queen Anne shingle homes that blended colonial designs and European accents; he commenced the 1890s with the Century Association building on West 43rd Street, whose design he modeled on a Veronese Palazzo, and whose interior decoration reflected the turn toward an imperial idiom.[26] In 1891, he started work on the Metropolitan Club, using Renaissance principles and the Roman Palazzo Farnese as inspiration.[27] In 1893, White designed his most soberly classical edifice yet, the Cullum Memorial at West Point.[28] The jovial twenty-four-year-old traveler comically impersonating an ancient Roman had become a driven forty-year-old professional intent on bringing the grandeur of ancient Rome to his fellow Americans.

The apex of White's love affair with imperial aesthetics was 1893, timed perfectly to coincide with a national cultural event unlike any before or since: the World's Columbian Exposition in Chicago. Ostensibly celebrating the 400th anniversary of Columbus's expedition and "discovery" of the New World, the World's Fair more demonstrably celebrated and promoted the U.S. discovery of itself as an empire.[29] Thirty years after the Civil War had torn the country asunder, the nation's power brokers and boosters were attempting to forge a new national identity in the crucibles of dizzying industrial growth, pseudoscientific white supremacy, and international expansion. The World's Fair served as a kind of public unveiling of the new United States they envisioned; the White City, a complex of buildings dominated by the architectural styles of classical Greece and the Roman Empire, was its chrysalis. In privileging imperial designs, Daniel Burnham, the Fair's architectural director, sent a powerful message that the United States could and would have a public architecture worthy of the international stage, for it was on *that* stage that the new United States intended to act.[30]

In a sense, the World's Fair signified a trend in American architecture that finally began to meet Stanford White's hopes—indeed, his father's hopes—that the United States might develop a substantial art and architecture on par with Europe, thereby becoming a truly great nation aesthetically as well as industrially. Visitors hailed the White City as an ideal to which every American city should aspire, arguing forcefully that healthy communities required higher standards of public beauty, the core belief of the City Beautiful movement. In a serendipitous coincidence of history, White's need to surround himself with wealth and beauty had become consonant with good citizenship. Replicating imperial visions in public architecture was his private inclination, but he and the firm could sell it as patriotism and civic duty as well.[31]

There is little reason to believe that Stanford White thought extensively about the political impact of his designs on public life, but he made his understanding and support of America's imperial position perfectly explicit through his work. Responding to critics who later accused him of having pilfered European treasures for an insufficiently appreciative American nouveau riche, White wrote, "In the past, dominant nations had always plundered works of art from their predecessors. . . . America was taking a leading place among nations and had, therefore, the right to obtain art wherever she could."[32] White endorsed American power abroad, and he intended to wield that power himself to bring beauty to his native shores.

It was in this context of White's passion for the Roman ideal, his endorsement of American dominance in the world, and the public's delight with the White City that McKim, Mead & White won the commission for the Bowery Savings Bank building. And so White set out to re-create his most recent successes in a very different context: instead of a phantasmagoric White City on the shores of Lake Michigan, he brought a vision of empire to the Bowery slums—in the name of progress.

White's hand, however, was not the first to touch the Bowery. Nearly 250 years earlier, the neighborhood already bore the firm stamp of imperial power. Little more than a dirt trail in the seventeenth century, the Bowery was the only dependably dry path connecting the Dutch settlement in lower Manhattan to the rest of the island. Waterways and marshes impeded any other land crossing, making the Bowery the only possible overland attack route. In partial defense against potential raids from the local Lenape tribe, the Dutch West India company freed a number of aging African slaves and settled them on small farms along the northern reaches of the Bowery path. As one historian notes dryly, "The motive behind these measures was far from being purely benevolent."[33] In addition to the explicit conditions of their freedom—annual rent due to the company in harvest and livestock, and their children's continued slavery—their location on the upper Bowery burdened them with a third obligation: serving as human shields and advance runners to warn the white settlers in lower Manhattan of any imminent Lenape assault.[34]

The space of the Bowery had witnessed the play of class and racial tensions since the beginnings of European settlement, and little changed in that regard over two and a half centuries, though practically everything else did. Wealthy families like the De Lanceys, Bayards, and Stuyvesants transformed the Bowery's small farms (*bouwerij* in Dutch, handed out as an incentive to settlers) and modest homesteads into vast agricultural estates in the seventeenth century, worked by slaves and hired hands. The Bowery began to break down again in the eighteenth century when speculators such as Anthony Rutgers first broke up their estates, dividing the "pleasant thoroughfare of semisuburban, semicountry residences" into the 25 × 100-foot lots that would become notorious for their exploitative overcrowding.[35] Then the Revolution upended class dynamics once more. British occupation turned the neighborhood into a barracks, fertilizing the growth of saloons, taverns, playhouses, and "other resorts much less desirable." Lore has it that British officers "had horse races . . . they and the rank and file promoted dogfights and cockfights, and the tavernkeepers put on bull baitings for their amusement; and thus the street received another impulse towards the rowdy Bohemia which it afterwards became."[36] When the rebellion succeeded, the predominantly loyalist rich fled to Britain and abandoned their Bowery estates, leaving them to be colonized by the poor. As one period poem had it:

> At Delancey's deserted mansion he
> A moment paused to view the ruin'd dome
> Whose doors are left without a lock or key,

While saucy winds and dashing rains intrude
Where once Dalinda at her toilet sat;
Deserted rooms! that now can scarcely lodge
Secure from storms the beggar and her brat.[37]

Former colonial subjects found in the Bowery a ruin of empire, and claimed it for their own.

It was in the remnants of these dubious surroundings in 1833 that a group of forty-one businessmen and artisans gathered to found the Bowery Savings Bank, expressing a desire to improve the community and encourage financial independence among its residents, assimilating the recent, mostly Irish immigrants to nascent American industrial capitalism. "When you help a man to save his first dollar," wrote grocer and bank cofounder Thomas Jeremiah by way of explanation, "you have started him on the road to self-respect and self-reliance."[38] Whether the founders' expressed desires for the bank accurately reflected their actual motives remains an open question: the significant overlap in personnel between the new Bowery Savings and the old Butchers and Drovers Bank led some to the conclusion that the existing bank opened the new one for its own benefit rather than in the interest of local residents.[39] In any case, on the Bowery Savings Bank's first day of business, June 2, 1834, its depositors reflected the neighborhood: butchers, a mason, and a shoemaker, as well as more modest workers such as domestic servants and seamstresses lined up to put away their savings. Their collective funds enabled the Bowery Savings, in a matter of a few years, to establish one of the principal mortgage businesses in New York, underwriting extensive building and expansion in and around the city. In other words, New York grew in part by leveraging the savings of workers and immigrants, deposited on the Bowery.[40]

As the city grew, so too did the bank's coffers; by the end of 1895, Bowery Savings maintained over 111,000 accounts whose assets exceeded $60 million, making it "one of the wealthiest corporations on Manhattan Island."[41] The bank's wealth, however, had not translated into the kinds of local transformations its founders had claimed to envision. Just as they had been in 1834, late-nineteenth-century Bowery residents were struggling immigrants, the hard-working former subjects of kings, kaisers, and emperors. Tailors from Sweden and Ireland, barbers from Italy and Prussia, cooks, carriage makers, carpenters and carmen from every corner of the earth surrounded the bank, scraping to make a living. In 1880, the occupants of the tenement house at 112 Elizabeth Street, soon to be the location of the bank's new vault, were working-class Irish and Prussian immigrants, a saloonkeeper, a driver, a cabinet maker, and a barber, all married and with ten children among them.[42]

The buildings these residents occupied were rough, ramshackle tenements whose dumbbell design made natural light a distant dream. Indoor plumbing, not to mention enforceable zoning, was practically nonexistent. One of Gilder's Tenement House Committee inspectors testified about a nearby building whose ground floor housed a grocer, fishmonger, and baker, and where the sink that provided water for the baker's bread and a washtub for the fishmonger's fish "was also used as [a] urinal by the tenants."[43] The cellars were incubators for disease, as John B. Devins, a local pastor, attested to the Tenement House Committee by recounting a program enacted the previous winter to engage unemployed men in sanitizing neighborhood tenements. They had intended to whitewash basement walls, "but often," he noted,

> so much refuse was discovered in the cellars that whitewashing would be of little avail. . . . [R]ubbish was thrown against the walls in piles of one foot, two feet and three feet high; we removed refuse from 491 cellars, the total number of barrels being 3,903, including 150 barrels of ashes, 100 barrels of rags, 54 of bones, 47 of leather, shoes, etc., 44 barrels of wet straw, 41 of excelsior, 29 barrels of old iron, 18 of broken glass and 18 of old tin; the workmen also removed a large number of dead cats, dogs and rat[s] in a decomposed state, and large quantities of decayed garbage, including in one house several barrels of rotten sauerkraut, also putrid meat, old mattresses, filthy bedding and stale milk, and in one house in Fifth street there was a can of milk that had been in the cellar for over a year.[44]

The dangers to local health and hygiene were acute.

The Lower East Side streets presented equally minimal evidence of the bank's near sixty-year influence and prosperity. The Third Avenue elevated train and its twin tracks ran up and down the Bowery, imposing a visual, aural, and olfactory nuisance to the roadway as the price of swifter public transport, muting the potential for passersby to be awestruck by—or even to notice—any architectural beauty.[45] The neighborhood resembled Bedlam more than Rome, particularly around the corner in Hester Street. Shouts of peddlers and rag-pickers hawking their wares and haggling with customers clashed with the clip-clop of horses' hooves; mothers shouted from fire-escapes for barefoot sons and daughters to get out of the path of creaking wagon wheels; periodic bursts of water rushing from open hydrants elicited cries of delighted and refreshed laughter from suddenly drenched children, or furious declamations from street merchants with soaked shoes.[46]

The proprietors of businesses on the blocks adjacent to the Bowery Savings certainly bore some responsibility for the neighborhood's continuing chaos. Far from sharing the bank trustees' putative desire to exert a calming, sovereign influence on the area, they tended to exacerbate the fractious elements already in place. The Bowery between Park Row and Cooper Union in the 1890s played host to a fifth of the pawnshops and a sixth of the saloons in the entire city.[47] Extralegal behaviors and disproportionate policing inevitably followed, as suggested by the fact that over a quarter of the city's recorded arrests occurred in the Bowery district.[48]

Observers remarked not only on the congestion and criminality of the Bowery, but on the profound and continuing foreignness of the neighborhood. In September 1894, a *New York Times* writer journeyed to the vicinity of Bowery Savings to investigate the "purliens [*sic*] of the east side," and what he found apparently shocked him. "One of the first lessons to be learned by the explorer," he wrote, "is that a vast difference exists between the Hebrew of the drama and the sensational romance on the one hand, and the Hebrew of stern laborious reality on the other. The investigator will find no richly-fed men, extravagantly attired, gleaming with diamonds, fat as Jeshurun, rubbing their hands and computing their tremendous and illicit gains with an oily satisfaction. He will find no one gloating over the monstrous profits of the middleman, the excessive advantages of the usurer." Instead, the reporter confronted "attenuated creatures, clad in old, faded, greasy, often tattered clothing." He explained that the "investigator . . . will have the way cleared for him with the most eager consideration—a consideration so eager that he feels ashamed of the sense and appearance of comfort and repletion on his own part which generates it—by men and youths whose cheeks are pinched and hollow . . . whose sad, lustrous eyes look at him pitifully, like the eyes of hunted and captured animals that press up to the bars of their cages."[49]

The *Times* writer's characterization of himself defines the neighborhood as a racialized space even more than the stereotypes he deploys—the caricature of the "oily" usurer and the specter of desperate, Yiddish-speaking "animals"—to describe its Jewish residents. The writer moves through the neighborhood either as an "explorer," a foreigner in a strange land, or as an "investigator," identifying with the power of officialdom, inspecting strange specimens through "the bars of their cages." In either case, his identity as an outsider marks the space as foreign. Another *Times* story published the following year declared, "The Polish Hebrews . . . have transformed the territory east of the Bowery into a vast Ghetto," while the old Irish residents on "the west side of Bowery have given place to the greatest Italian colony in the city."[50]

Ten years later, no less an "explorer" than Henry James would echo the sense of displacement, struck as he was from the Third Avenue El by the locale's "Hebrew faces and Hebrew names," remarking, "I was on my way to enjoy . . . some peculiarly 'American' form of theatric mystery, but my way led me, apparently, through the depths of the Orient, and I should clearly take my place with an Oriental public."[51] Contrary to the assimilationist hopes of the Bowery Savings Bank's founders, this area had indeed become the province of other races, other countries. At the close of the nineteenth century and the opening of the twentieth, the Bowery looked like something out of another time or place to many of its contemporaries, especially to dominant observers and meaning makers such as *Times* writers and Henry James.

Rowdy, loud, foreign, and down-at-heel, the Bowery and its residents nevertheless produced enormous wealth, most of which flowed unstintingly away from the district. The bulk of it probably bled out directly through rent paid to absentee landlords, but the Bowery Savings and its mortgage business had also been a constant conduit for the removal of that wealth, both by making its investments in other areas of the city or nation, and by providing its wealthier local depositors the means, through dividend payments, to finance their relocation to tonier areas. The bank invested primarily in non-New York municipal securities, railroad bonds, and uptown real estate.[52] This made responsible financial sense because property values on the Lower East Side were crumbling—and how could anyone fault a savings bank for providing its depositors with dividends ample enough to move to a nicer part of town? Yet these responsible financial decisions had the effect of further impoverishing and marginalizing the bank's own neighborhood, extracting both human and capital resources from an area desperately in need of both. In this, the bank mirrored the financial operations of the new American imperialism: claiming a progressive mission while systematically siphoning wealth out of less powerful areas.[53]

It is unlikely that the bank directors paid much heed to these ironies of capitalist logic as they oversaw the disbursement of handsome dividends, derived in large part from the bank's location amid a continually rising tide of potential depositors. It is important to realize, however, that they pursued this business model not only with profit in mind, but also with the understanding that their bank provided a progressive service to the community. Bank president Samuel Brown, facing the need to expand in 1876, and watching as other savings banks followed their long-time depositors uptown, exemplified this understanding when he observed, "[W]e are obligated by our charter and by our word to serve the people of this community; and to serve them where they live, we need adequate space."[54] Rather than relocate uptown, Brown ordered a $60,000 renovation and expansion of the bank's existing building on Bowery and Grand Streets.

This already sizeable investment in its own premises, however, was minimal compared to White's designs of 1893. In obtaining new frontage on Grand and Elizabeth Streets for this, the building's second expansion, the bank trustees hoped to invest not only literally in their own building, but figuratively in the neighborhood around it. They sought to provide a powerful vision of American wealth and beauty that might stir their immigrant neighbors' aspirations to succeed financially.

Their personal attitudes toward those neighbors, however, reflected all the ambivalence that such assimilationist hopes usually imply. The bank's building committee undoubtedly wished to exert a positive influence on its immigrant surroundings, but it conceived of its mission less in a spirit of collaboration with the Bowery depositors who had underwritten the bank's success than as a function of *richesse oblige*. The instructions to architectural firms competing for the commission noted that "an edifice ought to be erected which should impress the beholder with its dignity and fortress-like strength," emphasizing the necessity for such imposing qualities "on account of the neighborhood in which it is to be located."[55] In other words, even as the building committee sought to change the character of the neighborhood, it made its plans with a static conception of the Bowery's character as

Drawing of the Bowery entrance to Stanford White's Bowery Savings Bank. Collection of the New-York Historical Society.

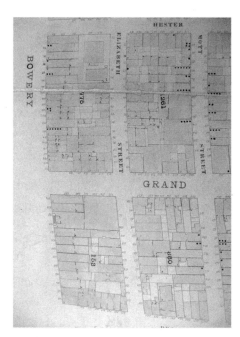

Detail from Lawrence Veiller, dir., "Map Showing Over-Crowding . . ." The large numbers at blocks' centers represent total population for those blocks in 1896. Each dot represents five different families in Charity Organization Society (C.O.S.) or Association for Improving the Condition of the Poor (A.I.C.P.) records who applied for charity aid from the address in which they appear. The Bowery Savings Bank vault is the largest footprint on the corner of Grand and Elizabeth St., and connects to the bank entrance on Bowery. Collection of the New-York Historical Society.

W. Louis Sonntag, Jr., "The Bowery at Night," as it was in 1895 after the completion of White's renovation. Print from the Collection of the New-York Historical Society.

undesirable and untrustworthy. The architects took their cue from the bank trustees, writing in the competition brief, "Owing to the fact that your bank is situated in a part of the city where you receive depositors from a very mixed population, it seems to us that light, air and cleanliness are important factors in the plan."[56] From the initial stages, the plans explicitly recognized that the new building must stand apart from the "very mixed population," imposing on its collective consciousness even while serving it.

The bank's set of guiding principles fit perfectly with the aesthetic ideas White was championing, fresh from the Chicago World's Fair. He envisioned progress imposed through finer aesthetics—a more beautiful public life realized through more beautiful public space. In a way, his vision for transforming the life of the Bowery by altering the streetscape paralleled Gilder's desire to achieve the same transformation by altering the tenements; but instead of fireproof construction, hallway lighting, and regulations governing running water, White imagined engendering behavioral transformation by projecting a classical standard of beauty, one that could usher a sense of grandeur into a declining neighborhood. It certainly was not a public idealism in the sense of allowing the public to participate, but White did hope to bring beauty into public space in a way that would inspire the man in the street. Richard Harding Davis, writing about White's entire body of work shortly after the architect's death in 1906, seemed to indicate that White had achieved his hope: "In New York it is impossible for the poor man, the rich man, the man of taste and the man with none, to walk abroad without being indebted to Stanford White, for something that was good and uplifting."[57]

One wonders if Lower East Siders present for the groundbreaking of the new Bowery Savings anticipated a more ambivalent legacy. In literal terms, the building required the demolition of three tenement lots on Grand Street, "all variously encumbered through May 1, 1893."[58] The working men and women encumbering those tenements may have learned to appreciate the bank's beauty eventually, but in the late spring of 1893 they faced eviction during a widespread economic catastrophe. The failure of the Pennsylvania and Reading Railroads a few months earlier had launched the Panic of 1893, and unemployment was surging, particularly in neighborhoods like the Bowery.[59] The construction of such a magnificent edifice in that moment, on that corner, offered a daily reminder to all who passed of the great fortunes still being piled high amid increasing poverty.

In more symbolic terms, White's design choices might just as easily have dominated a man in the street as uplifted him. He modeled the Corinthian capitals of the banking room's columns on those of Hadrian's Pantheon, imbuing the bank with the power of the Roman empire in its beholder's eyes. His richly coffered ceiling design echoed the barrel-vaulted aisles of Rome's Basilica of Constantine and Christianity's triumph over heresy.[60] These specific resonances may have gone unnoticed by many Bowery residents, but the overall effect would have been as purposefully overwhelming to anyone entering the bank from the hardscrabble streets outside.

The disconnect between White's designs and the daily experience of Bowery residents gestures toward other troubling inequities embedded in the political economy of the building's actual construction, particularly in the context of the financial panic. Not only was the bank using the wealth accumulated from working-class New Yorkers over decades to invest in a lavish new home for itself, but the developer on the project, David H. King, Jr., had a somewhat unsavory familial relationship to property in the area.[61] As construction moved forward on the Bowery project, King's father came up in the news as an absentee landlord who had allowed two of his tenement properties, at 182 and 184 Madison Street, to fall into a state of such decrepitude that the city declared them "dangerous to life and detrimental to health." Because the law refrained scrupulously from interfering with property rights and thus did not impose any direct penalties on King, the Board of Health took the only action it could: it evicted his tenants.

"It may seem cruel to turn these families out into the cold," the Sanitary Superintendent remarked, "but they are better off in the street than breathing the air in the house laden with sewer gas. Besides," he pointed out, "every family in that house was notified that the Health Department proposed to vacate the house, and a notice was posted on the building to that effect, and ample warning was given." Indicating the sort of circumstances that might have prevented tenants from heeding such warnings, one family with two children suffering from pneumonia was allowed to stay—that is, "until the children are in a condition to be moved."

So while King, Jr. followed White's designs to create a resplendent temple to American capitalism on the Bowery, his father's tenants reaped that system's capricious whirlwind a few blocks away.[62] As would be revealed in court the year following the temple's completion, Lizzie Jaeger had been a victim of the same tempest.

3

Prescribing Reform

> This is a very serious state of things. It shows that the children of these benighted or villainous people must be so exposed to American influences and so aerated by them as to be completely transformed before they can be regarded as trustworthy American citizens.
>
> —*The New York Times*

NEITHER DAVID H. KING'S impunity as an absentee landlord nor the city's response in evicting his tenants was unique, a fact demonstrated emphatically during the hearings of Richard Watson Gilder's Tenement House Committee, which were held on seven days between November 13 and December 7, 1894.[1] The Committee members spent nearly a fifth of the hearings cross-examining tenement owners, agents, and collectors for buildings that had failed to meet sanitary standards, almost invariably in the wake of devastating testimony from one of the Committee inspectors describing the filth they had encountered in a given property. This pattern of testimony illustrated common themes that reflected the scenario for King's properties on Madison Street. Inspectors presented evidence of neglect and sanitary violations so abominable as to endanger the lives of tenants. Owners, agents, and lessees then universally denied responsibility, blaming their underlings or the tenants themselves for the damage while refusing to commit to concrete, lasting remedies. Some were more contrite than others, but the overall attitude they struck was one of cool defiance, and occasionally contempt, toward the Committee.

Gilder's November 19 interview of Edward Rafter, the owner of the tenement house previously described in which the baker and fishmonger's sink doubled as a urinal for tenants in the building, was typical. When Gilder inquired if Rafter would like to deny any of the inspector's damning testimony, Rafter replied, "As far as the water-closet down stairs is concerned, the most of these people are Italians, and it is hard to make them keep their places clean; and as far as the man sleeping on his dough troughs, I can't control that at all."[2] This diffidence typified Rafter's response to all questions the Committee put to him. Could he prevent the sink's being used as a urinal? "I can't take any steps—what steps can I take[?]" Could he hire a housekeeper to do it? "I would have to leave her down there all day long." Could he keep the basement door locked to prevent the homeless from sleeping in the cellar? "I couldn't keep that door locked." Could he hire a housekeeper to ensure that the tenants did not break a lock on the cellar door? "It is a very hard matter to take charge of all the tenants in the house." Each time the Committee tried to corner Rafter into accepting some responsibility for the condition of the property, he slipped out of their rhetorical grasp, placing the blame on his tenants and remaining imperturbable in the face of the Committee's efforts to shame him.[3]

Rafter and witnesses like him knew the Committee could do nothing to punish them, not for the lack of laws governing space (various Tenement House Acts had proclaimed plenty of these), but for the lack of rules governing economic and personal accountability. Landlords had less financial stake in obeying the law than tenants did—the 1887 Tenement House Act actually decreed that the city must compensate landlords for various inconveniences associated with property upkeep, but could burn the clothing of the poor on hygienic grounds and offer no restitution. Edward King, the tenement resident who had objected to the inspectors' disrespect for privacy among the poor, declared this particular policy "an outrage" in his November 23 testimony, demanding that "the same consideration shown for the landlord should be shown for the tenant who loses his clothes and his bed."[4]

Landlords also seldom faced personal liability for the condition of their properties because they had, almost without exception, legally transferred that liability to various superintendents or collection agents, who in turn subcontracted *their* responsibilities for upkeep to the tenants. The Committee questioned several agents, one of whom, Richard B. McCotter, described his role in a string of subleases and diffused authority worthy of a limited liability corporation. One property he oversaw on Thompson Street belonged to the estate of Edward Anthony, executed by Richard A. Anthony, a photographer. McCotter had no knowledge of when the executor had last been in the house, and he admitted for his own part, "I have not examined the house lately." When asked to explain his neglect, he related, "The house was thoroughly overhauled about a year ago; it was leased to a new party and he thoroughly overhauled it, and papered and painted it throughout; he gave up the house about the first of September, and it was leased to another party; since then I have not been through the house."[5] Another property he oversaw, meanwhile, belonged to a Mrs. Julia Lucas, who lived in Saratoga, New York. McCotter knew no better when Mrs. Lucas had last visited her property. He had been there himself "within a week or two."[6]

Here the Committee thought they had McCotter on the hook. "What explanation have you to make of the filthy condition it is in?" one member asked.

"The condition was not called to my notice," he answered gamely.

"You were there a week ago?"

"Yes, sir; but did not go through the house."

"Did you collect the rent?"

"I did at the time, though we have a collector for that purpose."

"The rent of both those houses are collected by your firm on the premises?"

"Yes, sir."

As the Committee soon discovered, however, McCotter's "firm," in the person of his sublessees, did not exactly collect the rent either. After interrogating McCotter, the Committee called Anthony Lombardi, whom McCotter had indicated was the sublessee for the first property. McCotter had already explained that Lombardi did not live in the building, and that he operated a store on Bleecker Street, so it cannot have surprised the Committee members inordinately when Lombardi asserted about the filthy conditions in the house, "I don't know; I don't see it; I can't say."

"You have not examined the condition of that house?" Marshall asked.

"No, sir," Lombardi answered. "I don't examine it much."

"You make what you can get out of it, and you don't care whether the tenants die or not?"

"I send my man to collect the rent, that is all."

"You don't care what condition it is in?"

"I am very glad if it be in good condition; people don't like it to be in bad condition at all."

"Do you take any pains to see that it is kept in good condition?"

"I have something else to do."[7]

More than any specific policy, this structure of human relationships in the ownership, supervision, and occupancy of New York tenement houses seemed arranged to perpetuate criminal neglect, endangering the lives and livelihoods of tenants. Without any financial or legal incentives to invest in their own properties, owners and landlords predictably ignored (and may actually have remained ignorant of) sanitary violations while continuing to collect the profits such properties produced. Tenants were, for the most part, so itinerant that making the extra effort to nurture good relationships through prompt upkeep did not justify itself. Landlords made the same calculation that the Bowery Savings managers did when choosing to invest the bank's funds elsewhere in the city: pouring capital into Lower East Side residential property was a high-risk, low-yield, or at least long-term investment, and withholding that capital did not hurt their bottom line.[8] The Bowery Savings trustees, on the other hand, had a significant financial incentive to expand and renovate their institutional property; namely, it allowed them to accept more depositors, expand their business, and reap greater profits. Institutional investment could socialize cost and privatize profit, while residential investment in a poor neighborhood like the Bowery promised little additional private gain in return for hypothetical social or environmental amelioration.

This fundamental difference in the nature of institutional and residential investment seemed not to fluster the bank trustees, who insisted—despite significant evidence to the contrary—that the building project was both in the interest of the Bowery neighborhood and being achieved at minimal cost. In imagining the new building as the seamless continuation of its role as a progressive force in the neighborhood and a public fixture symbolizing the best of New York's and America's relationship between the wealthy and the poor, it produced quite a different achievement—it created a building

whose very presence, while inspiring and grand, would continue to underscore the checkered poverty of the surrounding area for decades after its
completion.[9] The trustees, rather than perpetuating what they perceived as
the bank's progressive purpose, revealed what had been its imperial effect
all along: to leverage the capital resources of poor foreigners while failing to
fulfill the promise of development in its depositors' own neighborhood.

Gilder's Committee and White's bank building, superficially different in
conception and execution, were actually a matched pair—not only in the
imperial-progressive ideology that drove them, but in their consequences
for the Lower East Side and for the class dynamics of space in New York
more generally.

The most lasting impact of the Committee was its success in convincing
the state legislature to grant property condemnation powers to the Board of
Health, powers that only nine years earlier had been declared unconstitu-
tional by the State Court of Appeals.[10] Those powers and others like them
became the basis of countless urban redevelopment plans for slum neighborhoods like the Bowery, plans that the wealthy or powerful imposed on
the poor for decades afterward in cities all over the country, often with a
spirit directly echoing the era-specific imperial progressivism of Gilder and
White. As with Gilder's Committee, experts in architecture and city design, often accompanied by eminent sociologists, would descend on a poor
neighborhood, analyze and diagnose its problems, and prescribe radical physical transformations while largely ignoring or misconstruing the political-
economic ailments at the root of the neighborhood's deterioration.[11] They
usually ascribed such ailments to the cultural inferiority of the neighborhood's residents.[12] Most eschewed low-income public housing solutions in
favor of private development, just as Gilder's Committee did.[13] Voluntary
open discussion or truly participatory consultation with such residents during the decision-making process occurred rarely, if ever.[14]

The building of the new Bowery Savings building in 1893 exemplified this
process in a microcosmic, private-sphere way. The project's wealthy boosters
such as bank president John P. Townsend justified it by asserting that it constituted both an aesthetic and capital investment in the neighborhood, yet its
first requirement was the eviction of tenement tenants on the block under

development.[15] While spending enormous sums of money on Indiana lime-stone and Italian marble for its new home, the bank made no discernible commitment to improving the tenements whose squalor was being so clearly demonstrated by Gilder's Committee. Instead, its operational investments sucked capital out of the neighborhood and put it to profitable use elsewhere, much as America's imperial financial policy would continue doing abroad.[16] Arguably the only direct "investments" the project produced for the Bowery were the small donations that the developer, King, Jr., made during construc-tion to a privately organized charity group, the Industrial Christian Alliance. This group aimed at softening unemployment's effects in the area during the depression by providing cheap—but not free—food to struggling men and women at "people's restaurants." It charged five cents for a meal.[17]

Nevertheless, Gilder and White imagined their respective projects as bringing the best of a new American identity into a neighborhood desper-ately in need of assimilation. Both men believed that a better life was pos-sible in the Bowery, if only through the right combination of regulation and splendor imposed on poor spaces, public and private. The proper pro-gressive regulations, behavioral modifications, and standards of imperial beauty, once firmly introduced by expert hands, could encourage the im-migrant residents to abandon their foreign "morals" and become upstand-ing participants in America's bright future.

Neither man grasped that the obstacle to improving space on the Lower East Side—and the reason that neither the Bowery Savings directors nor the landlords would invest systematically in the neighborhood—was a value central to American identity: the pursuit of profit. That value needed no promotion. Many foreign residents, following a well-trod path of American cupidity, had already begun to eye the profit-making potential in the spaces they inhabited.

Lizzie Jaeger's grandfather, Peter Rutz, was twenty-five years old when he stepped onto a New York pier from the deck of the *Margaret Evans* on Oc-tober 17, 1848.[18] He was among the first in a flood of immigrants streaming out of Europe in the wake of the social-democratic revolutions that had rocked the continent that spring. Whatever his initial attitude toward those revolutions, Rutz refused to remain in Bavaria to witness their failure, to subject himself to that bitterness (of whatever political stripe) that the German poet Joseph von Eichendorff expressed in 1849: "Truly, if I were younger and wealthier than I unfortunately am, I'd emigrate to America today. Not out of cowardice . . . but out of overpowering disgust at the moral rottenness which, to use Shakespeare's phrase, stinks to high heaven."[19] For Eichendorff, America represented the possibility of an escape from that rottenness, from what Karl Marx would soon describe—with that very historical moment in mind—as the nightmare of the past weighing upon the brains of the living. The would-be socialists and insurrectionist workers of Europe saw their revolutionary dreams overtaken by this nightmare; they awoke, bleary-eyed, to an age of industrial expansion, bourgeois retrenchment, liberal economics, and conservative politics. America beckoned as a bastion of relative freedom, but Eichendorff, and probably Rutz as well, failed to imagine how easily the nightmare and the reality that followed it might cross oceans.

After nearly a decade of living in New York, Rutz could have had few remaining illusions about the promise of an easier life in America. 1857 found him still working as a laborer, living at 86 Jackson Street, not far from where he had disembarked and a stone's throw from the East River.[20] His wife, a fellow Bavarian named Elizabeth, had given birth less than two years earlier to their first son, Peter, and would give birth again that year to their daughter Lizie.[21] Through successive homes and eight pregnancies, Elizabeth kept their house and raised the four children who survived— Peter, Lizie, Daniel, and Edward.[22] Theirs was the lot of most working-class German immigrants in New York: difficult work, rough living conditions, and family hardship perhaps mitigated only by thoughts that their children might have better luck should they live to see adulthood.

Yet luck was reluctant to show its face. Their eldest son Peter attended school briefly as a teenager, but he took a job with a livery service for a furniture company to supplement the family income and stuck with it. In 1880, Lizie was working in a millinery shop, and Daniel at a cigar maker's. Only thirteen-year-old Edward did not work, but neither did he attend school. After more than twenty-five years, the Rutz family still lived together on the Lower East Side, at 16 Clinton Street just below East Houston, eking out an existence along with their predominantly German neighbors—tailors, cigarmakers, lacemakers, and barbers.[23]

It remained that way a few years more, until the early 1880s, when Peter met a German woman with his mother's name and moved out to start his own family. The newly married Peter and Elizabeth had five sons over the course of twelve years from 1881 to 1893: William, Peter, Charles, Edward, and Jacob.[24] In the winter of 1891 to 1892, Peter's sister Lizie died, having given birth just over a year earlier to a daughter, Lizzie. Lizzie's father, Charles Jaeger, presumably daunted at the prospect of raising so young a child while working on his own, sent Lizzie to live with her aunt, uncle, and cousins.[25] And so it was that in 1894, Peter and Elizabeth lived with five sons and a niece on the third floor of a tenement building at 129 Suffolk Street, just around the corner from Peter's parents' old place on Clinton Street.[26]

Two generations of Rutzes had worked hard on the Lower East Side for almost half a century, and while they may not have experienced the rags-to-riches American dream, neither had they failed in spectacular fashion. They obeyed the law. They lived within their means. They were arguably the very diligent, upright, naturalized American citizens that Gilder and White hoped to see emerge, fully assimilated, from the foreign regions of the Bowery, and their rough northward trajectory on the Lower East Side seemed to indicate that, given time, they might do just that.

Their downstairs neighbor at 129 Suffolk Street, however, had set his sights higher. In 1886 at the age of twenty-three, Solomon Kleinrock, a Russian Jewish émigré, had set out from Hamburg on the *British Queen*. He had been a *Schneider*—a tailor or cutter—in his Galician hometown of Bolschowce (now Bilshivtsi, Ukraine), but within only seven years of his arrival in New York he was running a liquor store and saloon.[27] His was that fierce ambition for immigrant success in America, celebrated by Horatio Alger's stories and presented as a cautionary tale by Abraham Cahan in his later work *The Rise of David Levinsky*. In that novel, Levinsky, a teenage rabbinical student born in a Russian shtetl, emigrated to America after his mother's murder and, through years of bitter struggle, fashioned himself into a textile magnate, only to discover spiritual emptiness in his material success.[28] Like Levinsky, Kleinrock tried to strike pay dirt with his own business operation. Unlike Cahan's fictional protagonist, however, Kleinrock failed to prosper. By early 1894, his entrepreneurial drive had landed him on the edge of insolvency, yet every month like clockwork, the agent from the Budweiser Brewing Company in Brooklyn (improbably named

Abraham Kahn) dropped in to collect $35 rent on the saloon fixtures Klein-rock had leased.[29] As the months wore on and Kleinrock's cash reserves dwindled, he found it increasingly difficult to make the payments.

Kleinrock sought help from another Polish-speaking immigrant, Adolph Hershkopf. Born in Czestochowa, Poland, Hershkopf had been in New York longer than Kleinrock, and had moved further up the social and pro-fessional ladder. He had run a barber shop in Jefferson Street with his brother-in-law before going into the insurance line, first becoming a life-insurance agent, then a fire-insurance adjuster in the early 1890s.[30] With Hershkopf's wife, Anna, bringing in extra income from her dressmaking work, they seemed to enjoy a relatively successful immigrant life. Anna would later insist, "My husband and I have lived happily together. We have never seri-ously quarreled; he never struck me in his life. What he earned he brought home. I had nothing to blame him, and he was a good father to his chil-dren, and he was kind to me; he supported the children and I."[31]

Hershkopf, however, offered his friend Kleinrock a solution to his finan-cial woes that was somewhat at odds with Anna Hershkopf's portrait of her husband as a good family man: he suggested that they insure Kleinrock's sa-loon for as much money as possible, then burn it down and split the proceeds. As then-assistant district attorney Henry S. Davis would point out years later, "From 1890 to 1895 were the palmy days of the New York firebugs—companies were lax in the issuance of their policies. The adjusters who ap-peared for the companies in settling the losses were more often crooked than not."[32] Hershkopf, as the public discovered at his trial for the Kleinrock ar-son, ran with one of the biggest fire-insurance fraud rackets in New York. Davis later calculated that in five years, the gang (run by a man named Sam-uel Milch) had "engineered not less than 200 incendiary fires, most of them being in tenement houses."[33] At a rate of more than one fire every ten days, this was a small but not insignificant portion of all fires in New York.[34]

A series of witnesses at the trial revealed that Hershkopf made his living enticing struggling immigrants to commit insurance fraud, assisting them in taking out fat policies on their property, and letting his gang of "fire-bugs" torch their property. He then used a professional network of insur-ance adjusters to cash in on the destruction. If any trouble should arise, the gang's connections to the police and fire marshal's office helped to insulate them from suspicion.[35] These witnesses testified that Kleinrock visited with

Hershkopf repeatedly in the months before the fire at 129 Suffolk Street, planning the details of defrauding the Niagara Insurance Company out of the $1,200 policy Kleinrock had managed to secure (with Hershkopf's help) only weeks before the fire. They reported overhearing Hershkopf's instructions that Kleinrock fill the saloon with empty bottles and extra stock to magnify the claim because "the adjuster of the Niagara . . . is very hard to settle; he doesn't accept money neither." Two weeks before the fire, one eavesdropping witness heard an increasingly desperate Kleinrock say to Hershkopf, "You know I must have this fire this month, the present month." Hershkopf replied, "All right."[36]

The fact that these witnesses were, in the main, turning state's evidence as acknowledged arsonists and members of the gang themselves did not overshadow the villainous portrait they painted of Hershkopf as an arrogant sociopath, indifferent to murdering children in his quest for money. Max Gluckman and Scheyer Rosenbaum, the state's star witnesses, had been Hershkopf's accomplices, but both insisted to the court that they had refused to participate in the Kleinrock arson on ethical grounds. Gluckman testified first: "We told him he shouldn't go; he would regret it, because poor people are living there. I said, 'I know your material very well; there will be an accident.' [Hershkopf] said, 'You are big fools. In America people don't look at accidents. I am the boss; I am responsible.'"[37] Rosenbaum later corroborated this impression of Hershkopf's egotistical self-fashioning, claiming that he boasted, "I am the first mechanic here in New York— mechanic to make fires, meaning a professor, one who can make a good fire."[38] Louis Grauer, another Hershkopf recruit, described how Hershkopf had become resentful of Samuel Milch, the leader of the arson gang, asserting that after a fight with Milch over a payout, Hershkopf declared to Grauer, "I will show Milch that my name is Adolph Hershkopf."[39] In his own mind, at least, he was a man on the make.

In perhaps the most damning piece of testimony (partly because it came from a more credible witness), Joseph Biebergal, who co-managed a restaurant on Allen Street, testified that Hershkopf had tried to sell him on the idea of burning down his eatery in June 1894. Hershkopf had stood on the corner of Suffolk and Rivington Streets with Biebergal and said, pointing to the charred remains of 129 Suffolk, "You see that house burned down, and I will make a fire in your place and you needn't be afraid."[40] In other words, Hershkopf tried to employ the husk of 129 Suffolk Street as an advertisement for his services, indifferent to the fact that a child had died on that site only weeks earlier. Biebergal turned him down.[41]

Gilder's letter to Marshall upon investigating 129 Suffolk Street had mentioned the "suspicion of foul play," but it was not until months after the New York Legislature had enacted the new measures advocated by his Committee that the courts handed down an indictment for arson. In the meantime, the 129 Suffolk Street fire and the pathos of Lizzie's death had provided the perfect narrative justification for Gilder's insistence on new laws mandating fireproof construction and new behavioral regulations for tenement residents. The Committee's report included a multipage analysis of the fire and its progress through the tenement, complete with a foldout side-view plan of the building to better illustrate its tinderbox design flaws.[42] The conclusion seemed clear: the spatial arrangements and inadequate construction of tenements, as well as the irresponsible living and storage arrangements of the poor, were to blame for Lizzie's death. Unsurprisingly, of the various legislative initiatives emerging from the Committee's work, fireproof construction of new tenements and safeguards for existing ones were the most comprehensive.

This new legislation doubtless helped contain fires once they started, but it failed to get at the root of what had killed Lizzie Jaeger. Hershkopf's trial began to unearth that root, not only by revealing the immediate source of the Kleinrock fire, but also by describing the social and economic conditions that made tenement arson such a powerful temptation. Multiple witnesses—mostly poor immigrants testifying through a court interpreter—painted a picture of their itinerant living and working arrangements in New York's working-class immigrant districts, arrangements perpetuated by absentee landlordism and disinvestment. Anna Gluckman's testimony was typical: "I was born in Warsaw; I came to this country first six years ago . . . I lived two years in Delancey Street . . . I moved to 99 Willett Street, and lived there about six or seven months, and moved from Willett Street to Essex Street, and lived there one year . . . I moved from Essex Street to Eighth Street, Brooklyn; it is number 176 or only 76; I cannot tell exactly the number."[43] It seems safe to say that she felt little personal attachment to these consecutive residences.

Witness Meyer Brenner described a similarly unattached work life, explaining, "I have been a tailor for about twelve or thirteen years; I always

work as such when I can get work, and when I am not able to get work as a
tailor I peddle. I am working now as a tailor at home; I take work home,
finish it home." Despite admitting that he had taken out a $1,500 insurance
policy through Hershkopf in furtherance of an arson fraud, he had can-
celled the plan (and the policy), telling Hershkopf, "I don't want any fight
with my wife, and I don't want that kind of business." Under cross-examination
by defense lawyers, he insisted on his innocence, declaring, "Never in my
life I was a firebug [*sic*]. I am a working man."[44] Yet thousands of people like
Brenner and the Gluckmans, engaged in a constant struggle to find work
and without firm neighborhood ties were the ideal targets for fraud engineers like Hershkopf.

Moreover, the way Hershkopf applied pressure on these targets and reluctant fellow arsonists reveals not only his brilliance in playing on generic
dreams of material success, but also his skill in employing the adopted vocabulary of an explicitly *American* spirit of enterprise. When Gluckman
initially refused to participate in the Kleinrock fire out of fear that sleeping
tenants might be hurt, Hershkopf mocked him. "You are a big fool," he
said. "In America we don't consider those things. We only look to make
money. If nothing to eat nobody will give you anything. It will only take
about half an hour and you will earn fifty dollars."[45] In a few terse sentences,
Hershkopf distilled a certain essence of American capitalist ambition: profit
at all costs, self-reliance in the knowledge that no handouts are forthcoming, and an imperative to strike while the iron is hot.

Almost a year later, Hershkopf wrote to Gluckman in Germany trying to
persuade him to return to the United States for a few last jobs. "As I remarked
sometime ago I don't intend to remain in such a business," he assured Gluckman. "But as soon as we have made enough money. [*sic*] As soon as some
good business presents itself, all other business must cease and we will be able
to live in peace with our families here in America or in Europe."[46] The promise of a beatific future beyond the unpleasant but lucrative work available in
America spoke to the basic immigrant experience in the United States.[47]

On July 16, 1896, a jury foreclosed on Hershkopf's dreams, convicting him
of arson and allowing the judge to slap him with a life sentence; Kleinrock
had long-since fled back to Europe (although not before receiving his portion of the $750 insurance settlement).[48] The same day, the *New York Times*
ran an editorial entitled "Our Foreign Criminals," in which it declared:

The Supreme Court was yesterday, not for the first time, the scene of a striking illustration how alien and remote from any standards or customs with
which we are familiar is a considerable part of our population. . . . This is a
very serious state of things. It shows that the children of these benighted or
villainous people must be so exposed to American influences and so aerated
by them as to be completely transformed before they can be regarded as
trustworthy American citizens. . . . [I]t will be agreed that the whole procedure has a very foreign air and is calculated to admonish native Americans
of the existence among them of a large class of people with whom they can
scarcely be said to have anything at all in common.[49]

Echoing the Tenement Committee's prescriptive moral tone toward tenement residents, the *Times* editors blurred the distinction between immigrants
and criminals, equating foreignness with ignorance and villainy, and Ameri-
canness with normative morality. They advocated the core of an imperial progressive program: "aerating" foreigners otherwise incapable of self-government
with "American influences" to create "trustworthy American citizens." They
could not have more thoroughly misunderstood the affair.

Former assistant district attorney Davis, looking back on the phenomenon of fire-insurance fraud from more than a decade's distance, came to a
different conclusion. "Incendiary fires set for profit and gain are usually the
fault, at bottom," he wrote,

of the insurance companies, for they will write a policy for almost any reasonable amount merely upon the request of the applicant. In but few cases
do they survey the risk. . . . Thus they put a premium on arson. . . . Until
some such scheme is devised to protect the companies and to make arson
unprofitable incendiary fires will continue—will continue so long as the companies put a premium on crime by hanging the bait of dollars before the
noses of those men who find themselves financially embarrassed.[50]

This institutional interpretation hit closer to the mark (though not without
a whiff of anti-Semitism in "bait of dollars before the noses"). Still, inadequately regulated insurance company policies were just one thread in a complicated web of structural and human forces putting a "premium on arson."

The tenements had to be of so little actual material or sentimental value
to their inhabitants that they became worth more to them burnt to a cinder

than they were standing. A variety of political-economic factors contributed to bringing this reality to pass. Absentee owners and a small army of indifferent managers led to poor property upkeep and oppressive rents for tenants. The sporadic nature of most neighborhood residents' industrial jobs forced them to move with dizzying frequency. Capital and human disinvestment in the neighborhood, facilitated by banks like the Bowery Savings, further eroded property values in poor neighborhoods. And entrenched corruption in both the insurance industry and the city's regulatory structures (the police, fire marshal's office, Board of Health inspectors, etc.) facilitated organized criminal enterprises like the arson ring. It was not for a lack of laws stipulating better conditions that tenement hygiene and safety suffered, and Gilder's Committee, in successfully urging more such laws, did nothing to intervene in the larger structure of incentives and disincentives creating the undesirable conditions.

Although they may have been contributing factors, badly lighted hallways, fire escape obstructions, and lack of fireproof construction at 129 Suffolk Street were not ultimately responsible for Lizzie Jaeger's death. Nor did she die because poor immigrant Lower East Siders lacked a vision of imperial America to aspire to. On the contrary, her death came about through a series of market calculations in response to material circumstances. Solomon Kleinrock, an immigrant striver who could not make his saloon profitable in the midst of a severe depression, decided that burning it down for the insurance money was a better investment than continuing to run it. Because Adolph Hershkopf saw money to be made in incinerating buildings such as 129 Suffolk Street, he tempted hard-up owners and lessees such as Kleinrock into a profitable criminal enterprise. They pursued arson deliberately and carefully as a business venture, with the collusion of both insurance company personnel and prominent city officials. These two immigrants saw clearly what imperial progressives such as Gilder and White and the *Times* editors could not: the pursuit of profit, that most American of values, led logically to the further deterioration and destruction of their neighborhoods. Why, they concluded, should they not reap their portion of the spoils?

4

Loving the Poor with Severity

> It is better to love with severity than to deceive with lenience . . .
> more useful to take bread away from a hungry man if when he
> was sure of food he neglected justice, than to give bread to him so
> that, being led astray, he may rejoice in injustice.
>
> —St. Augustine

WITNESSES FOR THE PROSECUTION mentioned twice during Adolph Hershkopf's trial that the fraudster's intended victim, the Niagara Insurance Company, had retained the De Forest Brothers law firm as general counsel. This fact went unreported in the press and understandably so—the witnesses noted it in passing, and it seemed peripheral to the substance of the case. On the other hand, omitting it left a rich source of ironic reflection untapped. Only three years earlier, in 1893, De Forest Brothers had been entangled with fraud on a much larger scale.

Francis Henry Weeks, a former partner in the firm and uncle to its remaining partners Henry Weeks de Forest and Robert Weeks de Forest, had exploited his position in the firm's estates and trusts business to embezzle over $1 million from wealthy clients. He invested most of these funds in his own speculative mining and development ventures in Wisconsin. When the depression hit in 1893 and the money evaporated, Weeks realized the jig was up. He hastily resigned his club memberships and public positions, assigned his affairs to an attorney, borrowed money for traveling expenses, and fled to South America.[1]

It is farcical enough that the blue-blood law firm charged with defending the Niagara against "foreign" fraud had been party to a giant fraud itself, but the irony of Weeks's thievery ran quite a bit deeper. He had served, from 1885 to 1887, as the president of the Charity Organization Society of New York City (C.O.S.), a group devoted to the principle that easy access to alms led to idleness and moral decay among the poor. The group dispatched "friendly visitors," whom it initially hoped would be upper-class women volunteers, to foster advisory relationships with struggling New Yorkers, instructing them in thrift, sobriety, cleanliness, and other virtues, while simultaneously investigating them for profligacy, drunkenness, slovenliness, and other vices. Those investigations, supplemented by paid C.O.S. investigators and agents, produced meticulous files on individual alms-seekers that C.O.S.-affiliated charities could employ in deciding to disburse or deny aid.[2] Weeks had been industriously embezzling millions of dollars from his own clients after serving as the titular head of an organization prescribing morality to the poor while surveilling them. It was the kind of hypocrisy usually reserved for villains in Charles Dickens novels. Sadly, no one at the time seemed to take notice.[3]

Weeks only personified the Dickensian notoriety that the C.O.S. had acquired in some quarters of New York by the early 1890s. From its beginnings, the C.O.S. antagonized other New York charities by accusing them of wastefulness. The group's secretary, Charles D. Kellogg, typified this approach with his widely publicized claim, barely a year after the C.O.S. had been founded in 1882, that "65 per cent of the work done by . . . charity societies is misdirected."[4] His solution? Eliminate 65 percent of alms. This sort of logic led one notable Episcopal clergyman in 1888 to tag the C.O.S. with a sobriquet Dickens himself might have coined: "the meanest humbug in New York City."[5] Others began referring to it as the "Organization for the Prevention of Charity."[6]

Indeed, C.O.S. leaders *did* intend to prevent charity in what they saw as its corrupted form—namely, the careless and excessive distribution of alms to all the poor, regardless of merit. By applying their "scientific" methods of investigation, record-keeping, and communications networks among charities, they aimed to create greater consistency in providing charity to the worthy poor, while denying aid to the unworthy, whom they believed to be legion. Their stated hope in doing so was that denying aid to the unworthy would facilitate a process of reform, both at the individual and social levels. Drunks would be made sober, the lazy would become industrious, and the feckless would discover purpose, if only their vices were met with opprobrium and denial rather than leniency and aid. As a result, social health would improve, as, in Kellogg's words, the previously parasitic poor became "provident, thoughtful, self-respecting and contributing members of society."[7] It expressed the clearest kind of prescriptive entitlement—an assumption of the right to oversee, render judgment, and enforce reeducation upon the poor. It also reflected a powerfully modern impulse: to reform society by improving the individual.[8]

The C.O.S.'s "scientific" methods institutionalized long-prevalent, prescriptive cultural attitudes toward the poor, primarily the belief that excessive alms encouraged dependency and therefore should be tightly controlled and regulated by law and social custom.[9] Moreover, the group's trumpeting of the need for scientific methods in charity reflected a broader cultural shift from sacred to secular in nineteenth-century theories of social organization, positioning it to exert significant influence on professional social work and welfare policy in the twentieth century. The C.O.S. institutionalized this influence when it established the first comprehensive educational program for social work in the city, the New York School of Philanthropy, which ultimately became the Columbia University School of Social Work.[10]

Viewing the C.O.S. primarily as an agent in the secularization and professionalization of welfare practice, however, creates a misimpression of its actual operations and diverts attention from its central paradox: its pairing of modern methods and reform expectations with a medieval principle of charity, the theory of distinction between worthy and unworthy poor. In one form or another, this theory proposed that among the poor exist two broad types—those who possess qualities entitling them to the support of the community, and those who do not—and that the denial of support to the latter is at least as important to social health as provision of support to the former. Among "Worthy Cases," as specified in the C.O.S.'s *Hand-Book for Friendly Visitors among the Poor,* were the aged, the sick, and widows with young children and no means to support a family. The unworthy cases occupied a much larger range of categories, from those "where too much is paid for rent, or tobacco, or liquor, or dress, or in any unwise expense; and *economy needs to be taught,*" to those "Undeserving Cases," where "liquor, or thieving, or imposture, or any form of vice has got hold of a family."[11] The C.O.S.'s "scientific" methods of investigation and record-keeping may be the ancestors of modern social work, but the theory of distinction's entrenchment in the American imagination as a force for reform has been an equally powerful part of its legacy.

Of course, the theory of distinction between worthy and unworthy poor (hereafter, simply "distinction") long predated the Charity Organization movement. It had been the philosophical touchstone of nearly every poor-relief system in the Western world up to the society's founding, and remains for many an article of faith to this day.[12] Its longevity has largely insulated it from the kinds of critiques that organizational shifts in its application, such as those pioneered by the C.O.S., have attracted, granting its presence and assumptive validity an undisturbed veneer of timeless consensus—as if the systematic division of the poor into two broad categories of worthy and unworthy were a natural human instinct rather than an idea with its own history of development and application.[13]

As currently conceived, distinction is, in fact, a medieval Catholic concept with institutional origins in twelfth-century canon law. Its first statutory incarnations were religious, and had negligible prescriptive intent toward the poor. Distinction *became* prescriptive through application in modern schemes of social improvement or reconciliation. Examining the course of this philosophical shift through the experience of the C.O.S., in both its origins and daily operations, reveals how such prescriptive distinction not only failed to improve social health, but actually reinforced inequality.

Few individuals personified the swelling power of postbellum reform as fully as the C.O.S.'s guiding spirit Josephine Shaw Lowell. Born nine days before Christmas in 1843 to the evangelical Unitarian scions of two wealthy Boston families, she spent her childhood immersed in the society of transcendentalists, abolitionists, women's rights activists, and utopians of religious and socialist stripes, developing a rigorous ethic of civic obligation from a tender age. A widow at twenty-one, the first woman appointed to public office in New York State at thirty-two, and the founder of the most influential charity organization in New York City before her fortieth birthday, Lowell believed in the perfectibility of man and society. Hers was a religious faith, and even when it strayed from strictest doctrine into realms of science and political economy, its bedrock remained one of Protestant service and morality. That foundation played a determining role in everything she built atop it.[14]

Seeing her C.O.S. as a nonreligious or even antireligious phenomenon, however, makes reasonably good sense. The earliest of the organization's advocates explicitly declared it to be a system of nonsectarian "scientific charity," one that did away with the biblical dictum "the poor you will always have with you" and operated instead in the pursuit of poverty's total or near-eradication through rational methods of—as the name implied—organization.[15] They decried a system (as they saw it) of automatic, unthinking apportionments to the poor, a system whose origins they traced to church laws on tithing that named provision for the poor as among the primary duties of a Christian parish and promised spiritual redemption in return for the mere act of almsgiving. From the start, the C.O.S. seemed to be positioning itself squarely within contemporary scientific trends and against an outmoded, sentimental religiosity. This was to be a modern charity.

Moreover, the charity organization movement in New York had a central concern with earthly, local politics. The city's Department of Charities and Corrections (D.C.C.) under William "Boss" Tweed and his Tammany Democrats had doubled as an all-purpose engine of political corruption, providing patronage positions, cash to purchase votes, and the ballot-stuffing potential of easily bribed (or coerced) prison, workhouse, and almshouse residents. Even when employed in delivering the charity services that were its actual charge, the department reinforced Democratic partisan power. When Tweed's reign collapsed under the weight of its ill-gotten riches and well-deserved scandals, reformers such as Lowell leapt at the chance to ensure that the D.C.C. would never again become an instrument for political shell games, not just because they believed in a more utopian vision of charity but because they despised Tammany Democrats.[16]

In this political context, and in light of the C.O.S.'s own declarations of scientific nonsectarianism, viewing the group as fundamentally religious in its conception of charity might seem contrarian. Given that its contemporaries—from adherents to critics to marginal observers—saw it as a scientific and possibly irreligious departure from traditional charity, doing so might seem ahistorical. Yet for all its scientific rationalism and mundane political purpose, the C.O.S.'s vision for charity radiated Christian tradition. That it did so with so little notice, either historical or contemporary, indicates a collective blindness not only toward the C.O.S., but also toward the paradoxical origins and development of U.S. relief systems writ large— and, for that matter, toward the fraught contributions of Christian doctrine to American class relations.

In an address to the C.O.S.'s fourth annual meeting in 1886, Reverend H. L. Wayland spoke on "The Old Charity and the New," outlining the important strides that scientific charity was making in poor relief. "The Old Charity," he argued, "finds a man hungry and cold; and it feeds him, and gives him an order for a ton of coal." Wayland found this behavior horrifying. The "New Charity," by contrast, *"Imitating a great-hearted apostle* . . . takes the impotent man by the hand and lifts him up. To uplift, to set people on their feet, to enable them to stand, is the great effort of the New Charity."[17] His vision—and that of most C.O.S. advocates—was of a distinctly non-materialist charity captured in the C.O.S. motto, "Not alms, but a friend," and while the group's constitution prohibited "proselytism or spiritual instruction," its participants were perfectly explicit in their understanding of the religious inspiration for their work.

Indeed, the C.O.S.'s predecessors in New York's field of elite charities made a true secular break deeply improbable; invocations of divine purpose and piety flowed through the minute books and infused the operations of most major nineteenth-century charities in the city. For decades, the annual report narratives of the Society for the Relief of Poor Widows with Small Children (S.R.P.W., founded in 1797) consisted of elaborating the relationship of the group's work with and dependence upon God. The S.R.P.W. bylaws decreed that each fortnightly meeting begin with the reading of "a portion of Scripture."[18] The Society for the Prevention of Pauperism, founded in 1817 as a stern corrective to overly generous forms of both municipal and sectarian poor relief, referred to charity in an early official report as "that fair daughter of Heaven, that sublime attendant on true Christianity."[19] Robert M. Hartley, a leader of the C.O.S. forerunner the Association for Improving the Condition of the Poor (A.I.C.P., founded in 1843), had served for years as a city tract missionary and had succeeded in convincing the A.I.C.P.'s founders to hire its district secretaries from among his evangelist former colleagues. Their religious influence filtered down into

A.I.C.P. meetings with the poor, as a typical report from 1855 indicates: at a meeting with more than twenty poor New Yorkers, the visitor in question describes how "I read a chapter of Solomon's Proverbs, and dilated on the instruction to thrift and industry with which that remarkable book abounds; and closed our meeting with a singing and prayer."[20] Despite their claims of nonsectarianism, the C.O.S.'s founders swam their entire lives in a charitable milieu awash in Christian language and practice.

In answering the question "What is Charity Organization?" for the inaugural edition of *Charities Review* in 1891, C.O.S. president Robert Weeks de Forest cited neither Charles Darwin nor Edmund Spencer, but rather St. Paul: " 'Though I bestow all my goods to feed the poor, and though I give my body to be burned and have not charity, it profiteth me nothing.' " De Forest hardly de-emphasized religious inspirations when he averred, "Like St. Paul's charity, [Charity Organization] is love."[21] Even while insisting that their vision of charity was scientific, Wayland, De Forest, and their colleagues regularly defined it through references to Christian apostolic love, both in its attention to the moral causes of poverty and in its concern for the long-term (including eternal) effects of charity on all parties involved. "This Society," as the C.O.S.'s *Second Annual Report* stated, "seeks to establish a community of philanthropy, in which the experience of each enriches all; where charity is studied as the law of love, and that law obeyed as the voice of God."[22]

Even as C.O.S. leaders made plain their spiritual debt to Christian traditions, they also shared the widely held view that those same traditions had led to deplorable poor-relief practices in need of modernization. This view reflected the writings of Arwed Emminghaus, a German historian of European charity, and W. J. Ashley, an English economic historian, both of whom represented the nineteenth-century consensus that medieval church institutions had failed to discriminate between worthy and unworthy poor in dispensing relief. According to Emminghaus and Ashley, as one historian explains, "the [medieval] emphasis on the intrinsic virtue of almsgiving led to a complete neglect of the effect of the alms on the recipient, and . . . in turn caused nearly all the resources available for the relief of the poor to be squandered in 'indiscriminate charity,' which . . . was far worse than no charity at all."[23] The C.O.S. reformers saw parallels in their own era, both in religious institutions that provided relief to their poor congregants without serious inquiry, and in wealthy philanthropists or politicians who gave without considering the deleterious moral effects on the poor. By setting themselves up as the modern, scientific, disinterested alternative to religious, indiscriminate, self-interested precursors and contemporaries, the C.O.S. leaders tried to claim the mantle of scientific progress that for many had begun to define the late nineteenth century.

Emminghaus and Ashley, however, had provided a misleading account of the medieval period. They ignored and obscured aspects of the premodern poor-law tradition to which the C.O.S.'s vision of charity owed a profound debt.[24] Despite C.O.S. reformers' beliefs to the contrary, Christian thinkers had grappled with the potentially pernicious moral effects of indiscriminate charity since the time of St. Augustine, as suggested by the Augustinian dictum "It is better to love with severity than to deceive with lenience . . . more useful to take bread away from a hungry man if when he was sure of food he neglected justice, than to give bread to him so that, being led astray, he may rejoice in injustice."[25] European theologians were citing this passage as early as the twelfth century to justify codifying distinctions among the poor for charitable purposes. That there were advocates for indiscriminate charity among these medieval theologians and canonists is beyond doubt; that there were equally determined and influential advocates for defining categories of worthy and unworthy poor through canon law and institutional practice, however, is just as indisputable.[26] The resulting body of church law and local charity practice emerged from a dialectic between these two schools of thought, and it provided the foundation upon which the Elizabethan Poor Law of 1601—so often cited as the progenitor to U.S. systems of poor relief—established itself.[27] As one medievalist scholar argued decades ago, "Medieval canon law is no obscure eddy, outside the main stream of poor law history, but an important and neglected stretch of the main stream itself."[28]

The crucial inheritance, a Pandora's box borne safely along that stream's currents from twelfth-century religious thinkers to the nineteenth century and beyond, is the very principle of distinction that those medieval canonists were thought to lack: the idea that among the poor, there are those deserving and undeserving of relief, and that the givers of charity not only have the right but the responsibility to distinguish between the two. Historians of modern welfare systems have found a convenient source for distinction in the Elizabethan Poor Law, which drew a sharp line between family, community members, and the helpless as those entitled to relief, and strangers, vagrants, and the able-bodied idle to be denied relief. Indeed, Elizabethan Poor Law and its progeny developed far harsher *methods* of distinction than the medieval canonists had imagined, both in response to the violent dislocations of early capitalist development (more unfamiliar poor people impelled stricter rules), and in the context of consequent shifts in the common understanding of poverty from a natural state to a blameworthy or even criminal one.[29] But distinction itself in the codified practices of poor relief was the invention of premodern men in a premodern world.

The vital and profoundly consequential difference between the premodern and modern uses of distinction has been the social expectation of its practitioners. Distinction grew out of a conscious attempt on the part of medieval theologians to maintain the status quo, or, as the Augustinian dictum suggests, to "love with severity" in order to avoid inadvertently encouraging immorality or deviance.[30] Twelfth-century canonists and almsgivers treated social divisions between rich and poor as the work of God; the idea that church law or poor relief should or could dramatically *improve* the social landscape would have resembled blasphemy.[31] Distinction functioned within that system of social ethics, a system in which changing someone's earthly social status for the better through human policy was neither desired nor imagined. Instead, it meant to distinguish the worthy from the unworthy poor in order to maintain social equilibrium, preserve limited resources for the "truly unfortunate," and limit sin to a minimum.[32] Distinction was a lens through which to observe and distinguish poor people from one another. It was not an anvil upon which to shape them.[33]

Distinction's inheritors, meanwhile, from the English Parliament of the early sixteenth century to C.O.S. leaders and beyond, have sought more often to employ it (and to justify it) precisely as such an anvil, in the service of prescriptive social *improvement*.[34] They have used it recurrently as a means of punishment, discipline, or re-education—whether at the individual or communal level—to reduce the geographical mobility of the poor, chastise them for beggary or vagrancy, and conform their individual behavior to prevailing norms of work or gender.[35] From the author of a 1724 English poor-law tract who urged authorities "to Distinguish the Real Objects of Pity from the Counterfeits and Impostors" that they might "grant Relief to the one, give due Punishment to the others," to Kellogg's desire to "convert" the poor "into provident, thoughtful, self-respecting and contributing members of society," discipline and social transformation have been the running themes of distinction's modern history.[36]

Distinction's modern practitioners, in other words, took a tool designed to serve a world of unchanging social position and applied it to programs of personal and social amelioration. Critics have long attacked distinction as unjust, cruel, and inadequate to understanding or addressing social divisions under capitalism.[37] Few, if any, have noted that its premodern origins as a religious framework for *recognizing* social divisions have made it fundamentally counterproductive to the modern goal of secular social improvement or rehabilitation.

Philosophically speaking, then, the C.O.S. was a far less radical break from prior religious charitable practice than is commonly acknowledged. Its primary innovation lay not in its leaders' insistence on limiting charity more effectively to the "worthy" poor (the Society for the Prevention of Pauperism had been insisting on the same imperative over six decades before the C.O.S.'s founding), but in its methods of casework data accumulation and distribution. C.O.S. visitors and secretaries systematically assembled an ever-growing compendium of intimate detail on every person who applied for charity in New York, and they shared this information with cooperating charities. Predictably, this process eliminated hundreds of names from the charity rolls in short order. C.O.S. investigators often either directly identified previously undetected moral failings in those seeking relief or, by cross-referencing information from multiple organizations, exposed applicants who had accepted relief from several sources.[38]

Yet in the execution of its innovative casework system, the C.O.S. left a darker legacy: the entrenchment of distinction as the dominant interpretive framework of encounters between rich and poor in American schemes of poor relief. It is impossible to measure how drastically this framework curtails Americans' imagination for alternative forms of welfare policy. It is, however, possible to assess the social damage such a framework does in moments of prescriptive class encounters.

The C.O.S. undermined its own reformist goals and programs of class reconciliation by prioritizing the distinction between worthy and unworthy applicants. The counterproductivity of its approach appears most obviously in moments of contact between the Society's representatives and the poor. The individual case files the C.O.S. maintained on each relief applicant demonstrate with remarkable clarity how distinction continued to serve its twelfth-century purpose of recognizing—and consequently reinforcing—social place, despite the transformative hopes that men and women like De Forest and Lowell had attached to it. When the rich or their agents, guided by the principle of distinction, encountered the poor in C.O.S. offices or tenement homes, they powerfully bolstered the relative class positions of everyone involved. It is to a few of those encounters that we now turn.

Elizabeth Shaw had a difficult life by any measure. Born in 1854 in New York, she left home at sixteen after her stepmother slapped her in the face for asking permission to go to the theater. She was boarding with her sister's family on 40th Street and 4th Avenue less than two years later when she became pregnant with George, her first child, only to discover belatedly that the father was already married. She soon married Samuel Mortimer Carman, taking his name and having a daughter with him before he died in the mid-1880s. Her husband's death left Elizabeth Carman (neé Shaw) a widow with two young children, Mourna, now three years old, and George, an adolescent. Before reaching his tenth birthday, George had already spent over a year in the Five Points House of Industry, a juvenile reformatory. At fifteen, he ran away from home.[39]

Elizabeth Carman married again, this time to Joseph Hart, but she continued to struggle. In April 1890, agents of the Society for the Prevention of Cruelty to Children (S.P.C.C.) visited her basement apartment while she was out and deemed it "damp and filthy, and almost destitute of furnishing." They promptly committed Mourna, now eight years old, to the Five Points House of Industry. The S.P.C.C. superintendent later remarked that when Elizabeth Hart returned home and discovered her daughter missing, "it was found necessary to arrest the mother, on account of her abusive talk."[40] The Society returned Mourna to her mother two months later "on being convinced that a reformation had taken place."[41] In 1892, Elizabeth Hart had her third child, Jeanette. As the 1890s wore on, however, Joseph Hart became ill and less able to provide for his family. When he died mid-decade,

Elizabeth reclaimed her first husband's name, and as Mrs. S. M. Carman, a widow twice over, she renewed the applications for assistance she had begun in the 1880s.

On February 2, 1897, Elizabeth Carman stormed into the 8th District office of the C.O.S. at 214 East 42nd Street and threatened the group with a lawsuit in "most abusive" terms, warning the agent on duty "not to visit or make any further inquiries" into her family.[42] Before storming out, however, she delivered a longhand letter to the agent, the contents of which alternated between anguish and fury, describing much of her history under the heading "Synopsis of my Life." The threats and demands she had issued in person before leaving the office might have suggested she wanted nothing more to do with the C.O.S., but her letter sought vindication for the "lies" that the investigator at the Application Bureau had written "on your long Postal Cards" (the memorandum cards for recording casework) when interviewing her days earlier. Carman had correctly deduced the investigator's unfavorable assessment of her application for aid, and as she put it in her letter, "[T]here is always 2 sides to a question."[43] She may have stormed out the door, but she was still pleading for a favorable response.

Rachel Johnstone, a seamstress (when she could get work), had enjoyed a good reputation with the A.I.C.P. and the C.O.S. throughout the mid-1890s as a "respectable and deserving" recipient of aid.[44] Her adult son had lost an eye in a work accident, and his periodic inability to afford the new glass eye he needed annually meant he had trouble holding a steady job.[45] Her husband died in 1898 after a five-year struggle with tuberculosis that had consistently devoured the combined, meager earnings of Johnstone and her children.[46] Neighbors and acquaintances speculated about a secret fortune the family had acquired through a window-sash patent, but Johnstone continued to receive periodic help from the A.I.C.P., mostly in the form of vouchers for groceries or coal.[47]

In 1899, Johnstone appealed to Reverend E. E. Matthews, a local clergyman, for additional help; on October 24 of that year, at Matthews's request, C.O.S. Registration Bureau agent C. L. Reeds set out for 190 East 76th Street to visit and investigate Johnstone once again.[48] Johnstone explained to Reeds that she had moved her family out of a previous apartment on

82nd Street in haste because "the landlady's son, who collects rent at 82nd Street, insulted her daughter, Annie, in such a way that she thinks she has a cause for action in a suit for damages." Having lost a great deal of time and money in the quick move, Johnstone had applied for aid, but rather than receiving one of the $2 grocery vouchers the A.I.C.P. had occasionally given her, "a lady called and asked a great many questions; said they would have to investigate." Johnstone complained to Reeds that "she thought this very unkind, as she has been a respectable, hard-working woman all her life, and now when she is hungry . . . cannot obtain a few groceries without being questioned." When Reeds asked about Johnstone's relatives, whom John-stone's daughter Amy had just been visiting in England, Johnstone "at first refused to give the address, saying she would rather starve than have [them] know she had applied for assistance." After Reeds explained "as kindly as possible" that she needed the relatives' address if Johnstone was to have any hope of receiving aid, Johnstone finally relented.[49]

Maria Bates had a fractious relationship with the C.O.S. and A.I.C.P., which had begun at least as early as 1883 when she was forty years old. An Irish immigrant from Tipperary whom C.O.S. visitors initially classified as "colored," Bates (and her five children) seemed to rub nearly everyone the wrong way.[50] Landlords, housekeepers, clergy—practically everyone agreed that the family were imposters who "drink & fight," and that Bates herself was "quarrelsome, abusive and drinking . . . much inclined to beg of churches."[51] Even in an instance when the A.I.C.P. decided to provide her with "a bundle of clothing" in 1895, the recording agent felt compelled to remark of her eldest daughter, "The young woman Mary Bates has a very saucy tongue & is most demanding in her manner."[52]

On December 9, 1901, Maria Bates traveled from 1315 Third Avenue down to the United Charities building on 22nd Street to follow up on a visit she had received the previous week from C.O.S. visitor E. N. Wood. She in-formed the agent who interviewed her that Wood's visit had probably been "in connection with an application to Mrs. [William] Dodge or Mrs. [J. P.] Morgan" that Bates had made in late November. Bates had written to both Dodge and Morgan herself, as she had explained to Wood the previous week, because she had known and received help from Dodge for nearly two decades and had "made a number of pairs of mittens for" Morgan over the years. A week had passed since Wood's visit, however, and Bates had heard nothing.[53]

Each of these encounters encapsulates the C.O.S.'s tendency to reinscribe class difference rather than diminish it. Elizabeth Carman's visit and letter to the C.O.S. district office combined resentment with a clear recognition that the "long Postal Cards" comprising her case file would largely determine her ability to gain relief for years to come. She could hate the C.O.S. all she liked, but she still needed the good opinion of its agents; her anger was a veil for supplication. Rachel Johnstone, after insisting to Reeds that an earlier visitor's close questioning had offended her dignity, could not avoid submitting to similar questioning from Reeds. No matter how "kindly" Reeds may have explained the necessity of Johnstone's relinquishing information on her relatives, it was the duress of their unequal class and power positions, not kindness, that ultimately forced Johnstone to comply.[54] Maria Bates arrived at the C.O.S. Central Office desiring only to know the outcome of the previous week's visit. The fact that two wealthy ladies, Dodge and Morgan, already knew the C.O.S. visitor's determinations (Morgan having received the information within two days) while Bates herself remained in the dark over a week later redoubled the initial indignity of seeking aid, no matter how inured Bates may have been to it.[55]

In all three cases, the organizational imperative within the C.O.S. to uncover moral dereliction through interviews—the better to correct it, ostensibly—proved determinative in both disempowering the poor and in denying aid. In a broader sense, that imperative endlessly reproduced scenes in which the wealthy and their agents met the poor and working class on terms that reinforced the imbalance of power between them. C.O.S. representatives bore the perquisites of inquiry, judgment, and most importantly, record keeping; applicants bore only their individual powers of persuasion. In a perverse way, this meant that applicants' power to influence an encounter with a Society visitor or agent increased only as the pathos of their circumstances grew more acute.

The C.O.S., in other words, created the conditions in which poor and working-class applicants benefitted by acting as destitute as possible. If they

appeared too comfortable, the Society would deny them aid, in part because visitors reasoned that applicants should sell or pawn their remaining
possessions before receiving relief (Reeds's last note before leaving Johnstone's apartment was "The furniture looked quite good. . . . Visitor noticed
organ").[56] If applicants admitted that any family members had jobs, the
C.O.S. could deny aid on the basis that their relatives should be providing
support. If they were unemployed but able-bodied, the C.O.S. might only
provide aid in the form of tickets to work in the C.O.S. Wood-Yard, where
they could earn 50 cents per day chopping wood—barely enough to live on,
much less to support anyone else.[57] The principle of distinction drove an incentive for applicants to embody a particular idea of poverty. It is no wonder
that so few applicants for the Society's aid proved worthy.[58]

Many applicants may have found the process of applying for relief humiliating enough without attempting to enhance the impression of their
need (indeed, the indignities of the application process likely dissuaded many
from applying at all), but a recalcitrance to act appropriately "deserving"
would not help their chances.[59] Certainly, Maria Bates's chances of receiving C.O.S. aid diminished from the moment E. N. Wood walked into her
and her sister's apartment on December 2, 1901, and noted that "the rooms
were comfortably furnished and very clean; the women were eating a lun-
cheon which consisted of bread and tea; there was a good fire."[60] None of
these details had any bearing on the fact that Bates's sister was blind and
required home care (which prevented Bates from working outside the apartment), or that Bates's son was unemployed, but they undermined Bates's
subsequent ability—either in person or in the consequent C.O.S. record of
her case—to convince the group of her need.

Wood's visit to Bates provides an example of how the Society's procedures, intentionally or not, reinforced applicants' class position. According
to the *Hand-Book for Friendly Visitors,* C.O.S. visitors had a somewhat paradoxical mandate when interviewing applicants for aid. On the one hand,
they were urged to build relationships with the "poor who have the strongest claim on our sympathy . . . generally the silent, sensitive, painfully respectable people, whose clean and tidy rooms conceal to the utmost the evidence of their poverty."[61] These applicants, the handbook specified, "must
be sought out with delicacy, and treated with the utmost courtesy."[62] Fos-
tering relationships with them would, ideally, create space for the visitors to

offer useful advice without the "appearance of censoriousness or meddle-someness."[63] The handbook even enumerated examples of these "Worthy Poor," including the aged without solvent relatives, permanent or tempo-rary invalids unable to work, and widows unable to support families with young children.[64] On these terms, Elizabeth Carman, Rachel Johnstone, and Maria Bates all had some claim on a visitor's courtesy. Bates in partic-ular, with no husband, a blind sister, and no other relatives to provide sup-port, might have reasonably expected assistance.

This first part of the mandate, however, disappeared in the long shadow of the second. The *Hand-Book* admonished visitors repeatedly and in the strongest terms that "injudicious procurement of alms for the family of a drunkard, or a dissolute, idle, or shiftless person, will invariably do more harm than good."[65] It advised that undeserving cases "need to be treated with wise and firm severity. Wherever liquor, or thieving, or imposture, or any form of vice has got hold of a family, reform must be the main thing to aim at."[66] C.O.S. propagandists focused warmly on Society representatives' ability to sniff out fraudulent or immoral aid applicants, often drawing lu-rid pictures of such miscreants for well-to-do C.O.S. subscribers, as in the *Fourth Annual Report:*

> From the adroit begging-letter-writer who luxuriates in her fruits and flow-ers, her noon-day breakfasts and evening dinners, her elegant city apart-ments, and her summer relaxation at the choicest watering-places, to the pretended cripple who cringes and cowers upon the pavement by day, and drinks and gambles his nights away in the slums—all are fostered in their lives of deceit and self-indulgence by the easy-going selfishness of those who think it charity to supply the means therefor![67]

At bottom, after all, identifying such scoundrels was the C.O.S.'s raison d'être: misdirected charity had, in Josephine Shaw Lowell's view, created a scourge of charity frauds in New York, a class of idle and vicious poor who milked the misbegotten generosity of the wealthy to fund lives of excess and extravagance.

In practice, the C.O.S.'s organizational imperative to root out and deny aid to these undeserving poor meant that visitors leaned heavily toward the latter half of the dual mandate, so much so that the "reform" prescribed for the undeserving poor largely vanished.[68] Instead, once a visitor and a district committee had established an applicant's unworthiness, the common course of action seems to have been to close the case entirely, apparently without any notice to the applicant. Those, in fact, were the circumstances that brought Maria Bates to the C.O.S. Central Office in 1901. The C.O.S. had swiftly advised Mrs. J. P. Morgan that Bates had proven unworthy of charity, but had neither made any attempt to "reform" Bates, nor to inform her that help would not be forthcoming.

The Society closed Rachel Johnstone's and Elizabeth Carman's cases as well, providing the women with neither information nor reformation. Johnstone had warned Reeds that it would "be useless for [Reeds] to call at [her] previous address as because of this trouble [with the landlady's son] they will not speak well of her." Reeds went anyway, the very next day. Sure enough, the landlady painted a vicious portrait of Johnstone and her children, and Reeds referred the information to the District Committee members, who closed the case immediately. The testimonies to Johnstone's worthiness, gathered over years from various clergy, employers, and previous A.I.C.P. or C.O.S. visitors, might as well never have existed. Carman's anguished letter also failed to produce the vindication she desired. The same day she left the letter, in fact, her casework card bore the stamp "CLOSED BY THE COMMITTEE. CHIEF CAUSE OF NEED: NOT REQUIRING. DECISION AS TO RELIEF: Feb 2/97. Forwarded to [Registration Bureau]."[69]

"Closed" stamps effectively functioned as red flags for any future applications someone might make, and herein lies one of the most tragic ironies of the Society's operations. The group's narrow focus on distinguishing between worthy and unworthy poor, when combined with its meticulous documentation procedures, produced geological records of applicants' lives, in which successive moraines of behavior deemed immoral or improvident steadily accumulated. After a certain point, the accreting sediment of damning evidence, and the denials of aid they produced, buried the applicant's chances of obtaining a fair hearing upon reapplication. Applicants *became* their case files, and their case files inexorably became chronicles of misbehavior. This made unbiased consideration of any new circumstances much less likely.

Maria Bates's file suggests how the C.O.S.'s pursuit of distinction through "scientific" classification reproduced rejection and reified class position instead of stimulating reform.[70] When Bates applied for help in February 1896, the visitor's determination ran, "Case is undoubtedly identical with 1085.10 and 812.19. <u>closed</u>."[71] In January 1898, it said, "Woman believed to be identical with Maria Bates alias O'Reilly . . . **Closed**." Six months later, it ran: "[F]rom her description of woman's personal appearance visitor feels confident case is identical with I.D. 11633 . . . For filing." In May 1899, it said, "From statement made, visitor believed case to be identical with one at Bureau and on return found it to be the same . . . *closed*."[72] When E. N. Wood wrote up her report on Bates after visiting her on December 2, 1901, the very first line read, "Visited . . . and identified case as I.D. 11633."[73] The next entry, on December 4, said, "Report to Mrs. Morgan and bureau / closed."[74] Rather than providing a passive record of Bates's applications and the measures (whether moral or material) the C.O.S. took to address her needs (whether spiritual or earthly), the case file took on an active role, coloring successive visitors' impressions of Bates and becoming a tool that they used to justify denying her aid. The case file became a fulcrum around which the same prescriptive class encounter revolved, endlessly reproducing itself year after year, decade after decade.

Few if any charity applicants could consistently meet the high standards of the "worthy poor" as outlined in the *Hand-Book* for visitors. If continued applications for relief over the course of years were not evidence enough of an applicant's moral inadequacy, a paper trail such as Bates's, recording earlier "abusiveness" and "intemperance," certainly was. Consequently, the group Lowell had founded to reform the unworthy and nurture the worthy—a group committed to a dynamic idea of social amelioration through cross-class contact—effectively fashioned paper chains of "scientific" evidence that bound the poor more securely in want.

This operational tendency to accumulate and then defer to negative testimony when evaluating a case led to the C.O.S.'s reputation among critics as the "Organization for the Prevention of Charity." In particular, the Society's whole apparatus of "scientific" investigation seemed to contravene the cherished notions of charity as love that its leaders claimed to uphold. As early as 1888, an Episcopal clergyman in New York, Dr. B. F. De Costa, sparked a minor controversy when he accused the C.O.S. of degrading charity by "identifying [it] with the police and detective system." In De Costa's vision of charity, "Too much investigation is to be deprecated. Some methods are cruel . . . if you go by St. Vincent's Hospital . . . you will see about 400 poor men—tramps, beggars and outcasts; and the Sisters there give these poor people a hearty breakfast. We should rather be willing to take our chance of Heaven with those charitable Sisters than with the people who cautiously wait and delay and investigate before they give."[75] As De Costa's example suggests, his vision of charity did not necessarily extend to a wholesale social transformation. It seems unlikely that he expected the breakfasts from St. Vincent's to transform "tramps, beggars, and outcasts" into "provident, thoughtful, self-respecting and contributing members of society," as Kellogg had summarized the C.O.S.'s aims. His objection to the C.O.S., in other words, lay not with its failure to produce the reform it claimed to pursue, but with its cruel, stingy treatment of the poor. Most of all, he objected to the C.O.S.'s using tens of thousands of dollars in charitable contributions to fund such clinical cruelty, rather than using the money to feed the hungry, clothe the naked, and heal the sick as the Bible instructed.

Compounding De Costa's attack on the C.O.S.'s stinginess, the *New York Times* published a full-page critique later that year of the group's allegedly scientific methods under the heading "The Charity Organization Society 'Estimates' in Rather a Queer Way."[76] The article launched a withering statistical assault on the first six C.O.S. annual reports, demonstrating that if the Society's figures and methods of calculation were truly scientific, the reality they reflected would indicate "a rate of increase [among relief-seekers] which in the course of another six months is certain to include even Jay Gould unless he is wise enough to take the hint and establish himself permanently on his yacht. Evidently," it concluded, "New-York has nearly arrived at that exalted consummation held up as an ideal by Socialism in which every man is his own pauper."[77] To make matters worse, the article was anonymously reprinted as a circular and mailed to C.O.S. supporters, forcing the Society to draft an internal response.[78]

By the late 1880s, press skepticism and public animus (exemplified by De Costa's characterization of the C.O.S. as "the meanest humbug in the city of New York") were threatening to undermine the group's principal arguments—first, that giving unconditional material aid to the poor *only* satisfied the selfish emotional needs of the wealthy while doing harm to the poor, and second, that a systematic, clinical structure of organization to enforce distinction was the proper response to urban poverty.[79] The *Times*'s exposure of the group's dubious scientific methods made this latter claim particularly tenuous, and its "humbug" reputation became an even bigger problem after the depression of 1893 raised widespread doubts that individual moral deficiencies could satisfactorily explain such aggravated poverty or joblessness. That economic cataclysm and its manifestations contributed to a shift in Lowell's thinking on the origins of destitution, pushing her to consider more seriously the environmental and structural causes of poverty.

The C.O.S. was coming under intense pressure to rebrand itself for wider public consumption.[80] It did so first of all by shifting its *public* emphasis away from its efforts to investigate and remedy the moral failings of the poor. Internal disagreements within the reform community and sniping that targeted the C.O.S. at various charitable conventions partially explain this public shift, but publicized objections to the C.O.S. from other constituencies suggest an additional problem.[81] The success of the Society's operations depended upon smooth communication not just within the community of self-conscious reformers but with countless churches and neighborhood groups whose leaders and members, though they may not have followed esoteric debates over charitable methods, did read newspapers. In short, bad press interfered with business.[82]

The group also noticeably shifted tone in its New York annual reports, adopting a more conciliatory approach toward its colleagues and critics. One subtle measure was the removal, beginning as early as the 1887 report, of the injunction against "spiritual instruction" in its constitutional anti-proselytism clause, likely an effort to mollify distrustful clergy such as De Costa.[83] Later, with the appointment of Edward T. Devine as the general secretary in 1896, the annual reports frontloaded items that emphasized C.O.S. interventions in the material lives of the poor, such as programs to challenge evictions in court, or to reform tenement housing, while removing or downplaying staples that highlighted working-class depravity, such as "Mendicancy," or "Fraudulent or Questionable Schemes."[84] It still insisted on the danger of misplaced alms, and in fundamental ways continued to advance its program of abolishing public relief, but in the promotion of its own work, advancing material change had gained significantly on creating moral transformation. This dovetailed with Devine's own evolving understanding of poverty's causes, which placed greater weight on environmental impediments to social mobility than C.O.S. orthodoxy previously would have allowed.[85]

Moreover, the C.O.S. started instituting stricter oversight of its visitors and agents to combat periodic scandals involving unprofessional behavior. In February 1887, the *New York Times* told the tale of Edward Chiardi, a C.O.S. agent who first succeeded in having Annie Deprez of 197 Elizabeth Street imprisoned for "begging and vagrancy," then tried to extort $25 from her husband to "procure a discharge for his wife."[86] The police ensnared the would-be blackmailer, and the C.O.S. Central Council replaced him as "Special Out-door Officer of the Society," but the C.O.S.'s reputation took an embarrassing public hit.[87] The following year, the *Times* published another story about a Society agent in Poughkeepsie whose zeal in obtaining arrest warrants for supposed vagrants led to the police's detaining a woman subsequently identified as the daughter of a London innkeeper. The woman, Caroline Satcher, had fallen on hard times, but still had the wherewithal to sue the C.O.S. agent for false imprisonment. The jury awarded her $60, and the judge issued a scolding to the police, declaring (somewhat anomalously for that time), "It is no crime to be poor."[88] In the battle to maintain a polished public image, stories of such corruption or incompetence did real damage. In response, the C.O.S. executive committee began to monitor work at the district level more closely, sometimes intervening to remove agents when they judged their work inadequate or irresponsible.[89]

Led by Devine's efforts, the C.O.S. also began to spearhead more professionalized, academic training for charity and poor relief workers. An initial course in "applied philanthropy" during the summer of 1898 transformed within three years into the Summer School for Philanthropic Workers. Visiting experts gave lectures to C.O.S. trainees, as when Boston C.O.S. visitor Zilphia D. Smith delivered a speech on friendly visiting as part of a New York Class in Practical Philanthropy.[90] By 1904, these various initiatives helped establish the foundation for the New York City School of Philanthropy, which "provided systematic instruction for the full academic year of eight months designed to meet the needs of beginners wishing to prepare themselves for social service either as professional or volunteer workers."[91]

Devine was appointed the director, and while continuing in his capacity as general secretary of the C.O.S., he guided the institutional formation of the school destined to become the Columbia University School of Social Work, which remains among the most prestigious social-work academies to this day.[92] Each internal reform addressed some aspect of external criticism: removing the injunction against "spiritual instruction" from the constitution conceded ground to religious traditionalists who objected to the Society's "science"; drawing more attention to its material work among the poor combated its reputation as a purely investigative body bent on denying alms; and instituting greater oversight of agents while spearheading academic innovation in social work enhanced the impression of its professionalism.

It was this organizational reconsideration of its public image and greater attention to the power of public opinion that resulted in C.O.S. leaders' attending the Salvation Army's 1899 Christmas Dinner. Eight years earlier, Robert Weeks de Forest had expressed reservations in *Charities Review* about an eerily similar event for poor children held at Madison Square Garden for Christmas 1891, organized by a group called the Christmas Society. At that event, thousands of poor children and their mothers filed into the Garden arena, guided and monitored by 200 policemen, to receive presents donated in advance by wealthy children. They did so "while some of the patrons of the [Christmas] Society were quietly seated in the upper tiers, looking down from their high places at the animated scene below."[93] The Christmas Society had hoped to draw a much more sizeable crowd of wealthy spectators, but "the boxes and seats which it was believed that the rich and the children of the rich would purchase were not purchased" and so more of the poor were allowed entry.[94]

Of that event, De Forest wrote, "While giving toys through the machinery created by the Christmas Society doubtless 'has its reward,' that reward is greater just in proportion as the [rich] children's charity is personal service, not mere largess [*sic*], and is given in such a way as to minimize class distinction and recognize most fully the common brotherhood of all children, 'rich' and 'poor.'"[95] De Forest's concern with minimizing class distinction and maximizing direct, personal contact bespoke the C.O.S.'s ideal of personal service. It also implied an awareness of the potential in such an event for alienating the poor through class voyeurism. His leeriness found similar articulation and endorsement, alongside rebukes of the Christmas

Society, in a letter to the editor of the *Tribune* and in editorials of the *Evening Post* and *Times* the week before the event. A reader going by the name "E. H. V. W." warned the *Tribune* that the Christmas Society would stoke class animosity:

> The mere fact of bringing them together in such large numbers in the same building, with an impassable barrier separating the rich from the poor, the wealthy children clad in their velvet and furs seated aloft in their boxes, the poor children in humble and meagre garb in the arena below, subjected to the curious and critical gaze of their prosperous brothers and sisters assembled to behold the results of their condescension and so-called generosity, will not, I think, tend to produce more contentment among the poor or true Christian charity among the rich.

In any case, E. V. H. W. argued, "I know of no deserving poor children who will not be provided for at the Christmas season . . . by the various agencies that have hitherto been and will be employed in their behalf at Christmas-tide."[96] The *Evening Post* editorial concluded (and De Forest reprinted): "We must not allow charity in this great city to become the plaything of fashion or vanity."[97] And the *Times* editors warned, "Such an exhibition would not only be highly unchristian, but it would also be highly uncivilized." This "spectacle," they averred, "would be indecent and demoralizing."[98] Such criticisms reflected the C.O.S. position, both in their exhortations for a more personal form of charitable contact between rich and poor, and in their insistence that such events would tend to pauperize the poor.

Editorials beforehand, however, could not compete with coverage of the event after the fact, which largely praised the Christmas Society and testified to the happiness of the poor participants.[99] The *Tribune* story called the event "a decided success," absolved the Christmas Society managers of blame, and added simply, "They succeeded in attracting under one roof the biggest crowd of poor children ever brought together within four walls in this city . . . and in dismissing them all happier for coming."[100] The *Times* story likewise acknowledged, "There was not a hitch or a halt anywhere" in the proceedings, and that "nobody who assisted in the distribution was unhappy for having done so, for all of these saw smiles light up hundreds of pinched little faces as the result of their labors."[101] Whether these reports were accurate or merely pandering to the sentimentalism of a feel-good Christmas readership is immaterial. They made of the event a public success.

By 1899, the popularity of events like this one forced C.O.S. leaders to recognize that public opinion—or more precisely, the public opinion of those who mattered, namely, donors—would not brook the appearance of stinginess or half-measures at Christmas. Such close-fisted behavior, even when justified through appeals to "true" charity, seemed somehow less scientific at Yuletide than simply mean-spirited. Realizing this, the Society's leaders began carefully to include their group in activities that would have been antithetical to its principles in the 1880s, including mass distributions of food, spectacles, and sectarian Christian displays.

The Salvation Army's 1899 Christmas Dinner exemplified this shift toward more spectacular, commercialized charitable methods, which concealed the medieval influence of distinction in social welfare practices. Spectacle and commerce, however, could not remove that influence below the surface. Despite all the internal reforms the C.O.S. had undertaken by late 1899, and all the public-relations benefits it would garner from participating in the Army's apparently open-handed Christmas Dinner, its daily procedures still led investigators such as C. L. Reeds to blacken the previously worthy names of applicants such as Rachel Johnstone and to deny them aid. For Johnstone and her three children, Christmas 1899 brought neither alms nor a friend from the Charity Organization Society of New York.

What ever happened to Francis Henry Weeks, the blue-blooded C.O.S. president and embezzler? The discovery of his thievery was a high-society scandal of epic proportions. The whole affair played out over six months in New York's papers: the revelation of his misdeeds and flight from justice, the hiring of private detectives to track him down, his evasion of capture in Colombia, his rediscovery in Costa Rica, the special arrangements made for his extradition (for which no formal agreement existed with the Costa Rican government), and finally, his guilty plea and imprisonment. Before sentencing him to ten years at Sing-Sing, Judge Frederick Smyth, who had been a fellow club member and friend of Weeks's, addressed him sternly, "You are a member of a respectable family upon whom you have brought a lasting disgrace."[102]

Smyth's prediction of "lasting disgrace" proved as overwrought as his high opinion of Weeks's family was overgenerous. Weeks's nephew, Robert Weeks de Forest—who became the C.O.S.'s longest-serving president— does not appear to have debated the conflict of interest between his stance on the morality of the poor and his attitude toward the moral poverty of his uncle. When Weeks was dashing around the city preparing to wriggle out of the law's imminent grasp in April, he went De Forest begging for money.[103] One can only imagine what Weeks's "Memorandum Card" might have looked like from such a visit had he been truly poor. Would he have been denied aid for "Lack of Judgment," as was Rachel Johnstone?[104] Would he have been instructed to take in a boarder, as was Maria Bates?[105]

But Francis Henry Weeks was not poor; he was a well-connected, prominent, and recently rich man who happened to have lost all his (and quite a bit of other people's) money. Robert and his brother Henry gave their embezzling uncle a loan of $55,000, thereby helping to finance his temporary escape to South America.[106] As the president of the C.O.S., a paragon of morality, and the "first citizen of New York in philanthropy," De Forest must have been disappointed in his uncle.[107] But blood and class usually run thicker than principle. Within a week or two, De Forest was chairing a meeting of the C.O.S. Central Council, waiting for the appropriate moment to announce his uncle's resignation. His timing could not have been more fitting: he offered the news as the meeting's final agenda item, just after Otto T. Bannard reported on behalf of the Committee on Provident Habits.[108]

Long after Weeks had served his prison sentence (reduced from ten to six-and-a-half years, partially in recognition of his efforts while incarcerated to systematize the prison's bookkeeping) and rejoined his wife in Salt Lake City, the default position for the C.O.S., at least, remained the summary judgment of the poor.[109] Very occasionally, a few people still found such presumption irksome. Mornay Williams, a prospective C.O.S. donor, wrote to Edward Devine in 1906 to complain about a C.O.S. circular that solicited subscriptions to the Wood-Yard. The circular encouraged subscription by admonishing that when charitable people give to street beggars, they do so "knowing that it is wrong in principle, knowing that most mendicants are imposters, knowing that it tends to increase their number and create a nuisance to the city." Williams, after objecting to this position as contravening "our Lord in the synoptic gospels" and declaring his own belief that "investigation should be always subordinate to the disposition to give relief," made the following, incisive point: "I am of the opinion that the attitude taken by the society, perhaps unconsciously, in many of its circulars, does more to create a division between the poor who need relief and the well-to-do classes who ought to give it, than it does to diminish pauperism."[110]

Indeed, Williams's point finds ample support in the C.O.S. case files, which consistently reflect rage and resentment among applicants directed at C.O.S. representatives, whom they took to be the "well-to-do" of Williams's letter. "[I]f you don't destroy that Wicked Statement about me," wrote Elizabeth Carman, "I shall pray for that Woman's fingers that wrote it to paralize [*sic*] for I have suffered <u>too much for my Honor to be condemned in the end</u>."[111] Rachel Johnstone's daughter expressed a similar level of anger, but through sarcasm: "I thank you for your kindness to my mother," she wrote; "I wonder if God will treat you . . . with such kindness when you get to the gates of Heaven how will you feel when God will say go down to hell a week until the comitee [*sic*] meets to see if you . . . are worthy enough to enter Heaven."[112] In Maria Bates's case, she carried a grudge for years, berating visitors and physically ejecting them from her house when they announced themselves to be from the C.O.S. Applying for relief at St. Bartholomew's Parish in late July 1911, she told her interviewer that "she was known to C.O.S.," and declared all its representatives "Black-Guards."[113] Such anger, however, concealed a helplessness and frustration better expressed by two sentences from an unsigned, undated letter written in Elizabeth Carman's handwriting and kept in her C.O.S. file: "Oh God Deliver Me from Such Charity Organizations. My Own Experience is enough."[114]

5

The Business of Godly Charity

We do not propose to give tickets away indiscriminately, oh no!

—Frederick de Latour Booth-Tucker

A CHEERY ATMOSPHERE REIGNED inside Madison Square Garden on December 25, 1899. Salvation Army officers and police had maintained complete order throughout the basket-dinner giveaway during the morning and early afternoon. Consul Emma Booth-Tucker had stood for hours at the head of the orderly breadline, offering holiday wishes to the poor beneath American-flag bunting and fresh mistletoe as she distributed the baskets full of "fat chicken, potatoes, assorted vegetables, a can of prepared soup, a luscious plum pudding and plenty of fruit."[1] During the evening feast, the cooks had fed thousands more people than originally anticipated, and the entertainments had, to all appearances, gone off without a hitch.

Of equal importance, happiness did not belong solely to those eating or serving the feast but had spread to those watching as well, an audience that had begun to arrive in the late afternoon. As the front page of the *New York Times* reported, "In the boxes and gallery of the great building . . . sat many thousands of well-fed and prosperous people, among them many women who had come in carriages and were gorgeously gowned and wore many diamonds, who looked on in happy sympathy."[2] These spectators had paid $1 for admission to observe the evening meal, and their approval would doubtless produce a flood of further donations to Salvation Army coffers before year's end.[3]

Nearly two decades earlier, when the C.O.S. and the Salvation Army first appeared on the New York charity scene, they had differed sharply in many respects. The C.O.S. declared itself "completely severed from all questions of religious belief" and prohibited any of its representatives from using "his or her position for the purpose of proselytism or spiritual instruction."[4] The Army's first U.S. representatives, meanwhile, inaugurated their arrival from England on American shores by attempting to turn the Castle Garden immigration facility into a Christian revival meeting.[5] The C.O.S.'s founders, officers, and much of its personnel came from the most privileged strata of New York society, and they enjoyed a state charter for their organization, thanks in part to Josephine Shaw Lowell's membership on the New York State Board of Charities. The Army's leader, William Booth, had been apprenticed at thirteen to a pawnshop owner in East London, and his organization not only wore its working-class identity as a badge of honor, but also fought frequent court battles with the state over "disorderly conduct" regulations throughout the 1880s and early 1890s. Perhaps most conspicuously, the C.O.S. idealized restraint in all its endeavors— indeed, restraint and control practically defined the group, as its central avowed goal was the restraint of indiscriminate almsgiving to the unworthy poor—whereas the Army thrived on provocative public exhibitions to convey its message in as indiscriminate a manner as possible. The C.O.S. practiced distinction to the utmost. The Army, at least initially, largely ignored it.

Nevertheless, Army leaders shared the Society's prescriptive stance toward the poor. Both organizations aimed to reintegrate the poor into the wider community by developing direct, personal contact, establishing authority, and providing behavioral instruction. The Salvation Army pursued a literal religious conversion whereas the C.O.S., in Kellogg's words, aimed only to "convert" the poor in a behavioral sense. Yet these different conversions had a similar purpose: to effect a spiritual transformation of the poor that would foster both a renewed social investment, and an inculcation of the industry, sobriety, and thrift presumably lacking in their personal behavior.[6]

In other senses, however, the Army initially represented a much more radical approach. Conversion for the Army meant not only a discreet personal transformation, but a new commitment to the Salvationist movement.

It meant marching in the streets. It meant giving loud, theatrical, public testimonials about the benefits of conversion and the need to change the world. It meant, in other words, a transformation not only into a functioning member of existing society, but into a very public, unconventional agent of change within that society. It meant empowering the working class and poor, indiscriminately, as agents of social change.[7]

Those invested in society's conventions had little to gain and much to fear from incitement to activism among the working class, especially in an age when dynamiting incidents, anarchist speeches, and pitched battles between industrial workers and the state were regular features of the national landscape.[8] In the streets, Salvationists faced taunts, interference, and sometimes violence, particularly when they carried their message of Christian temperance near or even into saloons. Saloonkeepers, worried about losing revenue, used their clout with municipal officials to ban the Army from their premises. When Salvationists persisted, gangs of hired thugs frequently attacked them, precipitating chaotic scenes that police either aggravated or observed impassively before arresting the battered Army officers.[9] These activities touched off a series of court battles over the Army's right to demonstrate in public. Although the Army won most of these cases, it also earned itself a reputation as a rabble-rousing group, given to antagonizing the state and violating bourgeois notions of appropriate public behavior.[10]

Even as it grew in popularity within pockets of the working class, winning tens of thousands of converts, organs of establishment opinion continued to view the Army askance. In 1892, the *Times* wrote that "Salvationists entirely disregard all pretense of dignity, and it may be said of reverence. . . . Whoever joins the Salvation Army from the nature of the case bids goodbye to respectability as much as if he went upon the stage of a variety show."[11] The *New-York Tribune,* reporting on an 1893 Army meeting, reiterated this distaste: "From small and despised beginnings, the work of the army has been extended so that to-day it plays no mean part among the poor in the great cities. Its uniform is the same as ever, and its methods are still grotesque."[12] Because the Army depended on women's participation in all aspects of its work, critiques such as these that threatened its "respectability" and attacked its methods as "grotesque" stung in both class and gender terms.[13]

The Army's leaders began to realize that legitimization by the courts would constitute a pyrrhic victory if their tactics continued to alienate potential

financial and public support, and so over the course of the late 1880s and
1890s, they increasingly appealed to a more high-toned sensibility. First, they
concentrated greater efforts on the Salvation Army Auxiliary Leagues, fund-
raising and influence-building wings that cultivated relationships with
wealthy patrons, particularly women. Forging alliances with ladies of unim-
peachable "respectability" directly addressed many of their critics in the press.
By 1896, these Auxiliary Leagues outnumbered local Salvation corps eight to
one, and the Army counted Mrs. John Wanamaker, wife of the prominent
Philadelphia department store owner, among its staunchest allies.[14]

Second, after 1890, they separated the rowdier evangelical work from
their incipient and growing social work practices in slum neighborhoods,
which included rescue houses for "fallen women," and "slum brigades" of
Salvationist women who moved into tenements and provided various
forms of assistance to neighbors in need—a cross between the C.O.S.'s
friendly visiting and the settlement-house work being pioneered at the time
by women such as Jane Addams in Chicago and Lillian D. Wald in New
York.[15] This separation responded to the criticism the group had endured
for its occasionally "sacrilegious" religion, while also reflecting Army
leaders' growing recognition of the political-economic impediments to
their evangelical mission.[16] William Booth's son Bramwell put it succinctly
in a pamphlet published in 1900, quoting an Oxford reverend: "The response of the poor to a religion which has no concern or cure for poverty is
neglect of religion."[17]

Both these initiatives constituted an appeal to more traditional notions
of charity and class relations as appropriately prescriptive. The Auxiliary
Leagues reestablished the wealthy as primary actors in the charitable relationship to the poor, and the slum brigades engaged in services designed to
mollify or contain residents in poor neighborhoods rather than agitate them.
Army leaders had realized that popularity among the poor would not pay as
well as respect and recognition among the bourgeois.

As such, they also began to shift their position on distinction, catering to
the widespread concern among the wealthy over charity's being misdirected
to the unworthy poor (a concern continually stoked by the C.O.S.). William Booth's earlier writings had adamantly rejected the logic of distinction, arguing that any charity favoring "an elect few who are to be saved
while the mass of their fellows are predestined to a temporal damnation"

was un-Christian.[18] As the 1899 Christmas Dinner approached, however, Frederick de Latour Booth-Tucker, the Army's American commander, went on record in the Army's main New York publication, *The War Cry,* offering emphatic reassurance that the Army's reputation for free-wheeling methods would not result in the feeding of unworthy poor. "We do not propose to give tickets away indiscriminately," he announced, "oh no!"[19] And yet Booth-Tucker walked a fine line, caught between the desire to use the Christmas Dinner as a promotional event for the Army's year-round work, and the particular public calls for charity during the Christmas season, which tended toward a more forgiving attitude than at any other time of year.[20] Trying to balance these competing demands led Booth-Tucker into contradiction. In another Army publication, he noted,

> As a rule, the free distribution of food or clothing is discountenanced by us. The poor man must either work or pay for whatever he receives. . . . We feel, however, that Christmas is the one exception which must serve to prove the rule. On this occasion our doors are thrown wide open and we welcome all who come.[21]

Here, in trying to capture the Christmas spirit of open-handed generosity, he suggests that perhaps the Army *will* distribute the tickets indiscriminately, softening his previous statement.

Nevertheless, the central intent of his later remarks was the same as his previous one: to remove suspicion that the Army might use donor money to give food or cash away year-round without consideration of recipients' worth. Booth-Tucker denied this suspicion unequivocally. Indeed, in the very same publication, he explained in detail how distinction actually *did* remain in operation for the purposes of the Christmas basket giveaway. "Tickets for these basket dinners," he wrote, "are carefully distributed through our officers and through the various religious and philanthropic agencies, so that the really needy poor are reached and helped."[22] During the dinner, he reiterated the point, unprompted, to a reporter from the *Tribune:* "There is another point to which I would like to draw attention. That is that the readers of The Tribune who have helped to supply these dinners need not have the least fear that their generosity will tend to pauperize the poor. As a rule, we never give anything without an equivalent either in work or cash, and this is thoroughly understood."[23] Distinction was not only very much in operation, but the Army's leadership was taking pains to ensure that people noticed.

This shift on distinction was only one aspect of the Army's brilliant publicity and rebranding campaign to integrate itself more effectively with the accepted norms of charity in the consumer capitalist landscape. Its promotion and fund-raising techniques for the 1899 Christmas Dinner exemplified the group's ingenuity at turning the spaces and practices of such consumption to the ends of charity. It executed a comprehensive strategy to advertise the Christmas Dinner that combined sidewalk collection pots, "mercy boxes" set up in local businesses, a letter-writing campaign to New Yorkers prominent in social or missionary circles, and multiple stories about the dinner in the *War Cry*. Each of these tactics was designed to create maximum exposure for both the Christmas Dinner and the Army's year-round work; each also contained a crucial visual element designed to integrate social work and missionary activity with the natural flow of urban capitalism.

Salvationists staffed the sidewalk collection pots with young women volunteers dressed in demure Army bonnets and regalia, or unemployed men dressed as Santa Claus, arresting the eyes of pedestrians without harassing them as its previous public performances had done.[24] The mercy boxes appealed to consumers' charitable inclinations at the very moment they reached into their pockets for money—when paying for goods. Making arrangements to place the mercy boxes also enabled the Army to forge cooperative relationships with businessmen, a goal it explicitly pursued through its Christmas Dinner letter-writing campaign. When the letters elicited favorable responses and donations from the clerical, municipal, or business elite, the Army publicized excerpts from the replies (and sometimes the amount of the contributions) in the *War Cry*, alongside stories about the Christmas Dinner.[25] By weaving itself into the existing social and economic fabrics of New York rather than disrupting them, the Army aimed to make itself and its activities a more respectable fixture in the bourgeois New York landscape.

Both the C.O.S. and the Salvation Army were converging on a presentation of charity and class relations more saleable to a broader public—and, in particular, to wealthy donors—than they had originally advocated.

"Raising the Money for the Salvation Army's Christmas Dinner," *Leslie's Weekly*,
Jan. 6, 1900.

C.O.S. leaders such as Devine transformed their group's public face from that of cold, hard "science" and unsentimental nonsectarianism into academic professionalism, material practicality, and thoughtful spiritual instruction. Army leaders such as Maud and Ballington Booth, and Emma and Frederick de Latour Booth-Tucker softened the Army's pugnacious working-class evangelism by appealing to the rich and influential with greater humility and restraint, while crucially modifying the Salvationist position on distinction.

The Salvation Army's 1899 Christmas Dinner packaged the essential elements of these new visions: a greater emphasis on material intervention in the lives of the poor, a seamless, unobtrusive mixture of religious and state participation in charitable enterprise, the maintenance of visibly hierarchical, pacific class relations, and the continued adherence to the principle of distinction between worthy and unworthy poor. The only thing left to do with this more saleable vision of charity and class relations was to sell it. For Christmas of 1899, New York's wealthy proved eager buyers.

"In the course of the year Madison Square Garden is the scene of many . . . spectacular happenings, but none could be more unique than the feast given yesterday," declared one newspaper account.[26] "From the gallery the guests looked out on the Garden as brilliantly lighted as for the circus or the French Ball," exclaimed another.[27] "I have been connected with the Garden for years," asserted a Madison Square Garden official, "and have seen a great many big affairs, but this is the greatest and best thing I ever saw. It will do a great deal to remove prejudice, and show the people what your organization is doing."[28] These comments and countless others confirm that the Salvation Army had not been engaging in false advertising when it said that it intended to deliver "a sight calculated to produce an indelible impression."[29] Inside the walls, Frederick de Latour Booth-Tucker's grandiose declaration that the event signified a "new era, the bridging of the gulf between the rich and the poor" might have seemed plausible, at least to certain participants.[30]

Such optimism, however, would not have extended very far. As the *New York Times* reported the next day, "after all this multitude had been fed and the tremendous stores of provisions had been exhausted to the last morsel, there still remained thousands of hungry mouths unfed, and men, women, and children were perforce turned back into the streets, hungry, friendless, and cold." Approximately three thousand poor New Yorkers faced locked doors and "were turned away without anything."[31] Indeed, from the selection of poor people invited to take part, to the scheduling of the program, to the physical arrangements of the hall, the evening's encounter between rich and poor served primarily to reinforce divisions, reaffirming the prescriptive principle of distinction through practice and spectacle.

The Army had choreographed a program of events designed to drape an aura of industrial efficiency and uniformity over a poverty that remained unbounded and unpredictable in its unvarnished state. The wealthy crowds that had begun to gather outside the Madison Avenue entrance during the early afternoon "entered first, by the thousands," filling up the lower levels of seats where they gained a vantage to watch when, at 4:30 P.M., the poor filed in from the Fourth Avenue entrance.[32] The whole process of assembly mimicked the prelude to a play or musical in which the audience settles down on one side of the hall before the curtain rises and the players appear from the other. As if to underscore this parallel, a large Army band in the wings provided a musical overture from start to finish. The visual and physical effect radiated order and competence, all packaged in a form recognizable as part of ordinary, entertaining cultural life, with definite divisions between those consuming the entertainment and those providing it.

This is not to say that the Army made no explicit efforts to "bridge the gulf" through its evening program. Once both groups had taken up their positions, the agenda proceeded with an eye not only to impressing the audience with the Army's organization, but also to infusing both audience and "players" with a gradually increasing sense of solidarity. The most basic strategy to this end involved the band's continuing to play as the poor ate and the finely dressed crowds watched, providing a common auditory experience. As the meal was concluding, Booth-Tucker eased along a sense of communion by directing his speech to everyone in the arena, dismissing differences and invoking a common blessing.[33] Then, completing the transition to more universally participatory undertakings, Booth-Tucker led them in communal song. As the *Sun* observed pithily, "Even the fat policemen lifted their helmets and sang."[34]

After rich, poor, and fat policemen alike sang "Nearer My God, to Thee," "Praise God, From Whom All Blessings Flow," and recited the Lord's Prayer in unison, the Army treated them all to a "stereopticon" presentation of Christ's Passion and the Salvation Army's good works. The screen onto which the Army projected this cinematographic display hung from the ceiling, so all were looking skyward at images of God and charity. The schedule of events had superficially unified everyone under the roof, first through shared song, then through common vision. These two bodies of people had entered from opposite sides of the building—indeed, from opposite realms of existence—but they ended the evening in a collective posture of passive rapture, mesmerized by a single vision projected on a screen.

Yet this sense of solidarity neither intended nor achieved a challenge to class arrangements within or outside the Garden's walls. Despite a definite desire to improve sympathetic links between rich and poor, the Army's leaders were eager to show their ability to forge such links without questioning or undermining their prescriptive basis. The dinner most obviously replicated existing social hierarchies in the physical arrangement of the crowds. The poor, after entering the arena under the supervision of Army personnel and the police, took their appointed, subordinate places either at the tables under the direct scrutiny of the wealthy, or in the upper mezzanine out of sight. This meant that only the poor actually eating—and thereby performing the headlining act produced with the money of the spectators—gained any kind of officially sanctioned visibility. The rest were relegated to the shadows of the upper deck.

This positioning emulated the spatial reality of New York, etched in stone on Fifth Avenue and vividly depicted in Edith Wharton's *House of Mirth,* in which the wealthy progressively insulated themselves from the public sight of the working class by moving uptown and indoors, away from the lower Manhattan tenements.[35] In the usual course of life, the elite only voluntarily encountered the working class in the form of service-economy workers such as cashiers or domestic servants or, for industrialists, their employees—in other words, when paying for their labor. In a sense, they replicated this dynamic in the Garden: wealthy audience members at the Christmas Dinner could simply choose not to turn around and crane their necks upward, thus avoiding the sight of the poor New Yorkers waiting above for their crack at the food. That vision would have been distinctly less reassuring than the one they had paid for, directly below them. As the *Sun* noted, those eating on the floor appeared cheerier than those in the upper mezzanine, where "bitterness, hatred, malice and all uncharitableness, sorrow, wretched pride, despair, plain starvation and stolid indifference were all there crowding one another."[36] The visual expression of any one of those emotions, much less all of them, could easily have dampened any "happy sympathy" among the moneyed audience.

Still, if the occasional bejeweled lady did happen to steal a glance away from the main event to the more ominous figures above and behind, she might take comfort in the authoritative presence of police interjected between the rich and the poor on all sides. Just as they did out on the streets of New York, the "bluecoaters" in the Garden acted as a visual reenforcement of society's boundaries. If the event was "bridging the gulf between the rich and the poor" as Booth-Tucker claimed, the state still vigorously monitored those bridges. By engendering illusions of solidarity within these frames of hierarchy, the Salvation Army granted legitimacy, as well as a healthy dollop of compassion, to the system that already held the loyalty of the moneyed spectators. Ideally it would also convince the poor that the rich already had their best interests at heart, even if sometimes the cards of civil, financial, and cultural power seemed stacked against them. In the course of less than two decades, the Army changed from a charity perceived, rightly, as disruptive of wealth's prescriptive social power over poverty, to one that used public endorsements of that power to solicit donations.

The purpose of these arrangements was not, however, to convince the wealthy spectators that they needed or were entitled to wield total social control over the poor. Wielding control would require exertion, effort, and sustained direction on the part of the elite, none of which the Army's vision suggested or encouraged. Rather, by presenting the wealthy with a carefully crafted picture of poverty that blended with quotidian commercial culture— methodically coaxing the constituent elements of that picture through certain entertaining movements and retaining the hierarchical structure of the status quo throughout it all—the event sold the idea that *any* exertion on the part of the elite was unnecessary so long as charity maintained adequate financial support. The beneficent rich and docile poor could be united in song under God and capitalism, without the slightest functional alteration in existing political-economic patterns. All it required on the part of the rich was a willingness to open their pocketbooks to the Salvation Army; all it required on the part of the poor was a willingness to accept the charity of the more powerful.

The fact remained, however, that this vision of social harmony was packaged and unreal, a figment of imagination played out in broad strokes under glitzy lights. The poor on the streets of New York did not always, or even often, agree to stand in line, mingle with police, or express gratitude and holiday wishes to their wealthy brethren. Upscale New Yorkers, for that matter, seldom consented (and even less frequently paid) to be in such close and ostensibly communal proximity to large groups of working people.[37] The Army's fabricated vision of harmony between rich and poor succeeded by almost any measure in masking those realities, but a few defects did appear in the façade. They went unrecognized or marginalized at the time, but on closer examination they emerge as suggestive indicators of both prescriptive class relations' less indulgent side, and the pervasive endorsement of distinction as an indispensable principle of charity and welfare practices.

Certain poor people who had collected basket dinners used them to exhibit a streak of capitalist entrepreneurship rather than the humble gratitude anticipated by the Army: they began selling the contents of the baskets on the street. The *Sun*'s account of this activity is revealing:

> Outside the Garden, as the [basket] line emerged, there were indications that some of the tickets had gone wrong, despite the pains the Army people had taken to distribute them economically and wisely. A number of Italian men and women and some East Side Poles had established a chicken market and were buying the fowls out of the baskets for five cents each and offering them for sale for 10, 15, and 20 cents each. . . . The miserable creatures who were engaged in the traffic had the grace to seem ashamed of themselves when their conduct was inquired into. The Italian women gave up their attempts and went away. Some of the Poles insisted defiantly that Christmas meant nothing to them and that if they could turn it to profit, they did well by themselves and by their faith.[38]

Rather than considering the possible economic logic driving such an impromptu chicken market—the easy calculation that a single chicken will last
for a day whereas the money obtained by selling it might purchase a durable
good or go toward rent—the *Sun* writer infers from the activity that "some of
the tickets had gone wrong," that the Salvation Army, far from being inadequately generous, had failed to be adequately selective in choosing which
poor to invite. The vetting during the ticketing process should have prevented
the intrusion of such "miserable creatures" (not subtly marked as foreigners
and Jews) who used charity to display a measure of self-reliance.

Some of the wealthy used the Christmas Dinner for purposes no less
unsettling to the packaged vision of their Army hosts, when they turned
what was meant as a demonstration of solidarity between rich and poor
into little more than the social event of the season. Despite Booth-Tucker's
triumphant claim in the aftermath that "the rich have faced the poor!" several news reporters in the crowd observed that the social luminaries remained more interested in facing each other.[39] The *Sun* evaluated their presence bluntly: "[These] people and many more like them had nothing to do
with the great dinner. They were simply there to see and be seen."[40] Perhaps
more perceptively, the *Times* regarded the elite as an intended adornment,
remarking, "To the Madison Avenue entrance came the spectators of the
extraordinary scene, in which they themselves were to add to its remarkable
character. They were to furnish the lighter shade to the picture, with their air
of contentment and prosperity, and perchance sympathy."[41] If the Army had
envisioned the elite's role as providing sympathetic gazes upon the poor, the
Times's "perchance" suggests that few played that role perfectly.

When they did "face the poor," the well-off seem to have done so as often in attitudes of horror, condescending indulgence, or rapt delight as in
the spirit of earnest charity and brotherhood the Army was selling. Three
examples stand out. One sensitive soul, a "well-dressed woman whose attention had been called to [the] horrible frieze [of poor in the upper decks]
by the man who had brought her into the garden burst into tears . . . and
broke down utterly. The man, greatly confused, led her to the door and took
her away in a cab."[42] Even a contained vision of mass poverty was too much
for some when they saw it in a non-performative state. Striking a somewhat
more positive note in evaluating that vision afterward, missionary maven

Adeline Countess Schimmelmann remarked, "It is a beautiful, a never-to-be-forgotten sight. It spoke to my heart when the people, by clapping and cheering, applauded the pictures of Christ in the Passion play, although at first, I must confess it jarred a little upon the finer sensibilities."[43] An aristocrat who had devoted her life to the spiritual salvation of the poor, the Countess betrayed her condescension toward them here.[44] On the other end of the spectrum, an "elegantly dressed gentleman," reportedly in a state of "comic despair," cried, "I cannot get my wife away from here! She is in smiles and tears alternately. We took a trip among the tables and came back without any money! This is perfectly delightful!"[45] Although this couple evidently took the call to material charity far more seriously than their peers who remained in the gallery, they seem to have done so in the spirit of diversion and emotional release. The Army's effort to make the poverty in the Garden appear as another element in the holiday decorations, albeit a prominent one that merited attention, abetted this attitude.

That the social problem extended further than the scope of the dinner could encompass manifested in the most glaring disappointment of the evening, observed succinctly but unobtrusively by the *New York Evening Post*:

> At a Christmas feast in Madison Square Garden, under the auspices of the Salvation Army, yesterday, nearly 20,000 people were fed and more than 3,000 received baskets of food to take to their homes for cooking there; unfortunately, the food gave out towards the end, and though there was money to buy them, supplies could not be obtained in the neighborhood in time, so many were turned away hungry.[46]

The declarations by the Army that "the order was perfect; the satisfaction unbounded," the assertions by the *Sun* that "all who had strength . . . received as much as they could eat," and the claim by the *Times* that "there was no limit to the food" amounted to rhetorical flourishes.[47] The *Times*, in fact, no more than two inches below the report of "no limit to the food," ran a subheading that read, "Food Supply Gave Out." This editorial contradiction gives some indication of what a show the Army had produced. It may have sent many away with empty bellies, but it sufficiently dazzled the *Times* to obscure that fact.

Still, one might expect either a certain critical mass of negative publicity for turning away petitioners on Christmas, or at least reporting as balanced as the *Post*'s. Only eight years earlier, after all, many of these same papers had published editorial warnings against a Christmas event sharing the same basic structure as the Army's 1899 dinner. Yet most papers devoted their coverage of the 1899 dinner to the love and gratitude ostensibly shared between rich and poor. None gave any indication that the deviations from the Army's vision suggested problems beyond the means of charity to address. A few accounts did mention the Army's failed effort to acquire additional supplies, but the *Sun* put a more revealing spin on the exhaustion of food: "At eight o'clock the doors were closed. But as late as 9 o'clock woe-begone, unshaven human wrecks came to the doors and asked the police whether they were too late. . . . They had been told to come at 5 o'clock and if they weren't hungry enough to be less than three hours late they deserved no dinners."[48]

Despite the Army's failure to feed all comers or induce every last person to play along, it apparently triumphed in projecting an image of success to the public. Most wealthy spectators, in any case, emerged from the show not with a sense of poverty's further needs, nor with an insight into charity's potential deficiencies, but with self-congratulatory confidence that they had participated in a great act of generosity and practical reform. Or, as at least one well-to-do man did, they exited the Garden with no thought of social dynamics at all, rather simply in satisfied awe of "the grandest sight [they had] ever seen."[49] The poor participants, meanwhile, were easily divisible into those who demonstrated appropriate meekness and gratitude, and those unworthies who either arrived late or failed to be satisfied with what they had received.

Only a few years earlier, C.O.S. president Robert Weeks de Forest had been bolstering criticism of such events in print. It is a powerful indicator of his group's own need for a more accommodating public image, and the Salvation Army's increasingly respectable reputation, that C.O.S. leaders and donors did not stay away. The overlap between Society donors and officials, and the underwriters or vice presidents of the Christmas Dinner was extensive. The Astor family, several members of whom were either Patrons (donors of greater than $500) or Life Members (greater than $100) of the

C.O.S., were involved in the event on at least two levels: Colonel John Jacob Astor donated $100 to the dinner fund, and his cousin William Waldorf Astor was a partial owner of Madison Square Garden.[50] New York Supreme Court Justice Charles F. MacLean was a vice president of the dinner; his wife was not only a C.O.S. donor, but a member of the C.O.S.'s 10th District Committee.[51] Governor Theodore Roosevelt sent a telegram to Booth-Tucker during the dinner that read, "Hearty Thanks! Warm Christmas greeting, and good wishes to all." At least five of his relatives (including his wife) were C.O.S. donors, and his uncle, J. Roosevelt Roosevelt, was both a Life Member and sat on the original C.O.S. Central Council.[52] John W. Keller, president of the Department of Public Charities, also served publicly as both a vice president of the Christmas Dinner and an ex officio member of the C.O.S. Central Council.[53]

The Salvation Army's ability to attract such luminaries speaks to its stunning success in rebranding itself—as recently as 1893, after all, it had been pilloried in the mainstream press as "grotesque," and lacking respectability. The C.O.S., meanwhile, which had built its own reputation on deliberative, parsimonious, nonsectarian distribution of poor relief, signaled a decidedly more relaxed attitude by effectively endorsing an openly religious public spectacle. The Christmas Dinner, the C.O.S., and the Salvation Army in New York are small parts of the Progressive reform story, but they indicate a shift in early Progressive-Era discourse about class and charity. In the early 1880s, idealist reformers such as Charles Kellogg and William Booth had argued that with enough rigorous science or religious spirit, poverty as they knew it could be all but eradicated in urban industrial settings like New York. Theirs were utopian, modernizing visions of charity's possibilities. By the end of the century, however, the organizational imperative to address bad press through downplaying more provocative ideas led them to shared participation in an event selling charity as warm-hearted material relief, and inequality as inevitable but manageable with the right people in charge.

The more utopian ideas—whether nonsectarian, scientific, and discreet, or public, passionate, and Christian—had given way, at least for Christmas, to a Madison Square Garden vision that seemed more governed by the dictates of the market. The market in charities had no space for a group that would deny poor people a pittance at Christmas because it could not investigate them properly first. It had comparably little market share for a charity that incited women and the working poor to march in the streets. What the market—in the form of donors—wanted was a charity that made visible, material use of donor money, provided assurance that it was not only filling bellies but swelling spirits, and studiously avoided uncomfortable questions about poverty's relationship to capitalism.

The material intervention of the dinner was clear. The Salvationists fed the poor by the thousands, a practice C.O.S. officials had once deplored without reservation but now seemed willing to countenance in public. Religious rhetoric and performance suffused the event, from the banners praising God to the performance of the Passion play, but the presence of prominent city and state officials—as well as a vigilant police force—testified to the fact that this particular religion aimed not to provoke but to ingratiate itself with civic authorities. Although the sheer spectacle of it all was in some respects designed to entertain rich and poor as equal spectators, the police drew a clear blue line between the poor on the arena floor and the wealthy in the stands, reinforcing class divisions for all to see.[54] This was not a vision of how charity could transform society. It was a vision of how the prescriptive influence of the wealthy made the lives of the poor more livable, while excluding the unworthy.

The historical arc of these two charities' transformations describes the larger tragedy of prescriptive class relations. Both groups imagined themselves to be renovating charity to battle the corrosive social effects of industrialization more effectively. Yet the cultural, social, and political underpinnings of industrial capitalism proved not only powerful enough to resist their "scientific" or religious innovations for charity, but actually co-opted them. Charity became geared more toward professionalism, public relations, fundraising, superficial efficiency, and spectacle—toward creating a soothing vision of class reconciliation worth paying for—than toward (as both the C.O.S. and Army had hoped) achieving actual class reconciliation through fundamentally destabilizing class assumptions.

There is still an overwhelmingly shared assumption in America that the poor have done something wrong. This belief is hardly unique to Americans, but it has achieved in the United States something approaching the status of national truism. In this Eden of opportunity, goes the reasoning, only personal mistakes or shortcomings can explain failure.[55] The implied and equally cherished belief is that wealth and power are the manifest rewards of right and imitable behavior, making affluent Americans the logical candidates to guide programs of correction for the poor.

Such prescriptive class relations necessarily involve a dearth of self-reflection on the part of the wealthy. These prosperous, would-be progressives generally fail to consider not only the countless sources of their prosperity unrelated to individual merit, but more importantly the way struggling men and women might experience their presumption, and how that experience might undermine progressive ends. Wealthy reformers of the Progressive Era were particularly prone to such obliviousness, steeped as they were in the collective vision of an ascendant, imperial America whose industrial and scientific supremacy would allow them to command a new social order. Fear distracted them as well: waves of unfamiliar immigrants crashed onto U.S. shores in those years; urban neighborhoods grew more crowded and derelict with each passing day; and percolating revolutionary thought among workers produced cascades of class violence, against a backdrop of four economic panics and collapses in the space of thirty-four years.[56] Dreams of improving downtrodden lives by applying scientific knowledge to the messy world of humanity seemed not only an increasingly realistic possibility, but also a vital and urgent necessity.

This combination of entitlement and urgency discouraged self-awareness, and whether the rich greeted the poor with a clinical will to assert power or a heartfelt desire to help their fellow man became, on a crucial level, irrelevant. Either way, those under the prescriptive impulse's sway could not grasp that their attempts to extirpate inequality and class animus might nurture them instead. Brilliant and dedicated individuals—including Richard Watson Gilder, Stanford White, Josephine Shaw Lowell, and Frederick de Latour Booth-Tucker—engaged in countless attempts to refashion society for a more hopeful future through schemes of prescriptive class relations. Their efforts shared at least one fundamental flaw: they reinforced class difference in the very attempt to mitigate it.

6

Reaching Out to the Rich

ON DECEMBER 9, 1909, eighteen-year-old Max W. Paley composed an earnest plea to Jacob Henry Schiff. "Dear Sir," wrote the immigrant office clerk in meticulous cursive, "knowing how philanthropic you are in cases of need, I am taking the liberty of writing you. I have a sister who is now sixteen years of age and is badly in need of an operation. She has had a tube in her throat ever since she was a child of four."[1]

Max's sister Jennie was the baby of the family, the only daughter, and the only child born and raised in the United States. Samuel and Emma Paley, Max's parents, had immigrated from the Russian Pale of Settlement in 1891 with Max and his two older brothers, Joseph and Philip. Jennie was born shortly after they arrived and, like so many children of immigrants in the city, became dangerously ill as a toddler. She contracted diphtheria, one of several highly contagious diseases that thrived in the dense living conditions endured by thousands of New York immigrant families. In the Lower East Side's Second Ward, yellow and scarlet fevers, tuberculosis, typhoid, diarrhea, and diphtheria contributed to a nearly 20 percent mortality rate (or "death-rate," in the less euphemistic language of the era) for children under five years old in 1894. Jennie Paley survived, but either lack of funds or the slow pace of her recovery prevented doctors from repairing the tracheotomy that had saved her life, leaving her to experience childhood and adolescence with a tube sticking from a scarred hole in her throat.[2]

The Paleys sought better luck upstate, moving to Rochester and settling on a street entirely occupied by other Russian Jews. Samuel worked as a peddler, while Joseph and Philip found positions in the neighborhood's main industry, tailoring. Together, they earned enough money at their three jobs to support the family, thereby allowing Max to attend school. Jennie's condition remained debilitating enough for the 1900 federal census to list her occupation as "Invalid." The Paleys established what they would later remember as a good home in Rochester, staying for at least a decade, but Jennie's suffering eventually uprooted them again. After saving what they thought would be enough money to pay for the operation to remove the tube from her throat, they packed their possessions in March 1909 and returned to New York City, where they hoped to take advantage of "greater medical advice."[3]

Events did not proceed as planned. The Paley men looked for work for months, and by the time they found it—Max as a clerk for a clothing concern, Philip as a cutter in a neckwear shop, Joseph as a tailor, and Samuel as an immigration official on Ellis Island—their living expenses had claimed all the money scraped together in Rochester. Compounding costs, Joseph had married a woman named Beckie, and so winter found the now seven Paleys (and more on the way) living in a small apartment on West 142nd Street, no money saved, and Jennie's ailment no closer to resolution. Max, having watched his parents and older brothers risk everything for his sister and come up short, decided to make an attempt himself. Using the education their industry had afforded him, Max wrote to a man he knew could help.[4]

Paley's letter to Schiff exemplifies a type of intersection between the wealthy and the poor distinct from scientific charity, class spectacle, or policy initiatives emanating from elites, those prescriptive forms of class contact more common to the age. Paley, a working immigrant, initiated contact in a form he controlled and on terms (at least initially) of his choosing. He did not put his faith in the city and its hospitals. He did not complete the C.O.S.'s exhaustive, humiliating application process. Far from trying to attract wider public attention to his sister's plainly sympathetic case of need, his postscript to Schiff reads, "We are a respected Jewish family and trust this will be confidential."[5] Although the request itself demanded humility on Paley's part, his desire for discretion conveyed pride and dignity undiminished by years of adversity. His letter, and thousands of other "begging letters" like it, constituted class contact of a different order, that of one human being in dire straits appealing to another who occupied a position of power and influence.[6]

Writers of these letters usually crafted their narratives painstakingly to resemble what they had learned were the cultural markers of the "worthy poor": principally industriousness, modesty, and respect for their "betters." In that sense, they still operated within the constraints of established cultural norms regarding poverty and wealth, nodding or bowing to realities of power. Yet their letters were also clear attempts to preserve some shred of power for themselves by evading the structural, bureaucratic, and ideological pitfalls of more prescriptive charitable channels. The letters were attempts to gain some control in overcoming their difficulties rather than submitting wholesale to an impersonal, often degrading charitable system endorsed by the city. Interacting directly across class lines, the letter writers retained a small but important measure of control and self-respect—precisely by remaining outside a system that demanded the surrender of both before it offered any assistance.[7]

Jacob Schiff also remained outside that system in more ways than one, despite the fact that he was a long-serving C.O.S. officer and one of New York's most prominent bankers, second only to J. P. Morgan in professional reputation. Most obviously, he was an immigrant Jew in a professional and social milieu populated predominantly by Old–New York Protestants, elites who moved in the same circles as Richard Watson Gilder and Robert Weeks de Forest. Schiff's resentment of the casual anti-Semitism he encountered on the charity circuit alienated him from establishment charities, but perhaps more significantly, his entire philosophy of giving expressed a different set of assumptions than those generally held by his fellow philanthropists. Schiff's analysis of poverty—and, by extension, his remedies for it—did not cleave blindly to laissez-faire economic doctrine, knee-jerk moralism, or Progressive "science." Instead, it drew from the tradition of *tzedakah,* the Jewish law that demanded every Jew minister to the poor in service of social justice, not social order or control. While cultural context inevitably colored his views and influenced his public statements, Schiff's bedrock ideas about social justice deeply informed his philanthropy, steering it frequently toward advocacy and activism. Those ideas brought him into much more direct and regular contact with the poor and working class than most wealthy New Yorkers, even prominent reformers, were willing to bear.

For Paley, contacting Schiff also meant engaging with Lillian D. Wald, one of Schiff's main collaborators and consultants on philanthropic work in the city. Indeed, many begging-letter writers bypassed Schiff and wrote directly to Wald, having discovered that in many ways she pulled the strings with Schiff's money. The Visiting Nurses Service and Henry Street Settlement, which Wald had founded, managed to be both active within and for the most part respectful of poor communities, offering innovative models of institutional poor relief at a time when the C.O.S. still sat in judgment of applicants and the city empowered elite committees like Gilder's to transform poor neighborhoods unilaterally from City Hall or Albany (via private homes and clubs). The Visiting Nurses Service sought out the poor in their homes to provide medical services, often for free, and the Henry Street Settlement opened a safe community space for Lower East Siders and their children to learn, play, and seek refuge. Poor and working families who knew about Wald had access to these resources largely on their own terms and, in the case of the Nurses Service, in their own spaces. Wald's philosophy of mutual human respect had earned her a reputation among the poor as an honest broker, while Schiff's endorsement of Wald to his wealthy friends and colleagues brought both positive attention and money to her work. Wald opened a line of communication between rich and poor in New York, metaphorically by using private wealth to make real partners of the poor in improving public health, education, and labor protections in the city, and often literally by inviting the rich to dinner at Henry Street to meet and break bread with the neighborhood residents.[8]

Wald and Schiff practiced effective, interactive alternatives to the prescriptive class contact of the C.O.S. and the city's public policy efforts. Neither sought an abdication of class privilege on the part of the wealthy, nor the creation of utopian cross-class relationships and perfect social harmony. The key to their work was a basic level of respect for other people—*all* other people. Near the end of her life, Wald put it simply, "I hold to my faith that the first essential to sound human relations is respect. No one who has that sense of respect will patronize, or insult, or feel alien to, human beings."[9] Working directly with and among the poor in that spirit of respect, Wald and Schiff gathered insights and made improvements to the city far beyond what was possible through other agencies. While traditional Progressives still followed the guidance of elite expertise and pseudoscientific principle in their work, Wald and Schiff listened closely to voices like Max Paley's. Their work offered a vision of class contact decidedly different and more promising than the traditional, prescriptive varieties.[10]

Anti-Semitism, lack of public funds, and a seismic shift in historical context, however, would subvert or undermine Wald and Schiff's ability to turn the broader culture of class contact in a more cooperative direction. Schiff fought battles with the C.O.S. over the discriminatory practices in its employment bureau—an agency he had helped establish—eventually resigning his responsibilities in protest when he met stiff resistance to providing equal services to non-Protestant, nonwhite applicants. Despite the benefits accruing to the city from the Settlement and Nurses Service, New York funded neither institution until 1917, so almost every year found both organizations struggling to meet expenses. In 1913, forced to make a broad public appeal to fund an endowment, Wald put on an open-air historical pageant in Henry Street to celebrate the Settlement's twentieth anniversary. Despite her efforts to create an inclusive event, Wald's pageant turned out to be the kind of class spectacle that reinforced rather than challenged the dominant understanding of class relations in the city. The xenophobia and American chauvinism that accompanied the Great War's onset soon thereafter effectively destroyed any chance Wald and Schiff had to challenge the prescriptive norm, particularly in light of increasingly violent class conflicts at home, and the Bolshevik Revolution abroad.[11]

Yet begging-letter writers like Max Paley, bankers like Jacob Schiff, and activists like Lillian Wald suggest that direct or cooperative class contact was possible on a wider scale in Progressive-Era New York than was ultimately realized. The memory of this lost promise has been obscured by the tendency to portray such figures in either adulatory tones of pride and triumph, or judgmental ones of deep skepticism. Such a tendency is understandable, after all. Paley's initiative in writing the letter and his eloquence in framing it underline the agency and dignity of the individual. A full catalogue of Wald's and Schiff's good deeds makes an even stronger case: each did more than almost any contemporary to foster basic respect for humanity in the city, and their partnership made inarguable inroads against two of New York's vilest social ills, disease and child labor.

Neither is healthy skepticism unreasonable. Resentment, both veiled and open, made frequent appearances in begging letters. Anger, servility, and desperation seethed beneath the surface or sprang off the page—whether expressing real sentiment or in service of a con game, it can be difficult to tell, because attempted fraud proliferated. As for Schiff and Wald, they supported vigorous efforts to assimilate recent immigrants through classes in subjects such as hygiene, cooking, and English, instruction that many in the Lower East Side community regarded as condescending and presumptuous. Wald's guiding philosophy of respect for humanity did not prevent her from supporting the eugenics movement for "defective" babies.[12] In an era of worldwide turbulence and doubt about capitalism's long-term viability, Schiff and Wald both understood that by actively mitigating capitalism's worst effects on the poor, their work acted as a bulwark against revolution and ballast for the political-economic status quo.[13] For Schiff, that status quo remained enormously profitable.

There is, however, a third mode of telling these stories, one that sees the power of individuals, the limits of their historical context, and their human imperfection: the tragic. Begging-letter writers tying themselves in knots to supplicate the rich individually because that was the *least* humiliating option available to them for relief; a private donor seeing his efforts to inject charity with a measure of Judaism's justice and humanism stymied by anti-Semitism; a forward-thinking community worker contorting her principles to attract the necessary private funding for publicly beneficial work—these narratives all have the makings of tragedy. In each case, dominant reactionary tendencies or traditional cultural currents within the Progressive Era foiled more honest class contact or comprehensive reform. Structural power and inertia subsumed or subverted cooperative human potential. Indeed, when examined against the backdrop of the obstacles set in its path, cooperative contact of any kind between rich and poor during this period appears fundamentally tragic. It is even more remarkable, then, for having flourished at all.

Direct appeals from the poor to the wealthy like Max Paley's to Jacob Schiff were not uncommon. Olivia Sage—widow of financier Russell Sage, heiress to his fortune, and founding director of the Russell Sage Foundation—received over three hundred such letters per day after public announcements of her inheritance. *The Washington Post* reported in 1913 that John D. Rockefeller's daily mailbag included five hundred begging letters. The Rockefeller Foundation (which requested its congressional charter in part to deal with Rockefeller's paper deluge) forwarded cases to Wald when its secretary felt the appearance of merit called for investigation, as did the Astor family on at least two occasions.[14]

Even less prominent New Yorkers received begging letters. In a 1906 letter to Wald seeking help to pay for rent and heat, Melke Clar perfectly demonstrates the phenomenon in neatly lined longhand and idiosyncratic style:

> Esteemd Miss, By a number of distinguisht persons differnt ranks of high standing as Orators of ethics, Journalists, theologists philanthropists sociologists Ect. My appeals did not found favor by them. I venture one's more which it will be of my last resort and of my great prospect as I am well convinced becous all the distinguist persons they do reffer me to you, and everyone says that you are very capable you are doing great deeds.[15]

As Clar's appeal conveys, Paley's note was only one drop in a constant stream of letters pouring into Henry Street, either forwarded by wealthy benefactors and their foundations, or springing directly from the savvier poor who knew that Wald was a gatekeeper for philanthropists and their money. That stream was only a small tributary in a vast delta of begging letters outside Wald's purview.

For Paley, writing to Schiff had a lot to recommend it, particularly given the potentially dangerous and demeaning alternatives left to his family after their savings and moving scheme had failed. Indeed, no matter who the author might be, writing a begging letter had at least two considerable advantages over applying to the C.O.S. or to United Hebrew Charities (U.H.C.) for relief: the retention of choices and the control of one's voice.

Begging-letter authors made clear, consequential choices unavailable to C.O.S. applicants. From the outset, they chose specific individuals or organizations to address for help rather than taking their chances with whatever Society member happened to be working in the C.O.S. office on a given day, or with whatever visitor or investigator might show up at their door. Even when basing their choice on knowledge gleaned from the press, word of mouth, or some other indirect source, this decision could be pivotal. Paley's decision to address Schiff meant that Wald and the Visiting Nurses Service would take charge of any investigation into his family's plight, which was vastly preferable to many alternatives. Other begging-letter writers were not so strategic or lucky. Olivia Sage eventually received so many thousands of letters that she turned to the C.O.S. for help in sorting and investigating them systematically. In her well-intentioned effort to reach out to as many people as possible, however, she subverted many writers' original purpose—to communicate directly with her and avoid the C.O.S. altogether. As a result, C.O.S. investigators frequently showed up at the doors of people who had written to Sage and encountered only "frigidity."[16]

The writers also chose, at least initially, what information to divulge about themselves and their families, rather than being forced to provide a predetermined set of personal data in an official interview. Despite being fairly forthright with Schiff about his family's situation and sister's condition, Paley omitted certain details—the fact that his father and both older brothers had jobs, for instance—that would have been required in a formal application for relief, and likely would have prevented the provision of any aid. Catholic Charities denied relief to Thomas and Bridge Kelleher, an elderly Irish couple who came within the Henry Street orbit, precisely because "they were so hesitant about giving history." In-person applications for relief required nothing less than total cooperation from applicants, and the charities, not the applicants, determined what aspects of personal history mattered, as Rachel Johnstone had discovered when being questioned by C. L. Reeds. Although letter-writers took a risk when eliding potentially adverse information from their requests (as the damning facts would probably come out eventually), the tactic could at least get a foot in the door; they could offer persuasive explanations later, by which time their wealthy correspondent may already have committed resources to their case.[17]

Given the details of his situation, Paley had little to hide, but other writers chose to show fewer cards for strategic reasons. One such writer's letter came directly to Wald in October 1905, begging on behalf of the Lipsky family from 187 Clinton Street. Various C.O.S. and police officers had warned or arrested Nathan Lipsky for begging in 1892, 1897, 1899, twice in 1903, and again in 1905. During the most recent arrest (in August of that year), the police had allegedly uncovered $500 on Lipsky's person, deeds to two properties on Clinton Street, and a "special pocket which Lipsky carries inside his trousers for the purpose of containing large amounts of change." The arresting officer informed the C.O.S., and the Society cut off aid to Lipsky's family immediately. The U.H.C., informed through the C.O.S., ceased aid as well.[18]

The unnamed supplicant to Wald, however, only alluded to "the recent occurence [sic] that . . . branded Mr. Lipsky as a man of means," perhaps hoping to avoid dredging up details. The writer lingered instead upon the family's suffering in an effort to pull at Wald's heartstrings. "If only these people [at the C.O.S. and U.H.C.] were aware what a great mistake was being made" ran the anguished account. "To seek charity that life may be possible is humiliating, but you can imagine how heartbreaking it is to have the minds of persons poisoned so unjustly who heretofore have extended a ready hand and the family left to its miserable fate." The letter, written from a third-person perspective, bears the dubious signature "Very sincerely yours, The Neighboring Lipsky Tenants."[19]

The writer may have actually been a neighbor or may have been Lipsky himself trying to assume a disinterested identity; the allegations against Lipsky may have been true, or they may have been result of anti-Semitic or nativist persecution by the police (which was entirely possible in this period). The letter evades such questions by choosing to present a narrative composed of suffering and grief: "As neighbors we have fed the little ones often and often they go to school with empty stomachs," it read, "and if you will accept the testimony of sympathizing neighbors, the Lipskys are in a most impoverished and wretched condition . . . anything you may do in behalf of this fallen family will live in our memories illuminated by gratitude."[20] Wald's case file does not reveal whether she intervened, but the letter certainly exhibits strategic narrative choices designed for that outcome, choices unavailable to the Lipskys (or their neighbors) in reapplying to the C.O.S. or U.H.C. With those institutions, a person's name, once sullied, remained mud.

Official charities were not the only institutions that begging-letter writers chose to avoid by contacting the rich or their proxies directly. Whether because they had personally undergone, or their neighbors had described to them nightmarish experiences of disease-ridden almshouses, discriminatory employment agencies, or other dysfunctional city-service centers, many poor and working people refused to engage with such institutions under all but the direst of circumstances. Hospitals in particular were to be avoided. Looking back on her early nursing work with Mary Brewster, Wald wrote, "My colleague and I realized that there were large numbers of people who could not, or would not, avail themselves of the hospitals." Even when working with life-threatening conditions such as advanced typhoid, she found that "overcoming hospital prejudice" required persuasion "with patients for whom the very idea of a hospital struck terror." For Paley, remaining independent from the public health care system meant that his sister would gain access to top-level care through personal connections instead of rolling the dice on a random referral. In fact, he intimated as much to Schiff, writing, "Naturally she will have to be in the hospital for about two months and will need the best of care." The phrase "best of care" subtly suggested Paley's awareness that most care in the city available to poor immigrants was decidedly not the best. By composing letters to wealthy individuals or their agents, petitioners reserved the right to reject undesirable public institutions in favor of alternatives, a choice closed to seekers of public aid.[21]

Another choice that begging letters afforded—unrelated to their content or outcome but no less significant in producing a preference for writing them among aid-seekers—was the decision of when and where to make an appeal. Choosing a private moment to write a letter in convenient surroundings certainly beat being surprised in one's home by a stranger's investigation, not to mention visiting the United Charities Building on 22nd Street in public and exposing oneself to potential ridicule from neighbors, condescension from officials, and shame in the eyes of family. The explicit request for discretion in Paley's letter to Schiff underlines the connection between dignity and privacy by connecting his request for "confidentiality" to his status in a "respected Jewish family." If Paley believed a piece of private correspondence could place his family's reputation in jeopardy, it seems fair to presume that publicly applying for aid (and undergoing the work test in the C.O.S. Wood-Yard to prove his willingness to work, as was required of all able-bodied young men) would have been anathema to him.[22]

Of course, the privacy enjoyed in writing a letter enabled fraud as well, or at least attempts at fraud. In the absence of immediate witnesses, a letter-writer could bend, break, or wholly reinvent the truth about themselves.

The case of Nathan Lipsky remains ambiguous, but some others were notorious. Frederick B. Jennings, writing the "Report of the Committee on Mendicancy" for the C.O.S.'s 1905 *Annual Report*, warned of "the forger-gambler Crawford with his begging letters and pleas so well calculated to move the average business man to hasty aid and equally hasty judgment." John P. Scott, "an American gentleman," admitted in the *Washington Post* to being conned by several such begging-letter writers, including one who claimed to be an "unhappy father who wrote regarding a dying daughter" but was "found to be a gentleman still enjoying the freedom of bachelor-hood, and following a highly lucrative business in the begging-letter line from a quite expensive office in the busiest part of New York City." Olivia Sage claimed that at least one quarter of the missives she received after her husband's death constituted outright fraud. Some rich folk were ripe for grifting, and begging letters were easy to write for an adequately literate, enterprising con artist. Whether they succeeded was another matter, but some clearly did.[23]

As both Paley's and Scott's experiences indicate, however, whatever privacy begging-letter writers enjoyed would almost always end in an investigation before any disbursement of aid. Yet in contacting the wealthy directly instead of the established charity services, begging-letter writers, whether fraudulent or sincere, had at least one more card to play in determining the nature of that investigation: they could craft their voice. Within certain limits imposed by language, education, and cultural context, they controlled the voice of their letters. Holding onto their own voices or creating new and utilitarian voices for the purpose at hand meant projecting a measure of personality and creativity into an act—asking for help—with bottomless potential for self-abasement. Confronting a system of charity that increasingly viewed applicants as faceless ciphers, dry numbers to be measured and categorized, begging-letter writers insisted on their own humanity.

"Having heard of you from many people of the good deeds you are doing," wrote Bessie Moskowitz to Wald in 1910, "I will make an attempt to relate a little of my history and see what you would advise me to do. I am a young lady of 19 years and a sufferer of a T.B. hip, for the last sixteen years. My parents died when I was quite young and I was left alone in the cruel world to battle with my life."[24]

"Your answer to this letter will mean a great deal to me," wrote a Brooklyn teenager, Philip Lubell, to Wald in 1915, asking for financial support to continue his "business school" studies. "Here's one chance to make good, and with your favor I can accomplish my aim. I am doing excellent work at 'school' and can show a statement of corroboration . . . I am almost certain that you will help me."[25]

"Since I was in your service . . . things have not gone well with me," Harry Heald mournfully informed the president of the B. Altman & Company department store, Michael Friedsam, in his letter of December 19, 1916. "I have been unable to secure congenial or suitable employment, though I have tried hard. . . . I am the sole support of my mother, sister, and young brother. We have had a year of great misfortune, my mother having been in hospital 9 weeks following a serious operation added to my sister, who since my mother's illness has been unable to follow her employment as seamstress owing to being hurt by a passing automobile which has left her very nervous. I trust, Mr. Friedsam," he genuflected, "that I do not bore you with a recital of these troubles, but know your great generosity in the past." After nearly three pages' worth of "these troubles," Heald closed the letter with this painfully modest request: "What would give me great help would be a few articles of your discarded wearing apparel, no matter how much worn. This would certainly be very welcome . . . with Best Wishes for your Health and Seasons Greetings, Yours Truly, Harry Heald."[26]

"Please do not place this aside after you get through reading it," wrote twenty-three-year-old Irving Ball to Mrs. Vincent Astor in 1917. "Things are very dark . . . for my mother and myself on account of me not working. My dear Mrs. Astor things would be very bright if I was only working. I know that you would enjoy to try to make another home happy."[27]

Letter writers like these begged, but they also cajoled, wheedled, pressured, and in some cases practically commanded correspondents to be compelled. In doing so, they fashioned their voices to appeal to the humanity in their addressees, a practical impossibility when engaging the records-driven bureaucracy of the C.O.S.

The voice Paley employed in his letter to Schiff blended self-respect, pathos, insistence, and affecting simplicity while establishing his family's bona fides of industry—it was inescapably the voice of an individual, not a caricature of poverty. After the initial lines acknowledging Schiff's renown as a philanthropist and introducing his sister's condition, he related the frustrating fact that "my father had a little money which would probably have been sufficient to see her through, but the operation which is to be performed now could not have been performed then. And since then father has lost all he had." Instead of veering into dramatic despair here, he reasserted himself: "I presume you realize that the girls [*sic*] life will be ruined if she doesn't have immediate care." Then he backed into reassurances that his family had seen specialists to determine that Jennie was ready to have the operation. Only the funds were wanting, and Paley made his request to Schiff simple: "as we haven't any money, I am going to ask you to see her through." Ending with a pledge to repay Schiff over time, he signed off "very respectfully yours," adding only his name, address, and a postscript mentioning their Jewish faith and asking for discretion. It was a near-perfectly calibrated voice, precisely because it did not seem to be *begging* so much as asking that justice be done for an upright, long-suffering family.

It also displays, however, certain niceties of form and content that reappear frequently in begging letters. The authors wrote letters in voices of their choosing, but more often than not those voices reflected cultural and historical circumstances as much as each individual's writing style or ability. The pervasive public image (all too frequently reflected in the documentary record) of the wealthy—their animosity toward aggressive working people, dismissiveness of the "idle poor," and Victorian moralism—created a framework within which almost every begging-letter writer, at least those with even a slim chance of success, tried to operate.[28]

This framework included honorifics for the potential benefactor, a description of abuses suffered, avowals of helplessness followed closely by insistence of industry (or willingness to work and repay debt), and finally requests coupled with declarations of despair should help not arrive posthaste. Many announced their own aversion to the very act of writing or asking for help. "I do not want charity," insisted Irving Ball to Mrs. Astor, "I only want a position." Melke Clar went further to Wald, stating, "Believe me if any person would stab my heart with a sword I believe I will not feel such payn, as I feel when I have to write an appeal for assistants." C. E. Sweeney, a former investigator who had been robbed by an employee in 1916, fit quite a bit into just one sentence to Wald: "I know that I have no right to annoy but in my desperation I was of the impression that with your large circle of influential friends and your charitable desire to assist worthy people you might be able to render me some assistance." Humility, despair, flattery, self-respect, and a request for help appear in turn.[29]

This language enacted a paradoxical ritual of pride and submission common to letters from the poor to the rich and their agents, a ritual that fit its practitioners into widespread notions of worthy poverty. Such language attempts to paint the author (or its subject, in the case of letters written on behalf of others) as harried but noble, in desperate straits but not constitutionally desperate. It impresses upon its reader that the impoverishment it describes arises solely from adverse circumstances, not from shortcomings of character. The authors knew that the act of reading their letters might be the first step in a more comprehensive investigation to come, an investigation that would involve a home visit, family interviews, and cross-referencing with other charitable organizations. The letter's voice, and the reader's impression of it, could determine what assumptions the investigators carried with them. Using common tropes of the "worthy poor," therefore, the writers fashioned images of families or individuals more likely to inspire a sympathetic hearing.

The contours of contact that begging letters represent suggest several aspects of class relations during the Progressive Era. Their sheer volume indicates that many poor and working people considered them a relatively viable and preferable method of seeking relief. This might say more about the unappealing alternatives available—hospitals, discriminatory employment agencies, and almsgivers, for instance—than about the true viability of writing begging letters, but for lucky or talented writers, any aid that arrived had the potential to come in a more agreeable manner. The advantages of choice and voice that begging-letter writers retained allowed them to impress their humanity and individuality upon the wealthy or powerful, usually ensuring in the worst case a respectful reply or none at all, and at best, much more favorable consequences.[30]

The commonalities of style and content in begging letters also suggest that most struggling New Yorkers recognized the dominant cultural conceptions of poverty with total clarity. Rather than allowing themselves to be objectified or categorized simply as "worthy" or "unworthy," those who wrote begging letters elaborated on such archetypes self-consciously, sometimes with great sophistication. Max Paley might have been a savant master of the form had he further occasions to write, his letter to Schiff paying homage without appearing obsequious, describing want without becoming maudlin, and requesting money without grasping for it. He and many others anticipated stock judgments from the well-to-do, and did their best through a set of linguistic steps to neutralize or take advantage of those judgments, breaking out of overdetermined categories to appear human on the page, and fitting themselves into an image of worthiness that transcended type.[31]

From a darker perspective, however, most begging letters did not meet the transcendent standard that Paley's did, and since those lesser letters could be the predominant form of contact the rich had with struggling New Yorkers' voices, many wealthy citizens' most direct impression of poor and working people was the refraction of an old stereotype. New Yorkers who wrote these letters took a proactive role in attempting to manipulate the stereotype in ways they could not through other methods, but they also knew that throwing it off completely, by departing a common frame of reference, would risk losing their potential patrons' attention. In the act of trying to break free of the charity system's structural and bureaucratic constraints, they placed themselves in cultural constraints of another kind.

The responses from the wealthy or influential to these letters varied widely, but they tended, with a predictably Progressive mentality, toward bureaucratization. The Rockefeller Foundation took on the project of privately organizing investigations, proposing to be a clearinghouse for begging letters that would "handle, not only that part of Mr. Rockefeller's correspondence, but the same kind of mail reaching other philanthropists with justice and dispatch." Olivia Sage, after unburdening the weight of her letters to the C.O.S., made a public announcement that scorned fraudsters and discouraged others, remarking, "I have been receiving ever since my husband's death several hundred letters a day containing applications of every conceivable kind. . . . To read them all would involve the total loss of eyesight, which a woman at seventy-seven needs to preserve." In fairness, Sage did continue to read many herself, and even occasionally broke her own rules by allocating money outside C.O.S. precepts, but the bulk of the work went to professional social workers at the "Sage Fund" set up and administered by the Society. These structures began to make begging letters simply another system of charity application, removing whatever more personal, cross-class contact the form offered, if not entirely the initial advantages of choice and voice.[32]

Max Paley's letter produced a happier outcome. His letter and the subsequent Nurses Service investigation induced Schiff to pay for Jennie Paley's operation and hospital stay, opening avenues for her future that almost certainly would have remained closed otherwise. Twenty years after Paley wrote to Schiff, Jennie was married to an apparently prosperous stockbroker, had two daughters, and was living in a $20,000 home in Westchester; her family even employed a live-in servant.[33] Undoubtedly, the path from a single begging-letter to wealth must have been rarely traveled, but Jacob Schiff took a rare tack in all his philanthropic endeavors, and his handling of Max Paley's request was only one indication of it.

7

Between Empathy and Prejudice

The ancient Hebrew lawgiver . . . knows no such word as
charity; to him even giving to the poor is only an act of justice,
and justice is the expression he solely applies, when he urges
his people to their duty to the needy and dependent.

—Jacob Henry Schiff

JACOB HENRY SCHIFF was perhaps not the likeliest of candidates to forge
cooperative, interactive bonds with the poor. Born in Frankfurt am Main
in 1847 to a line of prominent rabbis, intellectuals, and merchants, he could
trace his lineage at least as far back as the fourteenth century, and his family
had owned property in Frankfurt's *Judengasse* since 1608; these were hardly
humble origins. Schiff's father, Moses, lived up to the name, demanding
strict obedience in matters both religious and personal, and setting a stern
example that would resonate with Jacob for life. Schiff became a man of
compulsive routine and dictatorial temper in his business, observances of
faith, and family life, neither allowing himself indulgences nor brooking
them in others.[1]

His relationships with his daughter Frieda and son Mortimer, moreover,
suggest decidedly prescriptive instincts. He sent a trusted family nurse along
with his daughter and new son-in-law on their honeymoon to police the
proceedings. He, not Morti, decided what courses the young man would
take in college. Certainly Schiff's impulse to control the lives of his children
sprang from paternal custom and high expectations above all else—the

desire to see Frieda become a respectable woman of the New York gentry and to see Morti "rank with the good and solid men in his generation"— but his assertions of will could be peremptory. Even grandchildren were not exempt. When his little grandson Edward, on the advice of a nurse, plucked a flower to give Schiff during the Sabbath dinner, the agate-eyed, silver-bearded banker not only upbraided the boy for having broken Jewish law in taking life on the holy day, but banished Edward from the dinner table for two days. The punishment, Schiff told the child, was "so that you will remember this."[2]

Schiff's domineering parental style and privileged childhood did not, however, outweigh the tendency of his own experiences as a young immigrant to cultivate empathy and respect for the poor. He had embarked for New York alone as an eighteen year old, leaving behind family and friends in Frankfurt. He had a good education and prospects, certainly, but no prearranged job or home awaited him in America. Like many other immigrants, he stepped from a ship's gangplank into a land he had never seen, to be greeted by someone he had never met. Granted, the "someone" in his case was not a representative from a Lower East Side *landsmanschaft* waiting to corral and aid (or perhaps exploit) destitute Jewish immigrants, rather a family friend of means who put the young man up in a hotel. That first night, Schiff expressed the same nervous energy of any other new arrival. Urging his host to stay and talk about the "new land and the old place," Schiff managed to prevent his leaving the hotel room until the sun crested the East River. To feel that blend of homesickness and excitement, having left home behind for foreign soil and a new start as a teenager—this was an experience few other rich New Yorkers, but many poor ones, could claim.[3]

In his later interactions with or on behalf of the poor and working class, Schiff placed a premium on developing a greater understanding of their experience than his own life had afforded him. He said as much to journalist and activist Oswald Garrison Villard in replying to Villard's request for financial assistance on behalf of the Manassas School for Colored Youth. "While I willingly contribute to any deserving purpose which commends itself to me," Schiff explained, "I have made it a rule, where my personal information gives out, to carefully investigate . . . before I commit myself." While it might have been reasonable to write a check simply on the basis of

Villard's considerable credibility, Schiff insisted on the need to get his own information, on his own or "through others in whom I have confidence."[4] While this personal rule of Schiff's might seem merely part of the wider charitable culture in which investigation was a prerequisite of philanthropic giving, a principal goal of his inquiries was always to understand, not merely to judge. This set him apart.

His direct experiences with working people, both fleeting and substantial, also informed his civic engagements outside the realm of philanthropy. Schiff conveyed insight and humanist sensibilities regarding unemployment in a letter he wrote to New York's mayor, George B. McClellan, during a period of aggravated joblessness in the summer of 1908:

> I wonder whether you have observed in passing any of our public places, such as Union Square, the Recreation Piers, and other spots where the unemployed gather, how large a number of men are among the multitude, with that sad, far-away, despairing look upon their faces, men whose whole appearance betokens even now that they are making an effort to keep up an appearance of self-respect and dignity. Every day authenticated reports come to me of families on the verge of collapse, because their breadwinners, willing to do any kind of work, cannot find employment and would rather starve than ask for charity support.

Schiff's belief that many would starve to avoid charity and his sensitivity to working people's self-respect—in the flesh, rather than in theory—made his approach atypical among his peers in the financial world. Indeed, most prosperous New Yorkers—not just those in his profession—would have considered his proposed solution dangerously radical. Urging McClellan to enact a program of public works in response, Schiff continued his letter, "The parks, the streets, the speedways, and various other communal properties need work to be done upon them. . . . Several hundred thousand dollars thus put into circulation . . . would prevent a great amount of suffering and tend to maintain the self-respect of thousands of our people." In 1908, proposing structural and publicly funded solutions to unemployment was more the province of socialists than club men. When Schiff's proposal did not resonate with the city, he established a private relief subsidy instead. He called it the Self-Respect Fund.[5]

In a more standard upper-class mode, the *New York Times* had editorialized only a few months earlier against such plans for public works on the
premise that they would "manufacture paupers" by undermining the self-
respect of workingmen. Public employment, the *Times* argued, should be
limited to "sifting the lazy from the others among the professed unemployed. Actual hard work is an excellent test of character, and . . . should be
applied wherever charity is sought by able-bodied persons." This attitude
more closely reflected both the dominant political-economic theory of laissez-
faire among businessmen of the age, and the pervasiveness of distinction as
the driving force within leading charities. If charities or the state were to
provide employment or sustenance to the poor, the reasoning went, it had
to be on harsher or more humiliating terms than the worst private-sector
position, lest the working-class abandon their low-paid jobs and trample en
masse to charity and government offices with their hands outstretched.[6]

Schiff's personal interactions with poor and working people had taught
him the basic fallacy and class prejudice of this apocalyptic vision. For over
thirty years, he spent every Sunday (provided he was in New York) walking
the halls of the Montefiore Home and Hospital, talking with indigent patients, getting to know them, and following their medical progress. He and
his family ate regularly with Lower East Siders at the Henry Street Settlement. Schiff recognized the value of those interactions, writing to Wald
that he had "become more imbued with the spirit of responsibility wealth
should impose upon those to whom it is given by Providence, through the
opportunities you have often made for us to better understand the life of
those who have to struggle." His contact with "the life of those who have to
struggle," enabled Schiff to take a broader view of political and economic
realities than fellow members of the upper crust.[7]

At the core of Schiff's engagement with the poor was that sense of having a "responsibility . . . given by Providence," bespeaking his devotion to
the Jewish law of tzedakah in its traditional Hebrew meaning, which is
closer to "justice" than its Anglicized translation as "charity." Schiff unrav-
eled the distinction for a mainly Gentile audience in a speech he gave to
C.O.S. leaders in 1907, explaining, "The ancient Hebrew lawgiver . . . knows
no such word as charity; to him even giving to the poor is only an act of
justice, and justice is the expression he solely applies, when he urges his
people to their duty to the needy and dependent." Neither did the pursuit

of social justice through giving from a distance discharge that duty. True tzedakah required (then as now) that giving be undertaken and performed in an attitude of sympathy with the poor, preferably face to face. It was not enough for Schiff blithely to throw money at social problems from his plush Fifth Avenue home. His philanthropy expressed a commitment to his community better signified by his personal involvement in social reform than his financial investments in the same.[8]

It is worth noting that, in Schiff's case, the community in question covered the entire city of New York and the United States beyond it, not simply Jews. Many have characterized the world of Jewish philanthropy in Schiff's time as insular, depicting a stream of money flowing from Manhattan's Upper to Lower East Sides, from wealthy German to poor Russian Jews. In these accounts, the rich, assimilated German Jews such as Schiff used charity prescriptively to mold their motley East European brethren into a form that would not threaten the Germans' carefully accumulated cultural capital in the Gentile community. Even when affluent Jews donated to non-Jewish causes or institutions (as they did, significantly), most contemporaries and subsequent observers identified their primary motive as either a rearguard action against anti-Semitism, or an attempt to curry favor with influential Gentiles. While these interpretations do convey partial truth, they also carry a measure of prejudice all their own: they imply that the primary motivation behind Jewish charity was always to benefit the *Jewish* community above all others, and a particular segment of the Jewish community at that. It is beyond consideration, in the view of such interpretations, that Jewish philanthropists could ever be looking seriously beyond the Pale.[9]

Schiff did. While he gave generous support to Jewish charities and indisputably recognized himself as a leader (if not *the* leader) of the Jewish community in America, he also spread his wealth and time much more broadly, giving support and attention to New York parks, a variety of African-American uplift projects, the American Red Cross, and countless other nonsectarian local and national causes. He did so not only or primarily in his capacity as a Jew, but as a leader of the whole American nation. As he put it once, being an American Jew "means to be an American of the Jewish faith," just as Americans of other faiths were, in their civic identity, citizens first and worshipers second. Schiff engaged with all aspects of American life in which he had a stake as a citizen, from writing a letter to Woodrow Wilson protesting the segregation of the federal government—responding to the National Association for the Advancement of Colored People (N.A.A.C.P.)'s call for "fellow citizens" to protest—to advising successive presidents on economic policy, to taking leadership positions within the Gentile-dominated world of charity in New York.[10]

Because of his Judaism, however, Schiff bore a double burden that proved difficult to balance: promoting his vision of social justice and class relations to the Gentile majority as a fellow American, while simultaneously fielding requests from the Jewish community to battle Gentile discrimination against fellow Jews. Clearly Schiff could not maximize the persuasive power he had in the Gentile community if he was regularly chiding its members for their anti-Semitism, but neither would his adherence to tzedakah (or simple self-respect) allow him to turn a blind eye to bigotry.

The unemployment crisis of 1908 in New York and its aftermath proved emblematic of how those two priorities came into conflict. In addition to setting up and providing the bulk of the funding for the Self-Respect Fund loan operation, Schiff collaborated with the C.O.S. and U.H.C. to create the National Employment Exchange, an agency connecting job-hungry workers to employers with labor needs. Schiff's hope, as he described it to Robert Weeks de Forest, was that "an efficient employment bureau as an independent permanent organization" could significantly reduce "much undeserved misery . . . and also much of the existing social unrest." The banker's vision, again, transcended the immediate difficulties and imagined a lasting salve for more persistent social ills. In a model of interfaith cooperation, Schiff and De Forest made the leading contributions to the initial $100,000 fund for the Exchange.[11]

Little more than six years later, deluged with angry letters from Jewish job-seekers, Schiff discovered to his horror that the Exchange he had helped found and on whose board he sat was discriminating against Jews (in addition to African Americans and many foreign nationals, including the Catholic Irish, Italians, Slavs, and others not yet consolidated under the narrow banner of American whiteness). When he objected to the inequity, the Exchange's manager suggested dismissively that the complaints must be coming from the "lower grade" and not the "better class of Jews" because the latter did not use the service. At the board level, the vice president of the

C.O.S. Central Council, Otto T. Bannard, upheld discrimination as policy
on the grounds that many employers would abandon the Exchange were it
to stop screening out racially and religiously undesirable applicants. In
other words, Bannard defended the practices to Schiff as integral to the
Exchange's survival.[12]

Schiff not only resigned his membership on the board and took his complaint up the C.O.S. ladder to De Forest, he argued his position in language anticipating the "100 percent American" trend later in the decade. "I
wish to say," he declared, "with every emphasis I can give this, that the Exchange is serving in no way the purposes for which it was founded, and that
the spirit in its management is un-American and should no longer have the
acclaim or the support of those who founded the Exchange for the purpose
of rendering service to society." Positioning himself as an outraged American rather than an offended Jew obviously played to what he had in common with De Forest, but it also reflected Schiff's convictions about what it
meant to be an American. The "un-American" spirit of the Exchange's management resided in its willingness to be made "the handmaid of prejudiced
employers," violating the precepts of an egalitarian social justice while claiming to render "service to society."[13]

It was a losing battle for Schiff on many levels. In the immediate term,
his proposal to liquidate the Exchange rather than see it continue to discriminate against applicants elicited only a tepid response from De Forest.
In fact, De Forest initially defended the Exchange's anti-Semitic policies as
well, arguing that employers' wishes trumped Schiff's criticisms. After months
of wrangling, De Forest finally gave ground, arranging for the provision of
a form letter to employers explaining the Exchange's new nondiscrimination policy of recommending applicants regardless of religion. It was, however, little more than window dressing; employers were still free to reject
Jewish applicants. Far from cutting off access to the convenience of its services, the Exchange merely urged employers to interview Jewish applicants
before dismissing them.[14]

In a more general sense, the dispute with Bannard and De Forest signified Schiff's difficulties in exerting influence within the Gentile-
dominated world of reform, even when he worked actively within that
world. Bannard was no inconsequential charity bureaucrat—he was the
president of the New York Trust Company and a Republican mayoral

candidate in 1909 who sat on the city's Board of Education. During the dispute with Schiff, Bannard was engineering a loan of $500 million to Britain, beginning a global realignment of financial preeminence from London to New York. When he died in 1929, the *New York Times* pointed to his "civic and philanthropic work" in claiming he represented the "best type of New York citizenship." Yet to Schiff, he represented a racist impediment to social justice.[15]

De Forest, probably the most recognizable philanthropist and social reformer of his day, was of little more help. According to a colleague, he rarely if ever came into direct contact with an actual poor person, and his rigid adherence to ideals of efficiency meant that Schiff expended a great deal of effort gaining even superficial concessions to fundamental aspects of the American creed (as Schiff understood it). This was the caliber of men occupying New York's *elite* of social reform. If Schiff failed to convince them over the course of a year-long fight that nondiscrimination was the only defensible position for an American employment bureau, how could he possibly find traction for a more expansive, humanistic vision of class relations based on Jewish law? The primacy of elite, white, Progressive New Yorkers in the charity world—with their efficiency fetish and racial hierarchies in particular—obstructed such a vision as effectively in collaboration as it might have in opposition.[16]

This is not to say that philanthropic elites such as Bannard and De Forest were the only reformers who could not see past Schiff's religion to appreciate his larger vision for social justice. Schiff encountered racial and religious prejudice from Gentile progressives in the trenches of reform as well, even from those depending on his philanthropic largesse. When Jacob Riis wrote to Schiff in November 1906 requesting funds to cover a $2,100 deficit for the Theodore Roosevelt Gymnasium, a community children's center affiliated with the Jacob Riis Settlement, he raised Schiff's hackles by writing, "nor do I hesitate to ask you because the 'Gym' will increasingly benefit Jewish children. Therefore I asked Mr. Seligman and Felix Warburg for help, which they gave me last Spring. Up till that time you were the only one of my friends among your people whom I had asked for help." The back-and-forth that ensued demonstrates both Schiff's unwillingness to suffer prejudice lightly (even when inadvertently expressed by a putative ally), and the way that prejudice could infuse everyday communication among reformers, thus hindering Schiff's influence. Along with a $500 check, Schiff sent Riis this rebuke:

> May I say that it would not have been necessary on your part to emphasize the fact of the benefit which accrues to Jewish children from the good work in the settlement; in fact, appeals which come to me frequently, and the makers of which think they can gain my sympathy by specially calling attention to the Jewish clientele amongst their beneficiaries, appear to me as unworthy of people who desire to do their duty to their fellows.[17]

Riis returned the check immediately with a note revealing his mistaken belief that Schiff had impugned his purpose rather than the manner of his appeal. "I am not willing that the cause I stand for shall appear to you 'unworthy' even by mistaken inference," he declared, "for it does not deserve it." He continued in this vein of injured innocence by recalling objections Schiff and Warburg had previously made to Christian proselytizing in the settlement, suggesting that this proved their particular interest in the Jewish children (rather than their desire for a supposedly nonsectarian institution they supported to avoid facilitating missionaries). This self-justification only dug Riis deeper in the same hole. With the precision of a schoolmaster, Schiff retorted, "I have not said, even by inference, that the cause in question appears to me as unworthy," advising Riis that, had such been the case, "neither you nor anybody could induce me to offer any contribution to it."[18]

"What I did say," he continued, "and what I must adhere to is, that it is unworthy of people who, like you, I know, have the good of their fellows at heart, to claim support for a non-sectarian cause from others, whom they must believe big enough to ignore race or sectarian divisions, and at the same time emphasize it as a justification for such appeal, that they benefit those in whom the man applied to is supposed to be interested through racial or religious ties." Schiff was straining to be polite by acknowledging Riis's good intentions "at heart," but the double-standard and justifications Riis employed were all too familiar. In prose seasoned with irony, Schiff remarked, "I am frank to say, that I have never heard of a Jew interested in non-sectarian altruistic work to appeal to his Gentile neighbor, and giving it as a reason why the appeal should be heeded, that Gentiles are benefited through the cause the Jewish appealer represents." Despite closing the letter with a passing attempt at conciliatory civility, Schiff made his overriding message unambiguous on the last page: "I feel you have done me great injustice."[19]

Riis, it turned out, had more injustice to give. "I am doubtful whether I should consider it evidence of bigness in a Jew to ignore race and faith where the children of his people were concerned," he wrote Schiff the following day. "I for one am unwilling to endure suspicion and inuendo [*sic*] . . . when breaking, in an emergency, an established rule not to ask for Jewish aid . . . I have kept it till this season, though the number of Jewish children on our hands has doubled in the meantime. I shall not break it again." At a loss for a riposte to such a crescendo—Riis essentially put to paper that it was not worth his trouble to ask Jews for money—Schiff forwarded the "very unpleasant correspondence" to Wald, their mutual friend and collaborator. "I want to do injustice to no one and am most anxious to do right towards everybody," Schiff wrote, requesting she give him her "entirely unbiased judgment."[20]

Although a letter Schiff sent to Wald the next month indicates that he and Riis managed to reconcile, this November exchange demonstrates again that his religion constituted a central obstacle to his influence. Riis's letters suggest a belief common among non-Jews that Jews not only had a tendency, but an obligation to follow a different moral compass than Gentiles. His attempt to sting Schiff with his declaration that "bigness in a Jew" was not compatible with even-handed giving is succinct enough. It moved beyond simply reasserting that Schiff's philanthropy showed special concern for his coreligionists (as Riis had implied in his first letter and asserted in his second) and actually imputed that, even were it possible that Schiff's interests *could* transcend "his people," such a feat would be morally suspect. If Riis believed in the morality of Jews' demonstrating a preference for coreligionists, how could he, as a Gentile, ever take Schiff's moral example of nonsectarianism and nondiscrimination seriously?

In a cruel paradox, the very Jewish traditions from which Schiff drew inspiration for his universal sense of social justice and humanism rendered him fatally flawed as a vessel of such inspiration for the New York or the United States of his time. No matter how much or how often he donated in the service of social justice generally, or threw himself into the political life of the city and country beyond the Jewish community, his identity as a Jew would color his actions in the eyes of the Gentile majority. Schiff's devotion to tzedakah in the widest sense and his insistence that those using his money observe the spirit in which he had provided it would always be seen (and likely dismissed) in the wider community as the particularities of a Jew.

Cooperative class relations depend on the recognition or establishment of a powerful mutual interest, but such relations, by definition, do not occur on terms of equality: they assume the existence of at least two class positions. The question is, how long and how effectively can a given mutual interest displace the differences between people of goodwill? The correspondence between Schiff and Riis underscores the fact that class differences are only a portion of those differences requiring displacement if a cooperative class endeavor is to function. Racial, religious, political, and gender distinctions present equally nettlesome impediments.

Lillian Wald, a secular woman of Jewish heritage who shared Schiff's expansive humanism and broad view of social justice, did not experience religion as an obstacle to the scope of her influence in quite the same way. Money, however, was more of a problem. From the story of Wald's struggle to maintain the solvency of real, cross-class reform emerges another specter haunting those progressives dedicated to more cooperative modes of class encounter: the indispensability of private funding, and the reproduction of conservative cultural tropes often necessary to obtain it.

8

The Limits of Private
Philanthropy

> It was no effort to remember. She was interested in them and
> their lives were a part of her own.
>
> —George Alger

An undated manuscript among Lillian Wald's papers gives a fine indication of her driving perspective on social reform. One could, she wrote,
"generalize on intemperance, immoralities, physical poverty and heroic
virtues—all the so called problems of the 'other half' but this more scientific
information you may obtain from theorists and students who can . . . arrive
at conclusions in labeled and classified order." This ostensibly "Progressive"
approach did not appeal to her. "To me," she insisted, "my neighbors are
throbbing and vital men and women," not the products of "scientific information," rather "a procession of friends." They were immigrant "fathers and
mothers, too tired to take share in much besides their family life but coming . . . in hopes of the children." They were victims of exploitation and inadequate legal protections, like the "radiantly beautiful" girl who stitched
"white cotton flannel under-drawers" all day and remained illiterate because
she "has not been sent to school and no 'Compulsory education law' has
been enforced." They were casualties of bad luck, like the "sweetest little girl
of not quite four winters" who "plays on the fire escape while her mother
finishes knee pants" to support the family because her father's tuberculosis
kept him in a hospice.[1]

These "people who live in tenements," these "children of promise and the young men who declare now that the East Side should be discussed by East Siders," were prepared, Wald argued, to do their part in improving their own lives. Structural impediments, however, awaited removal first. She underlined this point by relating an anecdote about children in a Settlement class who announced, in response to a teacher's frustrated remarks on city conditions, "we'll do better when our turn comes." Throwing down the gauntlet to others and herself, Wald exhorted, "I am ready to believe that given a fair chance they will do better. But the change must be allowed. That is the responsibility of society at large. The people who in a measure control chances."[2]

As the head worker of the Henry Street Settlement and founder of the Visiting Nurses Service, Wald developed a talent for eliciting funding from "the people who . . . control chances," perhaps not least because she had been raised as one of them. Like Schiff, her predilection to empathize with the poor and working class grew out of experiences she gained in spite (and in some cases, because) of a privileged childhood. If anything, her Jewish ancestry was even more distinguished than Schiff's, including a sixteenth-century rabbi on her father's side who advised the Polish court, and a maternal line traceable to thirteenth-century Germany. She grew up in a well-to-do Rochester family, the daughter of an optical goods salesman and niece of successful textile factory owners. Her parents employed a servant, attended a tony Reform synagogue, and enrolled Wald in a non-Jewish private girls' school whose mission statement was to "make scholarly women and womanly scholars." On the rare occasions Wald referred to her upbringing in print, she dismissed it as "spoiled" and "indulgent," but her immersion in the etiquette of nonsecular bourgeois culture endowed her with a certain savoir faire that, when matched with Schiff's friendship network, proved indispensable to raising money.[3]

Wald's childhood provided her with not only fine manners but also multiple perspectives on class and gender relations in action. Her uncles took confrontational stands against their employees in repeated labor disputes throughout her teenage years, garnering approval from local press for their manliness in doing so. Her mother, meanwhile, devoted herself to keeping house, and gave out food to any unemployed men who came to the family's door. Wald clearly gravitated toward her mother's example of a genteel yet generous and nurturing woman who gave to anyone in need.

Correspondingly, she also acquired a conservatively naturalistic view of gender difference.

That view, however, in some ways contributed to Wald's particular brand of feminist humanism rather than hampering it.[4] Wald had a larger vision of what her mother's skills could provide to society than her mother did, and she desired a more systematic scope for her own talents than home-making afforded. She indicated as much in her application letter to nursing school in 1889, writing, "My life hitherto has been . . . devoted to society, study and house keeping duties. . . . This does not satisfy me now, I feel the need of serious, definite work." She found that work—and in the case of outpatient nursing, practically invented it—in New York, and she consistently referred or alluded to gender difference as a major reason that she excelled in it. In her view, women could take advantage of their inherent differences to produce powerful social change. One sentence from an article she wrote for the *Barnard Bulletin* in 1913 demonstrates this clearly. Trying to attract college women to nursing, she wrote, "Never before in the history of the world have women had an equal opportunity of dedicating themselves to a profession for which they are so essentially fitted, and which carries with it so many broad and deep social implications." The pairing of the terms "equal opportunity" and "essentially fitted" lies at the core of Wald's feminist thought.[5]

As her sympathetic portraits of tenement occupants indicate, Wald's feminist humanism translated into a model of personally involved social reform that differed profoundly from the moralistic data-gathering of Lowell's C.O.S., or the evangelical sentimentality of the Booth family's Salvation Army. The Henry Street Settlement took organizational inspiration from the original settlement at Toynbee Hall in London, offshoots in New York (the College Settlement on Rivington Street and the University Settlement on Eldridge Street), and Hull House in Chicago, but Wald infused Henry Street with her own inimitable spirit of humanism. George W. Alger, long-time chairman of the Settlement's board of directors and Wald's friend, described that spirit as "the daily application of love to life," illustrating it further with a story:

I will always remember a walk with her once on Clinton Street down in the slums. A young man greeted her on the street and they talked for a few minutes. She wanted to know something about his wife who had apparently had an operation or something like that. As I walked on I asked her perhaps a little maliciously, "Who does he work for and what does he make?" She knew and told me and added with a responsive gleam in her eye, "He pays $12 rent and has no running water." It was no effort to remember. She was interested in them and their lives were a part of her own.

Wald's willingness to share in the lives of her poor and working-class neighbors derived from her conviction that, as she put it herself, "no one class of people can be independent of the other."[6]

Mutual dependence and mutual interest required deep mutual involvement. At the Settlement and in the Nurses Service, that conviction translated into a greater willingness to investigate and understand the ways that hindrances of class—as opposed to the supposed moral dereliction, ethnic predisposition, or drunkenness her contemporaries often cited—might account for pathologies such as inadequate education or disease epidemics. Wald's motivation for establishing a service to provide medical care in people's homes stemmed in part from her recognition that many sick, poor New Yorkers resisted going to hospitals not out of superstition or an inability to pay medical bills, but because they simply could not leave their tenements. For many, doing so without access to affordable child care or some kind of medical leave arrangement from work risked, as she observed, "imperiling, or sometimes destroying, the home itself."[7]

Her tenement visits also taught her that the basic conditions necessary for effective schoolwork—space and relative silence—were practically unthinkable for most poor children, not because of negligent parenting, but as a result of the physical limitations that tenement living entailed. Those limitations could be so severe that they impinged not only on education, but on sanity itself, as Wald implied in a story about a textile sweatshop tenement: "The last time I called there the machines were going in almost every room of the house and it did not seem strange that the woman on the top floor (six flights of stairs for every time she needs anything) was neurotic." The New York Board of Education's decision to open regularly accessible study rooms in its schools grew out of Wald's provision of such rooms at the Settlement, a direct result of her tenement-visit insights and the testimony of local children, like the boy who told her "I can never study at home . . . because sister is always using the table to wash the dishes." Wald listened to poor New Yorkers in the spirit of cooperation, not as a favor or an act of charity, but because for her there existed no more expedient method of gathering the information necessary to address social ills.[8]

And for decades, address social ills she did. The modest project of nursing and social service Wald had started with one friend out of a Jefferson Street tenement in 1893 became, by the eve of 1913, a major agency of nonsectarian aid, medical treatment, and neighborhood advocacy on the Lower East Side. Among other triumphs, the Nurses Service grew from two volunteer nurses (Wald and Mary Brewster) covering a few blocks, to ninety-two nurses operating all over Manhattan and the Bronx out of more than a dozen locations. Those nurses made approximately 200,000 visits in 1912 alone, and their patients had a significantly better recovery rate from basic diseases such as pneumonia than did those who sought treatment in major New York hospitals. The Settlement established a network of country homes for convalescents, children, and new mothers that provided a temporary respite from the Lower East Side's sweltering summer streets. Using contacts and influence gained through the Settlement, Wald successfully spearheaded several drives for legislative reform as well, making inroads on problems of child labor, public health, and education, on both local and national levels. The Federal Children's Bureau, a division of the U.S. government dedicated to studying and safeguarding American children, finally became a reality with President William Howard Taft's signature in early 1912; Wald and Florence Kelley had discussed the idea for such a bureau over breakfast in the Settlement, back in 1905, and their relentless advocacy over the better part of a decade had in large part spurred its creation.[9]

Private donations fueled this reform juggernaut, and Wald's singular gifts as a fundraiser proved themselves time and again. She did not hector potential donors about their responsibilities to the poor, or, as a friend put it, "tell sad stories to her dinner swains until they burst into tears and gave her their pocketbooks." With the restrained manner she cultivated early in life, she instead provided "thumbnail pictures of people, mostly funny but with a bit of pathos in them which made her poor and sick people loveable to you as they were to her." These simple stories "made it easy to understand that public health nursing of the poor was a very fine and essential thing, and something to be supported gladly and she didn't have to ask you to do it. You did it because you thought you had suggested the idea to yourself." Her skill in soliciting donations face to face this way kept both Settlement and Service afloat for years.[10]

As both institutions continued to expand, however, Wald began to reach her limits. Despite their successes and evident value to the city and country, both the Settlement and the Nurses Service perpetually foundered in a sea of red ink, forcing her to spend precious time fund-raising rather than actually overseeing activities. On November 25, 1912, she wrote to Schiff, her most consistent and loyal benefactor, to follow up on an idea that might give her some relief, but would require his backing first. "I would like an opportunity to continue the conversation we had some time ago about the proper commemoration of our twentieth anniversary," Wald wrote. "In a way the most urgent matter to my mind," she admitted, "is that we take advantage of this occasion to get an endowment for the Settlement. As you stated last winter, this effort would doubtless lead to people's remembering us in their wills as well." Having discussed the idea of an endowment previously with Schiff and found him leery, she was careful to limit her vision. "I do not want our Settlement to live one day longer than it deserves," she conceded, "but I think that our work for the sick is analogous to the hospitals' . . . and that we ought not leave the thousand patients who now look to us entirely to the hazards of a precarious financial existence."[11]

Schiff knew that the Settlement's and Nurses Service's financial existence had long persisted almost entirely at the whim of philanthropic individuals, himself foremost among them, but this did not necessarily displease him. "I feel now more than ever that each generation must do its own altruistic and philanthropic work," he responded to Wald the next day, "and that endowments are a tax upon one generation, which results to a very great extent in the curtailment of the provision which the living must make for relief work of every nature of their own generation, and which there is always a tendency to do inadequately." In other words, establishing an endowment for institutions like Wald's might disincline or prevent the next generation's philanthropists from properly performing tzedakah (or its Gentile equivalent), crippling future social service enterprises that would likewise depend on private charity.[12]

Schiff's initial response to Wald reflected his assumption that the long-standing municipal neglect for welfare provisioning would continue. New York had abandoned public financing of "outdoor relief"—providing money and services to the poor outside institutions such as almshouses or workhouses—more than thirty years earlier, in large part at the urging of the scientific charity movement, whose advocates, Lowell and De Forest included, had insisted that outdoor relief contributed to the persistence of pauperism. The city had transferred the management of its meager welfare structure to the C.O.S., which spent most of its time and energy identifying applicants as unworthy in order to exclude them from benefits. (One of the "older members" of the C.O.S. had once quipped, "Our Society was on sure ground until it found a worthy case, and then it was all at sea.") Enterprises like the Settlement and the Service, indiscriminate by contrast to the C.O.S., could count on negligible help from the municipality, despite the mountains of evidence that its work served the public good. With no significant assistance forthcoming from the city, wealthy individuals had to step into the breach. For nearly two decades, their doing so had barely sufficed, and Wald recognized the need for something more.[13]

Other charity and social service organization leaders who struggled to tap private sources of funding had long since begun to adopt marketing strategies of publicity and self-promotion, advertising their fund drives in newspapers, setting up donation boxes at high-end retail establishments, and targeting prominent philanthropists for public endorsements. Celebratory cross-class events epitomized these strategies on a large scale. Like the Salvation Army's 1899 Christmas Dinner, such events tended to reinforce certain conceptions of poverty long held among the wealthy: that the poor, while culturally fascinating and picturesque, were a separate, properly docile class to be pitied; that they were helpless without the good offices of the wealthy; and that, somewhat paradoxically, they constituted a sore on the body politic in need of healing or excision. At the same time, cross-class events cast the wealthy as players in a drama that affirmed cultural conceptions of them (not infrequently reflecting their beliefs about themselves): that they were the rightful leaders of society, that private wealth held the proper solutions to public want, and that the poor—because they could never meet the wealthy as equal partners in public life—would be grateful and deferential to them when help was forthcoming.

These choreographed spectacles often constituted an elaborated version of slum tourism. Slum tourism during the period involved tours through the Lower East Side—the Five Points, Chinatown, Little Italy, the Russian Jewish neighborhoods—for the middle class and rich. The tourists, in whatever form, scrutinized the pathos, dirt, and vulnerability of the poor and working class, usually while managing the neat trick of congratulating themselves for anthropological intrepidity, empathy, and superiority. Like cross-class spectacle fundraising, slum tourism aimed not at enlightenment, but at squeezing money (whether for profit or charity) from preexisting notions of class. Slum tourism could be literary, appearing in magazines like *Harper's* and featuring virtual tours that casually dehumanized or objectified the locals under scrutiny. It could also be literal tourism by out-of-towners, encouraged by published guidebooks such as *The Better New York,* which appeared in 1904; the guide advised its reader on walking tours of New York, starting with about a hundred pages on the "slum district" in the lower wards. The most intense versions of such tours involved paying a slum resident a few dollars to show voyeuristic visitors through the streets and back alleys, taking them into opium dens, brothels, and sweatshop tenements for a closer look at (or sometimes a participatory experience with) the inhabitants. Whether it came in the form of hawking magazines, guidebooks, or tour-guide services, slum tourism offered a less mediated cross-class experience than the grander, more public cross-class event. Yet it traded on the same cultural conceptions of poverty and wealth.[14]

For two decades before the pageant in 1913, Wald had repudiated these conceptions and practices by demanding of everyone involved with the Settlement or Service, rich or poor, the same standard of decency and respect. In keeping with this faith, she had avoided the pitfalls of public fund-raising—the Settlement had never made a public appeal, much less produced a cross-class spectacle. That same year, in fact, she disapprovingly watched as the Y.M.C.A. and Y.W.C.A. rolled out a nationally publicized funding drive featuring celebrity endorsements and spectacles. Pressed to use such tactics herself, Wald wrote to Schiff, "Laying aside all questions of taste in using such publicity methods, the psychology of soliciting funds for the nursing service in this way would be bad. It has been uphill work to get the people who need the nurses most to accept their service without the feeling that they would be publishing their poverty." Advertising the Service openly as succor for the helpless would create a stigma that could interfere with its ability to reach patients.[15]

Wald had too much respect for her neighbors and their privacy to publicize their poverty, but a more far-seeing pragmatism drove her refusal to engage in such methods as well. She had recently succeeded in attracting modest but more regular underwriting for the Service from trade unions (to visit union members) and the Metropolitan Life Insurance Company (to visit its policy holders), structural sources of funding she was loathe to disturb. As she argued to Schiff, "To give wider publicity to the eleemosynary character of the nursing work would, I think, discourage self-respecting people who can pay a little and the insurance company which is willing to pay the full cost of each visit." Wald's ultimate hope was that "more and more . . . insurance plans and invalidity insurance will meet certain elements of the needs of the sick." Publicizing open funding drives might send the wrong signal to potentially more systematic and dependable funding sources than private philanthropy.[16]

The dinners Wald arranged for wealthy patrons at Henry Street, however, were not up to the task of creating an endowment, and Schiff, the frequent recipient of Wald's hospitality in the Settlement, knew it. Perhaps that was why he ultimately acceded to Wald's idea of pursuing the endowment, and why Wald gave ground on her principles in organizing a public pageant. Even with Schiff's blessing, though, Wald still faced the major challenge of appealing to the pocketbooks of the rich on a grander scale without appealing to prejudicial or narcissistic tendencies. She attempted to reconcile these imperatives in the settlement's twentieth anniversary celebration by creating a historical montage of Henry Street's contributions to the city. "I thought of a pageant for the neighborhood showing the historical past of this section of the city," she wrote to Schiff, "and the stories of the different races who have inhabited the lower east side with some reference to their past before they came to America, and their contribution to our community." She wanted to create a vision of symbiotic, multicultural class relations across time in New York, a vision that would bind the wealthy and poor together as partners in public life rather than as masters and supplicants.[17]

Moreover, she wanted the neighborhood participants to feel proud about both the pageant and their contributions to it. Wald pushed immigrants to assimilate through classes and clubs at the Settlement, but she did so with a kind of proto-multiculturalist sensibility. A former Settlement resident recalled how Wald taught children in the clubs "to be proud of their parents and their history . . . the background from which they had come—Lithuanian peasants, Polish or ghetto dwellers or what not, and the pride you could take in the history and contribution that had come out of that background." In Wald's fondest hopes, the pageant would provide a forum for her poor and working-class neighbors—in particular, the children—to promote the value they offered to the city, rather than attempt to trade on their poverty in soliciting donations.[18]

The preparations for the pageant reflected Wald's multiple purposes. Under direction from her close friends Alice and Irene Lewisohn ("two wealthy young women . . . among the many prominent non-resident workers for the Settlement," as the *New York Times* described them), hundreds of neighborhood residents sewed costumes, built props, and rehearsed dramatic roles. Wald even succeeded in advertising cooperative class relations in a few respects. As the *Times*'s promotional story the week before the celebration announced, the pageant "will represent the loving co-operation of all the varied forces of the settlement, from the little kindergarten graduates to the oldest beneficiaries, together with the various workers, residents, and many friends of the institution." It highlighted the class cooperation necessary to produce the pageant and sustain the Settlement financially, noting the many gifts that "represent the beautiful co-operative spirit of the donors. A newsboy, who had been connected with the Settlement, sent 25 cents for the pageant. A colored woman's club sent $5, and there has been a gift of $50,000 which will be the nest egg of a permanent fund."[19]

When the day came, on June 7, 1913, Henry Street had never seen anything like it—men, women, and hundreds of children performing history in the street, as a rapt crowd of thousands watched. Under throbbing electrical lights, figures adorned with feathers and face paint "smoked the pipe of peace" and "buried the hatchet" with white-skinned visitors, bringing "wampum and skins in exchange for bright-colored trinkets and garments." Scenes of strawberry-picking Dutch burghers gave way to dancing around a Maypole; Quakers founded the first public school for all New York's children; then the scene shifted again, and out of the crowd danced a group of young women in hoop skirts, men and boys accompanying them in "polkas and quadrilles." Finally, the new immigrants overtook them all: "Irish, Scotch, Germans, and Russians. They sang again the songs, and danced the dances of their native lands." The spectacle delighted the several hundred luminaries, including Mayor John Purroy Mitchel and many philanthropists, who sat in the grandstand built specially for the occasion. Altogether, the event appeared to be a triumph of warm class relations.[20]

The deeply gratifying history it presented, however, left a misleading impression of New York's past with unfortunate implications for the present. Despite her success in getting her neighbors to take ownership over the pageant, the historical vision on display necessarily concealed or prettified decades of class intersection and conflict. It presented what amounted to an alternative version of New York's class history, overlooking moments central to Henry Street and the city's class relations: mid-nineteenth-century labor and utopian socialist agitation, the nativist Know-Nothing craze, and the 1863 Draft Riots, to name a few moments directly relevant to the pageant's chosen episodes.[21] Wealthy pageant-goers could leave with the idea that class relations in New York had always been fundamentally sound, and that disturbances were historical anomalies.

The Settlement, of course, was under no obligation to provide an accurate telling of history, but the pageant's version obscured the very current class conflicts to which Wald had borne witness, and in which the Settlement and Nurses Service had played a mitigating role. It ignored the terrible flaws of the dominant private charity system (most notably the C.O.S.) and the central, humiliating role this system played in driving poor and working-class New Yorkers to Wald's door as a refuge. The powerful local nativism—and the hardship such xenophobia engendered daily in the lives of immigrants whom Wald knew—vanished behind a *tableau vivant* of various foreign ethnicities being welcomed to New York, offering the best of their cultures' theater, music, and dance in return. Most importantly, the pageant's historical vision obfuscated the intense struggles carried on by poor and working-class New Yorkers to gain recognition of basic municipal citizenship rights such as equal access to education for their children and health care for their ill. In fact, the *Times* promotional story implied that the Nurses Service had conclusively resolved questions of health-care delivery, asserting, "Poor mothers with large families who cannot under any circumstances leave home to go to a hospital now receive all the attention they need at home." The suggestion that there were major gaps in such a system was nowhere to be found.[22]

Wald had participated, and in some cases continued to participate, in many of those struggles, but she could not present their drama—nor the drama of the many class conflicts she had witnessed in the worlds of charity, immigration, and labor strife in New York—and expect the wealthy to shower Henry Street with money. She had to sell them a vision of the poor they would buy, and that vision was a powerful illusion of class harmony. Her own work belied that illusion, but the exigencies of the private funding structure had cornered her into the position of upholding it.

The coverage the pageant received in the *Times* purred over that illusion in a tone of condescension that Wald detested. The paper's editorial remarked on the participants being "of the lowliest origin, Russian immigrants and their children, who have profited by the educational advantages offered to them, have acquired knowledge of the history of this country and the meaning of its institutions, and are in the way to overcome the obstacles of poverty and become good and thrifty citizens." Practically the only reference to the neighborhood residents (beyond their roles in the pageant itself) was a jocular but telling observation that "the police were kept busy during the entire evening restraining the thousands of children who were eager to break through the roped-off lines and mingle with those participating in the pageant." This account casually reminded wealthy readers that the police department was all that stood between orderly poor people arrayed for their entertainment, and mayhem.[23]

As if to underline its desire for the poor and working class to remain quiescent, the editorial contrasted its appreciation of the fact that "no discordant note was sounded" in the Henry Street pageant with its disapproval of an Industrial Workers of the World (I.W.W.) event occurring at the same time, uptown at Madison Square Garden, in support of Paterson, New Jersey, silk factory workers. "Under the direction of a destructive organization opposed in spirit and antagonistic in action to all the forces which have upbuilded this republic," the column ran, "a series of pictures in action were shown with the design of stimulating mad passion against law and order and promulgating a gospel of discontent. The sordid and cruel incidents of an industrial strike were depicted by many of the poor strikers themselves, but with dominating and vociferous assistance from members of the I.W.W." In the *Times*'s view, the point of the Henry Street pageant was to celebrate "the triumph of civilization," whereas the I.W.W.'s event meant "to inspire hatred, to induce violence . . . and the institution of anarchy." Harmless, costumed, people "of the lowliest origin" acting in a drama depicting "picturesque social gatherings" garnered praise; an active, organized group of working-class men and women drew censure. An interpretation more defensive of the status quo—even an illusory one—is difficult to imagine.[24]

Wald found herself caught in a vicious cycle driven by historical circumstances typical of the Progressive Era. Without public funding, she faced the nearly impossible task of trying to support work that challenged existing class relations by soliciting donations from the people who had the most to gain by leaving those relations undisturbed. She might have hoped that the twentieth anniversary celebration would convey the humanity of her neighbors to those "people who in a measure control chances," but the pre-existing notions and interests of prospective donors almost inevitably shaped the reception of an event geared primarily toward attracting their money.

Wald did her best to highlight the potential social benefits in cooperating across class lines, in making equal partners of the wealthy and the poor. Instead, she saw the press describe the Settlement and Nurses Service as the products of her individual willpower ("Miss Wald's Settlement") and the generous donations of wealthy citizens, rather than as the collaborative, cross-class operations she understood them to be. Rather than highlighting the very real battles fought by the Settlement and Nurses Service every day, the broad interpretation of the pageant was that private charity kept New York class relations harmonious and stable. The final two paragraphs of the *Times*'s main story about the pageant, adhering to its standard practice for charity enterprises, listed the names of the wealthy and prominent citizens who had donated to the production and who supported the Settlement.

Their munificence proved insufficient. Schiff, four years later, was still petitioning Mayor John Purroy Mitchel for public funds. "The Visiting Nursing Service of the Henry Street Settlement," he wrote, "expends between $125,000 and $150,000 a year in home nursing among the less fortunate class of our population, many of whom otherwise would presumably become public charges." Schiff made it clear that private donations "do not suffice to cover its entire budget, which of recent years has closed with a

deficit of . . . $10,000 to $13,000," despite the "beautiful co-operative spirit
of the donors" heralded by the *Times's* coverage of the pageant in 1913. Given
that the Nurses Service had almost 30,000 patients under constant care,
"considerably in excess of the aggregate of patients treated annually by Presbyterian, St. Luke's, and Mt. Sinai Hospitals together," Schiff insisted that
"the Settlement should receive an allowance from the municipal treasury,
proportionate to its work." Mitchel heeded Schiff's call, and after years of
neglect, New York City's Board of Estimate finally inserted a $25,000 line
in the municipal budget for the Settlement and Nurses Service.[25]

By 1917, however, Wald's personal involvement in labor activism and, in
particular, the antiwar movement had begun to drive away some of her
more conservative, wealthy donors, making the public money more of a
stopgap than a true step forward. Private underwriting depends on deli-
cately negotiated relationships as well as historical circumstances that can
shift suddenly, a fact clearly illustrated by a 1919 letter to Wald from Mary
Stillman Harkness, who with her husband Edward had given nearly $15,000
annually to Henry Street. Harkness abruptly ceased her patronage, explaining to Wald, "For some time I have felt much disturbed concerning the
work you are carrying out at Henry Street because of the knowledge that
you hold such decided socialistic ideas. For this reason, I have, at last, reluc-
tantly come to the conclusion that I cannot . . . continue the contributions
I have made."[26] After fruitlessly entreating Harkness to reconsider, Wald
could only complain to her friend Lavinia Dock of the irony in being labeled
a subversive: "My political attitude is making some of our generous friends
uneasy. . . . Poor things, I am sorry for them—they are so scared. It is foolish since, after all, counting things in the large and wide, I am at least one
insurance against unreasonable revolution in New York." Nothing had
changed in the Settlement's operations, but the world around it, with industrial violence at home and revolution abroad, had changed dramatically.[27]

Wald had probably seen it all coming. Years before the Bolshevik Revolution, fear of "socialistic ideas" and preconceived notions of class had impeded another promising effort at cooperative class relations in which Wald
had been involved—and far more thoroughly than it did Henry Street.[28]
The Women's Trade Union League (W.T.U.L.), for a brief moment in 1909

and 1910, managed to entice the most glamorous and prominent Society ladies of New York to join in common struggle with thousands of immigrant working women, forging class cooperation on the basis of gender solidarity in a general strike of the shirtwaist industry.[29]

The remarkable level of violence both preceding and during that struggle, however, also demonstrates just how intertwined cooperative class relations were with their antithesis, conflictual class relations. Barely suppressed, mutual animosity between rich and poor could and often did burst forth in extraordinary incidents of violent confrontation. Sometimes, paradoxically, it also inspired remarkable episodes of class cooperation. Whether prescriptive, cooperative, or conflictual, the class encounters of the Progressive Era transpired amid a level of daily violence, particularly in the workplace, for which most contemporary Americans have little appreciation or understanding.

9

Killing Workers for Profit

> In any discussion of violence as a weapon of social action, we
> must begin not at the bottom at all, but at the top. For if there
> are any men today who genuinely believe in violence, and who
> are using it most dangerously, and defending it most shamelessly,
> it is these who are among the chosen of the land—the exemplars
> of virtue, the leaders of opinion, the custodians and champions
> of law and order.
>
> —John Haynes Holmes

THE TRIANGLE WAIST COMPANY FIRE on March 25, 1911, which killed 146 garment workers, mostly young women and girls, stands out as an iconic moment of violence in the history of American workplaces. Unsurprisingly, the Women's Trade Union League's annual report for 1911 to 1912 minces no words in expressing hatred for that particular firm and its directors. Yet the report's authors also made a point of casting their furious gaze through the flames of the Asch Building to an earlier moment, writing, "There is no block in the city of New York which the League members remembered, *before the great fire tragedy,* with such a sense of repugnance and loathing as the block running from University to Greene Street."[1] This "repugnance and loathing" emerged not from the ashes of the fire, but from the women's earlier conflicts with the Triangle and its owners on the shop-floor, in the street outside the factory, and sometimes extending into workers' homes. Those earlier conflicts expose a persistent element in American class relations:

the greater value and protection accorded to private property over workers' bodies in industrial disputes, and the unequal use of violence to enforce property rights over workers' rights.

This is not to say that violence was one-sided in struggles between workers and the wealthy. Many workers not only directed violence against wealthy employers and their property in self-defense, but explicitly advocated its use as the only effective path to economic concessions or industrial democracy. In the three decades before the 1909–1910 garment fights and for years afterward, newspapers overflowed with stories of worker violence—dynamitings, assassinations, and conspiracy plots executed and foiled. Such stories, some true and others conjured, created a palpable climate of fear and suspicion regarding worker violence, a general unease discernible in the public and private writings of contemporaneous observers.[2] Exacerbating such unease on the part of capitalists and managers was the fact that industrialism's demonstrable inequalities and brutal working conditions sometimes inclined local communities—or the broader public—to sympathize with, approve of, or even participate in worker violence.

Yet in scale and intensity, the violence springing from the ranks of the poor could only rarely rise to meet that of capital and the state; and in the realm of publicly perceived legitimacy, it never could.[3] This cultural imbalance, in which violence emanating from wealth (sometimes but not always via the state) enjoyed greater public endorsement, indifference, or simple invisibility than that emanating from poverty, reproduced class conflict. Not infrequently, in fact, it was the casual execution and popular countenancing of capital and state violence against the most vulnerable of the nation's inhabitants that goaded handfuls of poor Americans into choosing violence as their preferred mode of dissent.[4]

The wealthy had several distinct advantages over workers in their ability to mobilize violence. There was a longstanding complacency in the United States about violence done to workers' bodies, both in the workplace and outside of it. Such violence appeared to many as a natural function of industrial life, unrelated to (or at least only marginally a consequence of) managerial choice. Even many Progressive-Era reformers, by leavening their indictments of industrial conditions with blame for workers and exoneration for managers, reinforced public assumptions that physical harm to workers was inevitable. Such a calculus of exoneration and blame made workers appear more responsible for their poor working conditions than they were, insulating dangerous workplaces from more structural, political-economic critiques or policy solutions, and the managers of such workplaces from accountability.

Perhaps the most subversive advantage of wealthy belligerents was the ability to employ proxies in any violent confrontation, thereby obscuring their own role in visiting aggression upon the poor. Because their chosen proxies—strikebreakers, private security forces, police, the military, and even (as in the shirtwaist strike) prostitutes—often came from working-class or immigrant backgrounds themselves, this obfuscation had the potential added benefit to the wealthy of provoking divisive animosity within the working class. As financier and robber baron par excellence Jay Gould allegedly boasted in 1886, "I can hire one-half of the working class to kill the other half."[5]

Of course, differences among workers—the divisions of ethnicity, race, gender, nationality, language, and politics—were not simply superficial motivators of such proxy violence but had their own, often far more immediate logic of hostility. Such diverse motives for violence merged quickly and seamlessly with capital's hostility toward labor, serving the purposes of wealthy antagonists effectively while masking or confusing the material and ideological sources of conflict.

Nevertheless, some workers saw clearly that whatever the apparently immediate cause for their foremen threatening them, strikebreakers punching them, private security personnel kicking them, police arresting them, or judges fining them and sentencing them to the workhouse on unsubstantiated charges, the primary human movers of violence were almost always numbered among the wealthy. Not necessarily because the wealthy personally directed or were anywhere near the actual violence (though some did, and were), but because the structures of power they determinedly maintained over worker labor—whether through managerial control, the judiciary, or broadly accepted extralegal tactics such as the hiring of mercenary muscle—made such violent confrontations inevitable. We cannot properly evaluate class relations in the United States without demystifying the path from wealth's purse to poverty's physical and mental pain, and back again.

Isaac Harris and Max Blanck, the Triangle's owners, knew this path well, and used their advantage of accumulated economic power unsparingly.

Behind the daily, often invisible violence of the shop floor—which included refusal to address unsafe conditions, abuse of workers' bodies, and sexual harassment (a practice unrecognized in the language of the day, but experienced regularly)—lay the frequently realized threat of firing and economic privation. Behind the punches and kicks of the hired muscle awaiting picketers on the street lay direct payments from the company. And behind the arrest and sentencing powers of New York's legal system—at best unpredictable in its evidentiary standards, at worst antagonistic to workers—lay not only the probability of bribes to a police force renowned for its corruption, not only the state's disproportionate interest in protecting capital ventures whose tax payments on property helped fuel the engines of government, and not only politicians' cultivation of wealthy campaign donors. There also thrived an explicitly articulated ideology of class relations in which workers owed their lives and livelihoods to private property.

This ideology on its own constituted a tremendous advantage for those rich Americans with violent inclinations toward the poor, and its most renewable source was the broadly accepted orthodoxy of "natural" economic law. In a utopian world imagined by classical economists and their disciples, supply and demand alone could fairly govern questions of wages, benefits, and workplace conditions.[6] Even Henry Walcott Farnam, a prominent Progressive economist, described militant labor unions such as the Knights of Labor as evolutionary deformities, unacceptable violations of this supposedly natural equilibrium.[7] Those among the poor who violated this equilibrium's precepts by defying the supposedly invisible hand of the market consistently met with a much harder, plainly visible, and tightly clenched fist.[8]

This ideology and the uses of violence it countenanced reveal themselves with unusual clarity in the midst of New York's garment-trade battles from 1909 to 1910. Such clarity comes not from the exceptional nature of the violence—which by the standards of the era was relatively tame—but from the uncommon efforts at class reconciliation in the midst of those battles. The presence of rich women on streets and in courtrooms during the shirtwaist fight created a way to measure the significance of class as a predictor of violence. When rich women stood shoulder to shoulder with their poorer sisters, violence tended to dissipate, and court judgments grew more lenient. When the society ladies turned their attention elsewhere or simply failed to show up, force and harsh sentences returned with a vengeance.[9]

In both the uses of state and capital violence and in their rhetorical justifications, from the earliest stages of the garment-industry upheaval in the summer of 1909 and beyond, class emerges as the major determinant in the state's and public's willingness to countenance violence against workers. One can also begin to recognize patterns of rhetorical and ideological justification for state and capital violence against the poor that have survived into the twenty-first century.

To understand both the pervasiveness and widespread acceptance of violence against the poor at the turn of the century, one must first reckon with the inextricable relationship between violence and work in that era—on the street, in the workplace, on strike lines, in court, and even in workers' homes.

At some point, almost any low-wage worker in a late-nineteenth or early-twentieth-century American city found him or herself on the street without a job. Unpredictable business cycles, the seasonal nature of many professions, and unchecked managerial authority combined to render almost all such employment precarious. Whether in response to a depression or an economic dip, an annual low season, or an incipient union drive, factory owners often laid off huge tranches of their workforce, sending those erstwhile workers spiraling into poverty. Poverty among wage workers in this era, as one historian has observed aptly, was "the economic analogue to the common cold"—everyone was susceptible.[10] Since poverty had dangerous consequences for health, getting fired practically became a physical assault, a fact not lost on the workers. As Fannia Cohn put it when reflecting on that period in the history of the International Ladies' Garment Workers' Union (I.L.G.W.U.), "The worker's fear of losing his job was used by the employers as a weapon to prevent the workers from fighting. . . . The union realized, therefore, that the problem of maintaining standard conditions depended upon removing this club which the employers held over workers."[11] Her choice of warlike or policing metaphors here—weapons and clubs—is no accident. In an era with minimal labor law and no real public safety net, the threat of job loss closely resembled the menace of bodily harm.[12]

While looking for a job, unemployed men and women faced the regular threat of coercive violence on the street. One man remembered how after a fruitless wait for day labor in a slaughterhouse "one boy sat down and cried, just next to me. . . . Some policemen waved their clubs and we walked on."[13] Such threats escalated to arrests or assaults for any number of reasons, including municipal convenience. For the first few days of autumn 1909, being publicly unemployed in New York became de facto illegal. Under orders to clear the streets in preparation for the Hudson-Fulton celebration (an extravaganza of New York City boosterism marking the tercentenary of Henry Hudson's voyage up the river that would bear his name, and the approximate centenary of Robert Fulton's commercial paddle steamer), police rounded up hundreds of the unemployed and saw them arraigned for vagrancy. Police magistrate Peter Townsend Barlow, who would become notorious during that year's shirtwaist general strike for sending young girl strikers to the workhouse on dubious charges, handed down six-month workhouse sentences to many of these unemployed men and women. "Strange are the ways of 'justice,' stranger than fiction," mused the *New York Call*. "Because fifty men and women hunted for work in vain, that is, work for which they would be paid, they are given jobs in the workhouse without pay."[14]

A paying job, while clearly preferable, was if anything more likely to turn the threat of violence into its reality, since industrial wage work in the turn-of-the-century United States carried serious risks of debilitating injury and death. American industry averaged more than half a million worker injuries and 35,000 fatalities every year from 1880 to 1900, in a nation whose total population ranged from 50 to 76 million.[15] As grim as this average danger was when adjusted for the working population—approximately a 1 percent chance of injury, and nearly a 1 in 1,000 chance of death on the job—it paled in comparison with the risks attending particular industrial professions that formed the bedrock of America's economic expansion. Railroad employees had a nearly 4 percent chance of being injured at work in 1901, while almost 1 in 400 were killed. For operating trainmen, the likelihood of injury was almost 10 percent, and that of death was 1 in 137.[16]

Class ideology and cost considerations among the wealthy meant that these accidents continued despite technological advances that could have prevented them. Long after the early 1870s, when George Westinghouse invented and began marketing air brakes capable of coupling train cars automatically, rail company managers persisted in ordering workers to couple cars manually, regularly and unnecessarily placing those workers' flesh and bone between tons of swiftly converging iron and steel.[17] Paired with faulty coupling mechanisms, this practice continued to cleave bodies in half at the hips, crush internal organs, and unceremoniously amputate healthy limbs—a veritable production mechanism of agony and death.[18] Massachusetts theologian Lyman Abbott explained it as carnage by calculation: "So long as brakes cost more than trainmen," he said, "we may expect the present sacrificial method of car coupling to continue."[19] An early railroad manager was even more frank—and revealing about the class and racial politics of workplace violence—in dismissing self-acting car couplers. "Your device would be more expensive than Paddies are," he remarked.[20]

In New York, violence pervaded industrial workplaces in ways brutal and subtle. The national willingness to tolerate dangerous working conditions found minimal opposition in a city where most industrial workers were immigrants. The lack of enforceable safety regulations in the building trades meant regular exposure to death and dismemberment for predominantly foreign and African-American workers, whether they spent their days above the city streets balancing precariously on scaffolding beams, or below ground, drilling and detonating explosives in earth and rock to make tunnels for the banker August Belmont's new subway system.[21] *Christ in Concrete,* a semiautobiographical novel by Pietro di Donato about an Italian immigrant bricklayer's son, offers a vision of the grisly violence lurking behind daily work in such trades. A building collapse, precipitated by a manager's skimping on cement when mixing the mortar, buries the protagonist's father Geremio. Impaled through his genitals and immobilized by debris, Geremio struggles to survive:

> He tried to breathe, but it was impossible. The heavy concrete was settling immutably and its rich cement-laden grout ran into his pierced face. His lungs would not expand and were crushing in tighter and tighter under the settling concrete. . . . His mangled voice trebled hideously, and hung in jerky

whimperings. Blood vessels burst like mashed flower stems. . . . His bones cracked mutely and his sanity went sailing distorted in the limbo of the subconscious. With the throbbing tones of an organ in the hollow background, the fighting brain disintegrated and the memories of a baffled lifetime sought outlet.[22]

For di Donato, this was only nominally imaginative: his own father, also a bricklayer named Geremio, died in a building collapse in 1923, necessitating the future novelist's entry into his father's trade at the age of twelve. The novel makes it clear that the source of such butchery was both a system of class authority—the manager, Murdin, merely has to walk past Geremio on the job to silence his objections to the unsafe procedures, rendering him "no longer Geremio, but a machinelike entity"—and the fear of violence awaiting the poor who lost their jobs.[23] "The poor live in terror," di Donato said when asked about his portrayal of New York decades later, "and it's an insidious form of terror. It isn't something they could command with their hands. Then of course there's the law to back up this terror, the sheriff, and so forth."[24]

The manager, Murdin (a not especially subtle play on the word "murdering"), was a literary rendering of the all-too-real contractors who, whether through incompetence or unscrupulousness, often justified this terror in ways that rendered even minimal safety measures meaningless. Between January and June 1902, a single subcontractor for the Interborough Rapid Transit Company named Ira A. Shaler produced three major accidents: a powder house blast in January that killed five, injured 125, and defaced Grand Central Terminal (resulting in a manslaughter indictment for Shaler on grounds of having stored the explosives carelessly); a massive tunnel cave-in two months later that extended to street level, undermining the foundations of four properties; and the collapse, during a June inspection, of a half-ton boulder that snapped Shaler's neck, killing him.[25] Slightly more than a year later, another contractor ordered a dynamiting speed-up to finish the final hundred feet of excavation for the Washington Heights stretch of the line, dislodging a three-hundred ton boulder that killed ten workers. William Barclay Parsons, the chief engineer for the line, simply blamed the unstable geology of Fort George, reporting, "All possible precautions had been taken."[26]

This casual naturalization of worker death, and the associated assumption that no more could be done structurally to ensure safety on such jobs, extended well beyond employers and managers like Shaler and Parsons, into the ranks of Progressive reformers and industry experts. Frederick L. Hoffman, a statistician, argued strenuously in a 1909 paper that "the principle of social justice which shifts the trade risk upon the trade itself . . . is fully justified by both ethical and economic considerations"; he nevertheless concluded breezily that "a considerable proportion" of industrial death "results from risks which, in all probability, can never be entirely eliminated." The cause, he reckoned, was that "workingmen will often needlessly expose themselves to danger, and they are equally careless and indifferent in exposing their fellow-workmen to serious risk."[27] As Edwin W. De Leon noted with similar ease in the midst of a disquisition aimed at outlawing child labor, "Accidents to working children are due largely to illiteracy, and the incapacity to understand and appreciate the dangerous features of industrial life. The failure to read and comprehend rules and warning signs in factories is one of the most prolific sources of injury."[28] Prevailing wisdom, even from a critical perspective, suggested that workers (even child laborers) bore a significant measure of responsibility for their physical integrity on the job, even if, as worker compensation legislation came slowly into effect in the 1910s, employers increasingly bore the "trade risk."[29]

One might imagine that the finer nature and lighter materials of the textile industry would free its workers from much of this violence, but two intertwined factors largely erased the ostensible advantages of working with cloth instead of concrete: the lack of hygienic standards (or their enforcement) in the shops, and noxious systems of managerial control and oversight.

After a year of scrutinizing the entire industry from 1910 to 1911, tenement inspector and director of the Joint Board of Sanitary Control, Dr. George Price, admitted to confounded expectations regarding worker health. Despite the fact that, as he put it, "cloak workers are mostly men and women between twenty and forty-five years of age, [and] the general health of the trade should be above the average of workers in other industries," he had discovered to the contrary that "the majority of the workers . . . are not of a robust type, that they largely suffer from anemia, possess a more or less stooping gait, and are not, as a rule a very healthy lot of men and women."[30] Shops that observed basic health codes—legal requirements for garbage receptacles, cuspidors, or one bathroom per twenty-five workers, for instance—were a rarity. Tuberculosis ravaged the trade, earning its sometime nickname "the tailor's disease." One study of the industry's workers found the malady afflicting nearly 1 percent of the women and more than 3 percent of men.[31] The study's author, Dr. J. W. Schereschewsky, also noted the more prosaic but no less devastating problem of "faulty postures," warning that their "bad effects upon health" encompassed "pulmonary afflictions, including tuberculosis, hernia, displacement of the abdominal organs, digestive troubles, weak and flat feet, [and] habitual constipation."[32] Such symptoms, whether or not they could be fairly ascribed to "faulty postures," ravaged the garment-worker population.

Many such reformist studies, in their focus on immediate health and hygiene code violations, overlooked a major underlying source of a non-medical nature: management structures that intentionally withheld resources from workers, objectifying them to maximize profit. In addition to owners' refusal to budget for proper employee facilities when their absence constituted the industry standard, direct management choices exacerbated the dangers to workers' physical and psychological health. Paying piecework rates—less deductions for materials, mistakes, and rule breaking—drove employees to work harder and longer out of fear and economic necessity. As garment worker Sadie Frowne recalled, "The machines go like mad all day, because the faster you work the more money you get."[33] Managers further energized the frantic pace through verbal abuse, as Frowne noted, hurling epithets like "stupid animal" at workers who took a moment to look away from their tasks.[34]

Pauline Newman, an I.L.G.W.U. organizer and Socialist who played a major role in the Uprising of the Twenty Thousand (as the general shirtwaist strike became known), and who had worked in the Triangle for years, recalled how managers' control and attitude of impunity toward workers' bodies drifted easily into sexual insults. In an undated manuscript, she described how "[m]any of these girls pick up sufficient courage to tell the foreman or superintendent that they can't possibly get along on the wages they get, and they hope he will give them a raise." In response, "he looks at her, sizes her up from head to foot and asks, with a friendly smile, 'why don't you look for a friend on the side?'"[35] Such sexist lechery infuriated Newman, who had spent her childhood in Lithuania fighting for an education normally denied to girls. Before she turned ten years old, she later claimed, her simple observation of the injustice implicit in the town synagogue's separate sections for men and women "conditioned me to resent and fight all discriminations based on sex."[36] After emigrating with her widowed mother and two sisters in 1900, Newman's encounters with far nastier discrimination in the New York garment trade only hardened her resolve.[37]

Sometimes managers rationalized even more explicit abuse as a form of paternalism. One boss of a unionized shop defended his habit of pinching employees' buttocks whenever it pleased him by declaring innocently to Newman's comrade Rose Schneiderman, "Why, Miss Schneiderman, these girls are like my children." As Schneiderman recounted, the shop steward who had called the meeting to register workers' complaints replied, "Mr. Aptheker we'd rather be orphans."[38] This retort would have had a special, bittersweet resonance for Schneiderman. Her father had died of influenza less than two years after the family's 1890 arrival in New York from Poland, and the limited assistance forthcoming from United Hebrew Charities could not make up the difference in the family's collective income. Poverty had forced her mother Deborah to send Schneiderman's two brothers, and eventually Schneiderman and her sister as well, to the Hebrew Orphan Asylum; the girls had stayed there for a year, the boys even longer.[39] Schneiderman had personal knowledge of what it was like to be an orphan, and of how its indignities might be preferable to shopfloor abuse.

Supervisors' harsh discipline and objectification (always backed by the threat of arbitrary and immediate termination) drove workers relentlessly and had predictably violent results. "Sometimes in my haste I get my finger caught and the needle goes right through it," Frowne explained. "I bind the finger up with a piece of cotton and go on working. . . . Where the needle goes through the nail it makes a sore finger, or where it splinters a bone it does much harm. Sometimes a finger has to come off. Generally, tho, one can be cured by a salve."[40] Frowne's casual attitude toward the risk of amputation reflects a workplace culture, actively fostered by managerial structures, in which laboring bodies were not only considered unworthy of protection, but were commonly understood as intended for objectified expenditure of one kind or another. It was, as one historian of the trade concluded, an environment "of nagging, espionage, petty tyranny, favoritism, rudeness and discourtesy."[41]

Widespread subcontracting arrangements further obscured accountability for pay and encouraged the survival of technically illegal sweatshops, which rarely risked inspection at all. Inspectors generally understood that subcontracting increased health-code violations, but workers recognized it also as a major generator of more direct violence to their bodies through longer hours, lower pay, and harsher regimes of managerial authority.[42] Rose Cohen, a survivor of the Triangle fire, recalled how, as a child laborer, her first manager saw to it that she would enjoy no respite from her sore neck and aching back. When she tried to get up and leave at the end of the day, "feeling stiff in every limb and thinking with dread of our cold empty little room and the uncooked rice," she wrote, "he would come over with still another coat. . . . I understood that he was taking advantage of me because I was a child . . . more tears fell on the sleeve lining as I bent over it than there were stitches in it."[43]

Even in the more modern textile factories like the Triangle, hawk-eyed managers with sharp tongues ensured nearly unbroken attention to work whose endless physical repetition punished mind as much as body. Newman described the humiliations such oversight produced:

[T]here were conditions of work which in our ignorance we so patiently tolerated such as the deductions from your meager wages if and when you were five minutes late—so often due to transportation delays; there was the constant watching you, lest you pause for a moment from your work . . . you were watched when you went to the lavatory and if in the opinion of the forelady you stayed a minute or two longer than she thought you should have you were threatened with being fired; there was the searching of your purse or any package you happen to have lest you may have taken a bit of lace or thread. The deductions for being late was stricktly [sic] enforced because deductions even for a few minutes from several hundred people must have meant quite a sum of money. . . . That these deductions meant less food for the worker's children bothered the employers not at all. If they had a conscience it apparently did not function in that direction. As I look back to those years of actual slavery I am quite certain that the conditions under which we worked and which existed in the factory of the Triangle Waist Co. were the acme of exploitation perpetrated by humans upon defenceless women and children—a sort of punishment for being poor and docile.[44]

Workers like Frowne, Cohen, and Newman clearly recognized the way un-regulated managerial choices created the conditions observed by reformers like Price and Schereschewsky.

The doctors, however, arrived at a different conclusion. As Price averred, "The real menace to the health of the workers and the real dangers in their lives, lie not in the nature of the industry itself, but in the defective sanitary conditions of the shops."[45] Schereschewsky was equally blithe, to the extent of implicitly laying responsibility for health problems at the feet of the workers. "That the industry per se need not be responsible for faulty posture," he wrote, "was shown by the good effects upon the individual of previous military training in European armies or of physical exercise. In many such instances the posture remained excellent, and the influence of the previous training was prolonged."[46] In other words, in Schereschewsky's view, if the workers would only sit up straight at their sewing machines, so much pain could be avoided.

Studies such as Hoffman's and De Leon's undoubtedly led to greater public awareness of the terrible violence inherent in industrial labor, as did investigations like Davis's and Schereschewsky's, but they also ensured ambivalence in the public's new awareness by invoking workers' shortcomings and deflecting scrutiny from managerial sources of violence. Whether such invocations imputed personal blame to the workers (as in the suggestions of negligence or carelessness) or not (as when noting the widespread illiteracy and lack of proper training among employees), they reinforced disdain for the working poor while contributing to the naturalization—and therefore, the insulation from criticism—of industrial organization. Violence done to workers' bodies and minds in the workplace became a regrettable but ineradicable aspect of industrial life. Any unnatural, contingent, or historical origin for such violence—most prominently, the consistent determination of the wealthy to maintain unfettered control over workers and their bodies to increase productivity and profit—vanished in a haze of mystification for many Americans.

But not for all.

10

The Primacy of Property

> You are on strike against God and nature, whose prime law it is
> that man shall earn his bread by the sweat of his brow.
>
> —Justice Willard H. Olmsted

IN THE SUMMER OF 1909, shortly before studies of their working conditions appeared, New York garment workers began to reject the existing systems of industrial organization. When employers fought back, they did so not by denying the workers access to spittoons, shortening bathroom breaks, or demanding unpaid overtime at the risk of injury. They used naked force, and depended on prevailing leeriness in the general public toward striking workers and the immigrant working poor as rowdy harbingers of social chaos to shelter themselves from serious public criticism or scrutiny. They supplemented their disproportionate access to state sources of violence and punishment—the police and the courts—by hiring private security firms such as the Empire Secret Service Agency, self-described "Labor Adjusters" whose advertising flyer advised "Mr. Manufacturer" that in the event of a strike or lockout, "you would be constrained to seek ways and means by which you could commence work," including the use of strikebreakers and armed personnel.[1] The result was a summer of havoc in the name of law and order.

Remarkably, few people beyond the writers and readers of New York's socialist press (the *New York Call* and the Yiddish *Jewish Daily Forward*) seemed to take notice of the violence. In fact, with the exception of two tiny items that appeared in the *New-York Tribune* in July and August, the mainstream press apparently did not even observe that garment shops across the city were suffering a minor strike wave, much less take an interest in the strikers themselves.[2] During the same period from July to October that this fray was intensifying around Union Square, the *New York Times* ran at least four stories, two of them extensive front-page pieces, on worker violence in Pennsylvania, Nebraska, Indiana, and Missouri; it also editorialized on a colliery strike dynamiting in Nova Scotia, warning its readers that "this strike should be observed attentively on this side of the border" as an example of how unionist "terrorism" threatens workers otherwise "satisfied with the conditions of employment."[3]

The *Call*, by contrast, published multiple stories detailing abuse of garment strikers by management proxies.[4] On August 3, a "gang of thugs" attacked a group of neckwear workers on their way home from picketing A. W. Cowen's shop in Union Square. Rather than simply leave the workers—Morris Shafer, Hyman Stern, Ben Mermelstein, Max Itzik, J. Belinsky, and Hyman Bambor—lying "badly beaten up" in the gutter, the assailants "called cops and had Shafer, Stern, Mermelstein and Itzik arrested." Belinsky and Bambor escaped arrest, it seems, only because they required immediate medical attention. The desk officer at the Mulberry Street police station discharged the four other strikers when the arresting officer failed to offer "any definite charge against them," but the message to the workers was clear: go back to work, or barring that, stop picketing.[5] To underline the point, "plain clothes men" regularly stopped strikers passing the shop in question, and after searching their pockets, "slugged them, and let them go."[6]

A week later, "thugs under the direction of Dave Rosen," a co-owner of the Rosen Brothers firm at 33 East 10th Street, attacked strikers Robert Abelman, Philip Platinsky, and Jacob Futernick as they walked past the shop entrance. Abraham Cahan's *Forward* published front-page photos of the three workers, bandaged and battered, while the *Call* reported the union's protests that police had witnessed the beating from the shop hallway, but had done nothing to intervene.[7] The union's business agent speculated that the officers in question remained still because "they would have [had] to arrest the slugging thugs and the boss who were attacking peaceable passersby."[8] Absent any deterrent, such behavior continued, as a committee of the Central Federated Union reported three days later, attesting that "the strikers were being unmercifully beaten by thugs and hirelings of the bosses . . . armed with clubs and brass knuckles."[9]

Evidence of biased police action, or inaction, reflected more than just the failure to arrest bosses or the "hirelings of the bosses" beating workers on the street, or the willingness to arrest victims of such assaults on the word of the perpetrators. Two days after police failed to prevent Rosen and his men from attacking Abelman, Platinsky, and Futernick (or to arrest them for it), a Neckwear Workers' Union (N.W.U.) committee sent a delegation to the police commissioner to complain about an invasion of their office in which police either participated or were complicit. Apparently, plainclothes officers had forced their way into the union office with a strikebreaker in tow, to whom they accorded "the privilege . . . to point to anyone in the office and have him or her arrested."[10] In another such instance, reported a week later, a union representative tried to stop "a plain clothes man" and two strikebreakers from entering his office. In response, "the detective drew a pistol and threatened to shoot him. He then broke in the office" and arrested a union member for assault.[11] Whether these non-uniformed officers were New York cops or hired private security remains unclear, but the police department effectively endorsed the raids by upholding the arrests.[12]

Judicial responses to such incidents varied wildly, depending on the magistrate or court in question. One Brooklyn magistrate not only dismissed a Brownsville shirtwaist factory boss's charges of felonious assault leveled against three striking employees, but bluntly warned the arresting policeman, "Do not bring any more innocent strikers before me or I will fine you."[13] In a Manhattan night court two days later, magistrate Corrigan fined ten neckwear strikers $3 apiece—as much as a week's pay for some workers—for shouting "scab" at strikebreakers, despite the fact that the only witnesses against them (for a crime that was not, strictly speaking, illegal) were their boss and the arresting officers. The boss, in fact, became so confused during the defense lawyer's cross-examination that the magistrate suggested to him, "You had better take a back seat!"[14]

Regardless of magistrates' rulings, it is worth remembering that employers' efforts to suppress strike activity, whether through hired hands or the police, bore fruit at the moment of confrontation. Carting immigrant strikers into the intimidating surroundings of a police station or courtroom—where they frequently shared the company of prostitutes and petty thieves—added further insult to injury, but the initial injury of unceremonious arrest constituted a perfectly adequate disincentive to strike.

For the waning months of summer and into early autumn 1909, however, the incentives to strike continued to outweigh the drawbacks, and the violence and prosecutions connected with various shop-specific shirtwaist and neckwear actions escalated. On August 26, two hundred workers at the Rosen Brothers firm won a 20 percent raise after a four-week strike that included multiple assaults on strikers.[15] The following day, twenty-five neckwear strikers from Isaac Newman's shop at 301 Mulberry Street won a closed-shop union contract after a six-week strike during which "many strikers were slugged by thugs hired by the firm and twenty arrests were made at the behest of the employer."[16] Less than a week later on Thursday, September 2, one hundred workers struck at Louis Leiserson's West 17th Street shop; sixty more workers less than a block away at Solomon & Leffler followed them out on Sunday.[17] By Monday, union officials were accusing Solomon & Leffler of "employing thugs to assault the strikers," claiming that two strikers "were attacked by a band of these ruffians and so seriously hurt that they had to be attended by a physician." The four Leiserson strikers hauled into Jefferson Market Court by police that same Monday and charged with assaulting strikebreakers were immediately discharged.[18] Three days later on Thursday, September 9, several men attacked Clara Lemlich, a garment worker and union organizer destined to achieve fame in the coming months, as she made her way home from the picket lines at Leiserson's shop; they pummeled her so viciously that she was confined to bed for weeks.[19] The strike at A. W. Cowen's Union Square neckwear firm, begun in June, continued to rage unabated through September.

These strikes and their attendant violence passed relatively unnoticed outside the *Call*'s pages—and only one or two of these incidents have appeared in subsequent histories of the Uprising of the Twenty Thousand—but they are crucial to understanding the fierce daily reality that striking garment workers faced on picket lines during the summer of 1909, before the garment industry struggles earned serious, mainstream press coverage. The terms of engagement were set long before Lemlich initiated the general strike of shirtwaist workers by delivering a jeremiad from the Cooper Union stage in late November: employer-directed violence had dominated labor disputes for months, and confrontations between picketers, strikebreakers, private detectives, police, and bosses ebbed and flowed on the street with the dependability of the workday cycle.

With the strike at Leiserson's intensifying, the turmoil in the shirtwaist industry magnified significantly on the morning of September 27, when Harris and Blanck locked out hundreds of Triangle workers, precipitating yet another strike.[20] The number of violent incidents began to mount swiftly. About the same time as the Triangle dispute began, Mary Morgenstern, a Leiserson striker, approached an Italian woman heading into Leiserson's shop and pleaded with her not to go to work. Without warning, another strikebreaker named Dominick grabbed a fistful of Morgenstern's hair from behind and yanked her away from the woman. A "passing express-man" leaped from his wagon to Morgenstern's aid, chastising Dominick for assaulting a woman, but the rebuke apparently made no impression: Dominick was at it again the next day, when he "and other scabs badly slugged Miss Bessie Lipstein and Beckie Keller, strikers, as they were watching the scabs enter the shop."[21] Lipstein later testified that "Dominick attacked me, knocked me down and pushed me into the building, 26–32 West 17th Street. There he kicked me again several times, inflicting black and blue marks on my body."[22] The night of that assault, a Jefferson Market court judge dismissed disorderly conduct charges against six Triangle strikers "arrested at the behest of the boses [sic]," and warned the police, "Be careful in making arrests, strikers have a right to walk around near a struck shop." As an I.L.G.W.U. member named Abraham Bernstein discovered, however, that "right" offered insubstantial protection. After joining the Triangle picket line, he received a beating that left him in a doctor's care.[23]

Even taking the *Call*'s frankly propagandistic characterization of events with a healthy grain of salt, by October 1, 1909, the scene in the garment district within a radius of less than a half-mile was this: at least half a dozen shops comprising the better part of a thousand workers had struck or were on strike; hired security and strikebreakers, day after day, inflicted injuries on picketers—men and women, boys and girls—through street assaults both random and targeted; and police repeatedly arrested strikers on charges so flimsy that magistrates on at least two occasions paired their dismissals with reprimands to the arresting officers. It would not be an exaggeration to describe the vicinity of Washington Square East, University Place, Union Square West, and 17th Street between 7th Avenue and Broadway in

September 1909 as one of barely controlled chaos, troubled by regular out-
bursts of violence against strikers and clashes with strikebreakers, all caused
or directed with relative impunity by property owners and police. The authorities charged with maintaining order, in other words, made regular
class violence part of the order they maintained.

On October 1, the continental shelf of New York's garment industry lurched
sideways. After many weeks of only marginally successful shop walkouts,
persistent violence, and increasing frustration, the N.W.U. declared a general strike of the neckwear industry.[24] Like their sisters in the shirtwaist
industry, neckwear workers were predominantly poor, young, Russian Jewish immigrants, approximately 70 percent of whom were women and girls.[25]
They worked under conditions and for wages comparable to those prevailing in the shirtwaist trade. With 7,000 neckwear workers striking hundreds
of shops simultaneously, even the *New York Times* made desultory mention
of it, belatedly observing, "For the last six weeks there have been intermit-
tent strikes of neckwear workers in individual factories, accompanied by
more or less disturbances."[26]

   October 1, the day the N.W.U. began the general strike, was a Friday; by
the end of the weekend, eight shops had caved to striker demands. By Tuesday, October 5, the tally had risen to twenty-five shop concessions, and five
hundred more workers joined the strike in progress. By close of business on
Wednesday, nine hundred workers from forty-six shops had won union
recognition and terms favorable enough to return to work. Thursday's *Call*
included a ringing editorial endorsement of the job action.[27] In a city still
emerging from the financial panic of 1907 and subsequent industrial depression of 1908, these were noteworthy union victories.

   As the strike's success grew, the buzz began trickling into the pages of
mainstream newspapers in small but telling ways, presaging important aspects of the shirtwaist strike to come. That same Wednesday, October 6,
the neckwear strikers held a meeting in Clinton Hall at which "three richly
dressed women" representing the suffrage movement "occupied seats on the
platform." As the next day's *New-York Tribune* reported, they made statements of support to the strikers, which Lillian Plesser, the N.W.U. secretary,
translated into Yiddish. While these suffragists did not share their names

with the press, their leader told journalists that "a meeting would be arranged to take up the cause of the strikers."[28] A few days later, the *Times* ran a short item under the headline "Literary Neckwear Girls," conveying a message from "the women officers of the Neckwear Workers' Union, who are running the strike" that "the public must divest itself of the idea that the girl strikers are a frivolous lot who look on life as a holiday when they are not working. Instead they say the girls are great readers who are improving their minds while the men drink beer and play stuss." As Plesser attested to reporters, "the girls are fond of Shakespeare, and also read Goethe, Turgenieff, and Tolstoy."[29] As the shirtwaist strikers would in the months ahead, neckwear workers had begun to forge a cross-class alliance with the suffrage movement and to combat stereotypes of female workers as flighty and undependable.

A crucial demographic similarity linked the neckwear and shirtwaist strikes as well. Of the 7,000 neckwear strikers, the majority were Russian Jewish immigrants from the Lower East Side who shared streets and tenements—if not friends and family—with their shirtwaist worker compatriots and coreligionists. As the shirtwaist workers would in little more than a month, these poor immigrants sacrificed paychecks and endangered their jobs for a chance to win better wages, conditions, and a modicum of worker control on the shopfloor. They picketed in the same neighborhoods where the shirtwaist workers lived and worked.[30] The fact that thousands succeeded in winning significant concessions within the space of a twelve-day general strike of the trade—the N.W.U. declared victory and ended the strike on October 12 after over a hundred shops had settled—could not have been lost on shirtwaist workers, many of whom were engaged in their own, seemingly intractable strikes and shopfloor grievances.[31]

Much less would it have been lost on other union leaders, even if it went unacknowledged, that after months of ineffective shop by shop strikes, the N.W.U. had won an industrywide victory in less than two weeks. It strains credulity to imagine that when I.L.G.W.U. leaders issued their initial (abortive) declaration for a general strike in the shirtwaist industry just over a week later, they did not have the N.W.U.'s success in mind.[32]

There are a few possible explanations for the otherwise baffling fact that the neckwear workers' strike has escaped serious consideration as a contributing factor in histories of the Uprising.[33] Most obviously, the Leiserson and Triangle strikes provided a superficially compelling prehistory of the shirtwaist strike to eyewitnesses and participants themselves, not to speak of historians. The women whose testimony would be so important in reconstructing the shirtwaist strike's history—notably, Newman and Lemlich—were more focused on those battles in which they had participated and led, understandably privileging their role in retellings of the larger revolt.

Compounding this effect for both witnesses and scholars, the Triangle's owners—at practically the same moment that the N.W.U. declared its general strike—set a new bar for sensationalism in their efforts to crush the union drive in their own shop. The day after the neckwear workers walked out, Harris and Blanck deployed prostitutes along with the usual security personnel to attack and harass the picketers outside the Asch building.[34] "Prostitutes Hired to Beat Strikers" ran the headline in the *Call* the following Monday, diverting both contemporaneous and subsequent attention from the early stages of the year's first general strike. Given the gendered nature of this particular anti-union tactic and the centrality of women's solidarity to the ensuing shirtwaist strike, the outrages of early October at the Triangle have loomed large in both worker recollections and later treatments of the Uprising, and rightfully so.[35]

And, of course, the neckwear strike was not a Ladies' Garment Workers' strike. In telling the story of a pivotal moment in I.L.G.W.U. history, that union's members or officials would not have rushed to acknowledge another union's role in setting the stage. This may explain why Louis Levine, author of the I.L.G.W.U.'s most comprehensive early history, *The Women's Garment Workers,* offers such an unpersuasive account of the shirtwaist strike's origins. Recalling that by "the middle of October it looked as if the strikes against Leiserson and the Triangle . . . would have to be given up" in the face of the firms' aggression, and maintaining that the "fighting spirit of the strikers was breaking under the strain," Levine suddenly claims, "Under these circumstances, the officers of Local 25 and of the United Hebrew Trades . . . began thinking about a general strike in the entire trade."[36] Select I.L.G.W.U. officers had been advocating general strikes as a more promising tactic in theory for years, but with hundreds of strikers at two of the trade's largest shops feeling demoralized, with few actual dues-paying members and almost no money in their treasury, it seems unlikely that the

union's leaders would have deemed it a good time to call for a general strike
unless they had a more compelling reason to take heart. Of course, Levine
formed his account primarily on the basis of interviews with I.L.G.W.U.
leaders long after the fact.

Any one of these factors might have been enough to minimize the N.W.U.
strike's role in laying groundwork for the shirtwaist revolt; together they
have practically erased it. Yet the circumstantial importance of the neckwear workers' strike in October, especially in light of the summer's unrelent-
ing violence, provides an important layer of context in explaining the overwhelming and unprecedented response of shirtwaist workers to the strike
call in late November, which organizers at the time were at a loss to explain
satisfactorily. Even in the face of the Triangle owners' attention-diverting
shenanigans, the neckwear strike could not have escaped widespread public
discussion on the Lower East Side. The *Call* ran extensive articles detailing
its progress for the first two weeks of October, and most were far more jus-
tifiable in their tone of triumph than the *Call*'s usual triumphalist fare.[37]

Just as importantly for the course of the impending shirtwaist strike,
and for the violence that would in part define it, the neckwear revolt underscored two pressing needs for the manufacturers: to stiffen their resolve and
to organize themselves. They fulfilled the first need by ramping up their
violent proxy assaults against shirtwaist strikers. Harris and Blanck created
a perverse but effective team of union busters on October 5: first the prostitutes "and their procurers" (that is, their pimps) assaulted picketers, then
the police swooped in to arrest them. "There were no cops in sight while the
girls were being beaten," reported the *Call,* "but after they had been bru-
tally kicked and dragged around by their hair a number of cops appeared
and arrested them. No effort was made to corral their assailants."[38] When
one of the strikers, Ida Janowitz, demanded to know the cause of her arrest,
"she was insulted by the bluecoats and told to keep her mouth shut or she
would be clubbed."[39] Magistrate Finn discharged all ten arrested strikers,
but twenty-three other Triangle strikers arraigned the same day were not as
lucky. The Jefferson Market Court judge in their cases issued $1 fines to
each of them, a shadow of sterner measures to come.[40]

The Triangle's owners also took the initiative in getting the trade's employers organized. Neckwear manufacturers had failed to coordinate an anti-
union strategy, and opposition to the strikers' demands crumpled under a

succession of individual, caving bosses. Harris and Blanck had no intention of allowing such managerial pusillanimity in the shirtwaist trade. A week after the I.L.G.W.U. had declared for—and then postponed—a general strike in late October, the Triangle's bosses sent a circular letter "to the employers in the trade suggesting the organization of an Employers' Mutual Protective Association in view of the strike agitation."[41] Men such as industry lawyer Julius Henry Cohen had already floated the idea of a manufacturers' association, but Cohen, who became general counsel to the cloakmakers' association the following year, recalled that the idea initially met with ridicule. "In 1907, 1908, and 1909 a union of cloak *manufacturers* was something to poke fun at," he wrote. This was no less true in the shirtwaist industry. As Cohen bemoaned, "Anarchy on the workers side was matched by anarchy on the employers' side."[42]

Yet seventeen days after the neckwear general strike won historic victories for 7,000 workers, and one week after Local 25 declared for a general strike in the shirtwaist industry, the largest shirtwaist manufacturer—with ostensibly the greatest incentive to see its smaller competitors fail—actively sought to end the employers' anarchy. The lines were drawn for an uncommonly brazen class war: employers, the wealthy, and the aspiring wealthy arrayed in battle formation against workers, and workers flooding both streets and union rolls to fight their industrial masters.

But there was a fly in the employers' ointment. Wealthy women had not only begun to side with the strikers figuratively by providing financial and organizational resources and attending private rallies, but had also started placing their bodies on picket lines. This impeded the usefulness of street violence, the employers' bread-and-butter anti-union tactic, by making it visible to a much wider public and subjecting it to critique outside the *Call*'s and *Forward*'s pages.

On November 4, police arrested Mary E. Dreier on the complaint of a Triangle strikebreaker named Anna Walla. Walla claimed that Dreier had approached her outside the factory and declared, "I will split your head open if you try to go to work."[43] Dreier acknowledged having approached Walla but insisted that she had only said, "There's a strike in the Triangle," before Walla "became very angry and talked about my annoying her. Then she struck me."[44] When Dreier had asked a nearby policeman for protection at the time, Walla immediately claimed that Dreier had been threatening her, whereupon the cop arrested Dreier and suggested that Walla press charges at the station house. None of this was particularly remarkable in light of the previous summer's violence and evidence of bias among the police. But Mary E. Dreier was no humble seamstress—she was the president of the W.T.U.L.'s New York chapter and the daughter of a prominent bourgeois family. Accordingly, the next day's *Times* ran an extensive front-page story on the incident, its first coverage of the police abuse, reporting (on Dreier's word) that "last night was only the latest of a series of outrages which had been perpetrated by the men of the 'penitentiary precinct' for months."[45] Suddenly, after a summer of silence, the *Times* deemed police and employer violence on picket lines in its own city worthy of coverage. All it took was a bourgeois woman to be the victim rather than a working-class girl, and for that bourgeois woman to be the reporter's principal source.

While this increased visibility lessened the near-total impunity previously enjoyed by employers, private detectives, and police, it hardly meant that they stopped assaulting the strikers, or that judges became neutral arbiters of the law. Inez Milholland, who had graduated from Vassar earlier that year and was one of the wealthy "college girls" aiding the strike, incisively analyzed the employers' continued motivation for assaulting strikers.[46] "It is . . . the object of employers to have them accused of violence so as to discourage and intimidate them by arrests and fines, as well as to alienate public sympathy from their cause," she wrote in an undated speech manuscript, probably composed during the strike. "To do this they employ thugs and detectives at 'Fifty dollars a week' one employer declared, who bully, assault and molest the girls, who aggravate, push and shove them in hopes of making them retaliate violently."[47] Milholland acknowledged that the striking waistmakers occasionally gave in to temptation and retaliated, but in a statement remarkable for a woman of her class—and offering a compelling counterexample to those who have focused on the ways bourgeois women impeded or denied working women's political subjectivity during the strike—she defended such retaliation. "Personally I am inclined to agree with the Constitution when it establishes the 'right of revolution,'" she wrote. "I think there is a point where submission to unfair treatment becomes abject and slavish, and retaliation in one form or another is indicative of self-respect."[48] This explicitly American political formulation by a rich, native-born woman defending poor immigrant strikers' right to physical self-defense was itself a small revolution.

It is doubtful that Milholland's views were widely shared, but her involvement and that of other bourgeois allies certainly shifted some measure of public criticism, at least temporarily, onto employers and city officials. Complaints about prejudice among police magistrates, a staple of coverage in the *Call* all summer, also began to receive credence from the mainstream press. The day after the *Times* story appeared, the *Tribune* printed a smaller report conveying Dreier's announcement, on behalf of the W.T.U.L., that it would appeal some seventy fines levied on Triangle picketers, "ranging from $1 to $10," for disorderly conduct. Pointing out that at least one judge, Justice Blanchard, had assured strikers that "the right to maintain pickets is well established," she insisted that the strikers had maintained decorum, conscientiously avoided obstructing walkways, "and only tried to persuade strike breakers not to return to work."[49] Less than two weeks later, the *Tribune* published a longer story recounting how the police had refused to arrest a young Italian strikebreaker who ran out from a group of workers to kick Rose Berman, a Triangle striker. When the W.T.U.L.'s secretary Elizabeth Dutcher went to Jefferson Market Court to complain about the police and obtain a warrant to arrest Berman's attacker, Magistrate Cornell offered her a telling rebuke: "What were you doing in Washington Place?" he asked her. "You have no right to picket. If you go there you will get what's coming to you. I'm not going to interfere and I won't give you a warrant."[50]

As Cornell's statement suggests, even if the presence of wealthy women in the street made police and hired hands more cautious in meting out indiscriminate aggression, it demonstrably failed to lessen their belligerence in general terms, or to moderate the magistrates' notions about the justifiability of violence to protect property.[51] Police offered particularly astounding evidence of their continued hostility on December 21, when "Detectives Gallagher and Scott of the Union Market Police Station . . . burst into" a union meeting hall and arrested eight strikers for assault on the word of two strikebreakers who accompanied them. The union official in charge of the meeting, Philip Kove, recounted to reporters that one of the strikebreakers, Harry Berman, "was armed with a billy and for several minutes he and the detectives beat the unarmed strikers, who were taken by surprise and could offer no resistance. Then the men pointed out those they said had attacked them and the detectives arrested them." In fact, Kove noted, the one woman among the eight strikers arrested, Jennie Poision, "had Berman arrested on Monday for assaulting her in University Place and he is now under $500 bail for trial."[52] It seems fair to say that if the police were willing to enlist a man awaiting trial for assault to help raid a meeting of strikers that included his accuser, then they had not grown more restrained in light of the Dreier incident and the "mink brigade" surveillance of picket lines.[53]

It is all the more remarkable that this incident occurred only two days after the Association of Neighborhood Workers issued a statement, published in the *Times* over the signatures of reform notables such as E. R. A. Seligman, Mary Simkhovitch, Ida Tarbell, and Lillian Wald, declaring that "there is ample evidence . . . that the employers have received co-operation and aid from the police in place of that protection to which they, in common with all citizens, are entitled. The strikers, on the contrary, have been subjected to insult by the police and in many cases have been arrested when acting within their rights."[54] The strike had become an explicit site of contestation between public rights and private interests, and their relative protection under the law. The police could hardly have provided a clearer indication of which side in that contest they endorsed.

The judiciary was, in the end, equally frank. Despite the increasing awareness of unequal treatment, police magistrates became if anything sterner with shirtwaist workers after the Dreier incident, handing down more fines, harsher sentences, and issuing public warnings to strikers that confirmed ideological biases by either implicitly justifying or accepting violence toward strikers as natural, or blaming them for the violence regardless of the circumstances. One magistrate, Peter Townsend Barlow, informed a union lawyer that his leniency with strikers "had resulted only in increased disorder," and declared, "I will start sending these girls to the workhouse to-morrow."[55]

On December 30, in the most frequently quoted instance of this prejudicial phenomenon, Justice Olmsted of Special Sessions dismissed a striker's complaints against a strikebreaker's assault by invoking Genesis 3:19, the moment after the Fall: "You are on strike against God and nature, whose prime law it is that man shall earn his bread by the sweat of his brow."[56] The last word on this judge usually goes to George Bernard Shaw, who in response to a request for comment from Elizabeth Dutcher of the W.T.U.L., quipped, "Delightful mediaeval America always in the intimate personal confidence of the Almighty."[57]

Shaw's wit, though undeniable, missed the larger significance in Olmsted's statement. The judge's biblical justification for punishing the striker reeked of pious presumption, which Shaw ably ridiculed, but Olmsted also cited God "and nature" as twin movers of the "prime law," despite the fact that the Abrahamic deity, in the passage invoked, framed his punishment to Adam and Eve as something that would otherwise be entirely *un*natural.[58] That is, the naturalization of work—and the consequent perception of striking as a perversion of nature's law—is a cultural and historical creation of capitalism, not a throwback to medieval religious fanaticism.[59] Olmsted's dictum revealed him as not (or not only) a religious prig, but a believer in classical economic orthodoxy. Disrupting the "natural" flow of the commercial world by refusing to work, Olmsted and countless others believed, could only produce disorder.

After Shaw's stinging cable and its wide republication made Olmsted the butt of many jokes (more for his pomposity, one suspects, than for the substance of his views), the judge compounded this naturalization of workers' obedience, explaining to reporters, "These words of mine were spoken to children and for children, not for the world at large, nor for such astute minds as that of Mr. Shaw. What I said was uttered as a moral precept. And what could be better for an audience of children than the daily utterance of moral precepts? Mr. Shaw just didn't consider."[60] In an era before comprehensive child labor laws (and the strikers before Olmsted were indeed quite young), "worker's rights" meant the right to be disciplined as a child by property and the state acting in loco parentis. This reference to a biological relation to justify "moral precepts" only underscored Olmsted's belief that such authority was naturally determined.

Olmsted understood his duty toward petitioning workers not as a public servant protecting their rights and judging their wrongs, but as a parental guardian upholding a moral order of labor and property ordained by "God and nature." By extension, he naturalized the violence that workers suffered, suggesting that they themselves were responsible for it by virtue of rejecting "God and nature." What progressive investigators of workplace hygiene like Schereschewsky or Hoffman did less self-consciously or intentionally, Olmsted did explicitly: he blamed workers for the consequences of managerial decisions, both on the shopfloor and in the street. Milholland, in citing the Constitution to justify a "right of revolution," drew on one tradition in American politics; Olmsted drew on another, equally powerful piece of the American heritage: the capitalist conflation of the free market with natural law.

This conflation meant that the bar for public sympathy toward workers rose to lofty heights when clashes between rich and poor grew violent—the rich, after all, had a *natural* right to dispose of their property as they saw fit. Employers raised that bar even higher by paying to create more conflict, knowing it would reinforce the perception of the poor as rowdy, disruptive, and destructive, thus obscuring their expressions of democratic political will. No matter how much public opprobrium employers might risk with this strategy, some measure of blame would also stain the strikers, while legal statutes and widespread cultural predisposition would always respect the employers' property rights. As Olmsted's declaration suggests, a bloody trail might lead back to material incentives created by the wealthy, but the poor would always appear to be the ones violating nature.

At the source of that "nature" lay nothing more organic than power derived from rights in property. Karl Marx might as well have been directly analyzing the New York garment industry in the 1900s when he wrote, "the capitalist does not rule over the labourer through any personal qualities he may have, but only in so far as he is 'capital'; his domination is only that of materialized labour over living labour, of the labourer's product over the labourer himself."[61] Triangle strikers saw this theory made flesh when Harris and Blanck paid prostitutes and private detectives to assault them, using money that workers' labor had helped produce. They were hardly the only workers—either in New York of 1909, or in American history up to the present—to see the economic power of their own labor coagulated into another's property, then transformed into force and wielded against them.

And yet, occasionally, workers might also see that same economic power harnessed to their cause in a cooperative spirit of solidarity. One exceptionally wealthy woman would demonstrate that spirit very publicly throughout the conflict: Alva Belmont.

II

Sisters in Struggle

> I love women, all women, good or bad, right or wrong—even
> the anti-suffragists. I believe love wins more than hate, cordial-
> ity than exclusiveness, co-operation than competition.
>
> —Evalyn A. Burnham

A MONTH AND A DAY after Mary Dreier's spurious arrest, and after weeks
of primarily capital-directed street violence centering just north of Washington Square Park, an extraordinary instance of cross-class cooperation
took place in midtown Manhattan. Society matron, suffrage activist, and
millionaire widow Alva Belmont commandeered the Hippodrome, a mammoth theater spanning Sixth Avenue between 43rd and 44th Streets, for an
event meant to publicize the general strike of New York's shirtwaist industry that had begun two weeks earlier. Speakers included various clergy,
union leaders, and Rev. Dr. Anna Howard Shaw, the president of the National American Women's Suffrage Association (N.A.W.S.A.). Strike leaders
from the I.L.G.W.U., the W.T.U.L., and the Socialist Party had organized
thousands of strikers to attend, the vast majority of whom were young
women, many only teenagers. As the *Times* reported with its inimitably leery
conservatism, "Socialism, unionism, woman suffrage and what seemed to be
something like anarchism were poured into the ears of fully 8,000 persons . . .
in the interest of the striking shirtwaist makers of the city."[1]

The Hippodrome meeting on December 5, 1909, was something of a
coming-out party for a budding alliance of poor and wealthy New York

women. For a few months, this alliance mesmerized New York's newspaper-reading public and seriously discomfited the city's power-brokers in a way that the months of garment industry strife and street violence preceding it had failed to do. Public amazement and official trepidation were warranted, for in the Gotham winter spanning 1909 and 1910, it seemed as if women's solidarity might trump class divisions, destabilizing the entrenched social order of businessmen's patriarchy. A group of women, occupying the entire spectrum from grinding poverty to stratospheric wealth, came together in an unprecedented (and, for scale and sensationalism, unmatched) mutual struggle for women's and labor rights.[2]

This struggle represents a less common but profoundly more disruptive type of cooperative class relation than that which existed in the worlds of begging letters, individual philanthropy, and settlement work. In those arenas, individuals formed cross-class bonds that offered little if any sustained rebuke to the structures of power and inequality inherent in turn-of-the-century industrial capitalism. Begging letters worked very much within those structures to achieve their ends, usually emphasizing manifestations of inequality positively (the prospective donor's magnanimity and wealth, the poor writer's humble work ethic) as partial rationale for the relationship. Philanthropy sought to mitigate those structures' material effects without undermining their cultural foundations, providing philosophical or spiritual justification for inequality's existence by demonstrating how it could improve the souls of the rich and the material lives of the poor. Settlement work offered an alternative sphere that might serve as an inspiring example of how human relations could be different within those structures, but it would never directly challenge them beyond the realm of reform. As Wald's loss of Mary Stillman Harkness's patronage demonstrates, when settlements appeared even unintentionally to be flirting with the edge of a more direct, systematic challenge to the status quo, they endangered their financial viability.

More fundamentally, the cooperative class relations forged through begging letters, philanthropy, and settlements directly reflected the imbalance of power on either side of the class equation. While Paley claimed title to his own voice in writing to Schiff, the banker ultimately decided whether to pursue or continue—indeed, whether to constitute at all—the cooperative relationship, as he did in all his philanthropic endeavors. The poor in these relations were distinctly the more dependent party. Similarly, Lower East Siders who used Henry Street's resources or sought out its residents for counsel were petitioners to Wald's efforts, connections, and goodwill. That she treated everyone with respect, took their input seriously regardless of social position, and rarely denied anyone sources of assistance does not alter the fact that her discretion governed the allocation of those resources. The cooperative class relation in each of these instances lived or died on the basis of the wealthier participant's willingness and desire to provide the benefit of their power, wealth, or privilege to the poor. The cooperation was real, but it reflected, rather than subverted, the inequality upon which it rested.

By contrast, the cooperative class relations forged between poor and wealthy women during the 1909–1910 shirtwaist strike depended on a recognition of a shared oppression under identical structures (if not manifestations) of social power, and the potential for *mutual* assistance in altering those structures. The strike attracted Alva Belmont at least as much for what its poorest participants could provide to *her*—namely, a ready-made, publicly militant movement of radicalized women numbering in the tens of thousands—as for what she could provide to it—material resources, publicity, and a degree of normative legitimacy. Russian immigrant shirtwaist workers, likewise, could regard Belmont not merely as a gracious Lady Bountiful (or, as many Socialist women did, a cunning opportunist), but as a sister in struggle, a woman who, like them, had endured indignities in a patriarchal society and had decided to fight back. In the midst of that fight, further common ground would begin to emerge: wealthy women would confront the absence of an impartial judiciary or truly professional police force and be galled by it; poor women would begin to consider more seriously the value of demanding political enfranchisement for their sex not just in the workplace, but in civil society as well.

Certainly, this mutual struggle continued to reflect inequalities of power and purpose. The W.T.U.L.'s bourgeois founders explicitly envisioned an organization maintaining "a division of labor that gave trade unionists the role of technical advisors rather than policymakers," and those ladies' "power of the purse," along with sundry advantages of cultural capital, conferred disproportionate control within League structures.[3] This organizational model not infrequently drove devoted working-class W.T.U.L. members to protest, fume, or even resign from the League in anger.[4] These working women and the thousands of poor strikers who joined them also shared joyous and painful experiences—of ethnic and cultural origin, neighborhood life, and the elemental daily battle for control on the shopfloor—that bound them together in a comradeship to which the wealthy could never fully gain access.[5]

For some women, however, the common struggle loosened the bonds of pre-immigrant experience, narrow family or work lives and, most importantly, restrictive conceptions of class loyalty. Even if only for a short time, it made room for a more expansive and hopeful notion of sisterly solidarity. The very existence of such a cooperative class relation, not to speak of its evolution through joint struggle, posed a far more profound challenge to the status quo than the narrower solidarities of the mainstream suffrage or labor movements. If women could even temporarily privilege their common experiences *as women* over their divergent economic, political, racial, ethnic, or generational experiences, it would open doors of transgressive communication, rendering porous America's most basic hierarchical boundaries. Such transgressive communication could lead to empathy, and empathy to the formation of a collective. Such a collective could lead to more common struggles that not only transgressed boundaries, but dismantled them as well. This is what made the strike of 1909–1910 so potentially subversive, and consequently, such a remarkable and powerful moment of possibility for real change in America.

Of course, it is also what drew such intense resistance from the constituencies policing society's boundaries, and what made sustaining the struggle so difficult. Common experiences as women could not and did not simply erase or supersede differences within the collective. Those differences—economic, political, racial, ethnic, and generational—both influenced the calibration of goals for social change, and represented chinks in the armor of women's solidarity at which opponents could aim their blows. Natalya Urusova, an impoverished, sixteen-year-old Russian immigrant working twelve hours a day under abusive supervision, had a far greater willingness to embrace radical social restructuring than did Anne Tracy Morgan, the thirty-six-year-old daughter of J. P. Morgan, the most powerful financier in the world.[6] They shared a common experience of seeing their opportunities limited because they were women, certainly, and this experience briefly made them cooperating partners in the strike and the suffrage movement.

But Morgan had much more reason than Urusova to defend social structures in other areas, and much less reason to welcome their wholesale transformation or destruction. Opponents of the strike and what it represented could exploit such differences to divide the women from each other, and they did. Moreover, such external pressure was often unnecessary—internal differences, thrown into bold relief at moments of encounter, created ample friction within the alliance. Putative sisters with ideological axes to grind (on both sides of the class divide) whittled away at collective cohesion by publicly slashing each other with distrust, innuendo, and outright accusations.

Over the course of the strike, differences among these sisters in struggle would slowly set them at odds with each other, even as their collective efforts achieved consequential transformations in New York's shirtwaist industry, laying the groundwork for what would become one of the city's most powerful industrial unions for most of the twentieth century (the I.L.G.W.U.), and exposing the deeply misogynist, racist, and classist nature of New York's law enforcement apparatus.

Three crucial moments of class encounter during the Uprising of the Twenty Thousand tell the entwined stories of class cooperation and its unraveling: the December 5, 1909, Hippodrome meeting, the December 15, 1909, fundraiser and tea at the Colony Club, and the January 2, 1910, rally at Carnegie Hall to protest police and legislative abuse. Those encounters reflected the peculiar genius of individual women—Belmont, Morgan, Clara Lemlich, Mary Dreier, and Eva McDonald Valesh, among others— whose efforts and ambivalences first built, then dismantled one of the most potentially revolutionary moments of collective protest in postbellum American history.

On November 23, 1909, between 20,000 and 30,000 garment workers in New York flooded into the streets to strike. Huge crowds of workers, overwhelmingly young women, mobbed the offices of the W.T.U.L. and I.L.G.W.U. asking for union cards and instruction in how to proceed with the strike. Two days later, when the numbers had swelled even further and smaller shop managers had already begun to settle with their employees, Mary Dreier wrote to her sister, Margaret Dreier Robins, that Local 25 of the I.L.G.W.U. "did not expect such a tremendous answer to the call, and terrible confusion reigned." Dreier, however, was elated. "It is simply stupendous," she wrote, "—it is breathtaking."[7]

Dreier's excitement outweighed any "terrible confusion" she may have felt in part because, unlike the men in charge of the I.L.G.W.U., she had been privy to the months and years of organizing that produced such a mammoth walkout. Despite many contemporaneous accounts to the contrary, the shirtwaist strike of 1909–1910 was not a spontaneous outpouring of sympathetic emotion on the part of easily swayed young girls who followed their friends out on strike.[8] Rather, amid fortuitous circumstances provided by the neckwear workers' general strike, it was the culmination of painstaking organizing that had been carried out over years—by women—in hundreds of small garment shops, larger factories, and bourgeois parlors all over New York and Brooklyn. Women had driven every aspect of that organizing, but in particular three working-class, immigrant women—Clara Lemlich, Rose Schneiderman, and Pauline Newman—had been organizing shopfloors for practically half their young lives. The League's wealthier, college-educated leaders (known as "allies") including Helen Marot and Frances Kellor had provided administrative staff, fundraising, and indispensable material resources, from organizer salaries to the leaflets and pamphlets needed to inform and educate workers.[9] Together, these working and bourgeois women had already been guiding the smaller but significant strikes at the Leiserson and Triangle shops for weeks. It was a signal production of cross-class cooperation.

In many ways, it also represented the most substantive example yet of a cross-class women's solidarity that had been emerging for decades. A generation of bourgeois women born around the time of the Civil War—women such as Florence Kelley, Jane Addams, and Lillian Wald—began in their own lives to reject the repressive domesticity of Victorian femininity, and to seek a wider scope for their talents, energy, and often extensive educations.[10] They found such scope in social reform projects—legislative initiatives, settlements, and nursing, most notably—that brought them into regular, intimate contact with poor and working-class women, women who were bearing the brunt of industrialization's wrenching social transformations.[11] As these women began working together to improve the world and each others' lives, their reforms veered increasingly into the political arena around issues with gendered implications, including discriminatory pay, child labor, and a public culture of manliness celebrating a vision of femininity increasingly out of touch with the material reality of women's lives.[12] The W.T.U.L.'s founding in 1903 and its years of organizing drives before November 1909 were themselves preceded by arduous years of planning, preparation, and bridge-building between wealthy and poor women.[13]

This is not to say, however, that these women were quite prepared in practical terms for the scale and suddenness of their success in 1909, any more than the I.L.G.W.U. was. Money was a constant issue. On November 20, with the strike vote meeting in Clinton Hall only two days away, Dreier ended a letter to Robins saying, "I have to get out and hustle for money, we have none and it is so difficult to get any."[14] Newman echoed this years later, remarking that "there was no preparation for the strike. Furthermore, there was no money."[15] In the days and weeks after the November 22 strike vote, faced with the responsibility of leading shop meetings, signing women onto union cards, organizing pickets at hundreds of shop locations, defending strikers in court, paying for bail and fines, and devising new ways of attracting positive publicity for an undeniably chaotic phenomenon, both the League and the I.L.G.W.U. (whose treasury held $4 when the strike began) had to scramble to solicit donations for a strike fund. The strikers, Newman said later, "had to have heat, and they didn't. They had to have food, and they didn't. The questions, the major questions [sic], was to get funds to support the strike."[16]

One strategy entailed sending the best working-class organizers on speaking tours of the Northeast, gathering funds wherever they could find them. John Dyche, the secretary of the I.L.G.W.U., sent Newman on a tour of upstate New York to gather money from various union locals, but Newman also raised significant funds from wealthy women, whom she found "very generous, and very interested." She collected about $6,000 before she was through.[17] The League sent Schneiderman to Massachusetts with the same mandate, where she gave speeches and lectures at Faneiul Hall, Radcliffe, Wellesley, Mount Holyoke, and elsewhere, gathering some $10,000.[18] These sums were impressive for the time, and they spoke to a growing interest among wealthier women, well beyond Gotham's borders, in the shirtwaist workers' cause.

Yet expenses for the strike were astronomical, and such speaking tours could not sustain the basic needs of so many strikers over the long term, much less meet the legal fees and bail money associated with the hundreds of arrests and fines being incurred.[19] The strike needed to turn to deeper pockets.

Alva Belmont had such pockets, and League leaders had been developing a relationship with her at least a month before the strike began.[20] Belmont was neither the average middle-aged widow, nor the average, genteel New York society lady. Born Alva Erskine Smith in Mobile, Alabama, on January 17, 1853, and possessed (by her own account) of an "iron will" at birth, she later claimed to have had her first inklings of feminist consciousness at age four, when her older brother Murray died. Noticing that her father, relatives, and neighbors seemed far more distraught over Murray's death than they had been when her sister Eleanor died, she concluded, " 'So then . . . a dead son is worth more than a live daughter. Even when my Brother is dead, my Father cares more for him than for his girls.' . . . I did not suffer with tearful sadness but with violent resentment."[21]

That resentment may have contributed to her early rejection of what she later called the "static quality to a girl's life." She became something of a tomboy who lacked "a single intimate girl playmate," and instead relished the "life of a boy with its excitement, freedom, and adventure."[22] She insisted in hindsight that this attitude had nothing to do with gender confusion or envy, but instead reflected a refusal to deny herself the pleasures of behavior deemed, at the time, appropriate only for boys. Such behavior, she wrote, "belonged to human beings. Adventure, excitement, liberty, freedom from excessive restraint were the blessings which life offered to all irrespective of sex." Her parents predictably disagreed, but in spite of repeated whippings and punishments, they could not stifle what Belmont described as "a force in me that seemed to compel me to do what I wanted to do regardless of what might happen afterwards."[23]

Her father, a cotton merchant, moved the family to New York on the eve of the Civil War, and over the next fourteen years Alva's "force" descended upon the city's fashionable circles, culminating in her 1875 marriage to William Kissam Vanderbilt, scion of New York's wealthiest family. Their marriage lasted twenty years, during which she used her tremendous political acumen, creativity, and determination to ascend to the pinnacle of New

York and Newport, Rhode Island, Society.[24] In 1895, however, she scandal-
ized the conservative members of the "Four Hundred" by divorcing Vanderbilt for adultery and then marrying another millionaire heir, Oliver Hazard
Perry Belmont, only months later.

It is telling that, in advising her against pursuing the divorce, Alva's head
legal counsel Joseph H. Choate tried to persuade her that not only would it
be ruinous for her personally, but for the wealthy as a class. Belmont recalled,

> He saw the growing social unrest due to the piling up of immense fortunes
> in the hands of a few. He was wise enough to know that Wealth must expose
> itself to as little criticism as possible in order to hold its own. If the people
> saw that those who handled great fortunes were profligate in their living,
> incapable of nobly meeting their responsibilities, regarding themselves be-
> yond the reach of Law and subject to none of the standards of decency and
> honor by which others lived, the outcry against Wealth would be increased.
> The populace would rise against them. They would demand that these un-
> crowned kings be dethroned.[25]

Belmont's reference to Choate's wisdom suggests that she grew to appreciate
the naked truth of what he told her. She also found his solution of repress-
ing the wealthy's bad (or discountenanced) behavior from public view to be
morally reprehensible. Comparing Choate's logic to that of a notorious immigrant extortion racket, she wrote in retrospect, "I think his idea was that
there should be something of the same conspiracy of silence among the
Rich that exists among members of the Black Hand Society."[26]

Choate's warnings to Belmont regarding her personal situation were only
partially fulfilled: divorcing Vanderbilt and swiftly marrying O. H. P. Belmont resulted in a few "cold looks, insolent stares, or complete evasions," but
hardly in conspiratorial ostracism.[27] Whatever shunning of the newlyweds
occurred grew at least as much out of anti-Semitism (Alva was Episcopalian,
and Oliver a nonpracticing Jew) and Belmont's refusal to forego her alimony
from Vanderbilt upon her second marriage (which promptly alienated her
new in-laws) as it did from the controversy over her divorce. Regardless,
cold shoulders were powerless to interfere with what was the happiest period in Belmont's life. She succeeded in orchestrating her daughter's engagement to the Duke of Marlborough (much to that unfortunate young

woman's dismay), traveled freely between Europe and her mansions in New York, Newport, and Long Island, and most importantly, replaced a philandering husband with a devoted one. O. H. P. Belmont, she recalled wistfully decades later, "for a few short years completed life for me."[28]

Toward the close of the twentieth century's first decade, however, her happiness began to unravel. In the space of the four years before the shirtwaist strike, two friends, two sisters, a step-daughter, and her husband all died. O. H. P. Belmont's death of complications from appendicitis on June 10, 1908, devastated her, leaving her "ill for a long time."[29] Her sole surviving sister lived in France, and her daughter, now the Duchess of Marlborough, was unhappy in the marriage her mother had arranged. The Vanderbilt and Belmont families would have nothing to do with her.[30] She was isolated, bereft of practically all family and everyone dear to her. Yet she still possessed enormous wealth and social capital, and her sense of the world's injustice had been further stimulated. Searching for solace and new purpose, she gravitated to the women's suffrage movement.

Although she entered the movement through N.A.W.S.A. connections, Belmont quickly determined that the national organization had become both too conservative and too inconspicuous for her taste. Her judgment mirrored that of more militant women's rights activists such as Harriet Stanton Blatch, a dedicated feminist and pioneer of cross-class suffrage efforts. Blatch had formed a splinter group in New York in 1907, the Equality League of Self-Supporting Women, in frustration at N.A.W.S.A.'s unwillingness to include wage-earning women in either its vision for political equality, or its organizational strategy.[31] She wrote dismissively that the older group's effort at the time "was being wasted on its supporters in private drawing rooms and in public halls where friends, drummed up and harried by the ardent, listlessly heard the same old arguments."[32] Belmont, like Blatch, wanted to take more radical steps.[33]

While visiting England in April 1909 as a N.A.W.S.A. delegate to the International Woman Suffrage Alliance Convention, the millionaire widow acquired a different vision of what the American women's movement could look like, but not from the convention's "suffragist" proceedings. Instead, she was powerfully drawn to the militant actions—street meetings, public marches, demonstrations, and the like—of the local English "suffragettes," finding it "utterly impossible to concentrate on the international aspect" by contrast.[34] Belmont yearned to be part of building a force like the one she saw in the suffragette movement, describing her desire in the most universal terms:

> I saw and heard the terrific rush of the impulses of English women toward liberty. It was as if millions of atoms were being hurled toward a solution. . . . I became acutely sensitive to the oneness of myself with these atoms. . . . I saw that the value of the strength of each tiny, frail atom was dependent upon the complete whole. I longed to throw myself into this turbulent tide and to feel myself strengthened by the substance of the whole.[35]

The Society maven was receiving a firsthand lesson in the life-altering power of collective action, a lesson that culminated in her attendance, on April 29, at a rally in Albert Hall where the international suffragists "were the guests of the English suffragettes."[36] "What a revelation!" she wrote of the gathering. "Such electric fervor I had never seen nor felt in all my experience! This was not a suffrage meeting. This was a flowing together of humanity in the mass. . . . The thousands seemed to pour in from the highways and byways. . . . I was exalted."[37]

Watching these thousands engage passionately with women speakers recently released from prison and making unabashedly political appeals to a motley crowd of supporters and detractors, Belmont felt shame for the mainstream American women's movement she had come to London to represent—not only for its tactical timidity, but also for the limitation of its vision. "The tendency in all reform movements is to re-convert those already won," she wrote. "This is a sublime state and requires no fortitude. To go out and convert the multitude. There lies the path of self-denial and certain revilement."[38] The Albert Hall meeting drove home for Belmont that the absence of such "revilement" corresponded not to respect, but to irrelevance. Belmont returned to America determined to exert a politicizing, radicalizing influence on the U.S. suffrage movement, and with a far more inclusive vision of who should participate. As she said in September to the *New York Evening Journal*, "We are all equal—rich and poor alike— and all should join in this movement."[39]

It was undoubtedly that vision she had in mind when she rented the Hippodrome Theater, the "largest building of its kind in the world," for a rally in support of the shirtwaist strikers on December 5.[40] Although Belmont's writings do not specify her initial attraction to the strike, it is almost certain—especially in light of her contact with the League in October— that she would have been following its course in the news since well before the general strike vote, at least since policemen caused their front-page scandal by arresting Mary Dreier. When the general strike erupted, the press in the early weeks made it clear that it was overwhelmingly a fight of women against men. The day after the strike vote, the *Times* headline read "40,000 Called Out in Women's Strike."[41] The next day's headline ran "Waist Strike On; 18,000 Women Out," and the *Tribune*'s was "Army of Girls Idle."[42] Belmont had been hoping for an opportunity to radicalize the woman suffrage movement and to tie it to the struggle of women at every social echelon, and the strike was the perfect opportunity. The I.L.G.W.U. announced Belmont's support publicly on November 30.[43] The very next day, she announced the Hippodrome meeting.[44]

It was a fair, unseasonably balmy Sunday afternoon, and people began arriving at the Hippodrome early, in droves.[45] Once the doors opened, it took only half an hour for the crowd of somewhere between 6,000 and 8,000—well beyond the venue's seating capacity of 5,300—to pack itself inside.[46] As the *Washington Post*'s reporter put it, "there were enough people in the Hippodrome to provide a whole family of Cooper Unions with audiences."[47] Police outside the bulging building struggled to contain the rush and turned away hundreds still clamoring for entrance, while the audience inside, mainly young strikers, quickly overflowed onto the stage and into the orchestra pit, laying bodily claim to the space.[48] A band played throughout the seating process, and a collection for the strikers began going around the arena before any speaker took the stage.[49] In its sheer size, the event easily surpassed the Albert Hall rally which had so inspired Belmont earlier that year.

The auditorium and its settings, the *New York Times* reported, "were for a woman suffrage meeting. Flags of blue on both side walls carried the words in white, 'Votes for Women.' Three small drops hung down . . . carrying arguments in big letters. . . . 'We demand equal pay for equal work,' the audience read; and 'Give women the protection of the vote.'" Yet Belmont's

Political Equality Association (P.E.A.), the rally's sponsor, had anticipated the audience's predominant demographic of strikers, so many of the banners and hangings also proclaimed the endorsements of various unions for the suffrage cause.[50] Indeed, Belmont's statement to the press when she announced the event the previous week had clearly signaled that the rally was meant to be a merging of two movements, not the projection of one over the other: "The Political Equality Association recognizes the fact that women must organize politically as well as industrially if they are to permanently secure the benefits of industrial freedom."[51]

John Howard Melish, the rector of Holy Trinity Church in Brooklyn and master of ceremonies for the event, echoed this message in his opening remarks, noting, "There are two spirits abroad in our city today—one is the spirit of self-help, the other is the spirit of co-operation."[52] He explicitly referred to class differences by saying that "the meeting had been called to protest against the use of the police power by any one class in the community against another."[53] Yet circumstances made his mention of class differences ambiguous. Given the proliferating incidents of policemen abusing strikers, Melish might have been referring to the workers as the "class" suffering under unfair policing, but the mention of police power a month after Mary Dreier's widely publicized arrest suggested that the "class" against whom "police power" was being unfairly deployed consisted of not only an economic class, but all women.

He then celebrated both the emerging self-sufficiency of working women and their willingness to cooperate with the wealthy.[54] "The working women of New York," he observed approvingly, "are beginning to realize that they must help themselves. They do not resent the kindly interest in them on the part of some employers or philanthropic people. But they are beginning to realize that only as they help themselves will they be permanently helped."[55] Though congratulating the women on their lack of resentment toward the wealthy hardly qualified as a ringing endorsement of cross-class cooperation, the larger message of mutual help and solidarity fell on eager ears. As the *Call* reported, the audience warmed particularly to this message. "'Singly,'" Melish said, women "'can do little or nothing to lower hours, raise wages, or improve conditions, but together' (at this moment a flash exploded and there was tremendous applause). He then continued: 'Together they can do everything for themselves and for society.'"[56]

Six major speakers followed, the first of whom was William A. Coakley. A trade unionist representing New York's Central Federated Union, Coakley was probably a late addition to replace Samuel Gompers (who had been featured prominently in the P.E.A.'s press releases as a potential speaker for the event). Gompers had counseled against the strike at the Cooper Union strike vote itself, and preferred to be involved thereafter principally by proxy, or to play the role of mediator between the manufacturers and the I.L.G.W.U. (though his role would become murkier later).[57] Coakley, as the sole speaker from the mainstream trade union movement at the Hippodrome, aped Gompers's unsustainable balancing act between labor solidarity on the one hand, and conservatism regarding both strikes and social upheaval on the other. Coakley insisted that both rich and poor owed their sympathy to the shirtwaist strikers and urged the strikers to hold out for union recognition, but he also looked forward to a time "not far distant when there would be no further need of strikes, as the interests of labor and capital were identical."[58]

This earned a direct rebuke from the second speaker, Rose Pastor Stokes, a well-known socialist activist whose prominence among the speakers underscored Belmont's intention that the event be truly inclusive. Stokes dismissed Coakley's rose-tinted vision of a harmonious future, bluntly asserting, "The philosophy of Karl Marx has made clear to me where the struggle lies, not through the fault of any man, but because there are two great classes—those who own and control the land and industries of a country, and those who apply to them for work—between those who are exploiters and we who are exploited."[59] Belmont, the millionaire, had given a public platform to a staunch Marxist.

Then again, however deeply Stokes identified with the exploited, her relationship to the working class was slightly more complicated than her self-presentation might suggest, allowing her to make potentially inflammatory statements with less danger of alarming the bourgeois suffrage ladies in attendance. Her life story mirrored the plotlines of sentimental mass-market fiction, just then becoming popular with the Hippodrome's audience of young, working women.[60] After emigrating from Polish Russia and working for years as a child laborer in Cleveland cigar factories, Rose Pastor had moved to New York as a journalist and married the Progressive millionaire J. G. Phelps Stokes, becoming fabulously wealthy herself. Moreover, she converted her husband to socialism, the principles of which she had learned on the shopfloor.[61] In both her person and her rhetoric, she reinforced the strikers in their budding belief that they deserved better, and that they could claim it for themselves. Meanwhile, although her words may have unnerved the suffrage ladies somewhat, her marriage gave them reasonable reassurance that in the interests of self-preservation she would not advocate bloody revolution.

Stokes made at least a passing effort to articulate that reassurance by distinguishing her opposition to the economic system of capitalism from any personal animus toward wealthy individuals. She had, after all, become wealthy herself (and would struggle painfully with the implications of that transformation for the duration of her marriage to J. G. Phelps Stokes), so she could hardly have been insensible to the way stable access to funding could support efforts for social change. The *Times* reported that she "had no grudge against capitalists individually and personally," just that "she was doing all she could to destroy the breed of parasitic capitalists" who ruthlessly exploited workers—in this instance, the garment manufacturers of New York.[62]

More importantly, on the issue of suffrage, Stokes effectively repeated Belmont's own injunction from the P.E.A.'s press release that women—or, in Stokes's case, "working people"—must pursue a combined program of political and industrial liberation. "I believe that the ballot," she told the assembled crowd, "can do the working people of this country little good unless they use that ballot to free themselves industrially."[63] Stokes freighted the point with more militant undertones than the P.E.A. press release had done, but the common ground between the socialist and the millionaire was clear enough.

Anna Howard Shaw, effectively the headlining speaker for the event, continued in this vein of cooperative speechmaking, early on declaring to the strikers, "Our cause is your cause, and your cause is our cause."[64] She underlined this point by devoting large swaths of her address to vivid expressions of union solidarity, near-socialist critiques of contemporary inequality, and intense indictments of patriarchy. Belying the staid, conservative reputation of the suffrage movement, she sermonized to the crowd's delight, "So in this country today, in order to make millionaires richer, in order that they may have more palaces, more automobiles, and build more libraries, we are feeding to the mills of this country the little children who ought to be playing in our parks and going to our schools. And we call that a great nation?"[65] On union strength, her rhetoric approached the lyrical: "Personally, I believe in trade unions. You can't strike a blow with one finger or two fingers, but when you want to strike you put all your fingers together, clinch them hard, and then let drive."[66] Shaw even layered her suffrage advocacy—which defended a conservative, domestic ideal of womanhood—with an acknowledgment of industrial and material reality, declaring, "Men keep telling us we should go back to the home and do the work our grandmothers did. We can't; the men have taken that work out of the home, have put it in factories, and we must go out of the home to do it. . . . We don't go out to work because we like it. . . . We do those things because we have to."[67]

Of the three remaining speakers, Reverend Alexander Irvine and Publio Mazzella struck a similar note of awe and celebration at the unprecedented forces being joined under a single roof in common cause. Irvine pledged to the strikers, "We are here today . . . to demonstrate that New York is not dead and to tell you that behind every fight of every weak man and every weak woman stand the best people of New York."[68] Mazzella, speaking in Italian with both pride and provocation, reminded all assembled that "for the first time in the history of the Italian labor movement in this city an Italian speaker has been asked to speak at such a meeting as this."[69] It fell to Leonora O'Reilly of the New York W.T.U.L. to tell the story of the strike, of the terrible working conditions and disrespect that had driven so many young women into the streets to protest, and to identify the principal glue holding the different class constituencies together. "I am here by the right of three generations of shirt makers," she said, "my mother's mother having sung the song of the shirt when the potatoes went out in Ireland."[70] Her invocation of workers over generations was also an invocation of women—grandmothers, mothers, and daughters—reinforcing the spirit of female cooperation between Belmont in her box and the strikers packed into the general seating area.

O'Reilly probably had more right than any other woman in the Hippodrome that day to invoke the spirit of female cooperation: she had embodied it her entire life. She was a native New Yorker whose father, having lost all the family's money in a failed business venture, died a broken man shortly after her birth. His death meant that O'Reilly had to exchange classroom schooling for sewing collars in a garment factory at the age of eleven; by fourteen she had seen her wages cut in half, making her well-attuned to injustice by the time her mother and fellow garment worker, Winifred, began introducing her to radical and labor circles. O'Reilly quickly took the lead, joining the Knights of Labor at sixteen, persuading her mother to join as well, then promptly organizing the Working Women's Society, a cross-class advocacy group pledged "to secure better conditions for the working people" in part through "collecting statistics, promoting labor organizations, and pressuring for labor legislation."[71]

O'Reilly forged her first friendships with bourgeois women in this work and began to see the difference such cooperation could make. Among others, she befriended Josephine Shaw Lowell, whose experience engaging with working women as collaborators in the Working Women's Society instead of as supplicants to the Charity Organization Society began a long process of intellectual reorientation for the blue-blood widow away from the latter group's insistence on the moral sources of poverty.[72] O'Reilly spent much of her life educating bourgeois women like Lowell about the reality of working-class life, and organizing them to help improve it. In return, they periodically paid for O'Reilly to take breaks from her garment industry jobs, encouraging her to pursue continuing education, become a popular public speaker, and ultimately devote herself full-time to the W.T.U.L.'s labor and women's activism. She played the role of the loyal dissident, insisting that the League be a truly collaborative endeavor among women from all class backgrounds, and fighting the tendency among some League members, as she put it, to exhibit "the attitude of a lady with something to give her sister."[73]

O'Reilly radiated this insistence on women's collaboration from the Hippodrome stage, and the meeting was a success for the cooperative, inclusive spirit that she and Belmont hoped to foster—not because the speakers agreed with each other, which they clearly did not, but because the common interests of the strike and women's suffrage enjoyed universal support, and a spirit of women's solidarity across class lines ran high. The *New-York Tribune* gave perhaps the best indication of the rally's effectiveness by leading its story with a question and its answer: "Was it the cause of woman suffrage or the strikers? It was hard to tell."[74] As Shaw's declaration of common cause implied, both rich and poor women found any mutual class antagonism outweighed in the moment by the urgency of a shared purpose as women, and the utility of help forthcoming from the other side. Months earlier, Belmont had been explicit about this from a suffragist standpoint, telling the *New York American* that "many in society are not in favor of the suffrage cause because it has to deal too much with what is called the 'common people.' In my opinion, nothing will bring about success any more quickly than the fact that all classes of people stand shoulder to shoulder in the fight for the cause."[75] Bertha Poole Weyl, the Strike Committee's secretary, agreed on behalf of labor, remarking, "The industrial and women suffrage movement must go together in this strike."[76]

Some of the press about the rally in the following days underscored its success at creating both the impression and reality of collective ties between women of different classes. The *Washington Post* commented on the audience reaction more than most other papers, consistently indicating that speakers' messages of women's togetherness or condemnations of patriarchy elicited firm endorsements from the crowd. One of the *Post*'s subheadings ran "Women Pack New York Hippodrome to Demand 'Square Deal' for Strikers and for Sex in General—Denunciation of Male Dictation Arouses Excited Approval." The story noted that all six thousand women in attendance seemed "mighty serious in the belief that they had sense enough and ability enough to get the same kind of deal that men do."[77] Gesturing specifically toward the cross-class enthusiasm for women's rights, the writer observed, "Auditorium, boxes, and galleries rang loudly to their cheers whenever a speaker, especially a woman speaker, brought her two hands together with a smack and said that the time was past for man dictation."[78] The *Chicago Daily Tribune* underscored this sentiment by noting that the few "male persons" in the audience "seemed to sit stiffly and affect perfect composure . . . but when the 6,000 shirtwaists rustled ominously and the 12,000 hands came together with a terrible impact, the smiles tightened and the male persons looked as if they thought there was something in it after all."[79]

Even more evocative of the fact that women's solidarity fueled the cooperative class encounter of the Hippodrome rally was Evalyn A. Burnham's letter, appearing in the next day's *New York Call*. "I love women," Burnham wrote, "all women, good or bad, right or wrong—even the anti-suffragists.

I believe love wins more than hate, cordiality than exclusiveness, co-operation than competition."[80] Citing an ongoing debate within Socialist Party ranks, particularly in East Coast urban centers, about whether to support the mainstream suffrage movement, Burnham remarked, "It seems somewhat narrow as well as unnecessary to oppose a movement which is so progressive as the woman suffrage movement just because all of its members would not vote the Socialist ticket."[81] Arguing that the Socialist ticket would tend to attract women empowered with the franchise, making woman suffrage a political boon to the Party, she declared, "However, even if it did not all women are our sisters—Mrs. Belmont as well as the poorest working woman—and to have one set of sisters opposing another set, when both are working along progressive lines seems to me unwise."[82]

Yet in both the proceedings of the event, and in the reporting of it, some dissonant notes resounded as well, indicating the potential difficulties for such cross-class cooperation's longevity. Despite Anna Howard Shaw's own enthusiasm about the rally—she wrote to the N.A.W.S.A. board calling it a "tremendous success" and declaring that "it did more to reconcile the labor people with the Suffrage movement than anything that has ever happened"— she had appeared at the Hippodrome explicitly as an individual, not as a representative of the organization she served as president.[83] Thus, while Belmont succeeded in creating the appearance in the press of suffragists' full-throated sanction of the strike, many N.A.W.S.A. members remained apprehensive about yoking the suffrage movement to the far more radical (at least, as represented by the I.L.G.W.U.) labor movement.[84]

Such concerns were by no means exclusive to the bourgeois side of the potential cross-class collaboration. As Burnham's letter suggests, a significant faction within the labor movement and the Socialist Party viewed the suffragists' involvement in the strike as half-hearted at best, and hypocritically opportunistic at worst. Bertha H. Mailly, writing to the *Call's* "Woman's Sphere" column a few days after the Hippodrome meeting, noted that the president of the Interborough Teachers' Association, who occupied "a prominent position in the suffrage movement of the city" and whose organization's equal pay initiative had been prominently featured at the rally, had refused even "to entertain a resolution offering the sympathy and assistance of that body to the striking shirtwaist makers and protesting against the brutal treatment of the girls by the police."[85] In Mailly's view, the suffragists would use the strikers and socialists for their ends, but as in this instance, refuse to aid them in return. The reason was clear. These ladies, she argued, "although they believe in suffrage for women, advocate it from the sex-conscious rather than the class-conscious point of view." Such divergent visions pointed ominously to "the impracticability of working in close co-operation with a movement whose basic point of view is not the working-class one."[86]

Mailly had identified a profound potential source of misunderstanding, disagreement, and animosity within an otherwise promising women's coalition, but her point did not obviate the strikers' most basic, immediate need: money to carry on the strike. The Hippodrome meeting had garnered exceptional publicity, and both Belmont and the W.T.U.L. proceeded to capitalize on that publicity by organizing further fundraising events. One of those events would attract more quizzical public notice than any other: a tea at the Colony Club, the exclusive women's retreat for New York's most refined Society ladies. This event proved a crucial turning point for the strike, and for the cross-class women's collaboration undergirding it, not least because of who helped to organize it: Anne Tracy Morgan.

12

To Cooperate or Condescend

> They've brought me to their fashionable clubhouse to hear about
> our misery. To tell the truth, I've no appetite to tell it to them,
> for I've almost come to the conclusion that the gulf between us
> girls and these rich ladies is too deep to be smoothed over by a
> few paltry dollars; the girls would probably be the better off in
> the long run if they did not take their money. They would the
> sooner realize the great contrast and the division of classes; this
> would teach them to stick to their own.
>
> —Theresa Serber Malkiel

FINANCIAL INDUSTRY WORKERS sometimes referred to J. P. Morgan by
the nickname "Jupiter," the Latin cognate of the all-powerful, thunderbolt-
wielding Greek god, Zeus.[1] In most accounts of the Uprising, his daughter
Anne Morgan enters the narrative not so differently than Athena, Zeus's
daughter—sprung fully formed into the world, with no possible explanation
of her prior development.[2] This is misleading, for Anne Morgan had, in fact,
spent the better part of two years before the strike becoming increasingly
involved in campaigns to improve workplace conditions, wages, and benefits
for a variety of workers. She did not, as Margaret Dreier Robins speculated
in a letter to her sister a few days after the strike began, live "in deadly terror
of her father."[3] Counseled by her close friend (and, in all likelihood, lover),
Elizabeth "Bessie" Marbury, Morgan had entered "a brilliant international
demimonde of aesthetic appreciation, social activism, and female independence," years before the shirtwaist workers hit the streets.[4]

In March 1908, Morgan had helped form a Women's Auxiliary to the National Civic Federation (N.C.F.). The N.C.F. was a profoundly conservative organization that aimed to protect the existing structures of capitalism through collaboration between businessmen, labor leaders, and policy makers, but its women's auxiliary would focus more narrowly on conducting factory inspections and exerting pressure on "individual manufacturing firms in whose workshops are found abuses or unsatisfactory conditions."[5] Morgan hosted the founding meeting of the Women's Civic Federation in her father's Madison Avenue home, forging plans to reform industrial capitalism—albeit modestly—in that very system's inner sanctum.[6]

At least some of the wealthy women at this meeting had few illusions about their complicity in the injustices they sought to redress, and the presence of representatives from the American Federation of Labor (A.F.L.), the Firemen's Union, and the Teamsters did not make them bashful. As Florence Jaffray Harriman, wife of the banker J. Borden Harriman, declared at that first gathering, "Some of us are the wives or sisters of employers of large numbers of factory operatives, or perhaps ourselves are owners and stockholders in companies. Should not the woman who spends the money which the employes [sic] help to provide, take a special interest in their welfare, especially in that of the women wage earners?"[7] Her question reflected both a genuine desire "to remove the estrangement and want of sympathy out of which so much social prejudice, distrust, and class feeling have grown" and a clear maternalist condescension grounded in notions of appropriately nurturing womanhood and *richesse oblige*.

Eight months before the shirtwaist strike, the clumsiness of joining a desire for cross-class reconciliation with such a patronizing attitude came through powerfully in the public visit Morgan's group made to inspect conditions in the federal government's Bureau of Engraving and Printing. While their visit uncovered an unhygienic work environment and inadequate food for the workers, leading to improvements, speakers for the Federation also advised the women workers during their visit that self-help was the appropriate remedy for unwanted male attentions in the workplace. "If the working girl shows plainly that she will brook no familiarity from men they will soon desist," averred Mrs. Archibald Hopkins. Bessie Marbury advised the women to join professional unions, then she justified the advice by suggesting that refusal to join indicated a selfishness incompatible with being a good wife or mother.[8] Hopkins and Marbury provide a good index of Morgan's position—sufficiently invested in progressive reform to devote large portions of time, effort, and money to achieve it, yet also having no frame of reference for understanding the material reality of working women's lives, and harboring decidedly conservative notions of gender, class, and political action.

It was in this context and spirit that Morgan formed an interest in the strike, and helped organize a lunch under the auspices of the W.T.U.L. at the Colony Club, where the "girl strikers" could tell their stories to wealthy clubwomen. As she told members of the press, who were naturally licking their chops at the prospect of ragged East Side teenagers being welcomed into the most exclusive women's club in New York,

> The idea of inviting the shirtwaist makers to speak is a very simple one. We feel that what this strike stands for is not altogether understood and that the more people who hear their story the better it will be for their cause. That is all. There is nothing socialistic or suffragistic in the project. We feel that the shirtwaist makers are having a hard time and that they need the sympathy of the public.[9]

The difference between Morgan's framing of this event and Belmont's framing of the Hippodrome rally could not have been clearer. Where Belmont celebrated the potential alliance of the labor and suffrage movements in explicitly political terms, Morgan disavowed both. Where Belmont's P.E.A. had organized a program of speakers that included known socialists and encouraged strikers in the audience to embrace their own political power, Morgan seemed eager to cast the strikers as helpless victims in need of salvation through "the sympathy of the public." Indeed, it is unclear from her statement to the press whether, in her mind, "the project" containing "nothing socialistic or suffragistic" was the Colony Club tea or the strike itself.

Ironically, Morgan seems to have received her initial firsthand account of the strike from a socialist, though she may not have known it. After hearing Rose Schneiderman speak at a meeting of the Women's Education Society about how the poverty of working women could drive them to prostitution, Morgan sent her a note requesting a visit for the purpose of obtaining a more thoroughgoing explanation of the strike's goals.[10] Though Schneiderman, years later, recalled asking her League colleagues, "What does the daughter of that capitalist want from us?" she did meet with Morgan and found her "a very nice and intelligent person."[11] Presumably, Schneiderman emphasized the appalling working and living conditions that the shirtwaist workers faced as a result of the industry's abuses, rather than couching her arguments in explicitly political language. Whatever the socialist union organizer said, Morgan seems to have emerged from the meeting with a limited view of the strike's political implications, and a much more vivid, personal understanding of the shirtwaist makers' exploitation. She proved eager to sell that view to the press in answering questions about the Colony Club event. As she put it to another reporter, if wealthy women were "to fully recognize these conditions we cannot live our lives without doing something."[12] More than three weeks into the strike, however, with scores of employers already having settled on the union's terms, many strikers were now facing adversity with a far greater sense of empowerment than victimhood. The stage was set for an awkward experience.

After the ten strikers and their allies had entered the Colony Club's gymnasium, Florence Jaffray Harriman, president of the club, began the meeting by expressly insisting that the club had no official position on the strike and "could take none," but "was glad to offer its rooms for the meeting, so that individuals who might be interested could hear what the strikers had to say."[13] Then, apparently at the request of the event's three principal organizers (Morgan, Marbury, and Mrs. Edgerton L. Winthrop), Mary Dreier introduced John Mitchell, the former president of the United Mine Workers and an N.C.F. official, who read a letter that the garment manufacturers consortium had addressed to the clubwomen, and whose full text had appeared in the *Times* that morning.[14] Attempting to preempt the strikers' testimony, the employers claimed in the letter that they had agreed to arbitration to end the strike (which Mitchell refuted, pointing out that they refused to arbitrate the central question of union recognition), and accused Clara Lemlich of lying about receiving a $3 weekly salary when in fact she had been earning $15 a week. In other words, before hearing testimony from the workers, Morgan and her compatriots began the meeting by forcing their guests to sit through an articulation of the bosses' position.

It is unsurprising then, that when Lemlich stood up to defend herself against accusations of dishonesty, she did so "without a smile."[15] At twenty-three years of age, Lemlich had already endured the kind of life that disinclined her to suffer fools lightly. From her early childhood in the Ukrainian village of Gorodok, she had defied tremendous odds—the vicious anti-Semitism of tsarist Russia, Orthodox Jewish law, and parental prohibitions and punishments—to become literate in Russian as well as Yiddish. When her father found and burned the stash of Russian books she had bought with her earnings from sewing buttonholes onto shirts, she simply started it again, hiding the forbidden texts in a different place. Her determined self-education, pursued in secret and in constant fear of detection, led her not only to classic Russian literature, but to revolutionary thought, when a sympathetic neighbor began lending her anti-tsarist books and pamphlets.[16]

Her family emigrated in 1903, and the conditions of her first jobs in New York's garment industry inflamed her teenage inclination toward revolution. She enrolled in Marxist theory classes at the Socialist' Party's Rand School, joined with other immigrants eager to organize workers, and fomented unrest in shops all over the city. She brooked no disrespect, either from employers, or from men in the labor movement and Socialist Party, whose sexism and arrogance were a continual source of irritation and frustration.

By 1909, despite the oppressive patriarchy of the labor movement, Lemlich had risen to the executive board of I.L.G.W.U. Local 25, and had participated in multiple strikes and organizing drives. In September, she was hospitalized after a savage beating in which hired thugs broke her ribs in retaliation for her leadership of the strike at the Leiserson factory.[17] Undeterred, she mounted the Cooper Union stage two months later to deliver an impromptu address to a packed gathering of garment workers considering a walkout. After hours of vacillating speeches from male labor leaders, and in a moment that has acquired legendary status in U.S. labor history, she dismissed the men's hesitation with a few pointedly clipped Yiddish phrases and brusquely called for a general strike.[18] The crowd roared its approval. If Alva Belmont had an "iron will," Lemlich's was made of steel.

Facing a very different crowd at the Colony Club than she had at Cooper Union, she spoke with the same brevity and directness. "My dear ladies," she said, "I will tell you about myself . . . it is not true that I said I was making only $3 or $6 in a bad shop to work in. I said other girls were working that way. . . . I did not strike, dear ladies, because I myself was not getting enough. I struck because the others should get enough. It was not for me; it was for them."[19] Her explanation met with approval and applause. With the unpleasantness of the employers' accusations out of the way, however, the next order of business was a set of further "lectures on unionism" from Mitchell, Dreier, Rose Schneiderman, and a visitor from the Stock-Yard Settlement and Chicago's W.T.U.L., Mary McDowell.[20] The strikers' testimony, allegedly the focus of the event, came last.

When it did come, it was straightforward testimony, usually highlighting abuse, interspersed by questions from the wealthy women "in the balcony."[21] Without giving their names, workers told stories of supporting families on starvation wages, being docked for supplies and machinery malfunctions, and facing arrest and abuse from the police without legal cause. "We have twenty minutes for dinner because the boss he puts a piece of goods over the clock," said one, "and we do not know when to stop until the machinery stops."[22] Another explained that although she technically received an ample wage of $15 per week, this was "for only two months, when the season is steady. . . . Then I walk the streets."[23] One worker described how her company "hired immoral girls to attack us and they would approach us only to give the policemen the excuse to arrest us."[24] The *Call* seems to have been alone in reporting a story meant not to unsettle the audience's sense of justice, but of propriety: "Another little girl told how her boss had called on her at 7 o'clock in the morning in company of a detective, entered her bedroom and ordered the detective to arrest her. She began to scream and neighbors came running to her flat and insisted that the girl be given time to dress."[25]

Practically all the stories somehow cast the strikers as victims, and while the choice to withhold their names served the practical purpose of protecting them from possible retribution on the part of employers, it also magnified an impression of the workers as a victimized, petitioning, and subordinate class of humanity who needed help from above, rather than as individuals decrying injustice and asserting their rights. The physical arrangement of the workers—testifying on the gymnasium floor while looking up to the balcony where some of the rich women sat during their testimony—underscored a more conservative experience of class relations than Belmont's Hippodrome rally had promised.[26] Moreover, the workers' speeches were mediated, if not translated, by allies who had a greater ethnic, class, or political kinship with the clubwomen. Mitchell began the meeting; Dreier introduced striker testimony and periodically supplemented it; and after the Jewish workers (and one Italian) had finished telling their stories, the Reverend Percy Clay Moran served as witness to reconfirm everything they had said.[27] Undoubtedly, the strikers appreciated Mitchell's, Moran's, and above all Dreier's support, both on the picket lines and in the Colony Club, but the need for them to mediate communication between the poor and rich women suggests an assumption on the part of the latter that the statements of immigrant working women required corroboration to be believed or understood.

Certainly, a vast cultural, ethnic, and linguistic gulf separated the working women from their potential benefactresses and undeniably complicated the efforts to create mutual understanding. But the most powerful element that had undergirded the cooperative class encounter of the Hippodrome meeting, one that might have bridged that gulf—a sense of mutual dependency and need as women in a patriarchal society—was absent in the Madison Avenue clubhouse. Morgan, Marbury, and Winthrop had designed and executed the meeting in ways that both implicitly and explicitly reflected and reinforced that absence. Consequently, the proceedings were evocative of the wealthy ladies' tendency to see the strikers as petitioners to their court of mercy, rather than as sisters in a shared struggle. As if to underline that relation, it was only after all the strikers had proven themselves with their testimony that the clubwomen invited them down to tea.[28]

Despite this, the meeting itself seemed initially successful, raising over $1,300 in donations and pledges for the strike fund, and addressing various concerns and questions that the Colony Club members had for the strikers. Dreier, for one, was pleased. "The meeting was splendid," she wrote to her sister, "the girls so dear . . . if all the pledges come in 1500 [sic] almost will be won for the girls." In addition to the pledges (which she overestimated), Dreier noted the potential for badly needed legal help from Morgan. "Miss Morgan has been fine," she wrote to Robins, "& is helping us now in trying to get a big lawyer to take the girls' cases—3 more were sent to the workhouse today."[29] Press coverage of the event extended even across the Atlantic: a friend of Robins's wrote from Berlin on December 18 that "even today's *Paris European Herald* has a front page column about the strike, and the picketing, and a patronizing account of the Colony Club's interest in it."[30] By accruing money, direct assistance, and broad publicity for the strike, the visit to the Colony Club seemed to have been a worthwhile investment of a few hours.

Yet upon reflection, the gains from the meeting seemed either dubious, or offset by drawbacks. Alva Belmont, in a private appeal to fewer than a dozen friends two days earlier, had raised $1,525 for the strike, suggesting by comparison that there was no particular fundraising value added by bringing strikers into the presence of rich ladies for soliciting donations.[31] Newman and Schneiderman also collected many times the amount raised at the Colony Club when they toured New York and Massachusetts, appealing frequently to less wealthy audiences. Morgan's promise of legal help was encouraging, but she was joining an initiative already in progress that combined the resources of the labor movement, the Socialist Party, and the League in finding adequate legal representation for strikers facing fines and jail time. Ultimately, her contribution seemed not to have been the "big lawyer" Dreier had hoped for, but simply her participation in a meeting with other members of the New York W.T.U.L. on December 20, which issued a call for volunteer witnesses who might rebut employer agents' testimony in court. It was helpful, but hardly indispensable.

Indeed, it was Belmont who provided more direct legal help than Morgan, and quite sensationally so—she not only assigned her own lawyer to the Jefferson Market Court hearings on at least on one occasion, but taking the advice of the strikers and strike leaders, showed up to the court in person on December 18. With reporters eagerly tagging along, she stayed until the conclusion of the night's proceedings at three in the morning, when the final four strikers' cases finally came up.[32] Infuriated by the presiding judge's contemptuous attitude toward the strikers and the court personnel's general disrespect toward the most vulnerable defendants, she decried the "class feeling" in the courts, posted bail for all the strikers, and used the opportunity to propagandize for women's suffrage to the press.

Belmont's visit to court, however, exemplified how the Colony Club tea's most obvious benefit—publicity for the strike—was a double-edged sword. On the one hand, it certainly drew more attention to the strike, and with it the potential of new funding sources for the strike fund. On the other hand, the publicity overwhelmingly created the impression that the Society ladies had taken over the direction of the strike, implicitly denigrating or dismissing the women in the labor and reform organizations who had been coordinating the strike from the beginning, not to mention the strikers themselves. Headlines, even if they began to appear in greater profusion, showed an increasing tendency to emphasize the rich women's role in the strike: "Miss Morgan Joins Union" was the front-page splash for the *Washington Post* on December 14.[33] "Rich Women's Aid Gives Strikers Hope" ran the *New York Times* headline on December 17.[34] "Lead Girls on Strike: Mrs. Belmont and Miss Annie [*sic*] Morgan Plan for Shirtwaist Workers" declared the *Boston Globe* on December 20, accompanied by an artist's rendering of Morgan, whose caption read "Miss Annie Morgan, Who with Mrs. O. H. P. Belmont Assumes Charge of Shirtwaist Girls' Strike."[35] Each such headline had the paradoxical effect of garnering more attention for the strike while rendering the strikers themselves less visible in the public eye.

This type of publicity did not sit well with the strike's socialist and trade-union stalwarts. There is no direct testimony from the strikers who spoke at the Colony Club on how the experience made them feel, but accounts from leaders other than Dreier suggest a great deal more ambivalence. Schneiderman, who attended the event, offered a half-hearted defense of it to a meeting of Socialist women four days later, declaring, "I was responsible for taking those girls to that meeting. . . . Just as I think it will do good when the girls tell the reporters what has happened to them so I think it was good to have them talk to the people. You can't limit their education."[36] Years later, she would concede in her memoir, "We were disappointed because [the collection] was only a thousand dollars, and we had expected more from ladies of means."[37]

Theresa Serber Malkiel, who devoted herself to the strike and then fictionalized it as a work of socialist propaganda from the perspective of a worker in *Diary of a Shirtwaist Striker*, did not share Schneiderman's ambivalence, either at the time or in retrospect. In *Diary of a Shirtwaist Striker*, she wrote as if reflecting on the tea, "I couldn't forgive myself for sitting at this rich board . . . if they'd know what's good for them they wouldn't bring us in their midst, for, if anything will, this is sure to arouse the spirit of rebellion. I know it did in me. I felt sore for the rest of the day."[38] Malkiel, of course, had not been at the Colony Club, and the soreness she claimed on behalf of the fictional striker "Mary" more likely reflected her own resentments in the event's aftermath, which she expressed clearly at the Socialist women's meeting. There she warned, "You make a mistake if you think you can work hand-in-hand with the suffragists. . . . I was a suffragist before Mrs. Belmont ever dreamed of it. There is lots of work we can do, but why take the work on Mrs. Belmont's platform? Why not take it on our own?"[39] Morgan and Belmont were getting tremendous public credit for assistance to the strike that, compared with Malkiel's own work and that of many Socialist women, was minimal, far easier to perform, and, in Malkiel's view, of the Janey-Come-Lately variety. It was a bitter pill to swallow, both personally and ideologically.

Leonora O'Reilly offered a challenging response to Malkiel's complaint. "I want fair play and want to give fair play," she said. "If this is an educational work and these other women say, 'Come on our platform,' why not go and use it as a school for educating older people[?]" Advocating pragmatism over ideology, O'Reilly was blunt: "Sometimes you have to close your ears to the name of a school you don't like. If you can get work done with money why not let them do it? If you go on to their platform you may gain a stanch heart."[40]

Unfortunately, O'Reilly was the only woman present with two decades' worth of experience educating bourgeois women on the nature and consequences of their privilege, and seeing the rewards, both spiritual and financial, for the movement. More women seemed to share Malkiel's perspective that day than O'Reilly's and in an ironic twist, their anger toward the wealthy women made them commit the very sin they were accusing the wealthy of: grandstanding, and displaying insulting condescension toward the strikers. One speaker lamented, "I am ashamed of those poor girl strikers taken up among the Four Hundred. . . . Poor girls who only know enough to scream when they are hurt." Clearly the speaker, Dr. Anna Ingerman, did not have a particularly high opinion of the strikers' critical faculties, continuing, "When it is said that Mrs. Belmont pays for the meeting places of the strikers that is enough to blind the working classes."[41] In effect, Malkiel, Ingerman, and others like them thought that the rich women would dupe the workers.

Increasingly lost in both the Colony Club event, and in the recrimination and resentment following it, was the sense of sisterly purpose and solidarity that had seemed to infuse the Hippodrome meeting. In its place were widening gaps of understanding and trust. Every time wealthy and working women faced each other, these differences had the potential to create friction, impeding the movement of a collective, cross-class sisterhood. The Hippodrome meeting, despite foreshadowing some difficulties to come, had largely escaped the creation of serious friction, in part because the organizers and participants recognized and spoke explicitly about their mutual interests and basic equality as women. Doing so enabled them to acknowledge their class differences frankly, while also privileging their mutual interests in a way that rendered those differences less important. Moreover, the meeting had taken place in a relatively nonexclusive arena—a popular theater—in which everyone felt an equal right to be present, and everyone, wealthy or poor, occupied a common identity as a member of the audience.

The Colony Club tea differed in significant measure. The structure of the event involved workers and their union allies appealing to and performing for wealthy women, answering their interrogatory questions, at least some of which were formed on the basis of claims by management. From the start, then, the wealthy women took on a role less as sisters than as proxies for the employers. The space of the event and its physical arrangements—a sumptuous private club in which the workers appealed to the wealthy from a gymnasium floor—echoed stereotypical associations of workers with physical exertion, and of the wealthy with leisure. The question of mutual interest was almost entirely absent—and intentionally so. This was a charitable enterprise, and because of its sentimental focus on the workers' abuse, it called forth a sense of moral and emotional obligation among the affluent rather than a sense of political solidarity as women. The Colony Club tea seemed designed to inflame the embers of resentment and distrust on grounds of class.

The cooperative class relations of the strike's early weeks rested on a foundation of women's solidarity, but repeated manifestations of class difference were gradually eroding that foundation. The day after the Colony Club meeting, the *Call*'s "Woman's Sphere" section ran a column that argued tellingly, "The basic evil of modern conditions is not sex-privilege. [The Socialist] knows that the terrible oppression of the working woman is due almost entirely to the fact that she is a member of the working class, and only very slightly to the fact that she is a member of the female sex."[42] Class distinctions, the column dubiously argued, had "obliterated all sex distinctions, save primarily physiological ones."[43] Consequently, it concluded, the true Socialist "cannot afford to consider the right to the vote of the teacher, the professional woman, the property-owning woman, knowing that these women have all the prerogatives of their class, in spite of their lack of the ballot."[44]

Morgan believed that the working women desperately needed the help of upper-class ladies, but the working women and their more intimate allies had grown increasingly empowered by the strike on their own terms. These were dangerously mismatched positions, and on January 2, 1910, they would come to a head in Carnegie Hall.

13

Sisters at Odds

> It is very reprehensible for Socialists to take advantage of these
> poor girls in these times, and when the working people are in
> such dire straits, to teach their fanatical doctrines.
>
> —Anne Morgan

THE CARNEGIE HALL meeting's express purpose was to protest police brutality and miscarriages of justice in the police courts, where at least two magistrates, Cornell and Barlow, seemed bent on punishing strikers regardless of evidence. The initial public organizing committee for the event included the same combination of "mink brigade" allies, suffragists, and union activists that spearheaded the effort to have volunteer nonpicketers serve as witnesses in court, most notably Belmont, Morgan, and Eva McDonald Valesh, the close confidante of Samuel Gompers who had been assisting with strike publicity.[1] The move for a public meeting made good strategic sense: rather than merely fighting the police and magistrates on the latter's home turf—in the streets and courtrooms—these women decided to fight in the press by detailing their abuses for all to see and hear. Yet this committee's declared objects were limited, and couched in the technical language of constitutional and labor law. As it announced in advance, "Our condemnation of the Magistrates is not sweeping, but some of them have been encroaching unlawfully on the rights of the pickets and the right to free speech."[2]

This central organizing committee, however, delegated responsibility for writing resolutions denouncing those abuses to a subcommittee, and that subcommittee's members had no mink brigade allies on it.[3] Moreover, it included Morris Hillquit, a socialist lawyer and prominent public spokesman for the Socialist Party who had been volunteering as defense counsel for the strikers, and Mary Dreier, who herself had been unlawfully arrested in early November. Both Dreier's and Hillquit's direct experience of law-enforcement abuse and their awareness of its effect on the strikers inclined them toward the strongest possible condemnation of the authorities. As early as mid-December, Dreier was worried that failing to give the strikers' morale a boost in the face of police mistreatment might result in the workers actually beginning to break the law in frustration. As she wrote to her sister, "The girls are getting so terribly discouraged with the treatment of the police and the constant arrest that they are beginning to lose patience and are feeling that if they have to pay anyway to make the payment worth while by doing something for it."[4] Most strikers, Dreier and Hillquit suspected, would have little interest in parsing legal niceties.

Meanwhile, as the subcommittee drew up its resolution, Valesh was busily trying to engineer an end to the strike on some compromise basis, positioning herself in the press as the spokeswoman "for all the agencies at work for the aid of the strikers."[5] Although the employers' association denied having received any communication from her, and she had met an unreceptive audience at a December 29 union meeting when she tried to resurrect a proposed settlement recognizing the union in some shops while foregoing recognition and the closed shop industrywide (an arrangement strikers had unanimously rejected only days earlier), she continued to insist to the *Tribune* that "matters are now, I believe, shaping themselves toward a settlement."[6] To the *Times,* she said, "I feel more encouraged than I did two days ago, and I believe it will not be necessary to carry the fight to the finish."[7]

At the same time, Valesh gave a statement to the press on Morgan's behalf two days before the Carnegie Hall event that suggested both the doyenne's weakening resolve, and her desire to play savior to the strikers, whom she saw as held hostage by the strike rather than empowered by it. Morgan, Valesh explained, was "in full sympathy with the struggle of the shirtwaist girls to obtain recognition for their union," but urged that "any fair and reasonable proposition for a settlement ought to be carefully considered by the girls . . . in order that the suffering among the girls may be stopped by their going back to work with their union recognized and with better conditions than obtained before the strike."[8] In other words, on the eve of a major rally, Morgan and Valesh signaled to the public—and to the garment manufacturers—that while they hoped the union might win recognition, they did not necessarily support the demand for an industrywide closed shop. As Helen Marot observed in an article on the strike published later that year, "The strikers at this time lost some of their sympathizers."[9]

Although the meeting was scheduled to begin at eight o'clock in the evening, a crowd began gathering outside Carnegie Hall's doors by five o'clock in hopes of good seats, swelling to thousands. A full hour before the event, the *Chicago Tribune* reported, "there were such crowds in front of Carnegie hall that the quiet neighborhood began to wonder what was happening."[10] When the doors opened, the hall quickly filled beyond capacity, leaving many among the thousands of spectators only with room to stand. The boxes, meanwhile, held Society and suffragist luminaries: Belmont, Morgan, and former (and future) N.A.W.S.A. president, Carrie Chapman Catt among them. In an indication of both the diverse, cross-class coalition the strike had brought together, and the growing differences between the strikers and their wealthier sympathizers, one box was occupied by Mr. and Mrs. Frederick Taylor, the intellectual progenitors of scientific management and modern management consulting.[11]

The meeting's organizers tried in vain to minimize those differences from the outset. Mrs. Frank H. Cothren, the suffragist and ally who chaired the event, announced "that the gathering was not one of socialists or suffragists, but of just New York citizens anxious for their rights."[12] One newspaper, the *New York American*, reported that Morgan "gave up her box to some acquaintances" and with Bessie Marbury "went down unrecognized into the auditorium to sit with a group of working-girls," passing as working-class.[13]

These were forced attempts to mask waning solidarity. Both politically and culturally, a common identity as "New York citizens" was an unconvincing foundation upon which to build unity: aside from the fact that many of the strikers were recent immigrants with only a nascent sense of municipal attachment, the event explicitly recognized and denounced the disproportionate and abusive deployment of city power against one portion of the crowd and not the other. The atmosphere similarly belied Cothren's assertion of nonpartisanship. As the *New-York Tribune* reported, "from many of the boxes depended the banners of the various women's parties or groups— the Women's Henry George League, the Socialist Women's Committee of the Socialist Party, the Women's Trade Union League and others."[14] A flag displaying the yellow colors of Harriet Stanton Blatch's Equality League of Self-Supporting Women hung from a second-tier box, while another nearby ran "The Single Tax—Free Land, Free Trade, Free People."[15] As the I.L.G.W.U.'s *Souvenir History of the Strike* recorded, "Hearty applause greeted twelve of the women Socialist Committee when they dropped over the edge of their box a white silk banner worked in red."[16] It would have been evident to anyone that the audience comprised strikingly distinctive demographics and political agendas.

Moreover, the physical arrangement of the hall mirrored class hierarchy: wealthy patrons and suffragists disproportionately occupied boxes, while thousands of strikers sat or stood below—and most importantly, in contrast to the Hippodrome rally, the "performance" did not confer audience solidarity. Even if Morgan and Marbury did pass for the evening amid the strikers, photographs and reports in the next day's newspapers confirmed that the visual focus of the hall rested on the more than three hundred strikers seated on stage wearing sashes identifying them as "Arrested," or placards labeling them "Workhouse Prisoner."[17] Their seating on stage intended to honor them for their courage, but it also emphasized, in embodied fashion, the "class feeling" Belmont had observed in the police courts two weeks earlier. If those present in Carnegie Hall were all simply "New York citizens," it was inescapably clear that the perquisites of citizenship had been distributed unequally.

Despite the obvious divisions within the audience, the first speakers, lawyers Miles M. Dawson and Martin W. Littleton, framed their remarks as if addressing just the sort of unified crowd Cothren described. Dawson actually quoted statutes to the crowd detailing circumstances in which arrest without a warrant might be legal, concluding that—in most cases—the strikers' arrests failed to meet the legal requirements. While he at least animated this technical speech by inveighing against individual magistrates (whose names unfailingly drew hisses from the crowd), Littleton offered an argument better suited to an appeals court than a rally. Advising the absent police magistrates to consult "section 170 of the Revised Statutes of the state," he explained that the shirtwaist workers' employers actually had a right "to seek an injunction in a court of equity" against the strike; the fact that they had not done so "indicates that they are not sure they are entitled to an injunction against you strikers."[18] As one reporter commented, "The whole thing took on something of the aspect of a legal discussion tinged with emotion."[19]

Even less advisedly given his audience, Littleton proceeded to argue "that injustice to the working class was not inherent in the laws and legal procedure of the land, but that it was the result of the mistakes of individuals."[20] He offered a spirited defense of the American rule of law, reassuring the crowd (with inexplicable ingenuousness, given that he spoke at a podium flanked by hundreds of illegally and abusively arrested women) "that the institutions of the country were ample to guarantee . . . all the rights and liberties to which they were entitled."[21] He even asserted his own belief in the right, equal to the right to strike, "of every person to work when, where, and for whom and at what wages the person pleased."[22] Defending freedom of contract to a crowd overwhelmingly peopled by strikers who had recently rejected a settlement without a closed shop was an odd oratorical choice. These portions of his speech, one report observed, were "coldly received."[23]

Beyond any specific, infelicitous content in Dawson's and Littleton's addresses, their underlying messages struck a discordant note in the hall's marvelous acoustic space. Dawson deplored assaults of the police and magistrates on "the weakest and the most defenseless of our people."[24] Littleton pointed the strikers toward various legal or rational recourses—suing the magistrates for illegal prosecution and sentencing, suing the police for illegal arrest, or simply presenting employers with "Section 146 of the Labor Act" to demonstrate the legal grounds on which they should recognize the union.[25] He said of those sentenced to the workhouse for disorderly conduct, "Any girl so committed could gain redress through civil action." Each piece of advice further revealed a basic incomprehension of how the material and political reality of workers' lives made the pursuit of legal action practically impossible.[26] The first lawyer cast the strikers as helpless victims; the second advised them as he would individual clients. Neither saw their listeners for what they were: a powerful, seasoned collective made up of women who, on their own, lacked the resources to fight. Six weeks of striking (or, for some Triangle workers, three months) had undoubtedly taken a personal toll on each worker in the audience, but the events of the days previous to the Carnegie Hall rally—including the strikers' unanimous rejection of a settlement on December 27—also demonstrated that the experience had hardened their resolve.[27]

Morris Hillquit recognized the audience's collective power and had no inclination to defend the American legal system nor, for that matter, to assault it. Rather than make police and magistrate abuse the focus of his speech, Hillquit identified the fight for the union as "the very crux, the very heart of the question." Acknowledging that "individually, the shirtwaist makers are weak, defenseless, entirely at the mercy of their employers," he immediately rejoined that "collectively, as an organization, they are strong."[28] The proper recourse for injustice was not the legal system, Hillquit insisted, but collective struggle. The "wise magistrates" who indulged their "prejudice, personal vindictiveness, [and] personal partisanship" in trying and sentencing the strikers, he declared, "do not know the enthusiasm, the spirit and the courage of men and women engaged in a fight for a great and just cause."[29] Dramatically sweeping his arm toward the women seated on the stage behind his podium, he urged the entire hall, "Look at these girls; many of them have served their terms in the workhouse. We honor them here tonight for it. And the judges who pronounced that shameful sentence upon them thereby sentenced themselves to eternal disgrace." Hillquit's judgment carried the weight not of abstruse law, but of history. "Be of good cheer, sisters," he said. "You are not alone in the struggle, your fight is our fight, your cause is good, your fight is brave, your victory will be glorious." The crowd, for the most part, erupted joyously.[30]

Leonora O'Reilly more directly "administered a gentle rebuke to Martin W. Littleton for some of his views unacceptable to trade unionists" before joining her voice with Hillquit's in celebrating the strikers' empowerment.[31] More importantly, she identified the singularity of the strike in its ability to unite like-minded people across class lines. Hoping to salvage some of that unity, O'Reilly "boasted that this strike of six weeks had done more to make people of all classes in this city recognize their common bond of kinship than the preaching of all the churches and all the ethical schools had done in years."[32] It was an optimistic vision of cooperative class relations leading to real social transformation, and one that not at all incidentally chided established institutions of moral guidance.

Even Rose Perr, the diminutive sixteen-year-old striker who might have been the embodiment of feminine victimhood Morgan had described in her statement to the press on the eve of the rally, spoke defiantly about her five-day sentence to the workhouse on Blackwell's Island. She had asked a police captain to arrest a strikebreaker who assaulted one of her friends, and when she appeared in court to act as a witness found herself prosecuted and sentenced for assaulting a strikebreaker based on testimony from witnesses she had never seen before.[33] After recounting this story, she explained to the audience, "So that is why we want to ask whether we are criminals or not?"[34] It was a question that in another context might have seemed an expression of desperation or despair. Before a cheering crowd of thousands, however, and flanked by hundreds of women whose presence on stage demanded an answer to the same question, it seemed more like motivated outrage.

The crowd enthusiastically adopted the subcommittee's statement of resolutions, which was read aloud from the stage. The statement accused "a large number of police officers and several police magistrates" of "revolting partisanship, unfairness and cruelty," denouncing "the conduct of the police . . . as an indefensible abuse of power," and declaring "the city magistrates mentioned to be unfit for judicial office." It then resolved to send copies of the complaint "to all the constituted authorities, both state and municipal" who might provide a solution.[35] It seems impossible that this statement could have escaped prior scrutiny and vetting from those members of the mink brigade organizing the event, and perhaps they had imagined that its qualifications—"a large number" of police, and "several" magistrates—would lend it a tone of reasonable restraint. But in conjunction with Hillquit's, O'Reilly's, and Perr's speeches, amplified by the crowd's anger, the statement's content must have sounded far more incendiary than it had seemed in print. Dawson's and Littleton's speeches—and Morgan's public statement before the event—indicated that they had imagined the constituency adopting the resolution as a victimized, pleading group of individual girls, not a vigorous, furious collective of politically empowered women.

Whether motivated by the crowd's cool response to Littleton, its enthusiastic cheering for Hillquit's insistence on the closed shop, or O'Reilly's dig
at churches, Morgan had a negative reaction to the rally. She issued a statement to the press the next day denouncing Hillquit's and O'Reilly's speeches
as "Socialistic appeals to emotionalism." Again demonstrating her dim,
maternalist view of the strikers' capacity for critical thought and her investment in a more conservative brand of reform, she argued, "It is very reprehensible for Socialists to take advantage of these poor girls in these times,
and when the working people are in such dire straits, to teach their fanati-
cal doctrines. These doctrines are the more dangerous because they tend to
tear down all the good as well as the bad of our present social state."[36] She
continued (in a somewhat self-contradictory manner, given her earlier appeals to end the "suffering of the girls" through a settlement the strikers had
rejected), "Whatever protests are made should not be sweeping or condem-
natory or appeal to sentimentalities."[37]

The next day, the *New York Times* ran a story detailing the rift within
the strike alliance, and printing Hillquit's full reply to Morgan. While defending both himself and O'Reilly from charges of having introduced socialism into their speeches (there is no evidence, in fact, that either did), he
concluded,

> In this strike all supporters and sympathizers of the struggling shirtwaist
> makers, Socialists, trades unionists, settlement workers, suffragettes, and
> good people generally, have been working together harmoniously with the
> sole aim in view to help the striking girls to victory. The movement has been
> entirely free from partisan politics or controversies, and the attempt to intro-
> duce such controversies while the struggle is still in progress is, to say the
> least, rather injudicious.[38]

It was a firm rebuke, but it also recognized the value in holding the diverse
coalition of strike supporters together. But Hillquit could not resist coloring his ostensible attempt to shore up alliances with several digs at Morgan,
slights that implicated the wealthy allies more generally and spoke to sim-
mering resentment. Referring to his speech, he insisted, "I described the
conditions of the girls on strike without bitterness or exaggeration, and if
this description shocked some kind-hearted ladies of the more fortunate

spheres of life, they must blame the conditions described and not Socialism." Underscoring the point, he added, "Altogether I am inclined to think that Miss Morgan's active connection with the labor movement is as yet of too recent date to qualify her as a judge of the manner and methods in which its struggles should be conducted, and I, on my part, deplore her untimely and uncalled-for stricture."[39] The message to Morgan and to other wealthy allies was clear: class position compromised their judgment, and their inexperience rendered their opinion of the strike's methods irrelevant.

This spat may not have, on its own, escalated to the point of fracturing the strike alliance; indeed, there were certain hopeful signs of rapprochement over the following two weeks. Despite her criticism of O'Reilly, Morgan continued to work with the New York W.T.U.L. to aid the strike, attending a meeting on January 6 to discuss the distribution and sale of tickets for a benefit theatrical performance.[40] Furthermore, she traveled to New Rochelle on January 16 to attend a debate between Hillquit and Littleton on the merits of socialism that, according to one report, "at times broke down what might be called party lines or caused differences to be forgotten, and drew forth thunders of applause in which every one in the audience seemed to participate."[41] No other wealthy allies echoed Morgan's public objections to the radical tenor of the Carnegie Hall meeting; Belmont, several days after the event, actually called publicly for a general strike of women in the city to catapult the shirtwaist strikers to victory, a move much more plausibly deserving of the description "Socialistic call to emotionalism" than either Hillquit's or O'Reilly's speeches of January 2.[42] There was reason to hope that cooperative class relations in service of radical action might flourish anew.

But then, on January 21, Eva Valesh publicly denounced the W.T.U.L. as a Socialist front organization in a speech to the Women's Civic Forum, claiming later to the press that she did so on Morgan's behalf. Decrying the League's "dangerous purposes . . . masked by its perfunctory interest for the strikers," she announced the beginning of a campaign for "a new trade union movement" for women that would be free of Socialist taint.[43] She attacked the strike's executive committee as "eighteen men and two girls . . . the men all socialists, connected with the trade perhaps, but ignorant of what the girls want."[44] She then proceeded to undercut her defense of the "girls," on gendered grounds, by insulting them: "those girl strikers are actually grateful to the men who are using them for their own purposes," she said, mimicking them: "'It's so nice of the men, who know so much more than we, to serve on our committees,' they say."[45] When pressed by a woman in the crowd about why the suffragists' ulterior motives for aiding the strike were more legitimate, Valesh responded, "That's different. The suffragists have used the strikers, but they've helped them, given them spiritual vision, and besides, the suffragists say frankly to the strikers, 'We want votes for women,' while the socialists veil their purposes under all sorts of pretences [sic]."[46]

It was a bravura performance: Morgan had never authorized Valesh to make such a speech, but the heiress's subsequent public denial and protestation that she was still a member of the W.T.U.L. garnered much less attention than Valesh's fulminations.[47] If anything, the memory of Morgan's anti-Socialist statement after the Carnegie Hall rally lent Valesh's assertions credibility. Gompers's colleague managed with a single speech to sow distrust for the W.T.U.L. among the wealthier allies, dissension and resentment within the organization itself, and—when longtime League members angrily responded that their organization was absolutely not Socialist— bitterness among the Socialists who had played crucial roles in aiding the strike and the W.T.U.L. throughout.

While the Socialist allies do not seem to have been tricked by Valesh's claim to speak for Morgan (instead inferring, probably correctly, that she was acting as a proxy for Gompers and the A.F.L.), their public response further ruffled feathers among the League's leadership by claiming excessive credit for the strike, and accusing the W.T.U.L. of being inadequately grateful for their assistance.[48] As Margaret Dreier Robins wrote to Mary Dreier in frustration on February 12, days before the strike's official end, "The socialist women (in Chicago) . . . voted never again to co-operate with the Women's Trade Union League in any city because of the great discourtesy shown by the New York Women's Trade Union League to the socialist women." Referring to the Valesh speech, she noted, "This is also simply interesting in view of the great hullabaloo made by some of your New York executive board members." Privately, Robins wished a pox on both the suffragists and the socialists. "Some one [sic] said to me in New York that the Philadelphia [sympathy] strike was won by the suffragists as they were the only women who had helped," she recalled to her sister, "and I merely remarked that I thought the socialists and the suffragists might fight it out between them as both claimed absolute victory."[49]

In the end, the promising cooperative class relations of the strike's early days devolved into feuds over ideology, methods, and who deserved either credit for the strike's successes, or blame for its failures. Largely forgotten were the two elements that had made it such a powerful moment in the first place: solidarity premised on the shared experience of womanhood, and the collective power of the workers themselves. Those doors of transgressive communication that women like Dreier, Schneiderman, Belmont, and Lemlich had gingerly begun to open on the basis of shared womanhood and humanity suddenly slammed shut, blown back by the prevailing winds of class difference, distrust, and disdain.

The strike could not sustain its cross-class base of power long enough to achieve total victory. Drained of funds, with the vast majority of workers back in the shop under various settlements, and facing an intractable group of holdout employers among the Associated Waist and Dress Manufacturers, union leaders declared the strike over on February 15, 1910. The uprising had achieved a great deal, including industrywide wage increases, shorter hours, better working conditions in most shops, and a tremendous reduction in the widely hated subcontracting system.[50] It also expanded membership in the I.L.G.W.U. by the tens of thousands, setting that union on a course to transform the New York garment industry and become one of the largest and most powerful unions in the city.[51] For a group of workers widely considered unorganizable by the labor movement patriarchy, these women and their wealthy allies had waged one of the biggest, most militant, and most consequential strikes of the twentieth century.

Yet the strike failed to establish real bargaining power for garment workers on an industrywide scale, power that might have addressed more of the grievances that had led workers out on strike in the first place, many having to do with basic disrespect. One of those unresolved issues at whose core lay disrespect—locking workers in on the shopfloor to prevent theft—would prove horribly fateful when a fire broke out in the Triangle just over a year later. One hundred forty-six workers died—suffocated, trampled, burned alive, or leaping in agony to their deaths on the street far below.

Days after the fire, Schneiderman, who had since agreed to become a salaried organizer for the W.T.U.L., spoke at a memorial held at the Metropolitan Opera House, organized and paid for by Morgan, and chaired by Jacob Schiff. It was Schneiderman who had drawn Morgan's support for the garment workers in the first place, so it was appropriate that she would be the one to issue judgment on the cross-class cooperation's outcome— and, indeed, on the general public's response to workers' movements. Her words seared as hot as the deadly fire itself:

> I would be a traitor to these poor burned bodies if I came here to talk good fellowship. We have tried you good people of the public and we have found you wanting. . . . This is not the first time girls have been burned alive in the city. Every week I must learn of the untimely death of one of my sister workers. Every year thousands of us are maimed. The life of men and women is so cheap and property is so sacred. There are so many of us for one job it matters little if 143 [sic] of us are burned to death. We have tried you, citizens; we are trying you now, and you have a couple of dollars for the sorrowing mothers and daughters and sisters by way of a charity gift. But every time the workers come out in the only way they know to protest against conditions which are unbearable, the strong hand of the law is allowed to press down heavily upon us. Public officials have only words of warning to us—warning that we must be intensely orderly and must be intensely peaceable, and they have the workhouse just back of all their warnings. The strong hand of the law beats us back when we rise into the conditions that make life bearable. I can't talk fellowship to you who are gathered here. Too much blood has been spilled. I know from my experience it is up to the working people to save themselves. The only way they can save themselves is by a strong working-class movement.[52]

Schneiderman gazed unforgivingly on the shambles of the cooperative class enterprise that had seemed so promising and inspiring eighteen months earlier, and identified a major source of its ruin: the devaluation of workers' lives relative to private property, and the uses of violence to enforce that relation.

In the face of that violence, the Triangle workers and other shirtwaist strikers fought back primarily through the few legal avenues open to them. Schneiderman and the W.T.U.L. allies continued to argue strenuously, along with other Progressives, that those avenues must be widened and cleared of roadblocks. "If the present discontent is met effectively," they argued in the League's annual report for 1911–1912, "if the working women as well as men are to be given legitimate avenues through which they can express their will, the movement which represents them must be adequately manned." This admonition came with a bleak warning that working people could take only so much abuse. "If co-operation is withheld and organization prevented or delayed," they maintained, "the discontent will express itself more rather than less in forms of violence."[53] They knew whereof they wrote. In those same years, in the same city, other workers were proving the validity of the warning: in 1916, worker violence would come close to paralyzing New York.

14

Hard Fists, Short Fuses on the City Rails

> If the Mayor will assure you . . . that we will receive adequate protection we can win. If he will not give that assurance we will all be at the mercy of the mob.
>
> —Theodore Perry Shonts

A LITTLE AFTER half past four o'clock, in the brisk predawn air of Thursday, October 26, 1916, an ice-delivery man named John Mittlekauf was driving past Lenox Avenue and 110th Street when he saw a group of men dashing from the subway station. His eyes followed them as they vaulted over the Central Park wall and disappeared into the shrubbery.[1] Mittlekauf turned back to the road, but only got a block farther before he felt a powerful detonation behind him.

Dynamite deposited under the edge of the subway platform ripped through the concrete, tore up the roadbed, bent a steel rail out of shape, collapsed part of the ceiling and sidewalk above, and inflicted minor injuries on four people in and around the station. The blast smashed the windows out of surrounding buildings, including, to the glee of opportunistic looters, those of a nearby jewelry store and tailor's shop. Mittlekauf was the only witness, and although he had not eyed the perpetrators long enough to determine their identities, neither the police nor the next day's papers evinced any doubt about who they were. As the *Los Angeles Times* put it in its front-page headline, "Bomb Set by Strikers Wrecks New York Subway."[2]

The Los Angeles newspaper's anti-union owner and publisher Harrison Gray Otis would have been only too happy to print this banner headline, since it shared the front page with a smaller item about rumors that John J. McNamara—the former secretary-treasurer of the International Association of Bridge and Structural Ironworkers Union who had been convicted five years earlier with his brother James of bombing the *L.A. Times* office—planned to file an appeal for parole from San Quentin prison.[3] It must have occurred to Otis that the more labor violence abounded in the country and the more public opinion turned against labor, the less inclined a parole board would be to grant McNamara (whom Otis understandably loathed) early release. The paper characterized the possibility of the imprisoned unionist's plea for parole with one word: "Effrontery."[4]

In truth, the explosion in Gotham was probably superfluous for Otis's purposes because the early-morning dynamiting of a New York City subway station with none killed barely approached the high-water mark for sensational (or sensationally reported) worker violence in the six years since the *L.A. Times* bombing. Just a small sampling of incidents between 1910 and 1916 that received more press and far more subsequent historical attention than the Lenox Avenue subway bombing would include the first skirmishes in the West Virginia mine wars, which lasted for years and ultimately pitted U.S. Army veterans against the state militia in guerilla warfare; the deadly battles for control of the Rockefeller mining concerns in Colorado, in which workers responded to the Ludlow massacre by arming and mobilizing hundreds to take over entire towns; and the Preparedness Day bombing in San Francisco, which killed ten people and wounded dozens.[5]

Despite legislative efforts to restrict the distribution and accessibility of dynamite in various states, there were scores of other labor-related dynamiting incidents in these years, mostly forgotten today, but hardly ignored at the time.[6] On February 24, 1911, two bombs damaged the Iroquois Iron Company's new facility in South Chicago, shattering building windows for blocks around.[7] A month later in the same city, seventy-five strikebreakers working for the Chicago Telephone Company skirted death when a bomb narrowly missed a gasoline storehouse adjoining their company-provided sleeping quarters.[8] In Black Diamond, Washington, on March 30, Rasmus Christiansen, a disliked assistant manager with Pacific Coal Company, and his wife survived "a vengeful attempt to blow them into eternity" in the form of a bomb planted beneath their house as they slept.[9] Less than three weeks later in Elizabeth, New Jersey, someone—a striker or strike sympathizer was the presumption—tossed dynamite beneath a wagon carrying six strikebreaking lead molders into the Colwell Lead Works, demolishing the wagon though the intended victims escaped.[10] June and July saw nearly half a dozen bombings of electrical conduits belonging to the Commonwealth Edison company of Chicago, whose employees were on strike.[11] Striking shopmen of the Illinois Central Railroad in McComb City, Mississippi, attacked state troops who were attempting to quell "a series of riots and bloody fights culminating in an attempt to dynamite a [train] car occupied by 100 strikebreakers."[12] All this happened within the span of eight months in 1911.

1912 saw a dynamite assault in May on a copper smelter in Murray, Utah, and bombs laid on Boston trolley tracks in June.[13] In 1913, arson visited a Standard, West Virginia, coal mine in early January; in April, a railroad trestle of the International Railway Company near Buffalo, New York, exploded.[14] In June 1914, Butte, Montana, suffered a series of dynamitings, the result primarily of interunion conflict between the I.W.W. and the Western Federation of Miners.[15] 1915 witnessed not only the sensationally reported and well-remembered attempt to assassinate J. P. Morgan Jr. in July (motivated by antiwar Germanophilia, not union politics), but the far less extensively recalled attempts by anarchists to blow up Andrew Carnegie's Fifth Avenue home in June, and the Tarrytown estate of John D. Archbold, president of Standard Oil, in November.[16]

Many well-known political radicals and labor leaders at the time eschewed dynamite, but some did not, and mainstream newspapers usually ignored any distinction between them, rewarding restraint with strident editorials condemning the violence of unions generally, and with lurid news stories of anarchist and union conspiracies.[17] Managers understood that magnifying this perception strengthened capital's hand with both the state and the public. Indeed, between iconic moments of labor violence and the profusion of less famous anarchist or strike-related dynamitings, anyone— whether living through that time or looking back on it from the distance of a century—might get the impression that early twentieth-century American workers preferred to employ explosive devices as their primary mode of anticapitalist violence.

They did not. For most working Americans, class violence was *not* a matter of carefully calculated propaganda by deed with revolutionary ambitions. Neither was it philosophically justified terrorist violence, or part of a systematic program of assaulting corporate holdings that risked noncombatant lives. Most of the violence to which ordinary workers resorted in their fights with the rich, and in which their fellows shared either knowledge or complicity, involved low-to-the-ground destruction of property, sabotage, or nondeadly attacks on strikebreakers—smashing a window, throwing a bottle, spiking a rail, or assaulting replacement workers with little more than fists. These were the kinds of daily interferences with the means of production that fell within an exceedingly narrow strategic scope, and earned correspondingly short-lived spurts of news coverage. It was also, overwhelmingly, reactive violence that emerged from encounters with company proxies rather than from premeditated design.[18]

The New York transit strikes of 1916 have eluded the gaze of most historians, but examining them from start to finish gives a more representative portrait of worker violence in the era than the higher-profile terrorist attacks.[19] They also represent violence at a moment of transition, when nationwide trends in corporate public-relations practices, welfare capitalism, and state mediation began to undermine workers' justifications for violent protest in the public eye. The transit strikes—which culminated in the last attempt at a citywide general strike in New York's history—consumed the city for months, at times crippling commuter transit, provoking a merciless press war, and inciting acts of class violence all over the city, up to and including the Lenox Avenue bombing. They reveal identifiable dynamics within the conflictual class relations of the time, stimulative of violence, that outlived both Progressive-Era reform and the state repression that followed during the Red Scare of 1919–1920.

Contextualizing such mundane, encounter-driven violence amid the 1916 transit strikes in New York illustrates how this kind conflictual class relation stirs, grows, and reaches a point of eruption from the side of the poor. It also recovers a sense of historical continuity, however attenuated, between the labor conflicts of the early twentieth century and today. Dynamitings have disappeared from the world of American labor, but less public, less astonishing forms of worker violence, deviance, and sabotage—perpetrated for similar reasons—have not.[20] The baseline prevalence of violence as part of daily life in the early twentieth century surely underlies Progressive-Era violence's comparative ferocity. A few inciting elements from the 1916 conflict, however, are readily recognizable analogues to today's labor-capital relations. Two in particular stand out: the "gulf of understanding" (as Frederick de Latour Booth-Tucker put it in 1899) between rich and poor Americans, and the Gordian knot of competing interests among big business, the state, and the public. They offer a warning that while overt violence on the scale of the Progressive Era is largely a thing of the past, the sources of such violence remain latent in American class relations.

Theodore Perry ("T. P.") Shonts, the president of the Interborough Rapid Transit (I.R.T.) and New York Railways (N.Y. Railways) companies during the strikes, offers the consummate portrait of an American manager in the Progressive Era. Admirers saw him as the fulfillment of the American dream, a man of middling origins who, by dint of grit and hard work, managed to become president or director of a dozen separate rail companies, including the world's largest metropolitan rail network, the I.R.T.[21] Detractors, on the other hand, saw him as a ruthless, opportunistic, and arrogant driver of men whose success depended on privileges derived from his whiteness, Protestantism, and connections to men of even greater power and wealth.[22]

The available record places Shonts somewhere between these caricatures. He was a pragmatic, hard-nosed businessman whose career benefited equally from making smart decisions and leveraging his (considerable) privilege to the hilt. He could also be cold-bloodedly calculating, as correspondence and public statements during his lifetime suggest, and as a posthumous scandal concerning his private life confirms. Regardless, his decisions during the 1916 transit strikes shaped a unique turning point in American class conflict: a single industrial dispute whose arc describes a pivotal delegitimization of worker violence.

Born to Dutch and Scotch-Irish parents in Pennsylvania but transplanted to the Midwest as a boy, Shonts attended public school in Iowa, where chance brought him his first quasi-managerial appointment. Local public school overseers, at a loss to find a teacher "whom the students would not 'induce' to leave," offered Shonts the position, despite the fact that he was only fifteen years old and still a student himself. Apparently the overseers knew what they were doing. The teenage schoolmaster proved his mettle, enforcing "sepulchral silence" in the classroom thereafter.[23]

Shonts went on to study civil engineering at Monmouth College and served a short stint as an accountant before joining the Iowa law firm of Drake & Baker. The senior partner there (and future governor of Iowa), General Francis Marion Drake, was busily acquiring Iowa farmland and developing railroads on his way to amassing a fortune of over $3 million—in today's terms, over $75 million.[24] Drake, whose life rivaled even that of his privateer namesake for death-defying adventure, took the younger lawyer under his wing, introducing Shonts to the railroad business. He also introduced Shonts to his daughter Millie, whom Shonts promptly married. Drake then encouraged his new son-in-law to leave the law firm and devote himself full-time to railroads, in 1881 appointing him manager in charge of a major track development for the Iowa Construction Company, of which Drake was vice president, and financier Russell Sage was president. Shonts had the track completed on schedule under difficult conditions, proving himself to these powerful, influential men.[25]

This potent combination of ability and nepotism enabled Shonts, by the age of twenty-five, to wield remarkable executive authority for a man so young, and to enjoy intimate ties to key players of the late nineteenth-century U.S. political economy. By the month of his twenty-sixth birthday, he was acting as general superintendent of the Indiana, Illinois & Iowa Railroad; Drake passed the presidency on to him in 1898, and he quickly acquired a controlling stake.[26] When he sold the company to the Vanderbilt railroad empire less than four years later, he became a millionaire many times over.[27]

His only detour from railroad management came just before he accepted the I.R.T. presidency, and it offers a suggestive glimpse of an emerging management style that combined aggressive public relations and paternalist benevolence with a firm refusal to make policy concessions to organized labor. In 1905, Theodore Roosevelt appointed Shonts the commissioner of the Isthmian (now Panama) Canal project, whose first commissioner had been unable to resolve innumerable, nagging problems of labor supply and basic engineering. Roosevelt granted Shonts "absolute authority as to both men and measures," a prerogative Shonts by now expected as his due. Some American unionists, however, had long been arguing that laborers on the canal project should enjoy basic, American-style work protections so as not to undermine labor standards in the United States. Shonts successfully resisted such arguments, giving speeches around the country trumpeting progress made in sanitation conditions and workers' housing in the canal zone, while threatening the debilitating cost overruns that would result from the "restrictions" being proposed.[28]

Cartoonist Samuel D. Ehrhart parodied Shonts's approach to labor relations (and lampooned prominent capitalists as well) in *Puck* magazine's October 18, 1905, issue, depicting Shonts as a whip-wielding foreman, mercilessly extracting manual labor from "superfluous citizens" such as John D. Rockefeller and J. P. Morgan. Shonts's own words to a gathering in Chicago suggest that, allowing for a slightly less august workforce, this image hit near the mark. Facing calls for labor law to hold sway on the Isthmus, Shonts averred, "In my opinion it is a mistake to handicap the Panama Canal by any laws save those of police and sanitation."[29] He, and only he, would be the final law governing the terms of work.

When he took over the I.R.T. presidency in 1907—and that of N.Y. Railways in 1914—Shonts combined carrot and stick with a bit more subtlety, while still refusing to concede a whit of his influence to employees. At both companies, he extended policies prefiguring the sort of welfare capitalism that would become commonplace in the 1920s: voluntary associations and internal welfare departments (funded by employee contributions but entirely administered by company management) conferring various benefits such as free rides for family, discounted lunch counters, company excursions, small pensions for senior workers, and a wellness fund to pay for sick, injured, or needy employees.[30] On the other hand, he also instructed I.R.T. and N.Y. Railways managers to enforce the micromanaging employee rulebooks, deploying an extensive network of company spies to ride undercover and report infractions.[31]

Some rapid transit workers may have appreciated the voluntary association's benefits (while at the same time resenting the implied disrespect of its paternalist administration), but they viewed the rulebook enforcement as a form of daily tyranny. As one man put it, "I wouldn't mind working at the rates as they stand if things were run fairly. But they're not, and the only defense we have is to stick together. You can see what chance one man has against the boss and all his spotters and investigators."[32] Once the war in Europe began to spark inflation, and the already meager buying power of their wages declined even further, these grievances began to spill over.

Shonts's career as an executive before 1916 had spanned thirty-five years and a continent, but it had not prepared him to respect employee grievances. He began his ascent to the heights of railroad executive power four years after the federal government had made clear to railroad barons—amid the Great Strike of 1877—that when push came to shove, it would come down hard on labor to protect private property. Local government had conveyed the same message, not least amid the Uprising of the Twenty Thousand in 1909 to 1910.

The trajectory of Shonts's life, the scope of his professional and social circles, and the idolization of railroad executives during the bulk of his career did not foster a wellspring of humility or empathy in him for collectives of working people. Indeed, one of Shonts's most personal public statements, a commencement address delivered to Drake University graduates in 1912, unreservedly celebrated the cult of individualism while inveighing against a "spirit of communism" abroad in the land that inspired dangerous forms of collectivism. Among the examples of nefarious collectivism Shonts cited were city employment bureaus, municipal firework displays, and public organ concerts.[33] Clearly, this was a man who took the most extreme version of classical liberal economics very seriously. If his political-economic views won him little love from workers, his appearance could not have helped. With his sharp nose, bushy mustache, narrow eyes, immaculate suits, and pince-nez, Shonts visually personified bourgeois privilege.

The men surrounding Shonts in 1916 exhibited no greater affection for worker collectives. The founder and owner of the I.R.T. was August Belmont, Jr., Alva's in-law, whom one historian has described as "arrogant, mean-spirited, and quick to anger," a "fat little banker," who "flew into a rage when not accorded the obsequious treatment he thought was due a gentleman of his elevated station."[34] Shonts's general manager, Frank Hedley, had long indulged a habit of disdaining both employees and the public—in a 1910 meeting with Washington Heights residents, for instance, he replied to questions about service expansion by informing the group, "I will study the situation . . . and then—do as I please."[35] Even a sympathetic obituarist noted of Frederick W. Whitridge, the Third Avenue Railway Company president, "He did not hesitate to express contempt for labor unions and for state interference in the affairs of his system."[36]

Facing off against such men, the Amalgamated Association of Street and Railway Employees of America (here, the Amalgamated) was an unusually militant national union.[37] It had been attempting to make inroads with New York rail-transit workers, or "traction" workers, since at least 1905, and its members, over 80,000 nationally by 1915, had participated in approximately ten strikes or lockouts annually since the early 1890s.[38] Although its lead organizer, William B. Fitzgerald, abjured violence during the strike, he also declared himself a socialist in its midst, indicted New York's most prominent capitalists in class terms, and helped organize rallies where other speakers were far less restrained than he in counseling assaults on property and persons under company control.[39] Meanwhile, some local union officials had barely entered adulthood. The impatience of their youth would betray itself, and the strike, in a series of increasingly rash decisions.

The complex web of private companies within New York's transit system also played a role in exacerbating the tensions that sparked violence, by obfuscating the question of who was responsible for various company decisions during the strike. Multiple corporations operated several modes of commuter transport on dozens of lines: N.Y. Railways ran streetcars and shared a board of trustees with the I.R.T., but it was technically a separate corporation with independent bond issues; the Third Avenue Railway Company (T.A.R.C.) was one of several other independent streetcar operations with its own subsidiaries in Yonkers. The I.R.T. operated subways and elevated trains in Manhattan, but it had not yet merged with the Brooklyn Rapid Transit Company (B.R.T.), though both had agreements with the city to expand service under what was known as "the dual contract." Each company's workers had differently calibrated relationships with their employer and their local union. Fitzgerald and the Amalgamated could not effectively coordinate or control those relationships, or the way they contributed to the production of violence.[40] The companies, meanwhile, avoided the potential disadvantages of their divisions by allowing Shonts and Hedley to coordinate a collective response.[41] Ironically (but not unusually in the days before the 1935 Wagner Act), capital enjoyed the benefits of collective action more thoroughly than labor.

The public-private division of physical and financial power over the transit system further complicated issues and raised tempers on all sides because everyone—managers, workers, and the public—expected city officials to intervene on their behalf. The city and state maintained a financial partnership role with the local rail companies, ostensibly both to foster expansion and coordination, and to protect the public interest.[42] Ideological opposition among key financial interests to any public control of the urban railways, however, limited the city's authority, while the public-private system also ensured that any major financial decisions faced imposing, if not insurmountable political obstacles.[43]

Most obviously, protecting the nickel fare had become an article of political faith. Despite the financial unfeasibility of running such a high-cost operation with such a low, relatively fixed revenue stream, any politician suggesting that the price of a ride should be higher than five cents invited public wrath. As Shonts put it during the strike, "The five cent fare is about as deeply imbedded in the habits of the American people as is the Constitution of the United States."[44] He neglected to add that it was the I.R.T., spurred by a fear of popular demand to *lower* the cost of a ride, that had successfully fought to enshrine the nickel fare in its contract with the city.[45]

This meant that both the union and the company could (and did) claim to be serving the public interest by engaging in all-out war with each other. Companies charged that the union's demands for higher wages and shorter hours would impose a huge financial burden on New Yorkers because, under the terms of the public-private partnership with the city, New York had to reimburse both the I.R.T. and B.R.T. for deficits and interest before reaping any financial benefit for itself. The union insisted that company officials were abusing their employees and endangering public safety for outrageous personal gain, and soaking the city treasury to do it.

On some level, they were both right. The strikes came with a giant price tag in property destroyed and commerce interrupted, not to mention the cost of a magnified, sustained police presence. The city was on the hook for all of it.[46] Meanwhile, "traction men" like Shonts enjoyed lavish compensation for operating networks whose service failed to meet the growing public need, and whose watered stock, generous bonuses, and imprudent, chummy, short-term loan arrangements with New York bankers would place the entire system on the edge of bankruptcy in a matter of a few years.[47]

The public-private partnership may have facilitated slightly faster expansion of the transit network than private enterprise would have undertaken on its own, but its conditions effectively guaranteed the privatization of profit and socialization of loss.[48] The inadequacy of public authority under its terms would prove a major drawback in the effort to settle the strikes without violence. So New York's transit system was neither rapid, nor really a system; it was merely lurching toward becoming both, with New Yorkers along for the extremely bumpy, gradually accelerating ride. In 1916, the wheels careened off the tracks.

Springtime brought shadows of trouble to come. On April 3, 5,000 timbermen and "muckers" in Manhattan and Brooklyn—workers charged with bracing new tunnels and sloughing off earth and stone to remove from the ground, among the most grueling tasks in the construction of the new rail lines—walked off the job. Michael Carraher, the secretary-treasurer of the Subway Constructors' Union, said of the mucker's pay, "We do not regard $1.60 to $1.75 a day as a living wage in New York."[49] The workers wanted the General Contractors' Association to raise the standard rate by 25 to 40 cents.

Newspapers generally referred to these men as "unskilled," but Pietro Pacelli, the president of the Tunnel and Subway Constructors' International Union, objected strenuously to the designation. Banging a fist on his desk to emphasize the point, he declared, "Aren't most of them graduates of the great tunnel system connecting Italy and Switzerland? Haven't many of them grown up in the business of excavating and shoring from childhood? I tell you they are as much entitled to be called skilled men as the miners of Western Pennsylvania."[50] The *Tribune* reporter relating the story dwelt on Pacelli's animation, describing how, "in his excitement . . . he jumped from his chair," a subtle wink to readers with doubts about workers' and foreigners' ability to govern their emotions or themselves.[51] Pacelli's allusion to Western Pennsylvania miners' enjoyment of greater respect, meanwhile, underlined the aspirational nature of the timbermen's and muckers' cause in both classed and ethnic terms. For Pacelli, at least, the strike was as much about respect as about wages.

Expectations of worker violence in the press were matter of fact, and managers did their best to raise them. A few days later, after characterizing the union's demands as "financially impossible" and breaking off a brief negotiating attempt, the General Contractors' Association announced that they would resume work on April 10. The Association's statement warned that if the strikers refused to return, strikebreakers guarded by private detectives would take their place. These "elaborate precautions," a spokesman claimed, "were made necessary by threats of intimidation and violence made by some of the strikers."[52] In fact, the Association's statement alleged that "75 per cent. of [the] men have expressed a desire to return to their places, and only remained away on account of the threats of violence made against themselves or members of their families."[53] Managers rarely failed to garnish public statements with such generalized accusations of union intimidation; even less frequently did they attempt to substantiate their accusations. In truth, there was no need. Newspapers overflowed with stories of union violence, continually offering circumstantial corroboration to anyone inclined to believe them.

Another contractor, John F. O'Rourke, admitted to having received no threats, but only after he had detailed how deadly a workers' dynamite attack *would* be on the East River tubes his company was building. He added darkly, "It is best to be on the safe side."[54] O'Rourke also accused the "sandhogs"—who had gone on strike a few days after the timbermen and muckers to demand improved working conditions and wage hikes—of breaking the contract they had signed the previous August. The secretary of the sandhogs' union, Henry Kuhlmann, issued a cool rebuttal, pointing out that O'Rourke's company had first violated the contract (and state law) by forcing workers to stay on the job for "illegal periods of time under air pressure" and arbitrarily slashing the wages detailed in the aforementioned contract. O'Rourke, Kuhlmann remarked, was in no position to complain if "the union has decided to take advantage of the occasion to correct other evils."[55]

It fell to Oscar S. Straus and the Public Service Commission (P.S.C.) to arbitrate an end to the two strikes. The state legislature had created the P.S.C. in 1907 to replace the Rapid Transit Commission (which had failed to expand subways fast enough for political or popular sentiment). The P.S.C.'s mandate included the supervision and regulation of subway operation and construction—it was the city's front line in rapid transit matters. Theoretically, this meant that it could play a vigorous role, enjoying full partnership in the "dual system" of subway management subsequently proposed in 1911 and put in place through contracts with the I.R.T. and B.R.T. in 1913.

In reality, the P.S.C. was hamstrung in multiple ways. Both before and after the dual system came into effect, executive direction of operations and construction stayed in the hands of private companies. Those companies and their directors maintained critical influence with the city's Board of Estimate, the Mayor's office, the Chamber of Commerce, and Wall Street.[56] Any efforts the P.S.C. might make to supervise or regulate company actions depended on support from at least one of those four bodies, and attempts to alter construction plans practically required approval from all. This relegated the P.S.C. to a fairly ineffectual advisory position, dependent on help from the Mayor's office and public opinion to enforce its decisions.[57]

Straus managed to mediate an end to the spring strikes with gains for the workers, but the subway construction walkouts were only the teaser for a much larger production. The central issues in the new dispute—wages, job control, the public interest, and basic respect—remained much the same; the stakes, however, on the city's active rail routes, magnified exponentially. Company managers responding to the summer strikes would, like their springtime analogues, warn either allusively or explicitly of an impending war while doing their utmost to stimulate violence.[58] This time, as the days grew hotter and patience shorter, workers and their sympathizers would prove much more willing to reciprocate the hostility.

On July 22, 1916, the motormen of the Yonkers Railroad Company and the Westchester Electric Railroad Company street car lines went on strike, paralyzing service in Yonkers, Mount Vernon, and New Rochelle.[59] They had been in negotiations with company president Frederick W. Whitridge, but he had refused (in violation of a 1913 agreement) to arbitrate their differences, broken off negotiations, and departed for a summer excursion to Europe.[60] On July 25, "the first violence . . . occurred" when a mob set upon three men who crossed the picket line to apply for work. When they emerged from the company office, "they took one look at the crowd and began to run. . . . Stones were thrown and a blow or two struck." Luckily for them, two strikers—a motorman and a conductor—held the crowd back until the police came to escort the strikebreakers away.[61]

The next day, July 26, trolleymen and conductors of surface rails in the Bronx answered the call from Yonkers to go on strike. They took the opportunity to make their own demands for increased wages and voluntary shift changes after ten hours of work, declaring that if these terms went unmet, then "the strike would be extended to Manhattan."[62] Edward A. Maher, the assistant general manager of the affected Union Railway Company, labeled ridiculous the assertion by the Amalgamated that 1,200 additional men had walked out, claiming instead that "motormen and conductors were simply terrorized . . . because of raids that had been made by armed strikers from Yonkers upon work cars in the early morning hours."[63] Fitzgerald denied Maher's accusations of violence completely, insisting later that in addition to "sympathy with their fellow-employes [*sic*] in [Yonkers]," the Bronx workers were all eager to strike because "the conditions of employment on the transit lines in the city are horrible. Men work from 5 o'clock in the morning until 9 and 10 o'clock at night. They are paid less than men in the same class of service in any other city in the country."[64]

Despite Fitzgerald's denials, six strikers faced fines and judicial warnings "for snatching the trolley poles of cars from the wires" on the first day of the Bronx strike.[65] In this instance, workers clearly intended to disable rather than destroy property; at 184th Street, however, at least three strikers stoned an empty trolley and were arrested.[66] In neither case did they attack individuals.

Undeterred, the Union Railway executive Maher told a different story. His initial sangfroid regarding the strike's impact in the Bronx having dissipated by July 30, he began ordering all the company's Manhattan cars into barns by 4 o'clock in the afternoon and the Bronx cars in by 9 o'clock, claiming that "motormen and conductors remaining at work were being intimidated by gangs of strikers."[67] Maher explained to reporters that the early shutdowns aimed "to prevent violence" against working employees. "Thugs have visited their homes," he said, "and told their wives if they went out on cars they would come back in caskets."[68] This too would be a recurring theme in company propaganda, the attempt to besmirch strikers in the public eye through loud allegations that they were violating codes of both gender and honor by threatening the "women folks" of "loyal" employees.[69]

Although Maher may have been embellishing his charge, intentionally furthering a steady drumbeat of management invective, the picketers were undoubtedly confronting conductors and motormen who stayed on the job in the Bronx, even while actively organizing the Manhattan trainmen. As Fitzgerald had announced at the outset of the Yonkers strike, the union aimed to "reorganize some of the lines of other companies in New York City."[70] Indeed, the Amalgamated had been trying to organize New York transit workers for years, but had failed to untangle workers from the sticky web of corporate-municipal ownership and competing loyalties.[71] It did not help that very few, if any, of the Amalgamated's senior leadership came from New York.[72] Nevertheless, they took steps toward their goal on July 30, the same night Maher was denouncing them to the press, by issuing a call to strike the Third Avenue elevated line, which would affect service on the B.R.T.'s and N.Y. Railways' lines as well. Seven work crews from the Manhattan Bridge crossing already "failed to report for work at 7 o'clock" that evening, and a "rioting mob of strikers which gathered at the Canal Street entrance to the bridge was dispersed by the police."[73]

Meanwhile, Hedley issued a warning to all employees at Shonts's behest, notifying them "that labor agitators from outside cities have announced in secret meetings that they have come to New York to tie up all street railway traffic, regardless of the hardships to the families of the men operating the cars and to the public in general."[74] Other company officials frequently echoed this notion that "agitators" from "outside" the ranks of their employees were responsible for any disturbances.[75] It was an obvious attempt to shore up company loyalty and public sympathy, while also encouraging the perception of the strike as a war zone with foreign invaders.[76] Four days later on August 3, after refusing to recognize the Amalgamated, submit to arbitration, or even meet with union representatives at the request of Mayor John Purroy Mitchel, Shonts reinforced that perception in a speech to a company-organized rally in Van Cortlandt Park. After he had maligned the

"outside labor agitators who sought to disrupt the traffic service of the city,"
he drew a direct link between the war in Europe and the possibility of a
New York rail strike:

> The world is full of war and the rumors of war. The dominating nations
> have gone mad to slaughter each other. We have hoped that we would es-
> cape the trouble and we still hope that we will. Some gentlemen have come
> into town to disrupt the cordial relations that have existed for four and a
> half years between the officers of the New York Railways Company and
> their employes [sic].[77]

It was an inelegant transition, but his intended comparison between the
Amalgamated and the Huns was clear enough. In any case, he was speaking at a rally attended by one hundred employees who had signed a pledge
of loyalty to the company (the beginnings of a company union that would
play a major role in the weeks ahead), so perhaps the invocation of battle
lines was not entirely misplaced.

The signed loyalty of a hundred workers in a system that employed thousands seemed to be of little worth in the early morning hours two days later,
however, when the strike hit Manhattan in earnest. In at least two meetings
attended by 2,500 workers, N.Y. Railways carmen voted unanimously to
strike, furious at Shonts's and Hedley's refusal to meet with the union.
Hedley told reporters that foremen and supervisors spying for the company
at the meetings saw fewer than two hundred employees, but the subsequent
course of the strike belied such flippant dismissals.[78]

Service interruptions began immediately.[79] "At 2 o'clock this morning,"
reported the *Times,* "several of the most important lines of the New York
Railways Company reported service badly crippled," including the Broadway, Amsterdam, and Seventh Avenue lines.[80] Between 1,000 and 3,000
strikers marched up to the subway barns on Lexington Avenue between
99th and 100th Streets and "halted cars on the way, pulled bell ropes and,
failing in those attempts, placed ash cans on the tracks."[81] After "sporadic
rioting," arrests, and breakdowns of service during the day, a major confrontation occurred when "police reserves charged a crowd of strike sympathizers said to have numbered at least 2,000, who were bombarding a car
with stones and attempting to separate a prisoner from a patrolman." The

strikers and their allies in the street-level confrontation had an auxiliary division in the fight, as "women and children hurled missiles from tenement house roofs."[82] This sort of populist violence among strike sympathizers, in which whole neighborhoods sometimes engaged to protect each other and attack company property, became a regular feature of the struggle, despite remaining officially unsanctioned by the Amalgamated.

Hedley maintained a stubborn public posture, insisting that not a single line had shut down completely, and if only the loyal employees had adequate police protection from the union's thuggery, "the company would have been able to operate a full quota of cars on all lines." Fitzgerald countered that fully two-thirds of those men had joined the strike, and that "if the company were not using strike-breakers the service would be entirely paralyzed."[83] He need only have pointed out that if Hedley were so confident of employees' loyalty, there could have been no reason to transport nearly 3,000 replacement workers into New York from Chicago at great expense, nor to offer double pay to motormen remaining on the job, both steps that Hedley took with Shonts's authorization.[84]

Either way, the public found Hedley's claims in ill accord with their experience. As a *Times* editorial observed mordantly the next day, "It is difficult to put much trust in the officers of the tractions who affirm that their men are their united and devoted admirers only a few hours before the men order a strike and proceed to put it into execution."[85] After two days of badly snarled service, sporadic street fights, and a fair amount of carping press, N.Y. Railways officials finally agreed to begin arbitration with Mayor Mitchel, Straus, the P.S.C., and the union. An agreement emerged quickly that guaranteed N.Y. Railways workers the right to organize, a raise to be determined, and formal negotiations to be undertaken no later than August 20, less than two weeks away.

Management's apparent willingness to make concessions to the union masked a flinty resolve. The very day the truce was declared, August 7, Shonts sent a telegram to Belmont urging him to hold firm in the negotiations. In effect, Shonts welcomed the prospect of a war as long as the police remained arrayed in defense of property. "In my judgment," he declared, "this whole matter is in the hands of the police. If the Mayor will assure you and your Committee that we will receive adequate protection we can win. If he will not give that assurance we will all be at the mercy of the mob."[86]

A short while later, he sent another message, informing Belmont, "Mr. Hedley just reports that out of a full normal operation of 702 cars we are now operating 331. Under these conditions the strike is already broken."[87] These were not the words of a man prepared to meet his workers as equals, or to go down without a fight.

The initial battle was over, but crucially the union had failed to win official recognition, which would have ensured the kind of bargaining power and public legitimacy the workers needed. This would prove a disastrous concession, both for the union, and for the city of New York.

15

Making the World Safe for Inequality

> We're trying every day to improve our methods, and we want the people of New York to realize deep down in their hearts that that is the spirit in which we are operating these lines.
>
> —T. P. Shonts

NEW YORKERS WERE STILL washing newsprint off their fingers from the celebratory reports of the August 7 arbitration deal and labor peace when T. P. Shonts dropped a public relations bomb: he announced that under the terms of the city's contract with the I.R.T., New York would have to pay the cost of the strike on the surface lines, which he estimated at an alarming $1,520,000 for N.Y. Railways alone.[1] This, of course, would be only a fraction of the total cost to the public, because any agreement on the city's part to pay would establish a basis for claims from other affected lines—including the B.R.T., Third Avenue Railway, Second Avenue, New York & Queens, and Staten Island companies. As one report put it, "Now that New York has been saved from the hardships of a city-wide transportation tie-up, the public is to be asked to pay the price of its own rescue."[2]

   Shonts's announcement illustrates a tectonic shift in U.S. corporate public relations strategy between 1900 and 1920. For at least the three decades before the twentieth century, industrial magnates made a habit of public relations blunders—whether through entitlement, obliviousness, or willful malice—that seemed to confirm the absence of corporate conscience regarding the public weal.[3] To many Americans, William Vanderbilt and J. P. Morgan spoke for successive generations of businessmen and bankers (apocryphally or not) when they said, in 1882 and 1901, respectively, "The public be damned," and "I owe the public nothing."[4]

It hardly mattered whether such statements were the considered expressions of ideological positions, careless utterances, or (more than likely, at least in Morgan's case) the fabrications of disgruntled reporters whom Vanderbilt and Morgan had rebuffed for comment; they reflected a pervasive failure of managerial imagination when it came to the uses of public relations to align corporate interests—seemingly—with those of ordinary people.[5] Frederick W. Whitridge, president of the Third Avenue Railway, had sparked the New York transit strike in a fashion that exemplified such blindness borne of entitlement: he not only refused to submit wage disputes to arbitration, as he had vowed to do in a 1913 agreement with his employees, but also salted his arrogance by wordlessly departing for Europe.

Shonts was a new breed of manager. His tactics after the August truce would help redefine corporate rhetoric and strategy—and the terms of conflictual class relations in America—for decades to come.[6] As the conflict progressed, he or his subordinates would release a series of public statements and pamphlets insinuating dastardly union violence, emphasizing the city's financial dependence on uninterrupted transit service, and lamenting the struggles of "loyal" employees and their families to reject the union "democratically."[7] Shonts gave the company a human voice to which some readers might relate—that of an aggrieved parent or struggling businessman, only trying to do what was best for his children, customers, and the public. He may have risked alienating New Yorkers by presenting them with the bill for the strike, but he also sent a clear message about whose interests were aligned in such matters: the public and the company, he implied, would pay an equally unpleasant price for tolerating militant labor unionism.

Meanwhile, he cast the Amalgamated as the sole author of violence, while identifying the I.R.T. with the more general public interests of law, order, and dependable transit service.[8] This proactive, multipronged communications program was a far cry from that of Gilded-Age industrialists such as Henry Clay Frick and Andrew Carnegie, who some two decades earlier had secretly deployed paramilitary mercenaries to crush employee dissent at

their steel plant in Homestead, Pennsylvania, without any serious, comprehensive attempt at public self-justification. Of course, Shonts *did* ultimately
hire thousands of armed strikebreakers, just as Frick and Carnegie had, in
full knowledge that such personnel specialized in perpetrating and provoking violence; crucially, however, Shonts made the effort—loudly and
repeatedly—to justify this step as necessary to protect the *public* interest,
not merely the rights of private property.

This belated public-relations strategy, by making it easier for the public
to identify with the transit managers' perspective, gradually created a less
forgiving public context for the violence directed by workers and the poor
against the companies. This had not been the case in late July and early
August, when Whitridge's refusal to honor his agreement with his employees almost entirely overshadowed instances of worker violence stretching
from the Upper East Side to Yonkers. Guerilla action such as throwing
stones and spiking rails practically justified itself in the face of such arrogance. After several days during which multiple reports of worker sabotage
and assault had appeared, however, even the dependably pro-business *Times*
still focused its editorial on a critique of the corporate principals, and the
Public Service Commission's decision effectively blamed the entire conflict
on Whitridge.[9] Yet as Shonts's campaign took effect over the remainder of
August—gradually convincing newspapers and the public that the companies were now abiding by their agreements, hewing close to the law, keeping
their wage hike promises, and remaining solicitous of worker democracy—
the ground shifted beneath workers' feet. Under these circumstances, violence would not be so easily regarded as an understandable response to executives' callous egotism. Shonts had repositioned himself for further battle,
and this time he would hold the high ground.

As he prodded the public with the cost of the previous strike, Shonts also
outflanked the Amalgamated on the organizing front. Anticipating the
union's organizing drive on the I.R.T. (which the Amalgamated practically
announced on August 6) and wishing to avoid the depth of internal revolt
gripping N.Y. Railways, he swung into action once again with both the carrot and stick of incipient welfare capitalism.[10] On August 12, managers delivered to all I.R.T. workers a "tentative"—yet remarkably detailed—structure,

constitution, and voting schedule for what they called the Brotherhood of Interborough Rapid Transit Company Employees. Both the secret-ballot election of representatives to this body and the negotiations on contract language were to take place before August 20, the deadline for beginning formal negotiations with Amalgamated officials representing the N.Y. Railways employees.

It was a bold move to establish a company union, "for further promoting co-operation between the Company and its employees," before the Amalgamated could get its independent organizing campaign off the ground. To ordinary New York commuters unfamiliar with the true purpose of company unions—to squelch actual workplace democracy—it also seemed to confirm the company's insistence that it wished to protect its workers' rights.[11] Shonts (over whose signature the entire message about the Brotherhood appeared), noted that "the workings of this plan has [sic] nothing to do with any union."[12] He left it up to workers to construe his remark as reassurance or menace.

The Amalgamated leaders had badly misjudged Shonts and Belmont in their expectation that the two men would allow unfettered union organization within the I.R.T. just because they had agreed to it in principle on N.Y. Railways (although in fairness, Hedley continually misled the union representatives on this point, telling them as late as the August 30 conference, "I do not see how under God's heavens they can give me one set of morals . . . and orders to live up to on the Railways and another set for the Interborough").[13] If there had been any doubt about the company directors' benevolent intentions, Hedley obliterated it by firing fourteen N.Y. Railways workers (and twenty-eight more on other lines) who had been active in the strike. The union officers began receiving reports of these firings only three days after signing the truce. Believing them to be a direct violation of that agreement, they were flabbergasted and enraged.[14]

Barely more than a week after Mitchel and Straus had emerged as triumphant peacemakers, Shonts effectively provoked another war. The union had lost the initiative and public support; as a result, it also forfeited a measure of workers' confidence that its strategies would produce victory. This shift in balance and its continuing aggravation through company publicity and organizing impediments would contribute to the slow creep of wildcat violence.

On the night of August 16, 1,500 N.Y. Railways union members gathered at Lyceum Hall on 86th Street and empowered their local executive committee to call a strike, pending the results of a meeting with Hedley the following morning, and to seek renewed arbitration through the P.S.C. in the days to come. They reckoned that I.R.T. managers had, in multiple ways and on countless occasions, violated the promise not to interfere with organizing. They deemed the establishment of the Brotherhood and the singling out of union men for dismissal to be the most flagrant abuses, both of which started practically before Shonts's signature had dried on the August 7 agreement. After the strike authorization vote, Fitzgerald added that should a strike on the surface lines become necessary, it would immediately trigger one on the I.R.T.'s subways and elevateds as well.[15] All the preliminaries of spring and midsummer were leading to a citywide showdown on the entire transit system.[16]

Shonts and Hedley responded in public through proclamations of good faith, and in private by stonewalling, buying themselves more time to establish the Brotherhood as a de facto entity. The meeting with Hedley on August 17 proved a wash. After fencing with the union's committee over whether the Amalgamated officials (as opposed to rank-and-file employees) should be allowed in the room at all, the manager and his two attorneys squabbled with the workers' delegation over the competing meanings of two sections in the August 7 truce agreement, one that dictated strikers would be restored to their positions "without prejudice," and another that entitled managers to maintain discretion about "matters of efficiency."[17] It was a dry legal argument, but one that neatly encapsulated the crux of the fight between workers' rights and managers' prerogatives. The union envoys, of course, argued that "without prejudice" meant total amnesty for every striker. Hedley retorted that the men in question had all been arrested or convicted as criminals, placing the issue of their continued employment squarely within management's purview over "matters of efficiency." Neither side would concede.

In the midst of the bickering, Fitzgerald interrupted to question Hedley about his authority to offer redress, revealing that in fact Hedley had no authorization to make any agreements; he was acting solely as a conduit to, not a representative of, Shonts and the N.Y. Railways Board of Directors.[18] When Fitzgerald requested a meeting with the board for the next day, Hedley underlined the privileges of wealth in his reply: "I don't think it will be possible to have that to-morrow because I don't know of a single member of the Board of Directors . . . who is in New York at the present time. I don't know exactly where they are but they will be found wherever the members of the four hundred [*sic*] congregate in the summer time."[19]

The board members' social engagements proved not as pressing as Hedley surmised, and Shonts managed to scrape together a quorum for a meeting the next day; he struck a disinterested attitude from the start, however, and the lawyers remained at loggerheads. After a lengthy discussion with everyone present, the board members sought privacy in an antechamber, where they produced a swift written rejection of the union's demand for the return of the fourteen fired men to work.[20] There followed several days of tense waiting for a summit with the P.S.C. and Mayor Mitchel, who was rushing back from military training in Plattsburg, which lent an appropriately martial air to the proceedings when they began on August 21.

Less the warrior in the end than the sober judge, Mitchel compelled Shonts and I.R.T. counsel James L. Quackenbush to reinstate the fourteen N.Y. Railways men and to submit the other twenty-eight cases to arbitration. The union conceded—for the purposes of reinstating the men and arbitrating other questions—the issue of the Brotherhood company union. When the men emerged from the negotiation chambers, Shonts was smiling and gracious with the press. Hedley's mien, by contrast, betrayed that this apparent second truce was nothing more than a tactical cease-fire. When a photographer requested a shot of the I.R.T. managers side by side with Fitzgerald and the other union representatives, Hedley "jumped aside" and snapped, "Not much. And have it shot all over the country?"[21]

Despite Hedley's transparent animosity, the possibility of a subway and elevated strike seemed to have dwindled, and for more than a week the fracas subsided.[22] But both union and management remained quietly at work.

A chill wind blew into the union's ranks at August's end. Word reached Amalgamated headquarters that I.R.T. managers had been circulating a "working agreement" that guaranteed wage hikes and a nine-hour day—more modest concessions than the union wanted—at frozen levels for two years. Allegedly, its terms had been negotiated and approved by the company union. Shonts was successfully creating the impression of democratic

negotiation he needed to bolster his position with the public and to delegiti-
mize the Amalgamated.

Managers encouraged workers to sign "as individuals," and many of them,
whether out of eagerness to receive improved pay and conditions (as the company insisted), some combination of fear and deception (as the union
charged), or both, were doing so, surrendering their right to strike. In the
midst of labor-management conferences on August 31, Louis Fridiger, the
union lawyer, complained to Hedley about reports that "in the majority of
those instances" where I.R.T. employees had signed,

> the men stated that this was the method followed in obtaining the signa-
> tures; a man gets off his run and is told by the man in charge of these work-
> ing agreements . . . "You have got an increase in wages, your wage is going
> to be $2.70 from now on, is that satisfactory to you?" "Yes." With the agree-
> ment folded up just your signature showing practically, and space for his
> own, he is asked to sign that. In any number of those instances when he was
> informed that that agreement called for his absolute employment . . . until
> August, 1918, the man not only was surprised but expressed amazement. He
> wanted to know, in any number of instances, whether or not he could get
> this paper back.[23]

Hedley refused to discuss the matter beyond asserting that he would "have
to be shown" that such deception had occurred in each and every case.[24] The
meeting ended with Fitzgerald fuming, "There is lots of difference between
what is moral and what is legal. Lots of things legally can be done that
morally will not be stood for."[25]

The following day, 3,000 subway and elevated employees gathered at Lyceum Hall on 86th Street and Third Avenue and issued an ultimatum to
Shonts and Hedley: cancel the "master-and-servant" contracts or face another
strike, this time of the whole transit system. Fitzgerald thundered, "This contract is un-American if anything ever was, and every man should revolt!"[26]

They had played directly into the company's hands. Hedley issued a grim
statement over Shonts's name on September 5 that threatened immediate
dismissal for anyone who struck, and he refused absolutely to void the individual contracts, noting the company's moral and legal obligation to honor
them.[27] In a "more than acrimonious" meeting that same day, Hedley—all

pretense of friendliness or respect for the union delegation having vanished—told union lawyers that any man wishing to void his contract could try his luck in court; he flatly rejected the notion of arbitrating the question through the P.S.C.[28] The union, taken aback by the now total intransigence of the managers, weakly sent a message to Plattsburg asking Mayor Mitchel to return once more to mediate. In the meantime, 5,000 new strikebreakers commanded by James T. Waddell's professional strikebreaking firm, Bergoff Brothers & Waddell, began rolling into town from Chicago and manning the subway barns.[29]

As the union wavered over the next few days, Shonts piled on in a published, comprehensive, and widely distributed statement entitled *The Effort to Tie Up the Street Railroad Systems of New York*, averring that the Brotherhood had authorized the disputed contracts through a democratic process.[30] "The men desired to form a nonunion brotherhood," he explained innocently, "and we told them to go ahead and organize."[31] A *Times* editorial endorsed this line fully, declaring of the subway workers that "they are now a democracy," and that the goal of any strike would merely be to put workers under "rules and . . . control" of the Amalgamated.[32] Shonts, sensing his advantage, declared the union's threat to strike a violation of the August 7 peace accord, and let it be known that the I.R.T. "would fight the union to a finish."[33]

The strike began on the night of September 6, immediately following a nine o'clock rally and vote in Plaza Assembly Hall at 59th Street and Lexington Avenue, where Fitzgerald made it clear that violence was not to be the union's policy.[34] He advised employees of both the I.R.T. and the N.Y. Railways, "to keep out of trouble," maintain calm on the picket lines, and avoid making the situation "harder for the police force than it is."[35] Fridiger seconded Fitzgerald, urging, "Leave the intimidation to them, and don't let them stir you to violence. Don't use force; don't do anything that will turn the public against you."[36] The audience initially followed the leaders' directions to refrain from attacking strikebreakers; at least on some train platforms that night, "strikers and strikebreakers mingled freely," and "there was no disorder."[37] Minor violence against property, however, began at once. The I.R.T. claimed that ticket and station agents had left their posts, leaving money and tickets unattended, and that in at least two instances, "ticket boxes were hurled to the street."[38]

At first, the strike's effectiveness beyond the surface lines seemed limited, but even isolated interruptions began to produce unrest among the public. Police reserves rushed to 53rd Street and Eighth Avenue "to quell a disturbance" arising from an overflow of passengers on the elevated platform. Passengers at Times Square, meanwhile, took advantage of a ticket agent's departure to stroll onto the platform without paying. The ticket chopper, who had remained at his post, was "severely beaten" when he tried to stop two men from entering the cashier's cage.[39] The P.S.C., whose members were growing nervous, issued subpoenas to both company and union officials, invoking "its right to investigate conditions of transportation service."[40]

It was no use. Shonts and Hedley were immovable, and now they had the editorial press on their side.[41] Shonts used his testimony at the P.S.C. hearings on September 7 as an opportunity to advertise how hard he was working to keep the trains running for the public. When he told Julius Henry Cohen, the P.S.C. counsel, that he had been working for two days straight, and expressed envy of Straus's and Mitchel's recent vacations, Cohen remarked that Shonts did not appear at all fatigued. The transit president goaded the union representatives in the room with his breezy reply: "Appearances are sometimes deceitful. . . . While I am debonair in appearance, my physical infirmities call for rest."[42]

With the tide turning against the union, incidents of worker violence began to multiply. Despite the *Times*'s sanguine assessment after the first full day of renewed striking ("it could almost be said that there had been no violence"), the day had seen "bricks thrown at elevated trains or surface cars, a few cases of slugging . . . decayed vegetables flung at strikebreakers, the spiking of surface car slots, the stoppage of elevated trains by the pulling of emergency breaks, [and] the routing of faint-hearted train crews."[43] On September 8, "bricks and other missiles were hurled from roofs at moving trains" on the Ninth Avenue elevated between 45th and 50th Streets, and someone allegedly shot at the train four times for good measure. A northbound train passed through this stretch under a hail of "bottles and other missiles hurled from a roof near Fiftieth Street," and as the celestial artillery continued to rain down, "policemen were ordered to the roofs in the trouble zone."[44]

Ninth Avenue elevated railroad at 24th Street. As this undated photo indicates, the "bricks and other missiles . . . hurled from roofs at moving trains" were coming from very close range. Collection of the New-York Historical Society.

Third Avenue elevated railroad, looking South from 42nd Street, April 1915. Collection of the New-York Historical Society.

Worker violence against property and dangerous skirmishes with the goal of sabotaging operations continued apace as the prospects for the strike's success grew dimmer. On September 10, strikers attacked a Madison Avenue surface car and threw stones, bottles, and other debris at police, injuring one. Police arrested eleven and opened fire to repel strikers trying to recover their detained comrades; Shonts again remarked grimly, "It is a war to the finish."[45] On September 11, bricks connected with trolleys and elevateds across the city; a crowd of strikers near 86th Street mobbed a trolley, subdued the two patrolmen guarding it, then dragged off the operators and chased them away. Philip Henrich, a N.Y. Railways strikebreaker, "incautiously left the circle of police protection . . . to get a glass of beer, and was set upon by a crowd" that administered a sound beating before letting up.[46]

Without endorsing (or acknowledging) any of this violence, Fitzgerald issued a statement that night nakedly appealing to class loyalty. He listed the multimillion-dollar interest earnings that J. P. Morgan's banking concerns had claimed from the I.R.T. over several years prior, publicized Shonts's $100,000 salary, and characterized Whitridge as "the type of Bourbon driven out of France in 1789."[47] Speaking at two Socialist Party meetings six days later and after far more violence, he pressed an ultimately vain appeal (despite pockets of initial enthusiasm) for a sympathetic, general strike of New York's unions. In a suggestive indication of the Socialists'—and possibly Fitzgerald's—sympathy for worker violence, he was introduced as "the man who is going to smash the corporations to smithereens."[48]

On September 19, after Shonts and the other transit executives rejected pleas from a "committee of merchants cooperating with the Mayor" to soften their position against arbitration, riots grew from dozens to hundreds of participants. Simultaneous attacks on car barns of the two busiest surface lines (42nd and 59th Streets) overwhelmed police, whose numbers had been thinned by reassignment to polling duty during the primary election. The attacks produced a few beatings of strikebreakers, and put "to flight all railway employees in the vicinity."[49] At Broadway and 42nd Street, a crowd turned the construction of new transit lines against old ones by gathering stones from a subway excavation and using them to barrage a passing streetcar, scattering the terrified passengers.[50] When police arrived, the crowd beat a retreat to the rooftops, whence they "attacked Elevated trains, showering bottles and bricks" from above.[51]

At 76th Street and Third Avenue, a striker hurled an iron bolt through a car window, badly injuring a passenger's leg. On 173rd Street and Southern Boulevard, passengers on a surfacing subway panicked and rushed for the doors as the train came under a hail of stones. At 59th Street and Sixth Avenue, two strikers and a friend emerged from behind a Central Park Wall and smashed all the windows out of a crosstown car as it passed. The policeman manning the car arrested them, but just after they arrived at the precinct, "a report was received of another attack on a Fifty-Ninth Street crosstown car at Third Avenue. A mob of strikers hurled bricks and iron bolts at the car, one of the missiles injuring Anna Pollock of 722 Park Avenue so severely that she had to be taken to a hospital."[52]

In addition to more sporadic attacks across the city involving hundreds of strikers, the next day brought ominous news of the potential for violence of a different order. Police claimed to have concluded a successful sting operation to capture a striker who, "it was said, had attempted to purchase explosives from a laborer in a new subway excavation." They told reporters that the prisoner had admitted under questioning that "he sought the explosives to 'blow up' a couple of Broadway cars."[53] As the *Evening Sun* put it, "This is no longer a strike; it is civil war."[54]

Mitchel and Straus, seeing the situation spinning out of control and facing the possibility of a citywide general strike, announced that they were prepared to call in the militia. Hugh Frayne, an A.F.L. organizer in charge of directing any sympathy strike activities, declared stonily in response, "We have made no threats of disorder and we cannot be held responsible for disorder."[55] As the question of a general strike consumed labor's ranks over the next week, the violence ebbed. When it became clear that most unions would not join the transit workers—either in deference to their own contracts, or because Samuel Gompers put the kibosh on a sympathy walkout—the majority of workers began to acknowledge defeat.[56]

Still, the violence persisted. October began with mobs in Yonkers demolishing streetcar windows with bricks and stones, then driving back repeated charges of club-wielding police officers. Fridiger begged strikers in Mount Vernon "to desist from violence, telling them they were merely hurting their own cause," but his words fell on deaf ears.[57] A crowd in Third Street used their bodies to block all traffic, and moments after a cavalry of motorcycle patrolmen finally dispersed them by riding directly through their midst, a car conductor received a blow to the head with a stone.[58] The next day brought more attacks by strike sympathizers in Mount Vernon, and more arrests.[59]

On October 5, the nearly eighty-year-old Mary Harris "Mother" Jones delivered a fiery sermon of rebellion in Mozart Hall on the Upper East Side, attended by Fitzgerald and W.T.U.L. representatives. Jones remonstrated strikers' wives, "You ought to be out raising hell. This is the fighting age. Put on your fighting clothes. America was not discovered by Columbus for that bunch of bloodsucking leeches who are now living off of us. You are too sentimental."[60] Shortly afterward, a crowd of two hundred women destroyed a surface car two blocks away, hurling "paving blocks through the windows," and using "fists, finger nails, bricks and other missiles" to repel police when they arrived on the scene.[61] Officers declined to arrest Mother Jones, however, and a "police matron" who had attended the rally attested that "the speaker said nothing of an inflammatory nature."[62] Testing the limits of what might be deemed inflammatory in a Harlem River Casino speech the next day, Jones labeled the police "uniformed murderers" and growled, "If police are organized to shed our blood we are going to organize to shed the other side's blood."[63]

Such threats of bloodletting were the cries of a radical whose moment had passed. Jones and her generation of labor stalwarts had come of age in an era whose corporate antagonists pulled no punches—robber barons who, in Shonts's place, might have successfully used political influence to call in the state militia and have soldiers open fire indiscriminately on picketing workers. Accordingly, Jones and her contemporaries had become accustomed to a mode of industrial warfare that called for—and to some extent, countenanced—violent tactics and retribution on the part of the poor. The unapologetic violence of capitalists had created the context for the same behavior from labor, a context in which a jury, in 1905, could acquit I.W.W. leader William "Big Bill" Haywood of murdering the governor of Idaho at least in part because Haywood's lawyer, Clarence Darrow, could credibly threaten the country with retributive revolution in the event of a conviction. Union violence may never have enjoyed the tolerance that violence in defense of property did, but it had at least enjoyed some measure of understanding.[64]

In the intervening years, increasing numbers of capitalists had begun to recognize the danger they were courting, as Joseph Choate had indicated already in 1895 when advising Alva Vanderbilt to refrain from divorcing her then-husband. Some made efforts to improve their image, and that of the wealthy generally, through philanthropy. As mining king Daniel Guggenheim told the federal government's Commission on Industrial Relations in 1915, "If it is not for what has been done and what is being done" by such philanthropists, "we would have revolution in this country."[65]

More capitalists and managers, however, simply devised ways of having their cake and eating labor, too: by initiating welfare capitalist policies that created the public appearance of benevolent employment practices; by actively cultivating popular support in the midst of conflicts (and in the normal course of business) through elaborate publicity campaigns; and by appealing patiently to a legal code that preferred private property to democratic political expression. In the new landscape of labor-capital relations, capital progressively bolstered its emerging role as defender of the public interest, assigning blame for any violence to the "alien agitators" of labor.

By October 13, 1916, progressives and academics had formed a Citizens Committee to "ascertain whether the traction strike is over," a clear sign of defeat for the union if ever there was one.[66] The next day, the police commissioner withdrew the police presence from subway and elevated stations.[67] Fitzgerald, loudly maintaining his belief that the strike might still succeed, at least had the grace to remark of the police, "Now the poor fellows won't be compelled to work overtime as they have been. Putting them on the cars was a piece of unnecessary stage play."[68] Twelve quiet days after Fitzgerald uttered those words, a small band of frustrated and furious young men would prove that it had perhaps not been an unnecessary stage play after all.

Fitzgerald instantly disowned the Lenox Avenue bombing. He "characterized the incident as deplorable . . . and pointed out that he had been a foe of violence throughout the strike."[69] This failed to satisfy newspaper editorial boards. The day after the bombing, the *Times* sputtered:

> Some will think it fortunate, and a few will think it unfortunate, that the application for pardon for Dynamiter McNamara should be announced on the same day with the explosion of the bomb in the subway. The connection

between the two incidents is the unregenerate temper of those guilty of outrages of this sort. No reluctance to profit by them is shown by those in
whose interest the lives of innocent persons are endangered, and stubborn
opposition is shown to every attempt to place responsibility for them. Not a
word is said by the strikers in this city in repudiation of what doubtless was
done by their express authority, but which can have been done for no other
reason than to help their lost cause, now further discredited.[70]

Fitzgerald had actually used the words (and the *Times* had reported them)
"of course, we repudiate the explosion"; but this was the smaller, less consequential bit of obscurantism contained in the *Times* commentary.[71] In their
zeal to connect the Lenox Avenue bombing to the McNamara dynamiting
of six years before, the editors fed the notion that class violence on the part
of workers and the poor was all of a piece: heedless of human life, fanati-
cally radical, and the product of a remorseless, "unregenerate temper."

In truth, there was quite a bit of variation. The Lenox Avenue explosion
was the work of men who defied the principled, bomb-throwing anarchist
stereotype, or that of the implacable and methodical union dynamiter: they
were James J. Murnagh and William Molsky, subway guards; Thomas J.
McGuire, a chauffeur; and Michael J. Herlihy, an elevated guard, who was,
at the ripe old age of twenty, the financial secretary of Local 731.[72] After the
first arrests on November 3, one reporter noted upon meeting them, "The
prisoners . . . did not look like plotters. They are young, some very young,
and they looked it. Merna [*sic*] . . . is of medium height, slender of build,
with rather large eyes and hair brushed back from his forehead. He sat ner-
vously twirling his derby hat about in his hands. Herlihy, the Financial
Secretary, has only reached manhood. All . . . were neatly dressed."[73] Murnagh, McGuire, and Herlihy had all been born in New York, and were in
their early to mid-twenties.[74]

These were neither hardened, foreign revolutionaries, nor systematically
lawless union officials—any more than had been the men and women throwing bricks, flinging rotten produce, or fighting with strikebreakers over the
previous weeks—and their behavior over the following months proved it.
The police captain overseeing their interrogation after the arrest said that
they "told their stories quietly and apparently with little idea of the seriousness of the crime they contemplated and had in part carried out." Murnagh,

who had proposed the bombing and was, by all accounts, the romantic idealist of the group, at first declared to the Captain, "I would willingly give up my life for the benefit of 11,000 workingmen!"[75] When the enormity of his predicament set in, however, he rethought his impulse for martyrdom and pleaded not guilty. The others followed suit.

They maintained their innocence for nearly six months. On Tuesday, March 13, 1917, Judge Tompkins in State Supreme Court sentenced Herlihy, the first to be tried, to a term of ten to twenty years at Sing Sing. By Wednesday, Murnagh and Molsky, who were awaiting trial, had reversed their pleas "with the hope, their counsel said, of receiving lesser sentences."[76] On Thursday, Herlihy reappeared in court to turn state's evidence against McGuire and the final indicted man, the former assistant financial secretary of the N.Y. Railways Local 722 George Pollock. At first, newspapers eagerly parroted the story from Herlihy's lawyer that "from the time of his arrest, Herlihy had shown a wavering disposition to tell all he knew, but not until the young woman whom he was to have married on the very day he was sentenced . . . visited him . . . was there real hope of getting him to be entirely frank."[77]

Fridiger (who represented Pollock, the only indicted man the union had agreed to defend) revealed a less romantic truth in court. On cross-examination, he "drew from Herlihy an admission that an offer of commutation of his sentence was made to him before he took the stand." Pollock was acquitted on Friday.[78] McGuire pleaded guilty on Sunday.[79]

Despite Murnagh's impassioned declaration (quickly recanted) of willingness to sacrifice his own life for the cause of the workers, neither he nor any of his co-conspirators gave any indication that they wished to sacrifice the lives of others. To the contrary, they took pains to explain that their purpose was solely to destroy property, and thereby create a crisis that would force the city to pressure the I.R.T. managers back into settlement talks with the strikers. This was not even a carefully crafted strategy of methodical destruction, along the lines of what the Structural Ironworkers had pursued for years before the *L.A. Times* bombing.[80] Herlihy, in all likelihood, was driven by little more than frustration, resentment, and desperation. As a rank-and-file member of the Amalgamated negotiating committee for the I.R.T., he had been a silent presence in the room for the "more than acrimonious" September 5 meeting between Hedley and the union; he was summarily fired before the strike began the next evening, allegedly for failing to show up to his post.[81] Pained at the strike's slow death in October, Murnagh had decided independently of Herlihy that "something ought to be done to convince the public and the Interboro officials that the strike was still on in earnest."[82] He enlisted the now unemployed Herlihy in his harebrained scheme.

In this respect, Murnagh's and Herlihy's instincts were little different than those of anyone blocking the tracks in Mount Vernon or tossing a bottle from a rooftop on West 50th Street onto an elevated train passing below. McGuire's only role in the attack was to allow Murnagh (his friend) and Herlihy to stay in his New Jersey home overnight on their way to buy the dynamite, a courtesy for which they allegedly paid him ten dollars.[83] According to their own initial confessions, "The men were ignorant of explosives, and . . . spent some time experimenting to find out just how long a foot of fuse would burn."[84] Master terrorists they were not.

Herlihy, to the end, was quite explicit on one point: "the purpose of the explosion was not to endanger life, but to injure the Interborough Rapid Transit Company."[85] Of course, the McNamara brothers had said essentially the same thing—but only after years of participation in methodical bombings that ended in the murder of twenty-one fellow workers.[86] These men, little more than boys, represented something different, simpler, and more widespread. It was also something that was coming to an end.

Superficially, the Lenox Avenue station bombing had been a symbol of anarchy. A flashy, startling act of violence, it received more extensive and sustained news coverage than any other single incident during the strike. But in the larger scheme of mayhem and destruction on the streets of New York that summer, it hardly rated such attention. No one died. The few injuries sustained were minor. Trains were back on the same tracks less than one hour after the explosion.[87] Meanwhile, in the weeks that preceded the bombing, the city hovered on the edge of a public transportation shutdown while tens of thousands of working men, women, and children wreaked havoc on the symbols and physical property of a widely despised corporate cabal.[88] According to a P.S.C. report, collisions more than doubled in the second half of the year, cresting at 1,288 separate incidents, while instances in which "vehicles" of the transit companies "were struck" skyrocketed from under 800 to nearly 10,000.[89] Riots seemed liable to break out at any time, and did. Nine people were killed: a strikebreaker, one supervisor for Bergoff Brothers & Waddell (apparently killed by his own men), and seven passengers or strikebreakers in transit accidents caused by inexperienced replacement operators.[90] During the course of the fight, the violence ebbed when a favorable—or at least, respectful—settlement of the strike seemed possible; then it flowed in a rush through floodgates opened by managers' antagonism, their interference with worker democracy, and their undeniably savvier tactics vis-à-vis the courts and the city.

In this light, the bombing was not a grand sign of imminent anarchy but a symbol of the conflict from which it emerged. Like that conflict, it was an expression of outrage over the abrogation of municipal responsibility to protect a public service from private rapacity, presaging an unending, often bitter struggle over the state's role in regulating corporate enterprises upon whose operations citizens depend. Like that conflict, it was a cry of rebellion from people who had grown tired of feeling helpless, cheated in their contest with rich men who seemed supremely empowered to determine the rules of the game for everyone else while enjoying the freedom to violate those rules with impunity.

After the strike ended (functionally, if not formally), Shonts continued to specialize in publicity that sought a personal connection with riders while tying the fate of the city and nation to the I.R.T.'s financial health. *Interborough Rapid Transit*, a public newsletter begun around the time of the strike, published exchanges of letters between Shonts and "persons in all stations of life" who responded to the company's open solicitation for suggestions.[91] A few months later, the newsletter highlighted the military service of 1,260 I.R.T. employees in the Great War and the company's $4 million purchase of Liberty Bonds, urging the public to buy bonds as well, and trumpeting the I.R.T.'s patriotism. By announcing that 10 percent of June 25, 1918, ticket sales would go to the Red Cross War Fund, Shonts invited members of the public to view their ridership on the I.R.T. as a joint philanthropic endeavor between themselves and the corporation.[92]

As he put it in the April 6, 1917, issue, "We're trying every day to improve our methods, and we want the people of New York to realize deep down in their hearts that that is the spirit in which we are operating these lines." Making real connections with the hearts of customers and citizens—this was the new corporate dream.[93] For publicly countenanced, anti-corporate violence on the part of the poor, it was practically a death knell.

Overt and violent class conflict may have dwindled over the last century, but violence, or the threat of it, has been a continual, common currency in American class relations. Indeed, the metaphor of "currency" suits the use of destructive force in American class conflict because rich and poor have often traded violence as a kind of monetary instrument, trying to purchase from each other certain goods beyond the capacity of ordinary money to afford: notably, complete docility from labor, or material concessions and respect from capital. Economic metaphors are also tempting because practitioners of conflictual class relations, rich or poor, often justify calls to violence—as Shonts did—either by defending the "natural" economic forces of the market or—as the Lenox Avenue bombers did—by rebelling against creeping or sudden economic deprivation.

Market language also lends itself to describing conflictual class relations because such encounters necessarily embrace competition or opposing interests as the basis of relations between rich and poor. If cooperative class relations depend on an ideal of mutual interest, and prescriptive class relations require a vision of social adjustment that (no matter how heedlessly pursued or differentially enjoyed) benefits all, then conflictual class relations express the recognition, explicit or otherwise, that success for capitalists depends upon the exploitation of labor, and for laborers upon militant resistance to such exploitation—and, in extremis, the overthrow of capitalism itself.[94]

Moments of class conflict in the United States, however, have rarely been grand attempts to realize utopian economic visions. Instead, they have most often been messy, historically contingent, and narrowly directed manifestations of the irrepressible tension between America's most cherished *political* ideal, democracy, and its dominant system of production, capitalism. Since the early nineteenth if not the late eighteenth century, American workers and the poor have couched their attacks on the wealthy in the language of democratic or republican freedoms, usually borrowing directly from the nation's founders.[95] The wealthy, meanwhile, have drawn equally from

American scriptures of freedom and democracy—often in the same conflicts—to protect their right to own and improve property without interference.[96] This friction between democracy and capitalism, obscured by a shared vocabulary of liberalism, is the most fundamental basis of violent conflictual class relations in American history.

Most contemporary Americans seem to assume that democracy and capitalism are symbiotic sides of the same political-economic coin. In fact, the divergence in their philosophies should be self-evident. Democracy and capitalism pursue incongruous priorities: the Enlightenment project of improving humanity through democratic relations of greater social equality and popular government, and the classical economic project of improving and protecting property.[97] It is a truth, near universally ignored, that creating the conditions for a society's maximum human fulfillment seldom aligns with extracting the maximum material benefit from human bodies, minds, and spirits.

Capitalism's fiercest advocates deny that these priorities are at odds by reversing the terms of comparison, insisting that capitalism's program of improving property complements democracy's program of improving humanity. The contemporary incarnation of this position holds that the maximization of productivity generates vastly greater stores of wealth, and that such efficiency, emerging as it does from democratic rational choice in a liberal economic order, weds material improvement to human freedom.[98] Even those more skeptical voices calling for regulation of capitalism and a more sophisticated understanding of human motivation take as a given that everyone will be better off under a regime devoted to property improvement— correctly adjusted or restrained—because, in layman's terms, a rising tide lifts all boats, a bigger pie feeds more mouths, and so forth.[99] The material side of this claim is not necessarily wrong. Capitalist systems of production, with more or less regulation, have indeed created wealth beyond the wildest imaginings of men and women living even fifty years ago, let alone five hundred or five thousand. The pace of growth has been historically—dare we say geologically—unprecedented.

That growth, however, has come with clear human costs, the most obvious of which over the past two centuries has been the violent eruption and suppression of democratic social relations interfering with capitalism.[100] Cycles of rebellion and suppression stemming from such relations render untenable, on its face, the notion that capitalism and democracy are essentially harmonious systems of social organization. They coexist in extreme tension, and in a constant, frequently bloody effort to get the better of one another.[101]

On the eve of America's entry into the war in Europe, at the height of a strike wave seizing the nation, and in a historical moment of revolutionary political imagination, the violence that workers directed at New York's rail companies predominantly reflected the more prosaic goal of demolishing property.[102] That the Lenox Avenue bombing emerged mainly in response to elite corporate managers' increasingly savvy public relations campaigns, internal attempts to disrupt worker democracy through welfare capitalist schemes, and subversion of state powers designed to mediate conflict allows us to see such acts as outgrowths of class tensions that are most assuredly still with us.

T. P. Shonts did not live to see his dream of corporate influence grow through the 1920s, fade in the 1930s and early 1940s, and then grow again over the remainder of the twentieth century; he died in late September 1919, leaving two scandals to play out simultaneously in his wake.

The first was personal. Shonts, it turned out, had named Mrs. Amanda C. Thomas, a young divorcée, as the chief beneficiary of his estate. Subsequent newspaper investigations and lawsuits clearly indicated that the transit chief—who had piously warned the Drake University graduating class of 1912 that the growing "spirit of communism" was threatening not just the state but the "sanctity" of marriage—had himself been an enthusiastic adulterer.[103] Shonts's widow, understandably displeased, sued Thomas and alleged through her attorneys "that Mrs. Thomas received several million dollars in money and property from Mr. Shonts prior to his death." Her suit demanded restitution of this fortune, claiming that Thomas "willfully and wrongfully . . . in or about the year 1906 and from then continuously to September, 1919 . . . did prey ruthlessly upon the said Theodore P. Shonts and by her artifices, immorality, and wiles enticed him from the society of the plaintiff and alienated his love and affection from her."[104] Though the jilted widow did succeed in regaining executrix power over her dead husband's will, she never recovered the bulk of the fortune. The court dismissed her suit against Thomas, and the deciding justice remarked drily, "The purely perfunctory prattle of fraud, duress, and intimidation in haec verba is ominous with dearth of facts."[105]

No equivalent dearth of facts, however, plagued the city's investigation into the I.R.T.'s finances as the rail company neared bankruptcy in 1919 and 1920. On February 3, 1920, the company auditor himself testified before the city's Board of Estimate that the I.R.T. had paid out nearly $3 million "in bonuses" since 1913, "partly charged to the cost of construction . . . partly to equipment and to the work under the elevated certificates." Over $18 million more had gone to pay "bankers' commission, discount, and expenses," and shareholders had reaped generous dividends for years.[106] The 1916 strikes alone had cost the company over $2 million, more than 10 percent of which had gone to Bergoff Brothers & Waddell for professional strikebreaking services.

Quackenbush, who attended the hearings in his continuing capacity as I.R.T. general counsel, "broke into the discussion" at this point to interject that "if the $2,000,000 had not been expended in the preservation of the railroad's property the city would have lost five times as much." According to the *Times,* the lawyer "heatedly declared that the trains were kept running and that 700 men had been sent to jail for dynamiting the subways and assaulting citizens and employes [*sic*]."[107] The young city council president Fiorello H. LaGuardia publicly derided Quackenbush's claims, but in the long term it would not matter. Quackenbush had perfected Shonts's dicta: remind Americans that the company is the unappreciated savior of public finances, the defender of constitutional rights, and, at the end of the day, all that stands between civilization and anarchy.

These dicta had even greater resonance in 1920 than they had in 1916, for the streetcar strikes had come at a pivotal moment in U.S. history. Indeed, the summer months of 1916 were practically the last during which collective expressions of antagonism toward capitalism could assert themselves in America vigorously, even violently, and still expect a real measure of public sympathy. The end to such sympathy had been drawing near for some time, at least since a series of dynamite incidents in New York beginning two summers earlier.

The unintentional explosion of a bomb in production killed three anarchists in a Lexington Avenue apartment on July 4, 1914. Then dynamite rocked St. Patrick's cathedral and St. Alphonsus church on the Lower East Side that October.[108] November saw the bombing of the Bronx Court House, and then an attempt to assassinate a Tombs Court judge in his own court-room with dynamite beneath his chair—this latter plot foiled at the last minute by a watchful patrolman who noticed the sputtering fuse.[109] No such patrolman was on hand, however, to prevent the dynamiting of Bronx Bor-ough Hall's southeast section less than six months later.[110]

Several of these bombings elicited press commentary decrying the vio-lent radicalism of socialists, anarchists, and the I.W.W., but many authority figures remained leery of responding too harshly or even accusing social radicals. Monsignor Lavelle of the Catholic Church repeatedly dismissed speculation that anarchists or the I.W.W. had perpetrated the church bombings, despite suggestive circumstantial evidence that they had.[111] They would have had no reason to do so, Lavelle protested, because "St. Pat-rick's Church befriends the poor." Assistant District Attorney James Dela-hanty, in the wake of the Bronx Court House and Tombs Court incidents, spurned the notion that harsher state policies would deter radicals. "In my opinion," he declared, "no good would result from repressive measures to-ward anarchistic meetings or parades, or toward the use of the red flag, which has been banned by Massachusetts. No benefit would be obtained from severe penalties that now exist. Capital punishment would not help matters." His reasoning is telling: "There would be no public sentiment back of it."[112]

This was no idle cynicism on Delahanty's part, at least in 1914. An esti-mated 5,000 New Yorkers turned out to Union Square a week after the Lexington Avenue bombing to memorialize the would-be anarchist bomb-ers as martyrs. Despite some queasiness about the event, the editors of the *New-York Tribune* had even editorialized in favor of granting the necessary public permit, a remarkable demonstration of how lenient "public senti-ment" really was. In fact, it was public sentiment that the editors cited spe-cifically as the reason that granting the permit would be safe. "We," they wrote, "do not believe a permit would lead to disorder, since New Yorkers, as a whole, are too busy to pay more than superficial attention . . . and too indulgent to interfere."[113] Speakers at the memorial did not hesitate to make use of such leniency. One of them put it plainly enough: "I want to say that it's about time the working class came out frankly and openly and said,

'Yes, we believe in violence. We will use violence whenever it is necessary to use it.' "[114]

The serial bombings that followed, however, came just as the shadow of the Great War was stretching across the Atlantic, and any lingering, laissez-faire public sentiment toward radical violence began to hit a wall. Various Germans, Germanophiles, or antiwar zealots had been pursuing periodic sabotage operations to interfere with American assistance to the allies, and increasingly sensational newspaper and magazine reports were whipping up anti-German, antiforeign sentiment in the United States.[115] In this climate—and only eight days after the Preparedness Day bombing in San Francisco killed ten and injured dozens of ordinary civilians, creating national outrage—the munitions depot on Black Tom Island in New York Harbor exploded, killing several and injuring hundreds. The blast wave shattered windows in Manhattan, Brooklyn, Jersey City, and Hoboken, and at least one report claimed that people felt the reverberation as far away as Maryland.[116]

Only a few hours before this explosion, the Amalgamated had issued its strike call for the Third Avenue elevated, so when Shonts tried to tie the strike effort to the passions of war four days later, he was doing so in a context primed for reaction. Employers had long attempted to identify democratic industrial movements with dangerous foreign elements, and the combination of nationalist war fervor, multiple bombings that smacked of antiwar sabotage and radical labor politics, and anarchist bravado in public finally created conditions that would translate this rhetorical conflation into state policy.[117] Already in 1915, Woodrow Wilson had denounced all "creatures of passion, disloyalty, and anarchy." When he made his war appeal to Congress on April 2, 1917—less than three months after socialist and laborite Tom Mooney received a death sentence for the Preparedness Day bombing—Wilson's declaration that "disloyalty will be dealt with with the firm hand of stern suppression" clearly applied to radical domestic dissent as well as saboteurs.[118]

The Espionage Act came into effect that June, threatening up to twenty years in prison for any speech encouraging draft resistance or interfering with the war effort. It augmented an immigration law passed by Congress in February that mandated deportation for anyone "found advocating or teaching the unlawful destruction of property, or . . . the assassination of public officials," and would itself be supplemented by the Sedition Act in May 1918.[119] This all happened with neck-snapping swiftness, culminating in Attorney General A. Mitchel Palmer's launching a campaign to deport hundreds of the most prominent anarchists, Communists, and socialists from American shores, including Emma Goldman and Alexander Berkman.[120]

Berkman had organized the memorial to the Lexington Avenue bombers in 1914, but as he awaited deportation five years later, the *Tribune*'s editorial board had no indulgence left for him, opining, "Instead of repression, there has been a false sympathy with destructive agitators, who have been excused as philosophic radicals, rather than as actual terrorists."[121] Failing to acknowledge their relatively recent complicity in such "false sympathy," they celebrated "the great transformation in American opinion . . . after so many years of contemptuous tolerance," remarking of Berkman and Goldman that "the United States is no place for them or for revolutionists of their kind."[122] They were right: the state had dramatically and progressively clamped down on the expression of radical politics through an ever tightening vise of surveillance, imprisonment, and forced exile, and it had done so with mounting public approval.

It did so, moreover, with the participation and approval of the mainstream labor movement. The Wilson administration's wartime policy ingeniously paired suppression of radical speech with the mechanics of liberal compromise on industrial disputes. The National War Labor Board (N.W.L.B.), established early in 1918, created an unprecedented federal mediation structure for labor impasses, on the basic principle that "there should be no strikes or lockouts during the war." Despite some caveats to appease employer participants, its founding agreement explicitly affirmed workers' right to bargain collectively, a giant step for American labor that still fell well short of revolution.[123] This drew the more conservative A.F.L. into the federal government's protective embrace, at a time when labor's ties to antiwar and more radical working-class activists were well on their way to dissolution because of friction over the war. The federal government, by pairing its draconian criminalization of radical speech with such a pathbreaking assertion of the state's prerogative to protect labor rights, consolidated the alliance between bourgeois progressives, the state, and nationalist unionists such as Samuel Gompers, while decisively marginalizing antiwar activists and the more radical American left.[124] It made the mainstream American labor movement into the handmaiden of nationalism, war, antiradicalism, and above all public order.

By the time the war ended, this realignment of progressive politics had produced three major legacies. Resistance to state incursions on free speech sparked the modern movement to protect civil liberties, including the founding of the organization that would become the American Civil Liberties Union. The example of the N.W.L.B., meanwhile, set a new baseline expectation for the public that managers should negotiate over worker grievances, gradually pushing most employers away from hiring professional strikebreakers to settle disputes through violence and toward the emerging playbook of corporate welfare and public relations. And finally, the public's willingness to understand or empathize with those practicing violent class conflict to challenge the status quo effectively disappeared.[125] The first two of these legacies, in one form or another, figure prominently in most histories of the Progressive Era and the early twentieth-century labor movement. They ostensibly represent the best of what was "progressive" about the era: namely, the democratic rejection of strictures on speech, and the government's willingness to restrain capitalist prerogatives in the interest of social harmony.

The third, however, remains inadequately recognized as a major countervailing force to otherwise progressive outcomes of the Progressive Era. Before World War I, the American public's greater willingness to suspend knee-jerk judgment and engage critically with the possible structural sources of radical violence allowed for both urgency and creativity in finding potential solutions. They experimented with new labor laws, supported national discussions on industrial relations that included nearly all interested parties, and for the first time took tentative steps toward policies of wealth redistribution.[126] Even if statesmen and citizens disapproved of violent class conflict, they recognized it as the result of festering industrial grievances, unsustainably asymmetrical power arrangements, and worsening material inequality that affected the lives, liberty, and happiness of workers. One need not (and most Progressives did not) embrace political violence as a desirable means of producing social change to recognize that in the face of such violence, trading circumspection and analysis for automatic recourse to state repression is a devil's bargain.

That, however, was the bargain that Americans struck.[127] The politics and corporate practices that T. P. Shonts debuted in 1916, which turned the tide of the transit strikes in New York, became the standard script of conflictual class relations in America by decade's end. The reactive violence from labor's ranks on display in 1916 subsided because Shonts and his managerial descendants, with the help of the Great War, succeeded so thoroughly in getting the public and the state to recite from that new script. "The public interest" became synonymous with the maintenance of efficient economic production, law and order, and growth at nearly any cost. That script provides clear answers to the questions the Lenox Avenue bombers were trying to raise with their foolish, desperate act—questions about the appropriate relationship between private business, the state, and the commonweal, and about the relative accountability of wealthy and poor Americans for violence. Defer to business, for business knows best, the script replies. Violence on behalf of workers and the poor must be unquestioningly vilified and eradicated, and violence emanating from capital and the state is always defensive of the public interest.

These answers, and the pervasive acceptance of them in the United States, are as much a legacy of the Progressive Era as is the reduction of industrial violence. By perpetuating a profound epistemological inequality, these answers sharply limit Americans' political imagination when confronting material inequality. They are, in their way, responsible for much of the tragic, progressive inequality that surrounds Americans today.

Recognizing Class in Ourselves

"Bartleby!"

"I know you," he said, without looking round—"and I want nothing to say to you."

"It was not I that brought you here, Bartleby," said I, keenly pained at his implied suspicion. "And to you, this should not be so vile a place. Nothing reproachful attaches to you by being here. And see, it is not so sad a place as one might think. Look, there is the sky, and here is the grass."

"I know where I am," he replied, but would say nothing more, and so I left him.

—Herman Melville

DESCRIBING AMERICAN INEQUALITY as tragic has its dangers. As literary critic Terry Eagleton observes, the concept of tragedy is so powerfully bound up with a sense of inevitability that describing events or conditions as tragic risks divesting their human protagonists of agency.[1] Tragedy in this vein conveys notions of transhistorical essentialism in place of contingency, hopelessness in place of idealism, and conjures spectres of human incapacity before the gods: we are but mortals, our victories and defeats foretold by the Fates, products not of our will, but of theirs. It should be evident that such a bleak notion of tragedy is not the stuff of American class relations, nor of any history worth the name.

Yet tragedy can also invoke the contradictions between human yearning and action—the unanticipated material consequences of attempts to reconcile our deepest convictions with an unyielding reality. This tragedy manifests usually through some inescapable quality possessed by the heroes, invisible or unknown to them, that frustrates their most ardent desires and brings their fondest designs to unforeseen, lamentable, and sometimes condemnable ends. This is the tragedy of a reformer's quest to reshape slums by employing the very ideological and structural tools that built them; the charity devotee's faith in uplifting aid applicants through a process whose method necessarily compounds their degradation; the settlement-house worker's catering to capitalist illusions of dignified poverty in order to fund her alleviation of capitalism's attendant miseries; the society lady's latent disdain for garment workers she would embrace as sisters; the businessman's endless pursuit of labor peace through ruthless war; the worker's reinforcement of capitalist power with violence meant to demolish its cornerstone. These are human tragedies, and despite their thwarted purposes, they retain a great deal of contingency, agency, and even hope.

The hope lies not in the tragedies themselves, however, but in what they can teach us about our own failures of vision. In this vein, Eagleton turns to Walter Benjamin's theory of tragedy when considering Arthur Miller's *Death of a Salesman,* remarking, "Sacrifice for Benjamin is an act of liberation: through the death of the hero, the community comes to consciousness of its subjection to mythological forces."[2] Through Willy Loman's many sacrifices—his manner of dying, certainly, but even more acutely his manner of living—Miller skewered the myth of the American self-made man, in the explicit hope of illuminating his audience's subjection to it.[3] The best tragedies, like Miller's, unveil our own blindnesses by revealing them through the dramas of others.

The class collisions recounted here, dramas in their own right, unveil a tragic blindness toward class that contributed directly to inequality's reproduction during the Progressive Era. Surely, no one can accuse the men and women who appear in these pages of apathy or inattention to inequality. They were in many ways bolder, more creative, and vastly more optimistic than contemporary Americans in combating inequality and its ill effects. And yet their efforts often failed or backfired over time, because their inability to recognize class in themselves—or to account for it in others—caused them to manifest and reproduce it, expanding inequality in the very attempt to shrink it.

A case could be made, of course, that these stories constitute not tragedy, but farce—that the driving forces behind such class collisions were arrogance, fear, cupidity, or rage. Undoubtedly, these played their part, and to deny the worst in human history is to deny history altogether, exchanging it for the sort of reassuring redemption narrative that has long plagued popular understandings of both the Progressive Era and American history more broadly. We do our forebears no favors by ignoring the worst in them, and we betray ourselves to boot.

Choosing to see only the basest motivations behind their strivings to forge a better world, however, unfairly caricatures these men and women, rich or poor. It insidiously encourages what E. P. Thompson called, with biting concision, "the enormous condescension of posterity." What Thompson said of Britons vying for the first time with industrialization is equally valid for these subjects: "[T]hey lived through these times of acute social disturbance, and we did not. Their aspirations were valid in terms of their own experience."[4] It may offer some fleeting satisfaction to pinion Richard Watson Gilder or Anne Morgan to the page for their presumptions, to bemoan again the maddening instinct for self-destruction ever stalking the ranks of American labor, even more to condemn the authoritarian inclinations of men such as T. P. Shonts or Max Blanck. There is, unequivocally, nothing tragic about 146 people burning to death because their employers refused to see them as human beings. The Triangle Fire was a crime, not a tragedy. Yet by piling on to the already considerable rebuke of history, and in celebrating our ostensibly superior recognition of their world, we blind ourselves to everything their world shares with our own.

Their blindness to class stemmed primarily from an endlessly renewable resource in American political and cultural life: the myth of classless democracy. American politicians continue to insist—and many Americans continue to believe—that in the United States, life, liberty, and happiness are the assured rewards of hard work; that "personal responsibility" is not only an equally applicable moral imperative, but also a universally effective tool for success. It is a set of assumptions that deny the existence of class altogether, upholding in its place a fervent faith in the market's natural logic, and the presumptive justice of drawing moral inferences from the material conditions of others. These assumptions have retained their beguiling power throughout the twentieth century, surviving—and perhaps overpowering—decades of significant political and social transformation from the 1930s to the 1970s. From the 1980s to the present, their star has remained on the ascendant, barely dimming at all through the greatest economic calamity since the Great Depression.[5] As a result, Americans' attempts to reduce inequality have remained deeply compromised, more often than not reproducing the very inequality they mean to combat.

Those assumptions may have a hoary lineage now, but they were hardly new to the Progressive Era either. In 1853, Herman Melville wrote a devastating but far more subtle literary indictment of the same belief systems pilloried by *Death of a Salesman* nearly a hundred years later. A story of close and sustained class collision, its original title was "Bartleby the Scrivener: A Story of Wall Street."[6] The genial, well-meaning narrator of the tale, who believes himself a magnanimous sort, defines his world from the start through "myself, my *employées,* my business, my chambers, and general surroundings"; he assesses his humanity, in other words, through his engagement with the market.[7] Nevertheless, he is an employer not insensitive to the "fellow-feeling" he might have with his workers, willing to cooperate with them, anxious to do them favors, and occasionally observing in them various faults distributed by "nature," for which he might helpfully prescribe some correction.

He comes into conflict, however, with Bartleby, finding himself endlessly vexed—indeed, spiritually tormented—by the scrivener's imperturbable *preference* to remain unproductive. With exquisite care, Melville unravels this employer-narrator's unexamined assumptions: that productivity is the *summum bonum;* that Bartleby (and by implication, his other employees) owe him gratitude for his "undeniable good usage and indulgence"; that, in the end, property rights trump all, providing the basis for a stable moral order.[8] Driven to "sudden passion" by Bartleby's refusal either to work or to leave the office, the narrator declaims, "What earthly right have you to stay here? Do you pay any rent? Do you pay my taxes? Or is this property yours?"[9] He has traversed each fault line of American class relations in the course of the story, all in an effort to improve his world, but his determined obliviousness to his own assumptions makes of *him* the tragic figure, not the scrivener lying dead in the prison courtyard at tale's end.

The narrator cannot see that, despite his "pained" denials, he *did* bring Bartleby to the Tombs: for though he did not call the constable, the one who did doubtless shared his predication of "earthly right" upon rent, taxes, and property ownership. Such assumptions form a social and intellectual prison far more confining than the one of stone and mortar in which Bartleby meets his demise. In the final encounter between employer and employee, the narrator urges Bartleby to take heart in the sky and the grass of his prison world. At the same time, he re-instantiates the class relation between the two when he says, "And to you, this should not be so vile a place. Nothing reproachful attaches to you by being here."[10] The implication, of course, is that something reproachful *would* attach to Bartleby were he a man capable of productive labor and not, as the narrator suspects, a "ghost."[11] An enigma made flesh, the scrivener harbors no illusions about his surroundings. "I know where I am," he replies. Tragically—despite having built Bartleby's prison from the stuff of his own assumptions, and being imprisoned by them himself—the narrator still does not.

Like Melville's narrator, the women and men of the Progressive Era described herein struggled to reconcile their experience of class relations with their notions of morality and justice, grappling with the unbidden material effects of their own unrecognized assumptions. After the reflexive ideological revanchism spurred by the Bolshevik Revolution, the domestic repressions and liberal concessions of World War I, and the state's systematic exclusions of those most vociferously challenging industrial capitalism's inevitability, the continuing dominance of those assumptions seemed assured.

Undeniably, Americans of the Progressive Era transformed their nation and their world, often for the better. Their most lasting contribution to relations between rich and poor, however, was to further embed the tragic assumptions of Melville's narrator in "Bartleby." Those assumptions continue to reproduce inequality today.

Americans tend to be forward-looking people, but they have arrived at a moment of vast, progressive inequality eerily reminiscent of the past. In 1916, the federal government's Commission on Industrial Relations enumerated "four main sources" of discontent roiling American class relations:

1. Unjust distribution of wealth and income.
2. Unemployment and denial of an opportunity to earn a living.

3. Denial of justice in the creation, in the adjudication, and in the administration of law.

4. Denial of the right and opportunity to form effective organizations.[12]

After a century's journey, Americans have arrived again at their point of departure.

Some important details of the landscape have changed, not least due to the upheavals of the Progressive Era. Prescriptive class relations usually take a smoother form now. In place of "not alms, but a friend," the mantra of prescriptive poor relief has become, "welfare to work." The ideology behind this altered rhetoric, however, has not changed, as Congressman and former Vice-Presidential candidate Paul Ryan revealed in a March 2012 statement that could have been lifted directly from a C.O.S. annual report: "We don't want to turn the safety net into a hammock that lulls able-bodied people into lives of dependency and complacency, that drains them of their will and their incentive to make the most of their lives."[13]

Conflictual class relations have transformed more definitively. The overt and violent class war of the Progressive Era is not only unthinkable in the face of state and private armies whose firepower and tactics have turned an already slanted field of battle onto a vertical axis, but the bitterness and desperation of men such as Michael Herlihy have been anesthetized (though not removed) by easy credit, home mortgage tax deductions, and evermore ubiquitous communications campaigns designed to equate responsible citizenship with consumption. Still, as inequality grows, moments of conflict arise, generating flashes of violent protest within otherwise peaceful demonstrations that have objected to the proposed neoliberal paradise: the Seattle protests at the 1999 World Trade Organization meeting, for instance, or even the Occupy Wall Street movement in 2011.

The Occupy movement, however, speaks directly to the quiet persistence of American class relations' fault lines in its slogan, "We Are the 99%!" By envisioning a vast, populist commonweal facing off against a tiny, avaricious minority, this slogan implicitly projects a near-perfect commonality of interests among Americans, suggesting that the elimination of the minority's special powers and privileges might confer equality and freedom upon us all. Given the disagreements and frictions within Occupy around race, gender, and class, it is all the more ironic that its most recognizable contribution to the popular lexicon of protest elides the deeply stratified landscape of everyday class encounters in America.[14]

Such elision makes true class cooperation impossible, and if American history is a fair guide, such cooperation will be a necessity for any effective, large-scale political movement battling inequality. Class cooperation depends on the frank acknowledgment of differences, and the resolution—or temporary, mutual acceptance—of those differences in service of common goals. The incapacity of Americans to recognize class in themselves and others continues to impede the promise of real class cooperation, and it is a major reason that the topography of American class relations has remained largely the same, the fault lines where we left them a hundred years ago.

The historical record of that journey, however, overflows with instructive tragedy. If Americans attend to that record honestly, and use it to recognize class in themselves as their ancestors failed to do, then perhaps the past can serve as a map for a new journey: a more successful, collective project of combating the progressive inequality once more stalking the land.

If tragedy remains, then so too must hope.

Abbreviations

Organizations

A.F.L.	American Federation of Labor
A.I.C.P.	Association for Improving the Condition of the Poor
B.R.T.	Brooklyn Rapid Transit Company
C.O.S.	Charity Organization Society of New York
C.T.S.	Church Temperance Society
D.C.C.	Department of Charities and Corrections
I.L.G.W.U.	International Ladies' Garment Workers' Union
I.R.T.	Interborough Rapid Transit Company
I.W.W.	Industrial Workers of the World
N.A.A.C.P.	National Association for the Advancement of Colored People
N.A.W.S.A.	National American Woman Suffrage Association
N.C.F.	National Civic Federation
N.W.L.B.	National War Labor Board
N.W.U.	Neckwear Workers' Union
P.E.A.	Political Equality Association
P.S.C.	Public Service Commission
S.P.C.C.	Society for the Prevention of Cruelty to Children
S.R.P.W.	Society for the Relief of Poor Widows with Small Children
T.A.R.C.	Third Avenue Railway Company

U.H.C.	United Hebrew Charities
W.T.U.L.	Women's Trade Union League
Y.M.C.A.	Young Men's Christian Association
Y.W.C.A.	Young Women's Christian Association

Archives and Libraries

ALL	Avery Architectural and Fine Arts Library, Columbia University, New York, N.Y.
BLYU	Beinecke Library, Yale University, New Haven, Conn.
CRBML	Columbia Rare Book and Manuscript Library, Columbia University, New York, N.Y.
KCILR	Kheel Center Archives, Martin P. Catherwood Library, Industrial and Labor Relations School, Cornell University, Ithaca, N.Y.
JJC	Lloyd Sealy Library, John Jay College of Criminal Justice, New York, N.Y.
LL	Lehman Library, Columbia University, New York, N.Y.
NYHS	New-York Historical Society, New York, N.Y.
NYMA	New York Municipal Archives, New York, N.Y.
NYPL	New York Public Library, Manuscripts and Archives Division, New York, N.Y.
SLHU	Schlesinger Library, Harvard University, Cambridge, Mass.
SML	Sterling Memorial Library Manuscripts and Archives, Yale University, New Haven, Conn.
TLNYU	Tamiment Library, New York University, New York, N.Y.

Manuscript Collections, Personal Papers,
and Unpublished Oral Histories

AAB	Adolf Augustus Berle. "Reminiscences of Adolf Augustus Berle: Oral History, 1970." Interviewed by Douglas Scott. CRBML.
ABP	August Belmont Papers, ca. 1880–1938 at NYPL.
CSS	Community Service Society Manuscripts at CRBML.

DAP   District Attorneys Papers at NYMA.
DSP   Doris Stevens Papers at SLHU.
FFP   Farnam Family Papers at SML.
GWA   George William Alger, "Reminiscences of George W. Alger:
                 Oral History, 1952." Interviewed by Harlan B. Phillips.
                 CRBML.
ILGWUR   International Ladies' Garment Workers' Union Records
                 at KCILR.
IMP   Inez Milholland Papers at SLHU.
LDWP   Lillian D. Wald Papers at CRBML.
MDRP   Margaret Dreier Robins Papers at TMNYU.
MHP   Morris Hilquit Papers at KCILR.
NYHP   Pamphlet Collection at NYHS.
PNI   Pauline Newman interview with Elizabeth Phillips Marsh.
                 Transcript included in "The Uprising of the Twenty
                 Thousand: A Study of Women and Trade Unionism."
                 Undergraduate Honors Thesis (Mar. 1, 1974) at SLHU.
PNP   Pauline Newman Papers at SLHU.
PWTUL   Papers of the Women's Trade Union League and Its Principal
                 Leaders
RPSP   Rose Pastor Stokes Papers at SML.
RWGP   Richard Watson Gilder Papers at NYPL.
SPP   Society for the Prevention of Pauperism Collection (SPP) at
                 NYHS.
SRPW   Society for the Relief of Poor Widows with Small Children
                 Collection at NYHS.
SWAC   Social Work Agency Collection at LL.
SWC   Stanford White Correspondence and Architectural Drawings
                 at AAL.
WP   Lillian D. Wald Papers at NYPL

Initials

MDR   Margaret Dreier Robins
MED   Mary E. Dreier
RWG   Richard Watson Gilder

Notes

Prologue

Epigraph: Louis Adamic, *My America, 1928–1938* (New York: Harper & Brothers, 1938), xii.

1. "The Weather Report," *New-York Tribune*, Dec. 26, 1899; "Salvation Army's Bounty," *New York Times*, Dec. 26, 1899; "A Feast for Thousands," *New-York Tribune*, Dec. 26, 1899. For further discussion of this event and its implications, see Chapters 4 and 5. For briefer accounts, see Stephen Nissenbaum, *The Battle for Christmas* (New York: Alfred A. Knopf, 1996), 219–57; Diane Winston, *Red-Hot and Righteous: The Urban Religion of the Salvation Army* (Cambridge, Mass.: Harvard University Press, 1999), 130–33; and David Traxel, *1898: The Birth of the American Century* (New York: Alfred A. Knopf, 1999), 305–6.
2. See pages 1 and 2 of the *New York Sun*, *New-York Tribune*, and *New York Times*, Dec. 26, 1899. For Mr. and Mrs. Lewis Cass Ledyard's Society particulars, see *Social Register, New York, 1900* (New York: Social Register Association, 1899), 250.
3. "Salvation Army's Bounty"; "A Feast for Thousands."
4. Timothy Noah, *The Great Divergence: America's Growing Inequality Crisis and What We Can Do about It* (New York: Bloomsbury Press, 2012), 10–15. As Noah notes, inequality dipped amid and after World War I in no small part due to inflation and labor agitation, but it continued to rise quickly thereafter.

5. This book takes as a given that vast inequality threatens democracy. Relevant scholarship supports this position. See, most recently, Joseph E. Stieglitz, *The Price of Inequality: How Today's Divided Society Endangers Our Future* (New York: W.W. Norton, 2012); Noah, *Great Divergence*.

6. See, for example, Jeffrey D. Sachs, "The New Progressive Movement," *New York Times*, Nov. 12, 2011.

7. William Graham Sumner, *What Social Classes Owe to Each Other* (New York: Harper & Brothers, 1883), 13.

8. Martin J. Burke, *The Conundrum of Class: Public Discourse on the Social Order in America* (Chicago: University of Chicago Press, 1995), ix–x.

9. Alexis de Tocqueville portrays wealthy Americans in *Democracy in America* as adhering publicly to republican principles while privately indulging anti-democratic passions; see Tocqueville, *Democracy in America*, trans. George Lawrence, ed. J. P. Mayer (New York: HarperPerennial, 1969), 178–79; see also Gordon Wood, *The Radicalism of the American Revolution* (New York: Vintage, 1991), 347–48. Wood's contention that the Revolution created a "Middle-Class Order" offers one expression of the classless myth in the early national period.

10. Sven Beckert, *The Monied Metropolis: New York City and the Consolidation of the American Bourgeoisie, 1850–1896* (Cambridge: Cambridge University Press, 2001); Edwin G. Burrows and Mike Wallace, *Gotham: A History of New York City to 1898* (New York: Oxford University Press, 1999), 1002–38; Herbert G. Gutman, "The Tompkins Square 'Riot' in New York City on January 13, 1874: A Re-examination of Its Causes and Aftermath," *Labor History* 6, no. 1 (1965): 44–70.

11. David Quigley, *Second Founding: New York City, Reconstruction, and the Making of American Democracy* (New York: Hill & Wang, 2004), 92–93.

12. Alice Kessler-Harris, *Out to Work: A History of Wage-Earning Women in the United States* (New York: Oxford University Press, 1982). For forerunners, see Christine Stansell, *City of Women: Sex and Class in New York, 1789–1860* (New York: Knopf, 1986).

13. Beckert, *Monied Metropolis*, 207–36, esp. 220–21. According to Beckert, this would have effectively disfranchised nearly 70 percent of the eligible voters in New York City. See also Sven Beckert, "Democracy and Its Discontents: Contesting Suffrage Rights in Gilded Age New York," *Past and Present*, no. 174 (2002), 116–57.

14. Beckert, *Monied Metropolis*, 207–36; "Democracy and Its Discontents," 116–57; Quigley, *Second Founding*, 137–60.

15. Beckert, *Monied Metropolis*, 207–36; "Democracy and Its Discontents," 116–57; Quigley, *Second Founding*, 137–60. For more on social Darwinism generally and Sumner's relationship to it, see Richard Hofstadter, *Social Darwinism in American Thought* (1944; repr., Boston: Beacon Press, 1992), esp. 3–66.

16. See Robert D. Johnston, "Re-Democratizing the Progressive Era: The Politics of Progressive Era Political Historiography," *Journal of the Gilded Age and Progressive Era* 1, no. 1 (2002): 68–92. The Progressive Era's continuing good name, as Johnston observes, has retained popular currency on both sides of the contemporary partisan divide: John Mc-Cain's attempt to claim the "progressive" Republican mantle of Theodore Roosevelt during his 2008 presidential campaign, the ongoing reappropriation of the word "progressive" by many Democrats (to avoid being tagged with the politically radioactive term, "liberal"), and calls for (or recognitions of) a new Progressive Era from across the political spectrum. For three drops in the bucket, see William McKenzie, "Limiting the New Progressive Era," *Dallas Morning News*, Sept. 30, 2008, 13A; Frank Rich, "Goldman Can Spare You a Dime," *New York Times*, Oct. 18, 2009, 8; and "Twilight's New Gleaming," *Economist*, Apr. 20, 1996, R3.

17. The variety of scholarly arguments buttressing this narrative of redemptive change is extensive; many are highly critical of Progressives in targeted ways, yet still manage to imply that the era redeemed the sins of the Gilded Age, democratically or otherwise. For useful historiographical overviews, see Steven J. Diner, "Linking Politics and People: The Historiography of the Progressive Era," *Magazine of History* 13, no. 3 (1999): 5–9; and Johnston, "Re-Democratizing the Progressive Era." Synthetic works that support this narrative are Robert Wiebe, *The Search for Order, 1877–1920* (New York: Hill and Wang, 1967); Arthur Link and Richard L. Mc-Cormick, *Progressivism* (Arlington Heights, Ill.: Harlan Davidson, 1983); Alan Dawley, *Struggles for Justice: Social Responsibility and the Liberal State* (Cambridge, Mass.: Belknap Press of Harvard University Press, 1991); Steven J. Diner, *A Very Different Age: Americans of the Progressive Era* (New York: Hill and Wang, 1998); Daniel T. Rodgers, *Atlantic Crossings: Social Politics in a Progressive Age* (Cambridge, Mass.: Belknap Press of Harvard University Press, 1998); Elizabeth Sanders, *Roots of Reform: Farmers, Workers, and the American State, 1877–1917* (Chicago: University of Chicago Press, 1999); and Michael McGerr, *A Fierce Discontent: The Rise and Fall of the Progressive Movement in America, 1870–1920* (New York: Free Press,

2003). Dawley, Diner, Rodgers, Sanders, and McGerr typify the later scholarship in that they acknowledge the era's obvious departures from positive change (including the vitiation of labor power, widespread poverty, eugenics, increased lynching, and the consolidation of Jim Crow), but still accord it a balance of progress. For a look at Wiebe's classic in a different light, see Kenneth Cmiel, "Destiny and Amnesia: The Vision of Modernity in Robert Wiebe's *The Search for Order," Reviews in American History* 21, no. 2 (1993): 352–68.

Multiple generations of historians have rewritten this narrative. The classic work revisionist work is Richard Hofstadter, *Age of Reform: From Bryan to F. D. R.* (New York: Vintage, 1955). Others include George E. Mowry, *The Era of Theodore Roosevelt, 1900–1912* (New York: Harper, 1958); Gabriel Kolko, *The Triumph of Conservatism: A Reinterpretation of American History, 1900–1916* (New York: Free Press, 1963); Aileen S. Kraditor, *The Ideas of the Woman Suffrage Movement, 1890–1920* (New York: Columbia University Press, 1965); James Weinstein, *The Corporate Ideal in the Liberal State, 1900–1918* (Boston: Beacon Press, 1968); Paul Boyer, *Urban Masses and Moral Order in America, 1820–1920* (Cambridge, Mass.: Harvard University Press, 1978); and Linda Gordon, *Pitied but Not Entitled: Single Mothers and the History of Welfare, 1890–1935* (New York: Free Press, 1994).

18. See, for example, Nell Irvin Painter, *Standing at Armageddon: The United States, 1877–1919* (New York: W. W. Norton, 1987); Noralee Frankel and Nancy S. Dye, eds., *Gender, Class, Race, and Reform in the Progressive Era* (Lexington: University of Kentucky Press, 1991); Theda Skocpol, *Protecting Soldiers and Mothers: The Political Origins of Social Policy in the United States* (Cambridge, Mass.: Belknap Press of Harvard University Press, 1992); Evelyn Brooks Higginbotham, *Righteous Discontent: The Women's Movement in the Black Baptist Church, 1880–1920* (Cambridge, Mass.: Harvard University Press, 1993); Kathryn Kish Sklar, *Florence Kelley and the Nation's Work: The Rise of Women's Political Culture, 1830–1900* (New Haven, Conn.: Yale University Press, 1995); Glenda Elizabeth Gilmore, *Gender and Jim Crow: Women and the Politics of White Supremacy in North Carolina, 1896–1920* (Chapel Hill: University of North Carolina Press, 1996); Roy Rosenzweig, Nelson Lichtenstein, Joshua Brown, and David Jaffee, *Who Built America? Since 1877, Volume 2,* 3rd ed. (Boston: Bedford/ St. Martin's Press, 2008).

19. Louis Adamic, *My America, 1928–1938* (New York: Harper & Brothers, 1938), xii.

20. See, for example, David Montgomery, *The Fall of the House of Labor: The Workplace, the State, and American Labor Activism, 1865–1925* (Cambridge: Cambridge University Press, 1987); Kathy Peiss, *Cheap Amusements: Working Women and Leisure in Turn-of-the-Century New York* (Philadelphia: Temple University Press, 1986); Gail Bederman, *Manliness & Civilization: A Cultural History of Gender and Race in the United States, 1880–1917* (Chicago: University of Chicago Press, 1995); Nan Enstad, *Ladies of Labor, Girls of Adventure: Working Women, Popular Culture, and Labor Politics at the Turn of the Twentieth Century* (New York: Columbia University Press, 1999); Robert Johnston, *The Radical Middle Class: Populist Democracy and the Question of Capitalism in Progressive Era Portland, Oregon* (Princeton, N.J.: Princeton University Press, 2003); Beckert, *Monied Metropolis;* Moses Rischin, *The Promised City: New York's Jews 1870–1914* (Cambridge, Mass.: Harvard University Press, 1962); Erika Lee, *At America's Gates: Chinese Immigration During the Exclusion Era, 1882–1943* (Chapel Hill: University of North Carolina Press, 2003). One notable exception to the practice of focusing on one class is Priscilla Murolo, *Common Ground of Womanhood: Class, Gender, and Working-Girls' Clubs, 1884–1928* (Urbana: University of Illinois Press, 1997). Those focusing on the period as a whole usually treat these groups consecutively or chronologically, rather than concurrently. See, for example, Painter, *Standing at Armageddon;* Diner, *A Very Different Age;* Glenda Elizabeth Gilmore, ed., *Who Were the Progressives?* (Boston: Bedford/St. Martin's Press, 2002).
21. Few if any U.S. labor historians would claim that late nineteenth- and early twentieth-century workers' movements did not transform labor relations in America. See Montgomery, *Fall of the House of Labor;* Melvyn Dubofsky, *When Workers Organize: New York City in the Progressive Era* (Amherst: University of Massachusetts Press, 1968). Likewise, no chronicler of the American elite can ignore the consolidation and pursuit of class interests among a previously less self-conscious U.S. bourgeoisie. See, for example, David C. Hammack, *Power and Society: Greater New York at the Turn of the Century* (New York: Russell Sage Foundation, 1982); Beckert, *Monied Metropolis.*
22. Namely, the refusal to work deserves scorn and punishment, regardless of circumstance.
23. Namely, a vision of America in which imperial white capital eradicates dangerous foreignness, and individualist private enterprise is the true expression of democracy.

24. See the works in notes 17, 18, and 20 for examples.

25. See especially Michael B. Katz, *Undeserving Poor: From the War on Poverty to the War on Welfare* (New York: Pantheon Books, 1989), and *In the Shadow of the Poorhouse: A Social History of Welfare in America* (New York: Basic Books, 1996).

26. Beckert, *Monied Metropolis*, 238.

27. Mary Louise Pratt's notion of "contact zones" informs this proposition. As she writes, "A 'contact' perspective emphasizes how subjects are constituted in and by their relations to each other. It treats the relations among colonizers and colonized, or travelers and 'travelees,' not in terms of separateness or apartheid, but in terms of copresence, interaction, inter-locking understandings and practices, often within radically asymmetrical relations of power." Pratt applies this analysis to explicitly imperial contexts, but it can be usefully transferred here to the relations between those at the center and peripheries *within* a "metropole." See Pratt, *Imperial Eyes: Travel Writing and Transculturation* (London: Routledge, 1992), 7. For a powerful contemporary expression of this process, see "Coming to Class Consciousness" the second chapter of bell hooks, *Where We Stand: Class Matters* (New York: Routledge, 2000).

28. E. P. Thompson, *The Making of the English Working Class* (1963; New York: Vintage, 1966), 9. My reading of Thompson echoes Marc W. Steinberg, "Culturally Speaking: Finding a Commons between Post-Structuralism and the Thompsonian Perspective," *Social History* 21, no. 2 (1996): 193–214. This essay resolves seeming differences between Thompson and poststruc-turalists in part by refuting readings of Thompson as a rigid materialist through an exploration of his historicist concern with discourse as a constitutive element of class.

29. This follows Seth Rockman's proposal to treat class as a "heuristic for the economic power relations of capitalism," albeit in a sense that encompasses more than the strictly "economic." See Rockman, "Class and the History of Working People in the Early Republic," *Journal of the Early Republic* 25, no. 4 (2005): 530–31.

30. For further explanation of the terms "capital-enhanced" and "labor-dependent," see Frederick R. Strobel, *Upward Dreams, Downward Mobility* (Lanham, Md.: Rowman and Littlefield, 1993), 15–17, 22; see also Strobel and Wallace C. Peterson, "Class Conflict, American Style: Distract and Conquer," *Journal of Economic Issues* 31, no. 2 (1997): 437–38. These definitions approximate Marx's division between those who own the means

of production and those who do not, but allow room for noneconomic (or indirectly economic) factors such as cultural capital. On cultural capital, see Pierre Bourdieu, *Distinction: A Social Critique of the Judgment of Taste*, trans. Richard Nice (Cambridge, Mass.: Harvard University Press, 1984).

31. There is a rich and illuminating—but to this author's mind, unpersuasive—body of historical and social science work attempting to define a "middle class" in cultural, economic, and political terms as a distinctive cross-section within the power relations of capitalism. For an overview, see Burton J. Bledstein and Robert D. Johnston, eds., *The Middling Sorts: Explorations in the History of the American Middle Class* (New York: Routledge, 2001), esp. Johnston's review essay (296–306).

32. Thompson, *Making of the English Working Class*, 9.

33. Of course, the threat of forceful coercion in response to noncompliance often hovered over such putatively nonviolent initiatives. This potential violence notwithstanding, prescriptive interaction must be considered qualitatively different from more violent forms of asserting class power, particularly in its more effective reinforcement of discursive control.

34. For more on reforms emerging from cross-class cooperation, see Dawley, *Struggles for Justice*.

35. Conflictual class relations embrace a much wider, subtler range of behaviors and discourses than violence: from territorial confrontations manifesting as little more than glowering stares, to looking away from the homeless on the street; from laughing at someone for wearing the "wrong" clothes, to spurning politicians for their "elitism." Yet these other behaviors, whatever other reaction they may elicit, predominantly seek to achieve alienation or distance. Violence, by contrast, seeks openly to gain an advantage, be it material or political, that only the other class can provide.

1 · Invading the Tenements

Epigraph: Stephen Crane, "The Fire," in *Tales, Sketches, and Reports*, ed. Fredson Bowers (Charlottesville: University of Virginia Press, 1973), 339. "The Fire" first appeared in the *New York Press*, Nov. 25, 1894.

1. Testimony of Peter Rutz, New York Supreme Court, Trial Term, Part 1, *The People of the State of New York vs. Adolph Hershkopf, impleaded with Meyer Dietchek*, JJC, Trial Transcripts, Court of General Sessions, Case 3109, Roll 372, 1–7.

2. Ibid., 5.

3. Ibid.; see also "Panic at Tenement Fire," *New York Times*, June 1, 1894; "Hemmed in by Flames," *Washington Post*, June 1, 1894; "Fire in New York Tenement-House," *Chicago Daily Tribune*, June 1, 1894; New York State Legislature, *Report of the Tenement House Committee as Authorized by Chapter 479 of the Laws of 1894* (Albany, N.Y.: James B. Lyon, State Printer, 1895), BLYU, 321.

4. Testimony of Peter Rutz, *People vs. Hershkopf*, JJC, 3.

5. Ibid.

6. "Panic at Tenement Fire" *New York Times*, June 1, 1894; "Hemmed in by Flames," *Washington Post*, June 1, 1894; "Fire in New York Tenement-House," *Chicago Daily Tribune*, June 1, 1894; New York State Legislature, *Report,* BLYU, 321.

7. Testimony of Charles Jaeger, *People vs. Hershkopf*, JJC, 8.

8. The year from July 1, 1893, to June 30, 1894, saw 2,415 tenement fires in New York, in which fifteen people died; over the ten years prior, tenement fires had killed or "fatally injured" 256 people. New York State Legislature, *Report*, BLYU, 329, 345.

9. The New York board of aldermen proposed renaming Clinton Place as West Eighth Street in 1897, and accomplished it shortly thereafter. See "Want to Change Street Names: Aldermen Make Recommendations about City Thoroughfares," *New York Times*, Dec. 10, 1897. On the *Century*, see Arthur John, *The Best Years of the Century: Richard Watson Gilder, Scribner's Monthly, and Century Magazine, 1870–1909* (Urbana: University of Illinois Press, 1981).

10. Richard Watson Gilder (RWG) to Edward Marshall, May 14, 1894, RWGP, Box 20, Letterbook 10, 2; RWG to Felix Adler, May 14, 1894, RWGP, Box 20, Letterbook 10, 6–7.

11. New York State Legislature, *Report*, BLYU, 4.

12. Rosamond Gilder, ed., *Letters of Richard Watson Gilder* (Boston: Houghton Mifflin, 1916), 255.

13. Although Charles Follen McKim was McKim, Mead & White's primary representative at the World's Columbian Exposition, architectural historians note significant elements of White's designs and tastes in the firm's work there (including the Agricultural Building). White was also the chief designer for the firm, whereas McKim specialized in overall composition. See Samuel G. White and Elizabeth White, *Stanford White: Architect* (New York: Rizzoli International, 2008), 231; Stanley Appelbaum, *The Chicago World's Fair of 1893: A Photographic Record* (New York: Dover, 1980), 8.

14. "World's Columbian Exposition—Entrance to the Palace of Agricultural Building," *Scientific American*, Aug. 26, 1893, 138.

15. Alan Trachtenberg, *The Incorporation of America: Culture and Society in the Gilded Age* (New York: Hill and Wang, 1982), 213.

16. Frederick E. Pierce, "Map No. 2 of City of New York Showing Distribution of Principal Nationalities by Sanitary Districts," insert to New York State Legislature, *Report*, BLYU, 256–57.

17. This term has appeared elsewhere, most prominently in discussing Theodore Roosevelt's worldview as president. The present definition renders it more widely applicable as a broad congeries of thought influencing U.S. domestic class relations.

18. "Imperial progressivism" offers an umbrella term for a variety of culturally imperial expressions: see, for example, Jacobson, *Barbarian Virtues*, and Bederman, *Manliness & Civilization*. Edward Said's *Culture and Imperialism* (New York: Knopf, 1993) also provides apposite analysis of cultural dialectics (or "contrapuntal" relationships) in imperial contexts. For more on American empire in these years, see Walter LaFeber, *The New Empire: An Interpretation of American Expansionism, 1860–1898* (1963; Ithaca, N.Y.: Cornell University Press, 1998); "U.S. Emergence as a World Power," *Political Science Quarterly* 101, no. 5 (1986): 705–18; Brenda Gayle Plummer, *Haiti and the Great Powers, 1902–1915* (Baton Rouge: Louisiana State University Press, 1988); Emily S. Rosenberg, *Financial Missionaries to the World: The Politics and Culture of Dollar Diplomacy, 1900–1930* (Cambridge, Mass.: Harvard University Press, 1999); Mary Renda, *Taking Haiti: Military Occupation and the Culture of U.S. Imperialism, 1915–1940* (Chapel Hill: University of North Carolina Press, 2001); Laura Briggs, *Reproducing Empire: Race, Sex, Science, and U.S. Imperialism in Puerto Rico* (Berkeley: University of California Press, 2002).

19. Renda, *Taking Haiti,* integrates more recent historiographies of Progressivism, gender studies, and race in discussing U.S. empire; Wexler, *Tender Violence*, explores the domestic refractions of imperialist culture. Vast and unwieldy is the literature attempting to define the Progressive Era, but for the purposes of this analysis, see Daniel T. Rodgers, "In Search of Progressivism," *Reviews in American History* 10, no. 4 (1982), 123. For more on U.S. imperialism in the Progressive Era, see the previous note.

20. RWG, "The New Tenement-House Law," RWGP, Box 23, Addresses. For example, as a precaution against fire, the new law determined that "no part of any tenement-house may be used for the storage of feed, hay or straw,

except by permit of, and under such conditions as may be prescribed by, the Fire Department" (4). Likewise, the law banned private schools and the "storage of rags" in tenement houses (12). Both measures made theoretical sense, but they proscribed behaviors in working-class spaces that went unregulated elsewhere.

21. Oscar Schisgall, *Out of One Small Chest: A Social and Financial History of the Bowery Savings Bank* (New York: AMACOM, 1975), 8–9.

22. LaFeber, *The New Empire*; "U.S. Emergence as a World Power"; Plummer, *Haiti and the Great Powers*; Renda, *Taking Haiti*; Briggs, *Reproducing Empire*.

23. See, for example, Josiah Strong, *Expansion under New World-Conditions* (New York: Baker and Taylor, 1900); Rosenberg, *Financial Missionaries*.

24. Strong, *Expansion;* Trachtenberg, *Incorporation of America*; Dorothy Ross, *The Origins of American Social Science* (Cambridge: Cambridge University Press, 1994); Hofstadter, *Social Darwinism in American Thought*; David W. Blight, *Race and Reunion: The Civil War in American Memory* (Cambridge, Mass.: Belknap Press of Harvard University Press, 2001); Eric Foner, *Reconstruction: America's Unfinished Revolution, 1863–1877* (New York: Harper & Row, 1988).

25. Matthew Frye Jacobson, *Whiteness of a Different Color: European Immigrants and the Alchemy of Race* (Cambridge, Mass.: Harvard University Press, 1998).

26. Some on the Lower East Side had been using savings accounts for decades; see Tyler Anbinder, "Moving beyond "Rags to Riches": New York's Irish Famine Immigrants and Their Surprising Savings Accounts," *Journal of American History* 99, no. 3 (2012): 741–70. Increasing and increasingly diverse immigration, however, demanded service expansion.

27. For a helpful recasting of "social control" theses of Progressive reform, see Boyer, *Urban Masses and Moral Order*. On "nonwhite," see Jacobson, *Whiteness of a Different Color*; David R. Roediger, *The Wages of Whiteness: Race and the Making of the American Working Class* (New York: Verso, 1991); Noel Ignatiev, *How the Irish Became White* (New York: Routledge, 1995).

28. Strong, *Expansion*; Rosenberg, *Financial Missionaries*.

29. Jacobson, *Barbarian Virtues*, provides analysis of a similar (and deeply enmeshed) paradox of the period's cultural and political ideals.

30. Physical dislocation resulted from both razing tenement properties under the new law and rising rents encouraged by development such as the

Savings Bank renovation. Of course, high rents and inadequate enforcement of sanitary laws induced people to leave of their own volition,
particularly once the city introduced comprehensive rapid transit. See
Kenneth Jackson, *Crabgrass Frontier: The Suburbanization of the United
States* (New York: Oxford University Press, 1985); Peter Derrick, *Tunneling
to the Future: The Story of the Great Subway Expansion That Saved New York*
(New York: New York University Press, 2001).

31. Gilder, *Letters*, 17.
32. Ibid., 3.
33. Ibid., 7–21.
34. Ibid., 19.
35. Ibid., 17–30.
36. Ibid.; John, *Best Years of the Century*, 5.
37. Any record of the cause of death remains elusive.
38. Gilder, *Letters*, 98 (photograph), 76–78, 88.
39. Ibid., 115.
40. John, *Best Years of the Century*, 125. This series appeared in the *Century*
from 1884 to 1887.
41. Gilder, *Letters*, 80–81, 119–20; Gregory F. Gilmartin, *Shaping the City: New
York and the Municipal Art Society* (New York: Clarkson Potter, 1995).
42. Thomas Bender adjudges RWG "a sincere but hopelessly naïve idealist,"
which misleadingly suggests a lack of practical method. See Bender, *New
York Intellect: A History of Intellectual Life in New York City, from 1750 to the
Beginnings of Our Own Time* (Baltimore: Johns Hopkins University Press,
1987), 213.
43. John, *Best Years of the Century*, 2–4. John writes, "[George Washington]
Cable, exploring the city's literary and publishing world, found that 'Gilder
is . . . the sweetest, gentlest, manliest, most interesting fellow I see.' . . . To
[Andrew] Carnegie, he was 'one of the sweetest, saintliest, yet most heroic
souls I have ever been privileged to know and love.' [John] Burroughs said
he had never encountered anyone in person or in books who made 'such an
impression of pure spirit.' . . . Gilder was unworldly only in that he lacked
guile. He went after what he wanted openly and persistently, displaying, in
the words of one who knew him well, a 'tactical hardihood' and a daunt-
less spirit" (2–3).
44. RWG to Marshall, May 31, 1894, RWGP, Box 20, Letterbook 10, 43–46;
RWG to Roger Foster, June 2, 1894, RWGP, Box 20, Letterbook 10, 43;
"Panic at Tenement Fire," *New York Times*, June 1, 1894; "Hemmed in by

Flames," *Washington Post*, June 1, 1894; "Fire in New York Tenement-House," *Chicago Daily Tribune*, June 1, 1894.

45. New York State Legislature, *Report*, BLYU, 4.

46. Richard Plunz, *A History of Housing in New York City* (New York: Columbia University Press, 1990), 22.

47. Plunz, *History of Housing*, 22–24. Over thirty years after the legislature mandated fire escapes, over a quarter of tenements still violated the code's provisions (ibid., 23).

48. Plunz writes, "The prolific use of . . . statistical analysis within the report served to push the 'scientification' of the tenement problem to new levels" (ibid., 37).

49. Ibid.

50. See, for example, Edward Marshall, "New York's Tenements," *North American Review*, no. CCCCXLV (1893), 753–56.

51. New York State Legislature, *Report*, BLYU, 85.

52. Ibid.

53. Marshall notes that several of the collegians were "accomplished sanitationists and engineers" (ibid.).

54. New York State Legislature, *Report*, BLYU, 85; on German resentment of temperance societies and related politics, see Richard McCormick, *From Realignment to Reform: Political Change in New York State, 1893–1910* (Ithaca, N.Y.: Cornell University Press, 1981).

55. New York State Legislature, *Report*, BLYU, 82.

56. Ibid., 448. It is unclear from the *Report* whether this is the same Edward King who was a labor leader and Lower East Side activist during the same period, but it seems likely.

57. Ibid., 81–82; for inspector testimony, see pages 387 (H. M. Leverich, 600–800 houses), 394 (T. F. Murray, 300–400 houses), and 534 (Julius Cohen, "1,500 at least").

58. Ibid., 91 (italics added).

59. Ibid., 97.

60. Ibid., 93–94.

61. Ibid., 158–59.

62. Stephen Kinzer, *Overthrow: America's Century of Regime Change From Hawaii to Iraq* (New York: Times Books/Henry Holt, 2006), 18.

63. Strong, *Expansion*. This was common practice for imperialism more broadly. See, for example, Edward W. Said, *Orientalism* (New York: Vintage Books, 1978), 31–33. Said uses the example of Balfour in British

Parliament justifying Britain's imperial power over Egyptians: "Knowledge means rising above immediacy, beyond self, into the foreign and distant. The object of such knowledge is inherently vulnerable to scrutiny. . . . To have such knowledge of such a thing is to dominate it, to have authority over it" (32).

64. For a more comprehensive consideration of archival technologies of rule, see Kirsten Weld, "Reading the Politics of History in Guatemala's National Police Archives" (Ph.D. diss., Yale University, 2010); and James C. Scott, *Seeing Like a State: How Certain Schemes to Improve the Human Condition Have Failed* (New Haven, Conn.: Yale University Press, 1998).

65. New York State Legislature, *Report*, BLYU, 94–95.

66. See Christopher Mele, *Selling the Lower East Side: Culture, Real Estate, and Resistance in New York* (Minneapolis: University of Minnesota Press, 2000), 31–75.

67. For example, see Valerien Gribay Edoff, "Living Pictures on Broadway," *Frank Leslie's Popular Monthly* XXXVIII, no. 6 (1894), 714; Kathleen Mathew, "New York Newsboys," *Frank Leslie's Popular Monthly* XXXIX, no. 4 (1895), 453–61; Edward Sanford Martin, "East Side Considerations," *Harper's Weekly* 96, no. 576 (1898), 853–63.

68. As quoted in Esther Romeyn, *Street Scenes: Staging the Self in Immigrant New York, 1880–1924* (Minneapolis: University of Minnesota Press, 2008), 57. Romeyn provides useful analysis of slum tourism.

69. New York State Legislature, *Report*, BLYU, 88.

70. Ibid., 88–89, 78 (italics added).

71. Ibid., 47.

72. Ibid., 98.

2 · Bank on the Bowery

Epigraph: John Jay Chapman, as quoted in Samuel G. White and Elizabeth White, *Stanford White: Architect* (New York: Rizzoli International, 2008), 6.

1. Claire Nicolas White, ed., *Stanford White: Letters to His Family, Including a Selection of Letters to Augustus Saint-Gaudens* (New York: Rizzoli International, 1997), 78.

2. Paul R. Baker, *Stanny: The Gilded Life of Stanford White* (New York: Free Press, 1989), 4.

3. Ibid., 5–6.

4. Richard wrote revealingly in an *Atlantic Monthly* essay, "To call a man an American because he happens to be born in America . . . is entirely to reverse the natural and logical order of things." See Michael G. Crowell, "Richard Grant White and Americanisms," *American Speech* 42, no. 2 (1967), 126.

5. Baker, *Stanny*, 4–5. For more on the economic impact of steam power on shipping, see T. J. Stiles, *The First Tycoon: The Epic Life of Cornelius Vanderbilt* (New York: Alfred A. Knopf, 2009).

6. Reprinted in George G. Foster, *New York in Slices: By an Experienced Carver, Being the Original Slices Published in the N.Y. Tribune* (New York: W. G. Burgess, 1849), 73–74.

7. Baker, *Stanny*, 33; see also "Education and Discipline," *New York Times*, Sept. 19, 1880, in which White argues the benefits of educating people to gain the qualities of good servants.

8. Baker, *Stanny*, 10.

9. Richard expressed this bitterness in a letter to his wife: "I am weary, so weary of this grind . . . Sampson in the mill, with his blindness and without his strength" (Baker, *Stanny*, 16).

10. Examples of Stanford White's easygoing snobbery abound in his letters, published and archival. See White, *Stanford White*, esp. 35–39; SWC, Letterbooks vols. 9 and 10 (Jan. 24, 1894–Nov. 3, 1894), Classics (Rare Book) Collection, AAL; e.g., Stanford White to Robert Goelet, Esq., SWC Letterbook, vol. 9, 459.

11. Charles C. Baldwin, *Stanford White* (New York: Dodd, Mead, 1931), 1–2.

12. Ibid., 3–4.

13. Baker, *Stanny*, 21–23.

14. Ann Jensen Adams, "The Birth of a Style: Henry Hobson Richardson and the Competition Drawings for Trinity Church, Boston," *Art Bulletin* 62, no. 3 (1980), 409–33; Lauren S. Weingarden, "Naturalized Nationalism: A Ruskinian Discourse on the Search for an American Style of Architecture," *Winterthur Portfolio* 24, no. 1 (1989): 43–68.

15. Baker, *Stanny*, 23; "The Artist in Our World" (reprinted from the *New York Evening Post*) *American Architect and Building News* 90, no. 1593 (1906), 6.

16. White, *Stanford White*, 25.

17. Ibid., 26.

18. Ibid., 25.

19. Baker, *Stanny*, 43–44; Gilder, *Letters*, 103–4.

20. White, *Stanford White*, 48.

21. Ibid.

22. Ibid., 51.

23. Ibid.

24. Baker, *Stanny*, 56.

25. Ibid., 85.

26. White and White, *Stanford White*, 250–52.

27. Ibid., 261.

28. Ibid., 234.

29. Trachtenberg, *Incorporation of America*; LaFeber, *New Empire.*

30. Trachtenberg, *Incorporation of America*, 208–34; James Gilbert, *Perfect Cities: Chicago's Utopias of 1893* (Chicago: University of Chicago Press, 1991); Erik Larson, *Devil in the White City: Murder, Magic, and Madness at the Fair That Changed America* (New York: Crown, 2003).

31. On the connection between imperial Roman aesthetics, the City Beautiful movement, and the influence of the Chicago World's Fair on New York architecture, see Margaret Malamud, "Ancient Rome in Turn-of-the-Century New York," *Arion* 7, no. 3 (2000): 64–108.

32. As quoted in Lawrence G. White, *Sketches and Designs by Stanford White: With an Outline of His Career by His Son Lawrence Grant White* (New York: Architectural Book Publishing, 1920), 24–25.

33. Alvin F. Harlow, *Old Bowery Days: The Chronicle of a Famous Street* (New York: D. Appleton, 1931), 10.

34. Ibid., 9–10. On this period and the relation of settlement to the natural environment, see Eric Sanderson, *Mannahatta: A Natural History of New York City* (New York: Abrams, 2009).

35. Harlow, *Old Bowery Days*, 50, 66–67.

36. Harlow, *Old Bowery Days*, 75–76. "Bull baitings" and bear baitings, as Harlow explains earlier, "meant that the larger animal, usually chained, was pitted against several vicious dogs." Tavern keepers, he writes, staged them to attract business (65).

37. Ibid., 84.

38. Schisgall, *Out of One Small Chest*, 9; Anbinder, "Moving beyond 'Rags to Riches.'"

39. Alan L. Olmstead, *New York City Mutual Savings Banks, 1819–1861* (Chapel Hill: University of North Carolina Press, 1976), 18; "Like the Bank of England," *New York Times*, July 9, 1893.

40. Schisgall, *Out of One Small Chest*, 15.

41. Ibid., 77.

42. Bureau of the Census, *Tenth Census of the United States: 1880*, New York City, New York County, New York State, Series 869, Roll T9: 7C–9A.

43. New York State Legislature, *Report*, BLYU, 389.

44. Ibid., 427.

45. For photographic and artistic illustrations, compare Detroit Publishing, "The Bowery near Grand Street" (www.shorpy.com/node/7418), and the W. Louis Sonntag, Jr. drawing on page 45. In the photograph, the Savings Bank is not present; in the drawing, it is.

46. See the photograph of Hester Street in Schisgall, *Out of One Small Chest*, 152–54. For two evocative descriptions, see Irving Howe, *World of Our Fathers* (New York: Galahad Books, 1976), 69–70; Crane, *Tales*, "The Broken-Down Van," 275–80.

47. Harlow, *Old Bowery Days*, 403.

48. Ibid.

49. "Not the Hebrews of Fiction," *New York Times*, Sept. 13, 1894. The reporter's story focuses on the corner of Orchard and Broome, about four blocks east and one block north of the bank.

50. "All the Bowery Aroused," *New York Times*, Apr. 12, 1895.

51. Henry James, *The American Scene* (1907; New York: Penguin, 1994), 146.

52. By 1904, nearly 80 percent of the Bowery Savings Bank's investments lay in real estate mortgages, railroad bonds, and municipal securities of cities other than New York. See "The Bowery Savings Bank—New York" (New York: Frank Presbrey, 1904), NYHP.

53. Rosenberg, *Financial Missionaries*; Plummer, *Haiti and the Great Powers*.

54. Schisgall, *Out of One Small Chest*, 57.

55. "The Report of the Committee on Plans and Buildings of the New Banking House," *BSB Minutes* 3 (Feb. 13, 1893), 513–25, as quoted in Landmarks Preservation Commission, Richard Brotherton au., "Bowery Savings Bank (Now Home Savings of America) First Floor Interior," August 23, 1994, 3.

56. Competition brief, *BSB Minutes* 3 (Feb. 13, 1893), 515, as quoted in Landmarks Preservation Commission, "Bowery Savings Bank," 5.

57. As quoted in Lawrence Wodehouse, *White of McKim, Mead & White* (New York: Garland, 1988), 243.

58. Landmarks Preservation Commission, "Bowery Savings Bank," 10n18.

59. For a sketch of the 1893 depression's onset and effects in New York, see Burrows and Wallace, *Gotham*, 1185–90.

60. Landmarks Preservation Commission, "Bowery Savings Bank," 5.

61. Burrows and Wallace, *Gotham*, 1188.
62. "Many Tenants Evicted," *New York Times*, Dec. 5, 1893.

3 · Prescribing Reform

Epigraph: "Our Foreign Criminals," *New York Times*, July 16, 1896.

1. New York State Legislature, *Report*, BLYU, 299–561.
2. Ibid., 387–91.
3. Ibid., 393.
4. Ibid., 422, 451.
5. Ibid., 396.
6. Ibid.
7. Ibid., 398.
8. Kalpana Sharma observes a similar dynamic today in Mumbai's largest slum, Dharavi: "Investment is always available to beautify the already well-endowed parts of the city. But there is no money to provide even basic services to the poorer areas." See Mike Davis, *Planet of Slums* (New York: Verso, 2006), 97.
9. Kevin Baker, "Palimpsest Street," *New York Times Magazine*, Oct. 5, 2003, 94–8.
10. Plunz, *History of Housing*, 33–37. Plunz claims that "the recommendations made in the report of the committee of 1894 had little effect on the Tenement House Act which was passed in the following year," but a comparison of the recommendations in the *Report* with that subsequent law contradicts this assertion. See RWG, "The New Tenement-House Law," RWGP, Box 23, Addresses.
11. See Plunz, *History of Housing*; according to Plunz, the *Report* itself "contributed to the genesis of the discipline of city planning" (37). On connections between reformers of RWG's era and subsequent urban renewal efforts, see Samuel Zipp, *Manhattan Projects: The Rise and Fall of Urban Renewal in Cold War New York* (New York: Oxford University Press, 2010).
12. One example of the latter-day imperial-progressive attitude is Daniel Patrick Moynihan's, "The Negro Family: The Case for National Action" (Washington, D.C.: Office of Policy Planning and Research, United States Department of Labor, 1965). For a critique, see Alan S. Berger and William Simon, "Black Families and the Moynihan Report: A Research Evaluation," *Social Problems* 22, no. 2 (1974): 145–61.

13. New York State Legislature, *Report*, BLYU, 119. This is only one instance of several in the *Report* when advocates of model tenements and housing reform reveal their dual objectives, as W. Bayard Cutting of the Improved Dwelling Association puts it, of proving that "comfortable and scientifically constructed buildings could be erected for the laboring classes, and rented at rates at least as reasonable as were received for less desirable accommodations elsewhere, *while the owners still received a fair profit on their investment*" [emphasis added].

14. The touchstone of urban renewal critique remains Jane Jacobs, *The Death and Life of Great American Cities* (New York: Random House, 1961). For more recent work and criticism, see Alison Isenberg, *Downtown America: A History of the Place and the People Who Made It* (Chicago: University of Chicago Press, 2004); Michael E. Jones, *Slaughter of Cities: Urban Renewal as Ethnic Cleansing* (South Bend, Ind.: St. Augustine's Press, 2004); Jennifer S. Light, *Nature of Cities: Ecological Visions and the American Urban Professions, 1920–1960* (Baltimore: Johns Hopkins University Press, 2009).

15. Schisgall, *Out of One Small Chest*, 75–76; Landmarks Preservation Commission, "Bowery Savings Bank," 10n18.

16. Rosenberg, *Financial Missionaries*.

17. "Meeting the Poor's Needs," *New York Times*, Dec. 30, 1893.

18. Ancestry.com, *New York, 1820–1850 Passenger and Immigration Lists* (Provo, Utah: Generations Network, 2003). Original data: New York. *Registers of Vessels Arriving at the Port of New York from Foreign Ports, 1789–1919* (Washington, D.C.: National Archives and Records Administration) Micropublication M237, rolls #1–95.

19. As quoted in E. H. Hobsbawm, *The Age of Capital, 1848–1875* (1975; repr. New York: Vintage, 1996), 9. For more on von Eichendorff's relationship to the revolution, see Anuschka Burkhardt, *Joseph von Eichendorff, die Revolution, und der Gedichtzyklus 1848* (München und Ravensburg: GRIN Verlag, 2006).

20. *Trow's New York City Directory, 1857* (New York: R. L. Polk, 1956), 715.

21. Bureau of the Census, *Tenth Census of the United States: 1880*, New York City, New York County, New York State, Series 881, Roll T9: 34A.

22. Ibid.; Bureau of the Census, *Twelfth Census of the United States: 1900*, New York City, New York County, New York State, Series 1097, Roll T623: 21A.

23. Bureau of the Census, *Tenth Census of the United States: 1880*, New York City, New York County, New York State, Series 881, Roll T9: 34A.

24. Bureau of the Census, *Twelfth Census of the United States: 1900*, New York City, New York County, New York State, Series 1097, Roll T623, 21A.

25. Testimony of Charles Jaeger, *People vs. Hershkopf*, JJC, 7.

26. Minor details vary from source to source. For "fourth floor" see "Panic at Tenement Fire," 8.

27. Ancestry.com, *Hamburg Passenger Lists, 1850–1934* (Provo, Utah: Ancestry .com Operations, 2008). Original data: Staatsarchiv Hamburg, Bestand: 373–7 I, VIII (Auswanderungesamt I) B 1 Band 066, Seite 1466, Mikrofilm Nr. *S_13149*.

28. Abraham Cahan, *The Rise of David Levinsky* (New York: Harper & Brothers, 1917).

29. Testimony of Abraham Kahn, *People vs. Hershkopf*, JJC, 37–38, 79–83.

30. Testimony of Isaac Feierman and Anna Hershkopf, *People vs. Hershkopf*, JJC, 155–156, 190.

31. Testimony of Anna Hershkopf, *People vs. Hershkopf*, JJC, 190–191.

32. Henry S. Davis, "The Inner History of the Great Firebug Gang That Terrorized New York and Brooklyn," *Washington Post*, Mar. 8, 1908.

33. Ibid.

34. New York State Legislature, *Report*, BLYU, 14. The *Report* notes that the year ending June 30, 1894, saw 2,415 tenement house fires in New York. Milch's gang probably set more fires toward the end of the five-year period as it grew more confident in its methods and built its connections to police and the fire marshal's office (and as desperation grew in the midst of economic depression), but even conservatively assuming the average rate of forty fires per year would mean that this single incendiary gang started almost 2 percent of all tenement-house fires in New York.

35. Davis, "Inner History." See also "Indicted for Conspiracy: Ex-Fire Marshal Lewis, R. F. Rice, and ex-Detective Zundt Held," *New York Times*, Mar. 14, 1896, 9.

36. Testimony of Max Gluckman, *People vs. Hershkopf*, JJC, 38–39. For insurance policy details, see the testimony of West Pollock, 22–24.

37. Testimony of Max Gluckman, *People vs. Hershkopf*, JJC, 45.

38. Testimony of Simon Rosenbaum, *People vs. Hershkopf*, JJC, 120.

39. Testimony of Louis Grauer, *People vs. Hershkopf*, JJC, 129–130.

40. Testimony of Joseph Biebergal, *People vs. Hershkopf*, JJC, 111.

41. Ibid.

42. New York State Legislature, *Report*, BLYU, 223–28. The title of this section (and the *Report*'s index) incorrectly refers to 129 Suffolk Street as "12

Suffolk," but the details of the fire described, including the death of Lizzie Jaeger, make the mistake apparent.

43. Testimony of Anna Gluckman, *People vs. Hershkopf*, JJC, 67.

44. Testimony of Meyer Brenner, *People vs. Hershkopf*, JJC, 61–62.

45. Testimony of Max Gluckman, *People vs. Hershkopf*, JJC, 43.

46. Ibid., 139–40.

47. Moses Rischin, *The Promised City* (Cambridge, Mass.: Harvard University Press, 1962); Hasia R. Diner, *Lower East Side Memories: A Jewish Place in America* (Princeton, N.J.: Princeton University Press, 2000). For a guide to U.S. immigration historiography, see Leonard Dinnerstein and David M. Reimers, "John Higham and Immigration History," *Journal of American Ethnic History* 24, no. 1 (2004): 3–25.

48. The preponderance of written evidence and testimony against Hershkopf was overwhelming. Seven years after his conviction, however, the district attorney arranged a pardon for him, having been persuaded in the interim that the true mastermind of the Kleinrock arson (and the gang leader) was Samuel Milch. For Kleinrock payments, see the testimony of John T. McCurdy, *People vs. Hershkopf*, JJC, 33–37. For the pardon, see Davis, "Inner History."

49. "Our Foreign Criminals," *New York Times*, July 16, 1896.

50. Davis, "Inner History."

4 · Loving the Poor with Severity

Epigraph: St. Augustine as quoted in Brian Tierney, *Medieval Poor Law* (Berkeley: University of California Press, 1959), 58.

1. "Francis H. Weeks Assigns," *New-York Tribune*, May 2, 1893; "Francis H. Weeks Missing," *New York Times*, May 13, 1893; "Henry W. De Forest May Be Liable," *New-York Tribune*, May 20, 1893; "Will Expel F. H. Weeks," *New York Times*, Aug. 14, 1893; "Probably under a Delusion," *New York Times*, Aug. 21, 1893; "Arrest of Francis H. Weeks," *New-York Tribune*, Sept. 12, 1893; "How the Embezzler Was Found," *New York Times*, Sept. 15, 1893; "Weeks to Be Tried Here," *New-York Tribune*, Oct. 22, 1893; "Hard Labor for F. H. Weeks," *New York Times*, Nov. 9, 1893; "Term of Ten Years," *Chicago Daily Tribune*, Nov. 9, 1893.

On fugitive embezzlers as a period phenomenon, see Katherine Unterman, "Boodle over the Border: Embezzlement and the Crisis of International Mobility, 1880–1890," *Journal of the Gilded Age and Progressive Era* 11, no. 2 (2012): 151–89.

2. On New York's Charity Organization Society, see Dawn Greeley, "Beyond Benevolence: Gender, Class and the Development of Scientific Charity in New York, 1882–1935" (Ph.D. diss., State University of New York at Stony Brook, 1995); Joan Waugh, *Unsentimental Reformer: The Life of Josephine Shaw Lowell* (Cambridge, Mass.: Harvard University Press, 1997), 149–83; Frank Dekker Watson, *The Charity Organization Movement in the United States: A Study in American Philanthropy* (New York: Macmillan, 1922).

3. In all the newspaper coverage of the scandal, the author found no mention of his C.O.S. affiliation.

4. "Charity in New-York: General Condemnation of Mr. Kellogg's Conclusions," *New York Times*, July 15, 1883. The Charity Organization Society's first branch was founded in Buffalo in 1877; see Watson, *Charity Organization Movement*.

5. "Why Dr. De Costa Was Angry," *New York World*, Jan. 28, 1888.

6. "Mr. Peters Attacks Charity," *New York Times*, Sept. 19, 1893; as quoted in Waugh, *Unsentimental Reformer*, 163.

7. Charity Organization Society of the City of New York, *Second Annual Report of the Charity Organization Society of the City of New York* (New York: John J. O'Brien, Steam Book and Job Printer, 1884), 15.

8. Marshall Berman, *All That Is Solid Melts into Air: The Experience of Modernity* (New York: Simon & Schuster, 1982). On the C.O.S. theorization of the relationship between individual casework and social reform, see Watson, *Charity Organization Movement*, 114–17. Watson claims, "The social case worker . . . never passes moral judgment on a patient. Once in a while one still hears the phrase 'the worthy poor,' or 'the unworthy poor,' but where found it marks the user as one unacquainted with the spirit of modern social work, which has long since outgrown it." C.O.S. case files suggest otherwise.

9. Boyer, *Urban Masses and Moral Reform*; Barry J. Kaplan, "Reformers and Charity: The Abolition of Public Outdoor Relief in New York City, 1870–1898," *Social Science Review* 52, no. 2 (1978): 202–14; Waugh, *Unsentimental Reformer*. For a different analysis of the term "dependency" and its pejorative uses, see Nancy Fraser and Linda Gordon, "A Genealogy of Dependency: Tracing a Keyword of the U.S. Welfare State," *Signs* 19, no. 2 (1994): 309–36.

10. See the Columbia School of Social Work's description of its own history at http://socialwork.columbia.edu/about-cussw/history.

11. Charity Organization Society of the City of New York, *Hand-Book for Friendly Visitors among the Poor* (New York: G. P. Putnam's Sons, 1883), 7 (emphasis in original).

12. See Brian Tierney, *Medieval Poor Law* (Berkeley: University of California Press, 1959); Thomas Max Safley, ed., *The Reformation of Charity: The Secular and the Religious in Early Modern Poor Relief* (Boston: Brill Academic, 2003); Walter Trattner, *From Poor Law to Welfare State: A History of Social Welfare in America* (New York: Free Press, 1974), esp. 1–29; James Brodman, *Charity and Religion in Medieval Europe* (Washington, D.C.: Catholic University of America Press, 2009), and *Charity and Welfare: Hospitals and the Poor in Medieval Catalonia* (Philadelphia: University of Pennsylvania Press, 1998); Sharon Farmer, "Down and Out and Female in Thirteenth-Century Paris," *American Historical Review* 103, no. 2 (1998): 345–72; *Surviving Poverty in Medieval Paris: Gender, Ideology, and the Daily Lives of the Poor* (Ithaca, N.Y.: Cornell University Press, 2002). For contemporary analyses of what the author is calling "distinction," see Katz, *Undeserving Poor*; Ange-Marie Hancock, *The Politics of Disgust: The Public Identity of the Welfare Queen* (New York: New York University Press, 2004).

13. Many historians trace distinction's origins to the Elizabethan Poor Law of 1601, interpreting it as an outgrowth of incipient capitalism brought on by land enclosures. The first chapter of Trattner's *From Poor Law to Welfare State* is a notable exception to the tendency among U.S. historians to ignore the years before 1601. For further critique of the Weberian break between premodern and modern social forms, particularly in charity, see Safley, *Reformation of Charity*.

14. Waugh, *Unsentimental Reformer*, 13–35, 101–2; Robert H. Abzug, *Cosmos Crumbling: American Reform and the Religious Imagination* (New York: Oxford University Press, 1994); Clifford S. Griffin, *Their Brother's Keepers: Moral Stewardship in the United States, 1800–1865* (Westport, Conn.: Greenwood Press, 1960); Lori D. Ginzberg, *Women and the Work of Benevolence: Morality, Politics, and Class in the 19th-Century United States* (New Haven, Conn.: Yale University Press, 1990); Beckert, *Monied Metropolis*, 75–77.

15. For the relevant biblical verses, see Deuteronomy 15:11, John 12:8, and Matthew 26:11. Ironically, C.O.S. advocates tried to claim biblical

provenance by plucking convenient verses out of context for an ideal of charity that would eradicate poverty. See Reverent H. L. Wayland, D.D., "The Old Charity and the New," addendum to *Fourth Annual Report of the Central Council of the Charity Organization Society of the City of New York* (New York: Stettiner, Lambert & Co., 1886), 1. In a note to this address, Wayland cites Deut. 15:4 as an example of God's framing law "to the end that there be no poor among you," and claims, "This is the charity of the Bible, both of the Old and the New Testament." He apparently did not lower his eyes to Deut. 15:11: "For the poor shall never cease out of the land." *Holy Bible: Authorized King James Version* (Oxford: Oxford University Press, 1967), 235.

On the evolving dialectic between charity as a moral responsibility or a tool of social reform, see Stansell, *City of Women*, 30–36.

16. This assault on the D.C.C. was itself a political shell game of sorts, both in executing the policy predilections of Tammany's opponents and in weakening a Democratic power base. On the Tweed Ring, see Alexander B. Callow Jr., *The Tweed Ring* (New York: Oxford University Press, 1966); on Tweed's charitable exploits, see John W. Pratt, "Boss Tweed's Public Welfare Program," *New-York Historical Society Quarterly* 45 (1961): 396–411.

17. Wayland, "The Old Charity and the New," 2–3 (emphasis added).

18. "Constitution and By-Laws of the Society for the Relief of Poor Widows with Small Children" (New York: Mann & Spear, Stationers and Printers, 1857), 12, SRPW; *Minutes of the Society for the Relief of Poor Widows with Small Children*, vol. 3, SRPW.

19. Committee on Idleness and Sources of Employment, "Report to the Managers of the Society for the Prevention of Pauperism in New-York," 6, Box 2, SPP. For more on the SPP and its influence, see Stansell, *City of Women*, 32–36.

20. As quoted in Dorothy G. Becker, "The Visitor to the New York City Poor, 1843–1920," *Social Service Review* 35, no. 4 (1961), 388.

21. Robert W. de Forest, "What Is Charity Organization?" *Charities Review: A Journal of Practical Sociology* 1, no. 1 (1891), 2.

22. C.O.S., *Second Annual Report*, 24.

23. Tierney, *Medieval Poor Law*, 47; on Emminghaus and Ashley generally, see Tierney, *Medieval Poor Law*, 46–54; Arwen Emminghaus, *Das Armenwesen und die Armengesetzgebung in europäischen Staaten* (Berlin: F.A. Werbig, 1870); W.J. Ashley, *An Introduction to English Economic History and Theory* (New York: G.P. Putnam's Sons, 1888).

24. At least one of Emminghaus's and Ashley's contemporaries, Cardinal Fritz Ehrle, wrote a rebuttal to their mutual position, but it apparently lacked either the persuasive power or popularity that their work enjoyed. See Tierney, *Medieval Poor Law*, 54.

25. As quoted in Tierney, *Medieval Poor Law*, 58. Tierney quotes from the Augustinian passage again, with a slightly different translation, in an article from the same year, "The Decretists and the 'Deserving Poor,'" *Comparative Studies in Society and History* 1, no. 4 (1959), 363.

26. Brodman, *Charity and Religion*, 14–25, 28–32; Farmer, *Surviving Poverty*; Michel Mollat, *The Poor in the Middle Ages: An Essay in Social History*, trans. Arthur Goldhammer (New Haven, Conn.: Yale University Press, 1986), 107–12; Tierney, *Medieval Poor Law*, 55; Tierney, "Decretists."

27. Brodman, *Charity and Religion*, 1–44; Brodman, *Charity and Welfare*, viii, 1–7, 125–26; Tierney, *Medieval Poor Law*, 131–32.

28. Tierney, *Medieval Poor Law*, 6. Again, Walter Trattner is an exception (although his work appeared fifteen years after Tierney's).

29. For a lucid treatment of capitalism's emergence in England and the early consequences thereof, see Ellen Meiksins Wood, *The Origin of Capitalism* (New York: Monthly Review Press, 1999). On particulars of early Elizabethan statutes, see Mollat, *Poor in the Middle Ages*; and *Laws Relating to the Poor, from the Forty-Third of Queen Elizabeth to the Third of King George II* (London: Henry Lintot, 1743).

30. Augustine was employing this phrase metaphorically to endorse *suppression* of a heretical sect, not its improvement; see Tierney, *Medieval Poor Law*, 58. Ambitions of social improvement through poor relief grew out of the Reformation. See Peter Slack, *From Reformation to Improvement: Public Welfare in Early Modern England* (Oxford: Oxford University Press, 1999).

31. Indeed, this view survived into the modern era. John Romeyn, a New York minister, declared in 1810 that "riches or poverty happen at the wise disposal of God." See Stansell, *City of Women*, 31–32; Raymond Mohl, *Poverty in New York, 1783–1825* (New York: Oxford University Press, 1971).

32. Mollat, *Poor in the Middle Ages*, 109.

33. See note 30, this chapter.

34. Trattner, *From Poor Law to Welfare State*, 8. Trattner cites a 1531 law of Parliament that decreed able-bodied beggars should be "tyed to the end of a carte naked and be beten with whyppes throughe out . . . tyll [their bodies] . . . be blody by reason of suche whypping."

35. See Penelope Lane, Neil Raven, and K. D. M. Snell, eds., *Women, Work, and Wages in England, 1600–1850* (Rochester, N.Y.: Boydell Press, 2004); Katz, *Undeserving Poor*. See also Stansell, *City of Women*, 30–36.

36. See the preface of *Poor-Laws: Or, the Laws and Statutes Relating to the Settling, Maintenance, and Employment of the Poor* (London: In the Savoy, 1724); C.O.S., *Second Annual Report*, 15.

37. Critiques range from satirical flyers, such as a circa 1845 English pamphlet entitled "An Interesting Dialogue between the Poor-law Commissioner and the Poor People That Apply for Relief" that skewers moralistic distrust of the poor, to scholarship such as that of Michael B. Katz.

38. See, for example, *Minutes of the Society for the Relief of Poor Widows with Small Children*, vol. 5, 199–200, SRPW.

39. The materials for reconstructing Elizabeth Shaw's life come from multiple sources in CSS, Box 239, Folder R9, esp. a letter: Mrs. S. M. Carman to C.O.S., n.d. (hand-delivered Feb. 2, 1897), various responses (from the S.P.C.C., Five Points House of Industry, et al.) to C.O.S. inquiry letters, and the numbered "Memorandum Cards" describing her casework. Some details of Shaw's autobiographical narrative are impossible to verify, but for a cross-reference on her leaving home at age sixteen, see *1870 United States Federal Census,* New York Ward 22, District 24, Series M593, Roll 1053, 74.

40. E. Fellows Jenkins to E. I. Scott, June 9, 1894, CSS, Box 239, Folder R9.

41. Ibid.

42. "Memorandum Card 5," entry for Feb. 2, 1897, CSS, Box 239, Folder R9.

43. Mrs. S. M. Carman to C.O.S., n.d. (hand-delivered Feb. 2, 1897), CSS, Box 239, Folder R9, 1–2.

44. Supt. of relief to James V. Chalmers, Aug. 11, 1899, CSS, Box 239, Folder R10.

45. Miss L. E. Lockhart to E. I. Scott, Oct. 2, 1895; and "Memorandum Card IV," entry for Dec. 18, 1896; both in CSS, Box 239, Folder R10.

46. "Memorandum Card VI and 7," entries for Oct. 24 1899, CSS, Box 239, Folder R10; on husband's condition, see, for example, "Memorandum Card II," entry for Nov. 27, 1895.

47. "Memorandum Card 7," entry for Oct. 25, 1899, CSS, Box 239, Folder R10.

48. Rev. E. Ernest Matthews to C.O.S., Oct. 23, 1899; "Memorandum Cards VI and 7," entries for Oct. 24, 1899; both in CSS, Box 239, Folder R10.

49. "Memorandum Card VI and 7," entries for Oct. 24, 1899, CSS, Box 239, Folder R10.

50. "Memorandum Card," entry for Nov. 17, 1896, CSS, Box 239, Folder R4.

51. "Memorandum Card 10," entry for "Synopsis," CSS, Box 239, Folder R4.

52. "Synopsis Card," March 6, 1896, CSS, Box 239, Folder R4.

53. "Memorandum Card VI and 7," entries from Nov. 30, to Dec. 9, 1901, CSS, Box 239, Folder R4.

54. Johnstone extracted a promise from Reeds not to contact the English relatives, but given the bureaucratic machine of the C.O.S., it seems unlikely that such a promise by a visitor in the field would be kept once the recorded information became separated from its source.

55. "Memorandum Card 7," entry for Dec. 4, 1901, CSS, Box 239, Folder R4.

56. "Memorandum Card 7," entry for Oct. 24, 1899, CSS, Box 239, Folder R10.

57. The purpose of the Wood-Yard was not to provide remunerative employment but to test willingness to work. See Johnston de Forest, "The Woodyard as a Labor Test," *Charities* 9, no. 18 (1902): 443–46.

58. See C.O.S. annual report data, for example, C.O.S., *Second Annual Report,* 49, where "Table II—Cases Treated" indicates only 165 of 2,765 (fewer than 6 percent of total applicants) were "Worthy of Continuous Relief" and another 688 (fewer than a quarter) were "Worthy of Temporary Relief."

59. Kaplan, "Reformers and Charity," 209.

60. "Memorandum Cards VI and 7," entry for Dec. 2, 1901, CSS, Box 239, Folder R4.

61. C.O.S., *Hand-Book for Friendly Visitors,* 2.

62. Ibid., 2.

63. Ibid., 3–4.

64. Ibid., 7.

65. Ibid., 1.

66. Ibid., 8.

67. *Fourth Annual Report of the Central Council of the Charity Organization Society of the City of New York* (New York: Industrial Printing Company, Stettiner, Lambert & Co., 1886), 17. It is important to note that C.O.S. annual reports also contained case studies that told stories of successful reform, in which the poor learned the error of their ways, found work with the C.O.S.'s help, or gave up alcohol and became "productive" members of society. These annual reports, however, largely functioned as internal organizational propaganda and as recruiting tools for prospective members. Their distribution was far more limited than the advertisements the C.O.S. placed in newspapers trumpeting their ability to sniff out frauds. Moreover, in the dozens of actual case files consulted in the CSS collection, the author found no clear instances of "success" such as those described (with

pseudonyms) in the annual reports. Instead, the individual case files reveal the alacrity with which district committees closed cases when they judged the applicant undeserving. Efforts at reform rarely went beyond a few minor suggestions from the visitor during an investigation. (Wood, for example, recommended that Maria Bates rent out a room in her apartment to a boarder; Bates explained that she was amenable to the idea but lacked the necessary funds to purchase necessities like an extra bed or linens.)

68. See previous note.

69. "Memorandum Card 5," entry for Feb. 2, 1897, CSS, Box 239, Folder R9.

70. The term "reified" gestures intentionally to Georg Lukács's theory of reification, or capitalism's reduction of relations between people to the appearance of relations between things. This seems apposite in the case of C.O.S. operations, in which relations between friendly visitors and the poor become mediated through things—the physical paper records of previous encounters. See Lukács, *History and Class Consciousness: Studies in Marxist Dialectics*, trans. Rodney Livingstone (Cambridge, Mass.: The MIT Press, 1967).

71. "Memorandum Card I," entry for Feb. 20, 1896, CSS, Box 239, Folder R4 (emphasis in original).

72. "Memorandum Cards V–VI," entries for Jan. 14, 1898; July 19, 1898; May 5–6, 1899; all in CSS, Box 239, Folder R4 (emphases in original).

73. "Memorandum Card VI," entry for Dec. 2, 1901, CSS, Box 239, Folder R4.

74. "Memorandum Card 7," entry for Dec. 4, 1901, CSS, Box 239, Folder R4.

75. "Dr. De Costa's Sneers and Jibes," *New-York Tribune*, March 5, 1888, 3. See also "Against Organized Charity," *New York Times*, Feb. 20, 1888, 8; "Friends of Charity Meet," *New-York Tribune*, Feb. 21, 1888, 2; "Questions for Dr. De Costa," *New York Times*, Feb. 24, 1888, 8: "Dr. De Costa Writes to Mr. Hewitt," *New York Tribune*, Feb. 26, 1888, 16.

76. "New-York City's Paupers," *New York Times*, Oct. 7, 1888, 10.

77. Ibid.

78. See the untitled letter "We have received from some of our friends anonymous circulars . . ." and the "Startling Extracts" circular, CSS, Box 156, "Lawsuit 1888" Folder.

79. "Why Dr. De Costa Was Angry," *New York World*, Jan. 28, 1888; clipping in CSS, Box 156, "Lawsuit 1888" Folder.

80. For more examples of both external and internal criticisms, see CSS, Box 92, Folder "Administration—Criticisms of Staff 1887–1903."

81. Boyer, *Urban Masses and Moral Order*, 143–61.

82. See the *Charities Bulletin* collections published by the Russell Sage Foundation in SWAC. Many of these documents, several printed exclusively for internal C.O.S. use, focus on case studies of investigations in an effort to further professionalize the process as central to C.O.S. work. See also Kaplan, "Reformers and Charity." Regardless, as the cases of Carman, Johnstone, and Bates show, the C.O.S. may have stopped highlighting its investigative efforts for the public, but those efforts remained at the core of its operations, becoming increasingly professionalized and subject to internal review.

83. CSS, Box 156. An unsigned note in the folder relating to the De Costa press and a related lawsuit against the C.O.S. reads: "Observe that a Society not recognized by the Church, and which in its constitution, expressly prohibits the offer of alms or 'spiritual instruction' by its visitors to the destitute in body and soul, is now seeking to make its way as an instructor, through schismatics and heretics, into parishes and places of worship set apart for the service of Almighty God, according to the Catholic Faith, as taught in the standards of the Protestant Episcopal Church. New York, May 1, 1888." Whether written by De Costa, a C.O.S. officer (much of the material in the folder bears Charles D. Kellogg's signature), or by someone else, its inclusion in this C.O.S. archive supports the connection suggested.

84. See the secretary's reports of Charles D. Kellogg and Edward T. Devine in C.O.S. *Annual Reports* for 1883 to 1899.

85. Edward T. Devine, *Misery and Its Causes* (New York: Macmillan, 1909).

86. "Blackmailing a Poor Man," *New York Times*, Feb. 24, 1887, 2.

87. *Central Council Minutes, C.O.S.*, vol. 2 (June 1884–Dec. 1887), CSS, Box 205, 139.

88. "She Was Not a Vagrant," *New York Times*, March 27, 1888. The judge's sanctimony about poverty's blamelessness, of course, followed his determination of Satcher's former bourgeois status.

89. See CSS, Box 92, Folder "Administration—Criticisms of Staff 1887–1903," for examples of such instances. The folder is marked "Should not be used in any study without careful disguise," presumably to protect the objects of criticism and the confidentiality of casework discussed in the context of that criticism.

90. CSS, Box 99, Folder "Friendly Visitors Course, Z. D. Smith-1898–1899." Despite the name of the folder, the earliest dated materials it contains are from June 22, 1899.

91. Watson, *Charity Organization Movement*, 308–10.

92. See Columbia School of Social Work's own history, at http://socialwork .columbia.edu/about-cussw/history.

93. From the *New-York Tribune*, as quoted in Robert W. de Forest, "The 'Christmas Society' and Its Critics," *Charities Review: A Journal of Practical Sociology* 1, no. 3 (1892), 112.

94. "Gifts for Many Children," *New York Times*, Dec. 26, 1891.

95. De Forest, "Christmas Society," 113.

96. Ibid.

97. From the *Evening Post*, as quoted in De Forest, "Christmas Society," 111.

98. *New York Times*, Dec. 20, 1891.

99. See, for example, "Gifts for Many Children," *New York Times*, Dec. 26, 1891; "Gray Christmas Weather: A Bright Day for Thousands, However," *New-York Tribune*, Dec. 26, 1891.

100. "Gray Christmas Weather," *New-York Tribune*, Dec. 26, 1891.

101. "Gifts for Many Children," *New York Times*, Dec. 26, 1891.

102. "Term of Ten Years," *Chicago Daily Tribune*, Nov. 9, 1893.

103. For Weeks's movements and his contact with his nephews in April, see "F. H. Weeks Traced," *Chicago Tribune,* Aug. 18, 1893.

104. "Memorandum Card IX," entry for April 5, 1900, CSS, Box 239, Folder R10.

105. "Memorandum Card VII," entry for Dec. 2, 1901, CSS, Box 239, Folder R9.

106. "F. H. Weeks Traced," *Chicago Tribune*, Aug. 18, 1893; "Francis H. Weeks' Downfall," *New York Times*, Sept. 12, 1893. Both these articles include Robert W. and H. W. de Forest as the last in a list of "secured creditors" for the amount of $55,000.

107. C. G. Poore, "Our Veteran Captain of Philanthropy," *New York Times*, April 22, 1928.

108. *C.O.S. Central Council Minutes*, vol. 3 (Jan. 1888–Dec. 1893), May 10, 1893, entry, CSS, Box 205.

109. "Francis H. Weeks a Free Man," *New-York Tribune*, May 9, 1900.

110. Mornay Williams to Edward T. Devine, Feb. 7, 1906, CSS, Box 92, Folder "Administration—Criticisms."

111. Mrs. S. M. Carman to C.O.S., n.d. (hand-delivered Feb. 2, 1897), CSS, Box 239, Folder R9, 3 (emphasis in original).

112. Unsigned note to Mr. Kenedy [*sic*] in Rachel Johnstone's file, CSS, Box 239, Folder R10.

113. "Record of Applicants for Relief," July 28, 1911, CSS, Box 239, Folder R4.
114. Unsigned, unaddressed letter in Mrs. S. M. Carman's handwriting, n.d., CSS, Box 239, Folder R9.

5 · The Business of Godly Charity

Epigraph: "Our Madison Sq. Garden Christmas: 20,000 Poor Will Be the Army's Guests: How It Will Be Done," *War Cry*, Dec. 2, 1899.

1. "Salvation Army's Bounty," *New York Times*, Dec. 26, 1899.
2. Ibid.
3. Ibid.; Salvation Army, *Harbor Lights*, Dec.–Feb. 1899; Frederick de Latour Booth-Tucker, *The Salvation Army in the United States, Christmas 1899* (New York: Salvation Army Publications, 1899). For a critique of Salvation Army finances, see, for example, T. H. Huxley, *Social Diseases and Worse Remedies: Letters to the "Times" on Mr. Booth's Scheme* (New York: Macmillan, 1891); John Manson, *The Salvation Army and the Public: A Religious, Social, and Financial Study* (New York: E. P. Dutton, 1906).
4. C.O.S., *Second Annual Report*, 2.
5. Lillian Taiz, *Hallelujah Lads & Lasses* (Chapel Hill: University of North Carolina Press, 2001), 25–26; "The Salvation Army: Arrival of the Pioneer Band in This Country—Their Peculiarities," *New York Times*, Mar. 11, 1880.
6. C.O.S., *Second Annual Report*, 15; Winston, *Red-Hot and Righteous*, 18–24; Taiz, *Hallelujah Lads & Lasses*, 14–15.
7. Winston, *Red-Hot and Righteous*; Taiz, *Hallelujah Lads & Lasses*.
8. Beverly Gage, *The Day Wall Street Exploded* (New York: Oxford University Press, 2010); Louis Adamic, *Dynamite: The Story of Class Violence in America* (New York: Viking Press, 1931); Richard H. Frost, *The Mooney Case* (Stanford, Calif.: Stanford University Press, 1968); Paul Avrich, *The Haymarket Tragedy* (Princeton, N.J.: Princeton University Press, 1984); Paul Krause, *The Battle for Homestead, 1880–1892: Politics, Culture, and Steel* (Pittsburgh: University of Pittsburgh Press, 1992); and James Green, *Death in the Haymarket: A Story of Chicago, the First Labor Movement, and the Bombing That Divided Gilded Age America* (New York: Pantheon Books, 2006).
9. See Booth-Tucker, *Salvation Army in the United States*; Diane H. Winston, "Living in the Material World: The Changing Role of Salvation Army Women, 1880–1918," *Journal of Urban History* 28, no. 4 (2002): 469–70.

10. See, for example, "Jersey City's Police Denounced," *New-York Tribune*, Sept. 11, 1893.

11. "The Salvationists," *New York Times*, Feb. 2, 1892.

12. "Fighting against Evil," *New-York Tribune*, Nov. 15, 1893.

13. For an example of an attack on its respectability, or lack thereof, see "The Salvationists, *New York Times*, Feb. 2, 1892."

14. Taiz, *Hallelujah Lads & Lasses*, 42–44.

15. Ibid., 40–44. For more on settlement house work, see Chapters 6 and 7.

16. "Fighting against Evil"; William Booth, *In Darkest England and the Way Out* (New York: Funk & Wagnalls, 1890).

17. Bramwell Booth, *Servants of All: A Brief Review of the Call, Character, and Labours of the Officers of the Salvation Army* (New York: Salvation Army Book Department, 1900), 59.

18. As quoted in Taiz, *Hallelujah Lads & Lasses*, 107; from Booth, *In Darkest England*.

19. "Our Madison Sq. Garden Christmas," *War Cry*, Dec. 2, 1899.

20. Contemporary observers can see displays of this annual call to a more forgiving charity in the phenomenon of the *New York Times* "Neediest Cases" stories, the idea for which grew out of *Times* publisher Adolph S. Ochs's encounter with a homeless man after "a big turkey dinner" on Christmas day in 1911. The appeal is calendar-specific (with the unspoken understanding that one should be more generous at the holidays) while the narratives are always of the painfully deserving (euphemized as "neediest") poor. See "The Neediest Cases Fund: A Brief History," updated 2010, www.nytimes.com/ref/giving/neediesthistory.html.

21. Booth-Tucker, *Salvation Army in the United States*.

22. Ibid.

23. "Feast for Thousands," *New-York Tribune*, Dec. 26, 1899.

24. As depicted on the cover of *War Cry*, Dec. 2, 1899; Nissenbaum, *Battle for Christmas*, 253.

25. See issues of the *War Cry*, Dec. 2, 9, 16, and 30, 1899. The Army's self-promotion through the use of prominent names continued in the Jan. 13, 1900, issue as well.

26. "Feast for Thousands," *New-York Tribune*, Dec. 26, 1899.

27. "Great Feast in Garden," *New York Sun*, Dec. 26, 1899.

28. *War Cry*, Jan. 13, 1900.

29. *War Cry*, Dec. 2, 1899.

30. See "Salvation Army's Bounty," *New York Times*, Dec. 26, 1899; "Feast for Thousands," *New-York Tribune*, Dec. 26, 1899.

31. "Salvation Army's Bounty," *New York Times*, Dec. 26, 1899; "Feast for Thousands," *New-York Tribune*, Dec. 26, 1899.

32. "Salvation Army's Bounty," *New York Times*, Dec. 26, 1899; "Feast for Thousands," *New-York Tribune*, Dec. 26, 1899.

33. "The Great Dinner," *War Cry*, Jan. 6, 1900.

34. "Great Feast in Garden," *New York Sun*, Dec. 26, 1899.

35. Edith Wharton, *House of Mirth* (New York: C. Scribner's Sons, 1905).

36. "Great Feast in Garden," *New York Sun*, Dec. 26, 1899.

37. For examples of wealthy New Yorkers' simultaneous disgust and fascination with the poor and their presence, see Josiah Strong, *Religious Movements for Social Betterment* (New York: Baker & Taylor, 1900); James, *American Scene*; John Grafton, ed., *New York in the Nineteenth Century: 317 Engravings from Harper's Weekly and Other Contemporary Sources*, 2nd ed. (New York: Dover, 1977); Boyer, *Urban Masses and Moral Order*; Lears, *No Place of Grace*; Susan D. Moeller, "The Cultural Construction of Urban Poverty: Images of Poverty in New York City, 1890–1917," *Journal of American Culture* 18, no. 4 (1995): 1–16; Mary Hellen Dunlop, *Gilded City: Scandal and Sensation in Turn of the Century New York* (New York: William Morrow, 2000).

38. "Great Feast in Garden," *New York Sun*, Dec. 26, 1899

39. "The Feast of Love!" *War Cry*, Jan. 6, 1900.

40. "Great Feast in Garden," *New York Sun*, Dec. 26, 1899.

41. "Salvation Army's Bounty," *New York Times*, Dec. 26, 1899.

42. "Great Feast in Garden," *New York Sun*, Dec. 26, 1899.

43. "Opinions of the Great Dinner by Spectators and Guests," *War Cry*, Jan. 13, 1900.

44. For more on the Countess, see Adeline Countess Schimmelmann, *Glimpses of My Life at the German Court, among Baltic Fishermen and Berlin Socialists and in Prison Including 'A Home Abroad' by Pastor Otto Funcke*, ed. W. Smith Foggitt (New York: Dodd, Mead, 1896).

45. "Opinions of the Great Dinner," *War Cry*, Jan. 13, 1900.

46. *New York Evening Post*, Dec. 26, 1899.

47. "To Our Auxiliary Friends," *Harbor Lights* 3, no. 1 (1900); "Great Feast in Garden," *New York Sun*, Dec. 26, 1899 ; "Salvation Army's Bounty," *New York Times*, Dec. 26, 1899.

48. "Great Feast in Garden," *New York Sun*, Dec. 26, 1899.

49. "Opinions of the Great Dinner," *War Cry*, Jan. 13, 1900.
50. C.O.S., *18th Annual Report* (July 1899–June 1900), 76–77; "Army News," *War Cry*, Dec. 30, 1899; Burrows and Wallace, *Gotham*, 1147. This dual relationship speaks to philanthropy's ability to make its generosity pay— Colonel John Jacob Astor's money effectively passed through Army hands on the way to his cousin's wallet.
51. For MacLean's vice presidency of the dinner, see "The Mammoth Christmas Dinner," *War Cry*, Dec. 9, 1899; for his wife's donations and committee membership, see C.O.S., *18th Annual Report*, 9, 98.
52. "Greetings from New York's Governor," *War Cry*, Jan. 6, 1900; C.O.S., *18th Annual Report*, 80, 103. See the list of officers in C.O.S., *Second Annual Report*.
53. "The Mammoth Christmas Dinner," *War Cry*, Dec. 9, 1899; C.O.S., *18th Annual Report*, 2.
54. See "Salvation Army's Bounty," *New York Times*, Dec. 26, 1899; "Feast for Thousands," *New-York Tribune*, Dec. 26, 1899.
55. For this cultural phenomenon's normative development, see Scott A. Sandage, *Born Losers: A History of Failure in America* (Cambridge, Mass.: Harvard University Press, 2005).
56. 1873, 1884, 1893, and 1907.

6 · Reaching Out to the Rich

Epigraph: Irving Ball to Mrs. Vincent Astor, Jan. 26, 1917, LDWP, Box 42, Folder 8.2.

1. Max W. Paley to Jacob H. Schiff, Dec. 9, 1909, LDWP, Box 44, Folder 1.1, 1; Bureau of the Census, *Thirteenth Census of the United States: 1910—Population*, New York County, New York, Manhattan Borough, Ward 12, Series T624, Roll 1021, 11B.
2. Bureau of the Census, *Twelfth Census of the United States, Schedule No. 1—Population*, Monroe County, New York, Rochester, Ward 7, Series T623, Roll 1074, 17A; Margaret Anderson to Lillian Wald, Dec. 15, 1909, LDWP, Box 44, Folder 1.1, 2; New York State Legislature, *Report*, BLYU, 278.
3. Bureau of the Census, *Twelfth Census of the United States, Schedule No. 1—Population*, Monroe County, New York, Rochester, Ward 7, Series T623, Roll 1074, 17A; Anderson to Wald, Dec. 15, 1909, LDWP, Box 44, Folder 1.1, 2.

4. Bureau of the Census, *Thirteenth Census of the United States*, New York County, New York, Manhattan Borough, Ward 12, Series T624, Roll 1021, 11A–11B.

5. Paley to Schiff, Dec. 9, 1909, LDWP, Box 44, Folder 1.1.

6. The term "begging letters" appears in both newspaper articles and charity-world publications as well as in secondary literature. I have retained it for clarity of reference, although the term itself warrants critical analysis. See Sandage, *Born Losers*, 226–57; Greeley, "Beyond Benevolence"; and Ruth Crocker, "'I Only Ask You Kindly to Divide Some of Your Fortune with Me': Begging Letters and the Transformation of Charity in Late Nineteenth-Century America," *Social Politics* 6 (1999): 131–60.

7. For alternative frameworks in which to consider begging-letter writers and writing, see Pratt, *Imperial Eyes*, esp. her discussion of "autoethnography"; James C. Scott, *Weapons of the Weak: Everyday Forms of Peasant Resistance* (New Haven, Conn.: Yale University Press, 1985); and Tera W. Hunter, *To 'Joy My Freedom: Southern Black Women's Lives and Labors after the Civil War* (Cambridge, Mass.: Harvard University Press, 1997).

8. Lillian D. Wald, *The House on Henry Street* (New York: Henry Holt, 1915); *Windows on Henry Street* (Boston: Little, Brown, 1934); Marjorie N. Feld, *Lillian Wald: A Biography* (Chapel Hill: University of North Carolina Press, 2008); R. L. Duffus, *Lillian Wald, Neighbor and Crusader* (New York: Macmillan, 1939); Clare Coss, ed., *Lillian D. Wald: Progressive Activist* (New York: Feminist Press, 1989); Doris Groshen Daniels, *Always a Sister: The Feminism of Lillian D. Wald* (New York: Feminist Press, 1989).

9. Wald, *Windows on Henry Street*, 10.

10. Some historians have touched on progressive alliances between the working class and a wealthier "middle class"; see Murolo, *Common Ground of Womanhood*; Dawley, *Struggles for Justice*; Johnston, *Radical Middle Class*.

11. For Schiff's fight with the C.O.S., see Naomi W. Cohen, *Jacob H. Schiff, A Study in American Jewish Leadership* (Hanover, N.H.: Brandeis University Press, 1999), 70–71; Cyrus Adler, *Jacob H. Schiff, His Life and Letters* (Garden City, N.Y.: Doubleday, Doran, 1928), 1:386.

12. Martin S. Pernick, *The Black Stork: Eugenics and the Death of "Defective" Babies in American Medicine and Motion Pictures since 1915* (New York: Oxford University Press, 1996), 6.

13. See Chapter 8, note 27.

14. Ruth Crocker, "From Gift to Foundation: The Philanthropic Lives of Mrs. Russell Sage," in *Charity, Philanthropy, and Civility in American History,* ed. Lawrence J. Friedman and Mark D. McGarvie (Cambridge: Cambridge University Press, 2003), 206; Ruth Crocker, *Mrs. Russell Sage: Women's Activism and Philanthropy in Gilded Age and Progressive Era America* (Bloomington: Indiana University Press, 2006), 200, 206; "World Asks His Aid: Rockefeller Receives over 500 Begging Letters Each Day," *Washington Post,* Jan. 19, 1913; Edwin R. Embree, LDWP, Catalogued Correspondence, Box 4, Folder 1; Henry Street worker to Mrs. Astor, Zeidner case, March 5, 1909, LDWP Box 44, Folder 1.16, 1–3; Irving Ball to Mrs. Vincent Astor, Jan. 26, 1917, LDWP, Box 42, Folder 8.2.

15. Melke Clar to Lillian Wald, Nov. 17, 1906, LDWP, Box 43, Folder 1.1.

16. W. Frank Persons to Robert Weeks de Forest, Nov. 21, 1906, as quoted in Crocker, *Mrs. Russell Sage,* 207, 424n.

17. Paley to Schiff, Dec. 9, 1909, LDWP, Box 44, Folder 1.1; "Kelleher, Bridge & Thomas," n.d., LWDP, Box 43, Folder 1.14.

18. "Neighboring Lipsky Tenants" to "Ms. L. Ward," Oct. 17, 1905, LDWP, Box 43, Folder 1.15; C.O.S. Special Agent and Chief Mendicancy Officer James Forbes to Lillian D. Wald, Aug. 29, 1905, LDWP, Box 43, Folder 1.15. Both 1900 and 1910 federal census records list Nathan Lipsky as a peddler, living at 187 Clinton Street; see Bureau of the Census, *Twelfth Census of the United States, Schedule No. 1—Population,* New York County, New York, Manhattan Borough, Ward unlisted, Series T623, Roll 1093, 22A; Bureau of the Census, *Thirteenth Census of the United States: 1910 Population,* Borough of Manhattan, City of New York, Series T624, Roll 1028, 4B. These records do not suggest a successful con-artist or thriving mendicant—the Lipskys stayed put at the decidedly un-posh address of 187 Clinton, and only one of the many children was employed (as a cigar-maker). Still, an unsigned, undated typescript note in Wald's papers (LDWP, Box 43, Folder 1.15) related testimony from a U.H.C. visitor who saw the home and found it "very comfortable, showing evidence of sufficient means." As further grounds for denying relief, this again suggests the dilemma for the poor discussed above—live in squalor, suffer condescension; keep house well, receive no relief.

19. "Lipsky Tenants" to "Ward," Oct. 17, 1905, LDWP, Box 43, Folder 1.15.

20. Ibid.

21. Wald, *House on Henry Street,* 28; Howe, *World of Our Fathers,* 91; Paley to Schiff, Dec. 9, 1909, LDWP, Box 44, Folder 1.1, 2.

22. Paley to Schiff, Dec. 9, 1909, LDWP, Box 44, Folder 1.1; Crocker, *Mrs. Russell Sage*, 208.

23. Frederick B. Jennings, "Report of the Committee on Mendicancy," in C.O.S., *Twenty-Third Annual Report, From July 1, 1904, to September 30, 1905* (New York: United Charities Building, 1905), 51; "The Ancient Profession of Street Beggar as Practiced in New York To-Day," *New York Times*, magazine section, June 19, 1904, 2; "Begging Letters: One of the Trials with Which the Rich Are Burdened," *Washington Post*, May 13, 1907; "Mrs. Sage Has a Tender Heart: No Sympathy, However, with Begging Letter Writers," *New York Observer and Chronicle*, Jan. 3, 1907, 25.

24. Bessie Moskowitz to Lillian Wald, Oct. 1910, LDWP, Box 43, Folder 1.16.

25. Philip Lubell to Lillian D. Wald, Feb. 10, 1915, LDWP, Box 43, Folder 1.15; Bureau of the Census, *Fourteenth Census of the United States—1920 Population*, Kings County, New York, Brooklyn Assembly District 4, Series T625, Roll 1149, 1B.

26. Harry Heald to Michael Friedsam, Dec. 19, 1916, B. Altman & Co. Papers, NYHS, Box 1, Folder 1.

27. Irving Ball to Mrs. Vincent Astor, Jan. 26, 1917, LDWP, Box 42, Folder 8.2.

28. Such tactics reflect those employed by authors of what Pratt calls "autoethnography": see Mary Louise Pratt, "Arts of the Contact Zone," *Profession* 91 (1991): 33–40. Pratt defines an autoethnographic text as one "in which people undertake to describe themselves in ways that engage with representations others have made of them" (35).

29. Ball to Astor, Jan. 26, 1917, LDWP, Box 42, Folder 8.2; Clar to Wald, Nov. 17, 1906, LDWP, Box 43, Folder 1.1; C. E. Sweeney to Wald, Aug. 17, 1916, LDWP, Box 44, Folder 1.5.

30. For instance, the Henry Street men's director helped Irving Ball find training and a job; Wald invited Bessie Moskowitz to meet with her and discuss employment opportunities; even Philip Lubell, who had previously bilked Wald out of money, received a firm but respectful reply. See relevant letters from Wald to Ball (LDWP, Box 42, Folder 8.2), Moskowitz (LDWP, Box 43, Folder 1.16), and Lubell (LDWP, Box 43, Folder 1.15).

31. This echoes Pratt's examination of autoethnography in both "Arts of the Contact Zone" and *Imperial Eyes*, with the autoethnographic text becoming the mediator of an encounter to come.

32. "A Begging Letter Bureau," *New York Times*, Jan. 19, 1913; "Mrs. Sage Has a Tender Heart," *New York Observer and Chronicle* (Jan. 3, 1907): 25; Crocker, *Mrs. Russell Sage*, 205.

33. For details on Jennie Paley, see the entry for the Nat Barrows family, Bureau of the Census, *Fifteenth Census of the United States: 1930*, Westchester County, New York, Mount Vernon, Roll 1662, 16A. The live-in servant's name was Mabel Channel.

7 · Between Empathy and Prejudice

Epigraph: As quoted in Naomi W. Cohen, *Jacob H. Schiff, A Study in American Jewish Leadership* (Hanover, N.H.: Brandeis University Press, 1999), 59.

1. Ibid., 1–3. For more on Schiff, see Adler, *Life and Letters*, vol. 2; Cyrus Adler, *Jacob Henry Schiff: A Biographical Sketch* (New York: American Jewish Committee, 1921); Frieda Schiff Warburg, *Reminiscences of a Long Life* (New York: Thistle Press, 1956); Ron Chernow, *The Warburgs: The Twentieth-Century Odyssey of a Remarkable Jewish Family* (New York: Random House, 1993); Cohen, *American Jewish Leadership*.
2. Adler, *Life and Letters*, 1:9–10; Stephen Birmingham, *"Our Crowd": The Great Jewish Families of New York* (New York: Harper & Row, 1967), 198; Chernow, *The Warburgs*, 53, 91.
3. Adler, *Life and Letters*, 1:6–7.
4. Ibid., 316.
5. Adler, *Life and Letters*, 1:294–95; Cohen, *American Jewish Leadership*, 60.
6. "Investigating Unemployment," *New York Times*, Mar. 31, 1908. The fourth of five principles in the original A.I.C.P. handbook instructs visitors "to give assistance, both in quantity and quality, inferior, except in cases of sickness, to what might be procured by labor" (as quoted in Becker, "Visitor to the New York City Poor," 383). Under Edward T. Devine's leadership, the C.O.S. was beginning to take a broader view just at this moment; see Devine, *Misery and Its Causes*.
7. Cohen, *American Jewish Leadership*, 66; Schiff to Wald, Jan. 1, 1905, LDWP, Box 9, Folder 9, 1–2; Beatrice Siegel, *Lillian Wald of Henry Street* (New York: Macmillan, 1983), 41–42.
8. Cohen, *American Jewish Leadership*, 59. For more on tzedakah, see Joseph Telushkin, *Jewish Literacy: The Most Important Things to Know about the Jewish Religion, Its People, and Its History* (New York: Morrow, 1991), 563–66; Reuven Kimelman, *Tsedakah and Us* (New York: National Jewish Center for Learning and Leadership, 1983).
9. Cohen, *American Jewish Leadership*, 41–81; Daniel J. Elazar, ed., *Authority, Power and Leadership in the Jewish Polity: Cases and Issues* (Lanham, Md.:

University Press of America, 1991); Arthur A. Goren, *New York Jews and the Quest for Community: The Kehillah Experiment, 1908–1922* (New York: Columbia University Press, 1970), 15–17; *National Leadership in American Jewish Life: The Formative Years* (Cincinnati: Judaic Studies Program, 1986). On recasting the "social control" thesis, see Boyer, *Urban Masses and Moral Order*. On "uptown" and "downtown" Jews, see Jacobson, *Whiteness of a Different Color*, 163–99. Cohen attributes Schiff's intense personal involvement in the institutions benefiting from his largesse to a "drive for power and public approval" and claims that he "dominated his subordinates and the beneficiaries of his gifts" (55). This squares ill with both Schiff's periodic, anonymous giving, and his personal correspondence with Wald, which became increasingly advisory and hands-off. It seems more plausible that he wanted to stay informed of his charities' activities with the purpose of ensuring his money was being used efficiently, not to exert dictatorial control.

10. Cohen, *American Jewish Leadership*, 71; Adler, *Life and Letters*, 1:274, 313, 315.
11. Cohen, *American Jewish Leadership*, 70–71; Adler, *Life and Letters*, 1:361.
12. Cohen, *American Jewish Leadership*, 70–71; Adler, *Life and Letters*, 1:363–65. On whiteness, see Roediger, *Wages of Whiteness*; Jacobson, *Whiteness of a Different Color*. On racial and religious discrimination in charity-organization precursors to foster-care systems (and subsequently, in state-administered foster care), see Nina Bernstein, *The Lost Children of Wilder: The Epic Struggle to Change Foster Care* (New York: Pantheon, 2001).
13. Adler, *Life and Letters*, 1:363–64. On the "100 percent American" propaganda campaign during World War I, see Stephen Vaughn, *Holding Fast the Inner Lines: Democracy, Nationalism, and the Committee on Public Information* (Chapel Hill: University of North Carolina Press, 1980); George Creel, *How We Advertised America* (1920; repr., New York: Arno Press, 1972).
14. Cohen, *American Jewish Leadership*, 71.
15. "Otto T. Bannard Looks for Big British Loan Here," *New York Times*, Sept. 3, 1915; "Otto T. Bannard," *New York Times*, Jan. 18, 1929.
16. James A. Hijiya, "Four Ways of Looking at a Philanthropist: A Study of Robert Weeks De Forest," *Proceedings of the American Philosophical Society* 124, no. 6 (1980): 414.
17. Adler, *Life and Letters*, 1:314–97; Jacob A. Riis to Jacob H Schiff, Nov. 20, 1906, LDWP, Box 9, Folder 20; Schiff to Riis, Nov. 21, 1906, LDWP, Box 9, Folder 20.

18. Riis to Schiff, Nov. 22, 1906, LDWP, Box 9, Folder 20, 1; Schiff to Riis, Nov. 23, 1906, LDWP, Box 9, Folder 20, 1.
19. Schiff to Riis, Nov. 23, 1906, LDWP, Box 9, Folder 20, 1–2.
20. Riis to Schiff, Nov. 24, 1906, LDWP, Box 9, Folder 20, 1–2; Jacob H. Schiff to Lillian D. Wald, Nov. 26, 1906, LDWP, Box 9, Folder 20.

8 · The Limits of Private Philanthropy

Epigraph: George William Alger, "Reminiscences of George W. Alger: Oral History, 1952," Harlan B. Phillips interview, GWA, 254, 261.

1. Wald, "The People Who Live in Tenements," n.d., LDWP, Box 16, Folder 4. This manuscript is paginated, but Wald repeats pages 4 and 5, creating the sequence 3, 4, 5, 4, 5, 6. . . . The quotes appear on the first page 5, second page 4, second page 5, 9, and 13. The manuscript appears to be notes for a speech, almost certainly intended for delivery at the Tenement House Exhibition of December 1899. The references Wald makes to a larger exhibit of photographs and maps align with the newspaper coverage of the Exhibition. See "Tenement House Exhibition," *New York Times*, Aug. 14, 1899.
2. Wald, "People Who Live in Tenements," 11–12, 17.
3. Alan Edward Reznick, "Lillian D. Wald: The Years at Henry Street," (Ph.D. diss., University of Wisconsin, 1974), 2; Feld, *Lillian Wald*, 27–31; Bureau of the Census, *Tenth Census of the United States, Schedule No. 1—Population*, Monroe County, New York, Rochester, Ward 79, Series T9, Roll 862, 132A; Daniels, *Always a Sister*, 12–13.
4. Feld uses the terms "civic universalism" and "ethnic Progressive" to describe Wald's approach, tying both to Wald's "firm notions of women's distinctive natures," whereas Daniels argues for "feminism" as a "vital ingredient" in all Wald's thinking (see Feld, *Lillian Wald*, 54–55; and Daniels, *Always a Sister*, 2, respectively). The term "feminist humanism" attempts to recognize the validity of Daniels's analysis while incorporating Feld's under a simpler rubric—one more reflective of Wald's own language of "human respect." On gender, feminism, and the Progressive Era, see Chapter 11, note 10 of this book.
5. Feld, *Lillian Wald*, 20–21, 27–36; Wald to George P. Ludlum, May 27, 1889, WP, Box 2, Folder 1; Lillian D. Wald, "New Aspects of an Old Profession," *Barnard Bulletin*, Oct. 20, 1913, 3; Daniels, *Always a Sister*.

6. Alger, "Reminiscences," GWA, 254, 260–61; "George W. Alger, Lawyer, 94, Dead," *New York Times*, Apr. 20, 1967; Lillian Wald, "The Nurse as Settlement Worker," *Cleveland Women's Journal*, May 4, 1918, in Wald Papers, NYPL, as quoted in Feld, *Lillian Wald*, 20.

7. Wald, *House on Henry Street*, 29.

8. Wald, "People Who Live in Tenements," 13–14; Wald, *House on Henry Street*, 102–3.

9. "Henry St. Settlement Celebrating Its 20th Birthday," *New York Times*, June 1, 1913. For the recovery rates of pneumonia patients in 1914, see Wald, *House on Henry Street*, 38–39. On the Federal Children's Bureau, see Siegel, *Lillian Wald of Henry Street*, 60–63; Wald, *House on Henry Street*, 163–67. On settlements' contributions to Progressive reforms, see, for example, Allen F. Davis, *Spearheads for Reform: The Social Settlements and the Progressive Movement, 1890–1914* (New York: Oxford University Press, 1967); Mina Carson, *Settlement Folk: Social Thought and the American Settlement Movement, 1885–1930* (Chicago: University of Chicago Press, 1990); Louise W. Knight, *Citizen: Jane Addams and the Struggle for Democracy* (Chicago: University of Chicago Press, 2005).

10. Alger, "Reminiscences," GWA, 265–66.

11. Wald to Schiff, Nov. 25, 1912, LDWP Box 9 Folder 108, 1–3.

12. Schiff to Wald, Nov. 26, 1912, LDWP Box 9 Folder 108, 2.

13. Kaplan, "Reformers and Charity"; "President's Address" in C.O.S., *Seventh Annual Report of the Central Council of the Charity Organization Society of the City of New York, for the Year 1888* (New York City: Charity Organization Society, 1889), 19.

14. For examples of slum tourism, see Martin, "East Side Considerations"; Dr. William H. Tolman and Charles Hemstreet, *The Better New York* (New York: Baker and Taylor, 1904); Romeyn, *Street Scenes*.

15. Sidney Ford, "Women's Work, Women's Clubs," *Los Angeles Times*, Feb. 6, 1913, (the same writer's byline of "Sydney Ford" appears over other editions of the same column); "Slow but Sure, Her Goal Near: Philanthropists Respond to Y.W.C.A. Call," *Los Angeles Times*, Feb. 10, 1913; "Y.M.Y.W.C.A. Fund Has Its Worst Day: Only $33,650 Obtained Yesterday, with Six Days Left to Get $1,410,000," *New York Times*, Nov. 19, 1913; "Y.W.C.A. Work in Pageantry: Spectacle That'll Visualize Society's Scope," *Los Angeles Times*, Dec. 21, 1913; Wald to Schiff, Nov. 9, 1915, LDWP Box 10, Folder 119, 2–3.

16. Wald to Schiff, Nov. 9, 1915, LDWP Box 10, Folder 119, 3. On Wald's arrangement with Metropolitan Life, see Feld, *Lillian Wald*, 164, 252n. On the private-public development of welfare and health insurance in the United States, see Jennifer Klein, *For All These Rights: Business, Labor, and the Shaping of America's Public-Private Welfare State* (Princeton, N.J.: Princeton University Press, 2003).

17. Wald to Schiff, Nov. 25, 1912, LDWP Box 9 Folder 108, 1–2.

18. Adolf Augustus Berle, "Reminiscences of Adolf Augustus Berle: oral history, 1970," Douglas Scott interview, AAB, 158.

19. "Henry Street Settlement Celebrating Its 20th Birthday," *New York Times*, June 1, 1913.

20. "Henry Street Settlement," *New York Times*, June 1, 1913; "10,000 See Pageant of Henry St. Life: Twentieth Anniversary of Miss Wald's Settlement Is Celebrated in Novel Way," *New York Times*, June 8, 1913.

21. Sean Wilentz, *Chants Democratic: New York City and the Rise of the American Working Class, 1788–1850* (New York: Oxford University Press, 1986); Stansell, *City of Women*; Quigley, *Second Founding*; Iver Bernstein, *The New York City Draft Riots: Their Significance for American Society and Politics in the Age of the Civil War* (New York: Oxford University Press, 1990); John Higham, *Strangers in the Land: Patterns of American Nativism, 1860–1925* (New Brunswick, N.J.: Rutgers University Press, 1955); Ray Allen Billington, *Protestant Crusade, 1800–1860: A Study of the Origins of American Nativism* (1938; repr., New York: Rinehart, 1952).

22. "Henry Street Settlement," *New York Times*, June 1, 1913.

23. "Two Pageants—A Contrast," *New York Times*, June 9, 1913; "10,000 See Pageant," *New York Times*, June 8, 1913.

24. "Two Pageants." *New York Times*, June 9, 1913. According to the *Times*'s news coverage, the I.W.W. event was actually a pep rally for strikers at the Paterson, New Jersey, silk strike. See "Haywood's Pageant Cheers Up Strikers," *New York Times*, June 9, 1913. On the Paterson strike, see Anne Huber Tripp, *The I.W.W. and the Paterson Silk Strike of 1913* (Urbana: University of Illinois Press, 1987).

25. Adler, *Life and Letters*, 1:386; "Henry Street Settlement," *New York Times*, June 1, 1913, 45.

26. Mary Stillman Harkness to Wald, July 3, 1919, LDWP, Box 56, Folder 1.19.

27. Wald to Lavinia Dock, Aug. 1919, Wald Papers NYPL, Box 3, Folder 4, as quoted in Siegel, *Lillian Wald of Henry Street*, 152.

28. The Henry Street Settlement rebounded from this period of financial difficulty and has thrived as a nonprofit community center with total net assets of over $25 million as of fiscal year 2010, most of which it derives from "grants and fees from contracting agencies." For recent financials, see Loeb & Troeper, LLP, "Henry Street Settlement and Affiliates: Consolidated Financial Statements and Auditor's Report," June 30, 2010, Exhibit A, 2, and Exhibit B, 1. More recent reports are available at www.henrys treet.org/about/financials.html. For more on Henry Street's subsequent history, see www.henrystreet.org/about/history/.

29. For more on cross-class gender solidarity in this period, see Murolo, *Common Ground of Womanhood*.

9 · Killing Workers for Profit

Epigraph: John Haynes Holmes, *Is Violence the Way Out of Our Industrial Disputes?* (New York: Dodd, Mead and Company, 1920), 6.

1. W.T.U.L., *Annual Report 1911–1912, March–March of the Women's Trade Union League of New York* (New York: The League, 1912, emphasis added).

2. See, for instance, "Dynamite in Brooklyn," *New York Times*, April 17, 1883; "Dynamite in California: Leaders of the Seamen's Union Using It against the Obdurate Vessel-Owners," *Chicago Daily Tribune*, Dec. 1, 1887; "A Dynamite Plot: Three Burlington Strikers Arrested, Charged with Attempting to Wreck the Railway's Property," *Los Angeles Times*, July 6, 1888; "Miscreants Use Dynamite: A Dastardly Attempt to Murder Non-Union Men at Homestead," *New York Times*, Oct. 8, 1892; "Bombs of the Anarchists: Commonplace Tin Cans and Pails Converted into Agents of Destruction," *Southern Planter*, June 1894, 340; "Martial Law Is Declared: Strikers Have Dynamite and Rifles," *Chicago Daily Tribune*, Sept. 24, 1896; "Confesses to Dynamite Plot," *Washington Post*, Aug. 21, 1901; "'Reds' Plot to Kill," *Chicago Daily Tribune*, Dec. 18, 1903; "Three Cars Dynamited: More Disorder in the Chester Street Car Strike," June 3, 1908; "Another Dynamite Bomb Exploded in Chicago's Lighting Company War," *Los Angeles Times*, July 3, 1911; "Dynamite for Judges," *New York Times*, March 13, 1914; "Find Dynamite on Springfield Rails," *Washington Post*, Sept. 16, 1917. For more comprehensive accounts of fear, suspicion, accusation, and documentation of worker violence, see National Founders' Association, *A Policy of Lawlessness: Partial Record of Riot, Assault, Murder, Coercion,*

and Intimidation Occurring in Strikes of The Iron Molders' Union during 1904, 1905, 1906 and 1907 (Detroit: National Founders' Association, 1909); Julius Henry Cohen, *Law and Order in Industry: Five Years' Experience* (New York: Macmillan, 1916); Adamic, *Dynamite.*

3. The perceived illegitimacy of violence enacted by the poor means that it often received (and receives) greater public notice than assaults of capital and the state, creating an outsized impression of its *relative* frequency (see the previous note). On the development and pervasiveness of revolutionary violence and responses from state and capital during this period of U.S. history, see Gage, *The Day Wall Street Exploded.* For two instances in which U.S. labor violence did, briefly, rival that of capital, see Andrews, *Killing for Coal*, and James Green's forthcoming work from Pantheon Books on the West Virginia mine wars.

   On theoretical questions of how legitimacy is established, maintained, and wielded, see Max Weber, "Politik als Beruf," in *Gesammelte politische Schriften* (München: Drei Masken, 1921), 396–450. Other influential explorations of the relationship between legitimacy and violence or violent coercion include: Hannah Arendt, *On Violence* (New York: Harcourt, Brace, & World, 1970); Frantz Fanon, *The Wretched of the Earth*, trans. Constance Farrington (New York: Grove Press, 1965); Michel Foucault, *Discipline and Punish: The Birth of the Prison*, trans. Alan Sheridan (New York: Pantheon Books, 1977). For an intriguing psychotheoretical formulation of relative legitimacy between the violence of "dominants" and "subordinates" in "expropriative social relations" (read: "rich" and "poor" in "capitalism"), see Mary R. Jackman, "License to Kill: Violence and Legitimacy in Expropriative Social Relations," in *The Psychology of Legitimacy: Emerging Perspectives On Ideology, Justice, and Intergroup Relations*, ed. John T. Jost and Brenda Major (New York: Cambridge University Press, 2001), 437–67.

4. Emma Goldman and William "Big Bill" Haywood exemplify this phenomenon—they similarly traced their embrace of revolutionary violence to the state's response to the Haymarket affair of 1886. This fits with Fanon's theory of reciprocal violence in *Wretched of the Earth.* See the first chapter of Goldman, *Living My Life* (New York: A. A. Knopf, 1931); Gage, *The Day Wall Street Exploded*, 71–72.

5. David M. Kennedy, Lizabeth Cohen, Thomas A. Bailey, *The American Pageant*, vol. 2, *Since 1865*, 14th ed. (Boston: Wadsworth Cengage Learning, 2010), 586.

6. On the origins and persistence of this view, see Fernand Braudel, *After-thoughts on Material Civilization and Capitalism*, trans. Patricia M. Ranum (Baltimore: Johns Hopkins University Press, 1977), 44–45.

7. Henry Walcott Farnam, "The Industrial Bugbear," FFP, Box 232, Folder 3130. Farnam delivered this speech in 1887 to an audience of Yale alumni gathered at Delmonico's in New York.

8. On a few of the limitations of understanding U.S. economic development through the concept of Adam Smith's invisible hand, see Alfred D. Chandler Jr., *The Visible Hand: The Managerial Revolution in American Business* (Cambridge, Mass.: Belknap Press of Harvard University Press, 1977).

9. Annelise Orleck, *Common Sense and A Little Fire: Women and Working-Class Politics in the United States, 1900–1965* (Chapel Hill: University of North Carolina Press, 1995), 62. Orleck observes the dissipation of police violence when the "mink brigade" joined the picket lines.

10. Melvyn Dubofsky, *Industrialism and the American Worker, 1865–1920* (Arlington Heights, Ill.: Harlan Davidson, 1985), 25.

11. Fannia M. Cohn, "History of I.L.G.W.U.," International Ladies' Garment Workers' Union Records, (ILGWUR), Coll. 5780/167, Box 1, KCILR.

12. Modern-day U.S. employers continue to threaten workers with layoffs, but the consequences are mitigated by labor law (when it works) and a more comprehensive social compact. See, for example, Josh Eidelson, "Labor Board Rules for Workers, Conservatives Freak Out," *Counterpunch*, May 20–22, 2011, www.counterpunch.org/2011/05/20/labor-board-rules-for-workers-conservatives-freak-out/.

13. Leon Stein and Philip Taft, eds., *Workers Speak: Self-Portraits* (New York: Arno, 1971), 74.

14. "Jail for Homeless," *New York Call*, Sept. 21, 1909; "134 'Vagrants' Get Six-Month Sentences," *New York Call*, Sept. 23, 1909; "30 More 'Va-grants' Sent to Workhouse," *New York Call*, Sept. 24, 1909. It is some indication of the fear of class violence that near the top of a list of "don'ts" issued by the police department for the Hudson-Fulton celebra-tion and published in the *Times* was "Don't look too prosperous while on the streets." See "Police 'Don'ts' for Fulton Sightseers," *New York Times*, Sept. 24, 1909.

15. Dubofsky, *Industrialism and the American Worker*, 22; Bureau of the Census, "Table 2. Population, Housing Units, Area Measurements, and

Density: 1790 to 1990," available at *Selected Historical Decennial Census Population and Housing Counts*, United States 1790 to 1990, www.census .gov/population/www/censusdata/hiscendata.html.

16. Dubofsky, *Industrialism and the American Worker*, 22. To put these risks in comparative perspective, the Bureau of Labor Statistics calculated that the incidence of fatal accidents in the workplace for 2008 was 3.6 per 100,000 workers, or one in nearly 30,000. In other words, an American worker in 2009 was nearly thirty times more likely than her 1900 analogue to go home alive at the end of the day. See U.S. Department of Labor, Bureau of Labor Statistics, "News: National Census of Fatal Occupational Injuries in 2008," Aug. 20, 2009, 1, www.bls.gov/news.release/archives/cfoi _08202009.pdf.

17. On an early mention of Westinghouse air brakes, see JQT, "Wonders of the Iron City," *New-York Tribune*, Aug. 12, 1871.

18. See, for example, "Brakeman's Injuries Prove Fatal," *Washington Post*, Mar. 5, 1898; "Accidents at and near Tifton, Ga.," *Atlanta Constitution*, Feb. 21, 1900; "Saving Trainmen's Lives," *Boston Daily Globe*, Feb. 19, 1910. This last article ends tellingly, "But even railroad managers are beginning to realize that it is cheaper to save lives than to sacrifice them."

19. Rosenzweig et al., *Who Built America?*, 2:41.

20. JQT, "Wonders of the Iron City," *New-York Tribune*, Aug. 12, 1871.

21. Clifton Hood, *722 Miles: The Building of the Subways and How They Transformed New York* (Baltimore: Johns Hopkins University Press, 1993), 85–90. For both contemporaneous and retrospective literary views, see Pietro di Donato, *Christ in Concrete* (1939; repr., New York: Signet Classic, 1993); Colum McCann, *This Side of Brightness* (New York: Henry Holt, 1998).

22. Di Donato, *Christ in Concrete*, 17–18.

23. Ibid., 9.

24. Dorothée von Huene-Greenberg and Pietro di Donato, "A MELUS Interview: Pietro Di Donato," *MELUS* 14, nos. 3–4 (1987), 39.

25. Hood, *722 Miles*, 87–88.

26. Ibid., 88–90.

27. Frederick L. Hoffman, "Industrial Accidents and Industrial Diseases," *Publications of the American Statistical Association* 11, no. 88 (1909): 567–70. Hoffman's view of worker carelessness reflected his predilection for sweeping judgments, best exemplified in his *Race Traits and Tendencies of the American Negro* (New York: Macmillan, 1896), which used flawed 1890

census data and social Darwinism to argue that African Americans would die out and were, therefore, uninsurable; he was working for the Prudential Insurance Company at the time.

28. Edwin W. De Leon, "Accidents to Working Children," *Annals of the American Academy of Political and Social Science* 33, Supplement (1909), 137. De Leon was an insurance company executive, but he delivered this speech at the Fifth Annual Meeting of the National Child Labor Committee. In attendance were, among others, Lillian Wald, Jane Addams, and Florence Kelley. Addams and Kelley delivered talks or participated in symposia as well (see 207–9).

29. As di Donato suggests in *Christ in Concrete*, worker compensation laws hailed as major advances in theory often failed to protect workers, especially immigrants, in practice (*Christ in Concrete*, 127–32). See also Christopher Howard, "Workers' Compensation, Federalism, and the Heavy Hand of History," *Studies in American Political Development*, no. 16 (2002), 28–47, esp. 36.

30. Dr. George Price, *Annual Report, Joint Board of Sanitary Control in the Cloak, Suit and Skirt and the Dress and Waist Industries* (New York: Joint Board of Sanitary Control, 1911), as quoted in Leon Stein, ed., *Out of the Sweatshop: The Struggle for Industrial Democracy* (New York: Quadrangle/New York Times Books, 1977), 182.

31. Stein, *Out of the Sweatshop*, 186–87. Byssinosis, another disease prevalent in the industry and caused by inhalation of textile dust, produced chronic bronchitis that mimicked tuberculosis, probably leading to excessive diagnoses of the latter. For the patient, of course, the difference was largely academic.

32. As quoted in Stein, *Out of the Sweatshop*, 186–87.

33. Stein, *Workers Speak*, 118.

34. David M. Katzman and William M. Tuttle Jr., eds., *Plain Folk: The Life Stories of Undistinguished Americans* (Urbana: University of Illinois Press, 1982), 52.

35. Newman, "Low Wages and White Slavery," PNP, Folder 114.

36. Orleck, *Common Sense*, 17–21.

37. Ibid., 25.

38. Rose Schneiderman with Lucy Goldthwaite, *All for One* (New York: Paul S. Eriksson, 1967), 86–87.

39. Orleck, *Common Sense*, 23–25.

40. Stein, *Workers Speak*, 118.

41. Hyman Berman, "Era of the Protocol: A Chapter in the History of the International Ladies' Garment Workers' Union, 1910–1916" (Ph.D. diss., Columbia University, 1956), 72.

42. For more on garment industry structures in this period, see Susan Glenn, *Daughters of the Shtetl: Life and Labor in the Immigrant Generation* (Ithaca, N.Y.: Cornell University Press, 1990); Berman, "Era of the Protocol."

43. Stein, *Out of the Sweatshop*, 29–31, 193.

44. Pauline Newman, "Memoir from PN to Hugh and Michael Owen," PNP, Folder 3.

45. Stein, *Out of the Sweatshop*, 183.

46. Ibid., 187.

10 • The Primacy of Property

Epigraph: "Mr. Shaw Sarcastic," *New-York Tribune*, Jan. 6, 1910; "Shaw Takes a Hand in Waist Strike," *New York Times*, Jan. 6, 1910; "Plan to Call Out 3,000 More Strikers," *New York Times*, Jan. 7, 1910.

1. Empire Secret Service Agency flyer, ILGWUR, Coll. 56, Box 9, Folder 15. Berman cites a similar letter reproduced in the *Jewish Daily Forward* of October 3, 1909. See Berman, "Era of the Protocol," 76. For more on private security forces in the era, see Edward Levinson, *I Break Strikes!*, eds. Leon Stein and Philip Taft (New York: Arno & New York Times, 1969).

2. "Necktie Makers Go on Strike," *New-York Tribune*, July 10, 1909; "Neckwear Workers Extend Strike," *New York-Tribune*, Aug. 24, 1909.

3. For stories, see *New York Times*, July 19, Sep. 23, Oct. 26 and 31, 1909. For the editorial, see "How to Lose a Strike," July 29, 1909.

4. Although these stories use overblown, propagandistic rhetoric, they also include verifiable details: names, dates, court proceedings, addresses, and so on. Every unequivocal or specific statement of fact in these stories tested through cross-referencing with subsequent newspaper articles, census records, published work, or union testimony in PNP, ILGWUR, IMP, and MHP has proven accurate.

5. "Pickets Beaten Then Arrested," *New York Call*, Aug. 4, 1909.

6. Ibid.

7. "Pickets Slugged: Three Striking Waist Makers Assaulted under Direction of Boss," *New York Call*, Aug. 11, 1909; *Jewish Daily Forward*, Aug. 11, 1909.

8. Ibid.

9. "C.F.U. after Police Again: Committee Protests against Beating of Striking Waist Makers by Thugs of Bosses," *New York Call*, Aug. 14, 1909.

10. "Police Invade Union Rooms," *New York Call*, Aug. 12, 1909.

11. "Nab Strikers at Behest of Boss," *New York Call*, Aug. 19, 1909.

12. On the private-public nexus of policing in the era, see Jennifer Fronc, *New York Undercover: Private Surveillance in the Progressive Era* (Chicago: University of Chicago Press, 2009).

13. "Would Fine Policeman," *New York Call*, Aug. 17, 1909.

14. "Nab Strikers at Behest of Boss," *New York Call*, Aug. 19, 1909.

15. "Waist Makers' Win," *New York Call*, Aug. 27, 1909.

16. "Neckwear Strikers Win," *New York Call*, Aug. 28, 1909. This story refers to "I. Newman"; for "Isaac," see "Union Must Pay for Jobs He Lost," *New York Times*, Dec. 21, 1911.

17. "Want Union Conditions," *New York Call*, Sep. 3, 1909; "60 Waistmakers Quit," *New York Call*, Sep. 6, 1909.

18. "Strikers Assaulted," *New York Call*, Sep. 8, 1909.

19. "Thugs Beat Strikers," *New York Call*, Sep. 8, 1909; David Von Drehle, *Triangle: The Fire That Changed America* (New York: Atlantic Monthly Press, 2003), 6–12.

20. "400 Locked Out for Joining Union," *New York Call*, Sep. 28, 1909.

21. "Girl Slugged by Leiserson's Scab," *New York Call*, Sep. 29, 1909; "More Violence by Leiserson Scab," *New York Call*, Sep. 30, 1909. The assault on Lipstein may have been intentional: she had identified Lemlich's attackers at their arraignment two weeks prior. See "Leiserson's Thugs Assault Strikers," *New York Call*, Sep. 16, 1909.

22. C.F.U. Committee Aids Waist Strike," *New York Call*, Oct. 13, 1909.

23. "Policeman Roasted, Pickets Discharged," *New York Call*, Oct. 1, 1909.

24. "Neckwear Makers to Strike," *New-York Tribune*, Oct. 1, 1909; "7,000 Neckwear Workers Strike," *New York Call*, Oct. 2, 1909; "Neckwearmakers Strike," *New York Times*, Oct. 3, 1909.

25. "7,000 Neckwear Workers Strike," *New York Call*, Oct. 2, 1909.

26. "Neckwearmakers Strike," *New York Times*, Oct. 3, 1909.

27. "Neckwear Workers Win Many Victories," *New York Call*, Oct. 5, 1909; "Neckwear Makers Winning Big Strike," *New York Call*, Oct. 6, 1909; "Neckwear Bosses Give in to Union" and "The Neckwear Workers' Strike," *New York Call*, Oct. 7, 1909; "Suffragists Enter Strike," *New-York Tribune*, Oct. 7, 1909.

28. "Suffragists Enter Strike," *New-York Tribune*, Oct. 7, 1909.

29. "Literary Neckwear Girls," *New York Times*, Oct. 11, 1909.

30. On the nexus between neighborhood and workplace as a laboratory for radicalism, see Ardis Cameron, *Radicals of the Worst Sort: Laboring Women in Lawrence, Massachusetts, 1860–1912* (Urbana: University of Illinois Press, 1993); Glenn, *Daughters of the Shtetl.*

31. "Neckwear Makers Win, 5,000 Strong," *New York Call*, Oct. 13, 1909; "Neckwear Workers End Strike," *Christian Science Monitor*, Oct. 14, 1909.

32. "25,000 Waist Makers Declare for Strike," *New York Call*, Oct. 22, 1909.

33. Von Drehle is alone in devoting even a single paragraph to the neckwear strike, but it mainly serves in his telling as a sidelight to the development of W.T.U.L. organizing and Local 25's growth; see Von Drehle, *Triangle*, 16.

34. "Prostitutes Hired to Beat Strikers," *New York Call*, Oct. 4, 1909; "Judge Discharges Ten Girl Strikers," *New York Call*, Oct. 5, 1909.

35. Alice Henry points to strikes in Boston and St. Louis as more important: see Henry, *The Trade Union Woman* (New York: Burt Franklin, 1915), 89. Berman, imitating Levine, traces the Uprising's origins to the Rosen Brothers strike in July, but then moves straight to the Leiserson and Triangle strikes, claiming (without attribution) that the success of the two hundred employees at Rosen Brothers inspired renewed hope in the industry. See Berman, "Era of the Protocol," 74; Louis Levine, *The Women's Garment Workers: A History of the International Ladies' Garment Workers' Union* (New York: B. W. Huebsch, 1924), 149–151. Orleck, Meredith Tax, Glenn, and Enstad adhere to the standard narrative beginning with the Triangle and Leiserson strikes (with minor wrinkles—Tax mentions a 1908 Triangle walkout, and both she and Glenn mention the Rosen Brothers strike). See Orleck, *Common Sense*, 58–59; Meredith Tax, *The Rising of the Women* (New York: Monthly Review Press, 1980), 212–14; Glenn, *Daughters of the Shtetl*, 167–68; Enstad, *Ladies of Labor*, 89–90.

36. Levine, *Women's Garment Workers*, 151.

37. "Neckwear Workers Win Many Victories," *New York Call*, Oct. 5, 1909; "Neckwear Makers Winning Big Strike," *New York Call*, Oct. 6, 1909; "Neckwear Bosses Give in to Union"; "The Neckwear Workers' Strike," *New York Call*, Oct. 7, 1909; "Suffragists Enter Strike," *New-York Tribune*, Oct. 7, 1909.

38. "Judge Discharges Ten Girl Strikers," *New York Call*, Oct. 5, 1909.

39. Ibid.

40. "Thugs under Bonds," *New York Call*, Oct. 6, 1909.

41. Levine, *Women's Garment Workers*, 152.
42. Cohen, *Law and Order in Industry*, 4 (emphasis in original).
43. "Arrest Strikers for Being Assaulted," *New York Times*, Nov. 5, 1909.
44. Ibid.
45. Ibid.
46. For more on Milholland's participation in the strike, see Linda J. Lumsden, *Inez: The Life and Times of Inez Milholland* (Bloomington: Indiana University Press, 2004), 44–53.
47. Inez Milholland, "The Shirtwaist Strike of 1909: A Communication from the NYTimes," 5, Inez Milholland Papers (IMP), Folder 31, SLHU.
48. Ibid., 6; Enstad, *Ladies of Labor*; Tax, *Rising of the Women*.
49. "Pickets to Appeal," *New-York Tribune*, Nov. 6, 1909.
50. "She Was Kicked," *New-York Tribune*, Nov. 18, 1909.
51. Orleck, *Common Sense*, 62.
52. "Police Break Up Strikers' Meeting," *New York Times*, Dec. 22, 1909.
53. Orleck, *Common Sense*, 62.
54. "Accuse the Police," *New York Times*, Dec. 20, 1909.
55. "Martyrs All Three," *New-York Tribune*, Jan. 3, 1910.
56. "Mr. Shaw Sarcastic," *New-York Tribune*, Jan. 6, 1910; "Shaw Takes a Hand in Waist Strike," *New York Times*, Jan. 6, 1910; "Plan to Call Out 3,000 More Strikers," *New York Times*, Jan. 7, 1910.
57. Ibid.
58. The God of Genesis 3 metes out a series of punishments—to the serpent, to Adam, and to Eve—all of which alter the previously existing natural order. This includes the injunction that Adam shall earn his bread by the sweat of his brow.
59. Weber, *Protestant Ethic*, 181.
60. "Plan to Call Out 3,000 More Strikers," *New York Times*, Jan. 7, 1910.
61. David McLellan ed., *Karl Marx: Selected Writings*, 2nd ed. (Oxford: Oxford University Press, 2000), 249. This passage comes from *Theories of Surplus Value*.

11 • Sisters in Struggle

Epigraph: Evalyn A. Burnham, "Socialist Women and the Suffrage Movement," in "Woman's Sphere" column, *New York Call*, Dec. 6, 1909.

1. "Throng Cheers On the Girl Strikers," *New York Times*, Dec. 6, 1909. For more, see "Thousands Applaud Battle of Striking Shirt Waist Makers,"

New York Call, Dec. 6, 1909; "Food for Strikers," *New-York Tribune*, Dec. 6, 1909; "Mrs. Belmont Aids Strikers," *Chicago Daily Tribune*, Dec. 6, 1909; "Cheers for Suffrage," *Washington Post*, Dec. 6 1909. For secondary treatments, see Enstad, *Ladies of Labor, Girls of Adventure*; Françoise Basch's introductory essay in Theresa Serber Malkiel, *Diary of a Shirtwaist Striker* (Ithaca, N.Y.: ILR Press of Cornell University Press, 1990); Tax, *Rising of the Women*.

2. For other considerations of cross-class organizing, race, and class in the women's movement, see Robin Miller Jacoby, "The Women's Trade Union League and American Feminism," *Feminist Studies* 3 (1975): 126–40; Nancy Schrom Dye, "Feminism or Unionism: The New York Women's Trade Union League and the Labor Movement," *Feminist Studies* 3 (1975): 111–25; Ellen Carol DuBois, *Woman Suffrage and Women's Rights* (New York: New York University Press, 1998); Lori D. Ginzberg, *Elizabeth Cady Stanton: An American Life* (New York: Macmillan, 2010); Kraditor, *Ideas of the Woman Suffrage Movement*; Vicki L. Ruiz and Ellen Carol DuBois, eds., *Unequal Sisters: An Inclusive Reader in U.S. Women's History* (New York: Routledge, 2008); Allison Sneider, *Suffragists in an Imperial Age: U.S. Expansion and the Woman Question, 1870–1929* (New York: Oxford University Press, 2008).

3. Tax, *Rising of the Women*, 110–15. Tax and Schrom Dye are particularly attuned to fault lines of money and political power within the W.T.U.L. See ibid., 110–15; and Nancy Schrom Dye, *As Equals and as Sisters: Feminism, the Labor Movement, and the Women's Trade Union League of New York* (Columbia: University of Missouri Press, 1980).

4. Schrom Dye, *As Equals and as Sisters*; Orleck, *Common Sense*.

5. Sydney Stahl Weinberg, *World of Our Mothers: The Lives of Jewish Immigrant Women* (Chapel Hill: University of North Carolina Press, 1988); Glenn, *Daughters of the Shtetl*; Orleck, *Common Sense*; Jennifer Guglielmo, *Living the Revolution: Italian Women's Resistance and Radicalism in New York, 1880–1945* (Chapel Hill: University of North Carolina Press, 2010); Cameron, *Radicals of the Worst Sort*; David Montgomery, *Workers' Control in America: Studies in the History of Work, Technology, and Labor Struggles* (Cambridge: Cambridge University Press, 1979).

6. On Natalya Urusova, see Sue Ainslie Clark and Edith Wyatt, "Working-Girls' Budgets: The Shirtwaist Workers and Their Strike," *McClure's Magazine* 36, no. 1 (1910), 70.

7. Mary E. Dreier (MED) to Margaret Dreier Robins (MDR), Nov. 26, 1909, MDRP.

8. This characterization pervaded mainstream press coverage of the strike (the *Times*, the *Sun*, the *Tribune*, etc.); for a historical example, see Graham Davis Jr., *Age of Industrial Violence, 1910–1915: The Activities and Findings of the United States Commission on Industrial Relations* (New York: Columbia University Press, 1966), 111. It is worth noting that even bourgeois allies in the League sometimes seemed not to appreciate the role organizing played in facilitating sympathy striking. For instance, MED wrote to MDR, "*Many* girls seem to have gone out just in sympathy, & there are many different situations which seem impossible of adjustment" (MED to MDR, Nov. 26, 1909, MDRP, emphasis in original).

9. Orleck, *Common Sense*; Tax, *Rising of the Women*; Enstad, *Ladies of Labor*; Schneiderman and Goldthwaite, *All for One*; Newman, "Memoir from PN to Hugh and Michael Owen," PNP. For more on W.T.U.L. history, see Schrom Dye, *As Equals and as Sisters*.

10. Ann Schofield, *To Do and to Be: Portraits of Four Women Activists, 1893–1986* (Boston: Northeastern University Press, 1997); Knight, *Citizen*; Victoria Bissell Brown, *The Education of Jane Addams* (Philadelphia: University of Pennsylvania Press, 2004); Sklar, *Florence Kelley*; Feld, *Lillian Wald*; Beverly Washington Jones, *Quest for Equality: The Life and Writings of Mary Eliza Church Terrell* (New York: Carlson, 1990); Daphne Spain, *How Women Saved the City* (Minneapolis: University of Minnesota Press, 2001); Linda Kerber, Alice Kessler-Harris, and Kathryn Kish Sklar, eds., *U.S. History as Women's History: New Feminist Essays* (Chapel Hill: University of North Carolina Press, 1995).

11. Jane Addams, *Twenty Years at Hull House* (New York: Macmillan, 1910); Florence Kelley, *Modern Industry in Relation to the Family, Health, Education, Morality* (New York: Longman, Greens, 1914); Wald, *House on Henry Street*; Addams, *The Social Thought of Jane Addams*, ed. Christopher Lasch (Indianapolis: Bobbs-Merrill, 1965); Murolo, *Common Ground of Womanhood*.

12. Bederman, *Manliness & Civilization*.

13. Elizabeth Anne Payne, *Reform, Labor, and Feminism: Margaret Dreier Robins and the National Women's Trade Union League* (Urbana: University of Illinois Press, 1988); Robin Miller Jacoby, *British and American Women's Trade Union Leagues, 1890–1925* (New York: Carlson, 1994).

14. MED to MDR, Nov. 20, 1909, MDRP.

15. Newman, "Memoir from PN to Hugh and Michael Owen," PNP.
16. PN interview with Elizabeth Phillips Marsh, transcript, included as "Appendix B" in Marsh, "The Uprising of the Twenty Thousand: A Study of Women and Trade Unionism" (undergraduate honors thesis, March 1, 1974), SLHU, v.
17. Ibid., v–vi.
18. Schneiderman and Goldthwaite, *All for One*, 93–95.
19. Helen Marot, "A Woman's Strike: An Appreciation of the Shirtwaist Makers of New York," *Proceedings of the Academy of Political Science in the City of New York* 1, no. 1 (1910): 126–27.
20. In an October 20, 1909, letter to MDR, May Rollaearthur writes, "You will have heard all about Mrs. Belmont by now—I expect she will send a subscription. Miss Marot says the League won't touch her money!" See May Rollaearthur to MDR, Oct. 20, 1909, MDRP. It seems safe, in light of the exclamation point, to read this last sentence either as a joke or a disbelieving dig at Helen Marot.
21. Peter Geidel, "Alva E. Belmont: A Forgotten Feminist" (Ph.D. diss., Columbia University, 1993), 2.
22. Ibid., 4.
23. Ibid., 4–5.
24. Geidel, "Alva E. Belmont"; Amanda Mackenzie Stuart, *Consuelo and Alva Vanderbilt: The Story of a Daughter and a Mother in the Gilded Age* (New York: HarperCollins, 2005).
25. Geidel, "Alva E. Belmont," 33.
26. Ibid. "Black Hand Society" refers to a late-nineteenth and early-twentieth-century extortion racket run primarily by Sicilian immigrants. It was a phenomenon related to but distinct from (and, in some respects, at odds with) the Mafia. For more, see David Critchley, *The Origin of Organized Crime in America: The New York City Mafia, 1891–1931* (New York: Routledge, 2009), 14–35.
27. Geidel, "Alva E. Belmont," 34. Geidel cites Belmont's later avowals that she felt shut out largely by women, but that Society men did not avoid her because they "would not deny themselves the spicy pleasure of conversing with a rebel" (35); later he refers to her being "ostracized from society" (36). The truth seems likely to have been a combination of titillation that kept Society men's devotion, and scandal that made Society's women leery. Either way, the ambiguity was short lived because within months Belmont (then still Vanderbilt) was throwing parties in Newport that no one in

Society could afford to miss, thereby reclaiming her preeminence. See Geidel, "Alva E. Belmont," 34–41.

28. Ibid., 42.
29. Alva E. Belmont, Memoirs (untitled), Matilda Young Papers, William R. Perkins Library, Duke University, as quoted in Geidel, 44–45.
30. Geidel, "Alva E. Belmont," 71–73.
31. Geidel, "Alva E. Belmont," 77–78; Ellen Carol DuBois, "Working Women, Class Relations, and Suffrage Militance: Harriot Stanton Blatch and the New York Woman Suffrage Movement, 1894–1909," *Journal of American History* 74, no. 1 (1987), 51–52.
32. Geidel, "Alva E. Belmont," 77; DuBois, "Working Women."
33. This did not necessarily make Blatch and Belmont immediate allies. Belmont had entered the suffrage movement through her friend, a N.A.W.S.A. member, Katherine Duer Mackay (see Geidel, "Alva E. Belmont," 76; DuBois, "Working Women," 58). Despite sharing many of Blatch's reservations about N.A.W.S.A., Belmont was still interested in reforming the organization from within.
34. Mrs. O. H. P. Belmont, "Why Women Went to Jail," mss., numbered page 2, DSP, Box 50, Folder 1. The manuscript, which has a foreword signed by Doris Stevens, also has a note appended to it that reads, "Prepared by Doris Stevens in 1920 at the request of Mrs. Belmont for possible publication in Mrs. Belmont's name." Researchers should be aware that the manuscript is mispaginated, and/or disordered.
35. Ibid., 2–2[a]. (Pages are in sequence, but both bear the number "2.")
36. "Medals for Suffragettes," *New York Sun*, Apr. 30, 1909.
37. Belmont, "Why Women Went to Jail," DSP, Box 50, Folder 1, 3. (Regarding pagination, see previous note 34.)
38. Ibid., 4.
39. *New York Evening Journal*, Sept. 20, 1909, as quoted in Geidel, "Alva E. Belmont," 97.
40. "Hippodrome to Open," *New-York Tribune*, Apr. 10, 1905.
41. "40,000 Called Out in Women's Strike," *New York Times*, Nov. 23, 1909.
42. "Waist Strike On; 18,000 Women Out," *New York Times*, Nov. 24, 1909; "Army of Girls Idle," *New-York Tribune*, Nov. 24, 1909.
43. Geidel, "Alva E. Belmont," 132–33.
44. "Suffragists to Aid Girl Waist Strikers," *New York Times*, Dec. 2, 1909; "Mrs. Belmont Helps," *New-York Tribune*, Dec. 2, 1909; "Mrs. Belmont Aids Strikers," *Chicago Daily Tribune*, Dec. 2, 1909.

45. "The Weather," *New York Times*, Dec. 5 and 6, 1909.

46. "Throng Cheers On the Girl Strikers," *New York Times*, Dec. 6, 1909. Estimates on attendance varied: the *Times* reported 8,000, whereas the *Chicago Tribune* estimated 6,000 in "Mrs. Belmont Aids Strikers," *Chicago Tribune*, Dec. 6, 1909.

47. "Cheers for Suffrage," *Washington Post*, Dec. 6, 1909.

48. "Throng Cheers On the Girl Strikers," *New York Times*, Dec. 6, 1909; "Thousands Applaud Battle of Striking Shirt Waist Makers," *New York Call*, Dec. 6, 1909.

49. "Throng Cheers On the Girl Strikers," *New York Times*, Dec. 6, 1909.

50. Ibid.

51. "Suffragists to Aid Girl Waist Strikers," *New York Times*, Dec. 2, 1909; "Mrs. Belmont Aids Strike," *Chicago Daily Tribune*, Dec. 2, 1909.

52. "Thousands Applaud Battle of Striking Shirt Waist Makers," *New York Call*, Dec. 6, 1909.

53. "Throng Cheers On the Girl Strikers," *New York Times*, Dec. 6, 1909.

54. Ibid.

55. "Thousands Applaud Battle of Striking Shirt Waist Makers," *New York Call*, Dec. 6, 1909.

56. Ibid.

57. Gompers was ambivalent, at best, about women in the labor movement, and W.T.U.L. leaders complained about his attitude over the years. His assistant, Eva Macdonald Valesh, took a leave of absence from her A.F.L. responsibilities to volunteer with the W.T.U.L. for the strike's duration. Later events suggest she may have been tasked with derailing the strike when it became too radical.

58. "Food for Strikers," *New-York Tribune*, Dec. 6, 1909.

59. Ibid.

60. On such fiction and its relationship to the strike, strikers, and popular-press presentations of the strikers, see Enstad, *Ladies of Labor*.

61. On Stokes, see Arthur Zipser and Pearl Zipser, *Fire and Grace: The Life of Rose Pastor Stokes* (Athens: University of Georgia Press, 1989); Rose Pastor Stokes, "I Belong to the Working Class," Rose Pastor Stokes Papers (RPSP). J. G. Phelps Stokes's journey to the left with his wife only went so far; he and Rose Pastor divorced in 1925.

62. "Throng Cheers On the Girl Strikers," *New York Times*, Dec. 6, 1909.

63. "Thousands Applaud Battle of Striking Shirt Waist Makers," *New York Call*, Dec. 6, 1909.

64. Throng Cheers On the Girl Strikers," *New York Times*, Dec. 6, 1909.

65. "Thousands Applaud Battle of Striking Shirt Waist Makers," *New York Call*, Dec. 6, 1909.

66. "Throng Cheers On the Girl Strikers," *New York Times*, Dec. 6, 1909.

67. Ibid.

68. "Thousands Applaud Battle of Striking Shirt Waist Makers," *New York Call*, Dec. 6, 1909.

69. Ibid.

70. Ibid.

71. Charles Shively, "Leonora O'Reilly," in *Notable American Women: A Biographical Dictionary*, ed. Edward T. James, Janet Wilson James, Paul S. Boyer (Cambridge, Mass.: Radcliffe College, 1971), 2:651–53; Susan Amsterdam, "The National Women's Trade Union League," *Social Service Review* 56, no. 2 (1982): 261–62; Joanne Reitano, "Working Girls Unite," *American Quarterly* 36, no. 1 (1984), 134; Alice Henry, "Mrs. Winifred O'Reilly: a Veteran Worker," *Life and Labor* 1, no. 5 (1911): 132–136.

72. Shively, "Leonora O'Reilly," 2:652; Waugh, *Unsentimental Reformer*.

73. Shively, "Leonora O'Reilly," 2:652.

74. "Food for Strikers," *New-York Tribune*, Dec. 6, 1909; This ambiguity manifested elsewhere as well. See, for example, the *Washington Post*'s subheading "Mrs. Belmont's Shirt Waist Union Meeting Enthusiastic" in its story "Cheers for Suffrage."

75. Geidel, "Alva E. Belmont," 117.

76. Ibid., 133. Weyl, it should be noted, was a W.T.U.L. member assigned early in the strike to act as an assistant to an I.L.G.W.U. officer. See Levine, *Women's Garment Workers*, 155–56.

77. "Cheers for Suffrage," *Washington Post*, Dec. 6, 1909.

78. Ibid.

79. "Mrs. Belmont Aids Strikers," *Chicago Daily Tribune*, Dec. 6, 1909.

80. Burnham, "Socialist Women and the Suffrage Movement," *New York Call*, Dec. 6, 1909.

81. Ibid. On the suffrage debate among Socialists, see Mary Jo Buhle, *Women and American Socialism, 1870–1920* (Urbana: University of Illinois Press, 1981), 216–26.

82. Burnham, "Socialist Women and the Suffrage Movement," *New York Call*, Dec. 6, 1909.

83. As quoted in Geidel, "Alva E. Belmont," 135; "To Speak Unofficially: Dr. Shaw Not to Represent Suffragists at Hippodrome," *New-York Tribune*, Dec. 3, 1909.

84. This partly had to do with N.A.W.S.A.'s internal politics, in particular a widespread mistrust of Belmont herself among N.A.W.S.A. leaders of longer standing. See Geidel, "Alva E. Belmont," 86–98.

85. Bertha H. Mailly, "Women Teachers and Girl Strikers," *New York Call*, Dec. 14, 1909 (letter dated Dec. 9, 1909).

86. Ibid.

12 • To Cooperate or Condescend

Epigraph: Theresa Serber Malkiel, *Diary of a Shirtwaist Striker* (Ithaca, N.Y.: ILR Press of Cornell University Press, 1990), 132.

1. Sebastian Mallaby, *More Money Than God: Hedge Funds and the Making of a New Elite* (New York: Penguin Press, 2010), 3.

2. Dye, *As Equals and as Sisters*; Orleck, *Common Sense*.

3. MDR to MED, Nov. 26, 1909, MDRP.

4. Jean Strouse, *Morgan: American Financier* (New York: HarperCollins, 1999), 524. On Morgan's and Marbury's relationship generally, see Strouse, *Morgan*, 521–31.

5. "Rich Women Aid Workers; Miss Anne Morgan Leads Movement to Improve Conditions," *Chicago Daily Tribune*, Feb. 25, 1908; on the N.C.F., see Marguerite Green, *The National Civic Federation and the American Labor Movement, 1900–1925* (Washington, D.C.: Catholic University of America Press, 1956), esp. 133–89.

6. "Women in Society Unite to Help Labor," *New York Times*, Mar. 7, 1908; "Rich Women Enlisted," *Washington Post*, Mar. 7, 1908.

7. "Women in Society Unite," *New York Times*, Mar. 7, 1908. On Harriman, the only woman whom Woodrow Wilson would appoint to the Commission on Industrial Relations in 1913, see Davis Jr., *Age of Industrial Violence*, 65–67.

8. "Meet as Sisters," *Washington Post*, Mar. 20, 1909.

9. "Rich Women Aid Strikers," *Baltimore Sun*, Dec. 13, 1909.

10. Schneiderman met with Morgan early in the strike. MDR wrote to MED already on November 26, "I have been told on pretty good authority . . . that Miss Morgan is very eager to serve the union women. . . . What would you think of asking her for money?" See MDR to MED, Nov. 26, 1909, MDRP.

11. Schneiderman, *All for One*, 93.
12. "Miss Morgan Joins Union," *Washington Post*, Dec. 14, 1909.
13. "Help for Strikers," *New-York Tribune*, Dec. 16, 1909.
14. "Critical Time for Shirtwaist Strike," *New York Times*, Dec. 15, 1909.
15. "Girl Strikers Tell the Rich Their Woes," *New York Times*, Dec. 16, 1909.
16. Orleck, *Common Sense*, 15–50.
17. Ibid. See also Drehle, *Triangle*, 6–11.
18. Orleck, *Common Sense*.
19. "Girl Strikers Tell the Rich Their Woes," *New York Times*, Dec. 16, 1909.
20. "Waist Strike Story Told to Rich Women," *New York Call*, Dec. 16, 1909.
21. Ibid.; "Help for Strikers," *New-York Tribune*, Dec. 16, 1909.
22. "Girl Strikers Tell the Rich Their Woes," *New York Times*, Dec. 16, 1909.
23. "Help for Strikers," *New-York Tribune*, Dec. 16, 1909.
24. "Waist Strike Story Told to Rich Women," *New York Call*, Dec. 16, 1909.
25. Ibid.
26. Belmont and other patrons were also in boxes at the Hippodrome, but they had shared mutual positionality with strikers as members of the audience gazing at the stage, and the "performers" were more diverse.
27. "Waist Strike Story Told to Rich Women," *New York Call*, Dec. 16, 1909.
28. Ibid.
29. MED to MDR, n.d., MDRP (emphasis in original). The context, and the fact that Dreier wrote the letter longhand, suggests that she wrote it on December 15 or 16.
30. Mary J. Quinn to MDR, Dec. 18, 1909, MDRP.
31. "Standing by Union," *New-York Tribune*, Dec. 14, 1909.
32. Geidel, "Alva E. Belmont," 136–41. Belmont had already bailed out the previous strikers, and as newspapers speculated the next day, the judge held the final four cases to the end of the proceedings in hopes that Belmont would leave and the remaining strikers would have no bail. Instead, she stayed and posted their bail by offering her 477 Madison Avenue mansion as collateral. She outlasted her lawyer.
33. "Miss Morgan Joins Union," *Washington Post*, Dec. 14, 1909.
34. "Rich Women's Aid Gives Strikers Hope," *New York Times*, Dec. 17, 1909.
35. "Lead Girls on Strike," *Boston Daily Globe*, Dec. 20, 1909. The *Atlanta Constitution* had the even clearer, and chiastically alliterative, "Society Leaders Leading Strike" (Dec. 21, 1909).
36. "Women Socialists Rebuff Suffragists," *New York Times*, Dec. 20, 1909; Buhle, *Women and American Socialism*, 225–26.

37. Schneiderman and Goldthwaite, *All for One*, 93.

38. Malkiel, *Diary of a Shirtwaist Striker*, 132–33.

39. "Women Socialists Rebuff Suffragists," *New York Times*, Dec. 20, 1909; Buhle, *Women and American Socialism*, 226.

40. Ibid.

41. Ibid.

42. A. C. B., "Woman Suffrage and the Socialist," *New York Call*, Dec. 16, 1909.

43. Ibid.

44. Ibid.

13 · Sisters at Odds

Epigraph: "Says Socialists Hurt Girls," *Los Angeles Times*, Jan. 4, 1910.

1. "More Aid for Girl Strikers," *New York Times*, Dec. 29, 1909; Elizabeth Faue, *Writing the Wrongs: Eva Valesh and the Rise of Labor Journalism* (Ithaca, N.Y.: Cornell University Press, 2002), 175–80.

2. "More Aid for Girl Strikers," *New York Times*, Dec. 29, 1909.

3. "To Talk on Strike," *New-York Tribune*, Dec. 31, 1909.

4. MED to MDR, n.d., MDRP. Other comments in the letter suggest the "mid-December" dating.

5. "To Talk on Strike," *New-York Tribune*, Dec. 31, 1909.

6. Ibid.; "Shirtwaist Strike Peace Plan Fails," *New York Times*, Dec. 28, 1909; "Strike May End," *New-York Tribune*, Jan. 2, 1910. It is worth noting the difference between "union recognition" and a "closed shop," terms that both contemporaneous newspaper accounts and historical studies tend to conflate. "Union recognition" means that the employer recognizes the union as the legitimate bargaining agent for union-member employees, while reserving the right to hire nonunion employees. A "closed shop" means that union membership is a condition of employment. The former, of course, leaves opportunity for a host of union-busting strategies (such as firing union leaders, dual unionism, diluting union density through expansion, and reneging on noncontractual agreements) that the latter precludes.

7. "To Censure Magistrates," *New York Times*, Jan. 2, 1910.

8. "Miss Morgan Talks," *New-York Tribune*, Jan. 1, 1910.

9. Marot, "A Woman's Strike," 126.

10. "Judges Scored and Hissed," *Chicago Daily Tribune*, Jan. 3, 1910.

11. Ibid. See also Jill Lepore, "Not So Fast," *New Yorker*, Oct. 12, 2009.

12. "Martyrs All There," *New-York Tribune*, Jan. 3, 1910.

13. "Wealthy Women Voice Protest for Shirt Waist Girls," *New York American*, Jan. 3, 1910. This story is likely fabricated—every other newspaper reported Morgan's sitting in a box.

14. Ibid.

15. "The Rich Out to Aid Girl Waistmakers," *New York Times*, Jan. 3, 1910.

16. Basch, "The Shirtwaist Strike," 45.

17. "Martyrs All There," *New-York Tribune*, Jan. 3, 1910; "Wealthy Women Voice Protest for Shirt Waist Girls," *New York American*, Jan. 3, 1910.

18. "Martyrs All There," *New-York Tribune*, Jan. 3, 1910.

19. Ibid.

20. "370 Arrested Waist Strikers on Platform at Carnegie Hall," *New York Call*, Jan. 3, 1910.

21. "Judges Scored and Hissed," *Chicago Daily Tribune*, Jan. 3, 1910.

22. Ibid.

23. "370 Arrested Waist Strikers on Platform at Carnegie Hall," *New York Call*, Jan. 3, 1910.

24. Ibid.

25. "The Rich Out to Aid Girl Waistmakers," *New York Times*, Jan. 3, 1910.

26. "Martyrs All There" *New-York Tribune*, Jan. 3, 1910.

27. "Shirtwaist Strike Peace Plan Fails," *New York Times*, Dec. 28, 1909; "Waist Strikers' Rejection of Open Shop Enthuses Women's Trade Union League," *New York Call*, Dec. 29, 1909.

28. "370 Arrested Waist Strikers on Platform at Carnegie Hall," *New York Call*, Jan. 3, 1910.

29. Ibid.

30. Ibid.

31. "370 Arrested Waist Strikers on Platform at Carnegie Hall," *New York Call*, Jan. 3, 1910.

32. "The Rich Out to Aid Girl Waistmakers," *New York Times*, Jan. 3, 1910.

33. "370 Arrested Waist Strikers on Platform at Carnegie Hall," *New York Call*, Jan. 3, 1910.

34. Ibid.

35. Ibid.

36. "Protests Are Heeded by Police and Courts," *New York Call*, Jan. 4, 1910.

37. Ibid.

38. "Strike Funds Low; Arbitration Fails," *New York Times*, Jan. 5, 1910. Hillquit's handwritten notes for the Carnegie Hall speech further exonerate him from charges of socialist divisiveness: he makes explicit reference to the class diversity in the audience just before this conclusion, writing, "The hearts of the entire working class and of many thousands [of] non-workers beat in warm accord with yours." See "Carnegie Hall Speech to Striking Shirtwaistmakers" (Jan. 2, 1910), MHP, Series II, Reel 5.

39. Ibid.

40. "Plan to Call Out 3,000 More Strikers," *New York Times*, Jan. 7, 1910.

41. "Argue Socialism," *New-York Tribune*, Jan. 17, 1910.

42. "Mrs. Belmont Wants All-Woman Strike," *New York Times*, Jan. 8, 1910.

43. "New Trade Union," *New-York Tribune*, Jan. 22, 1910; Faue, *Writing the Wrongs*, 177–78.

44. "New Trade Union," *New-York Tribune*, Jan. 22, 1910.

45. Ibid.

46. Ibid.

47. "Denial from Miss Anne Morgan," *New York Times*, Jan. 25, 1910. This tiny, eight-line item appeared on page 6, and read: "Miss Anne Morgan denied yesterday a statement that she does not indorse [*sic*] the methods of the Woman's Trades [*sic*] Union League, and proposes to start a campaign for a new trades union movement for women. Miss Morgan declared the statement untrue, as she is herself a member of the Woman's Trades [*sic*] Union League."

48. "Socialist Women and the Shirtwaist Strike," *New York Call*, Feb. 8, 1910. Although Gompers claimed to MDR that he "deplored [Valesh's] statement," he also "was not able to tell [MDR] whether she was officially connected with the American Federation of Labor or not," and he urged Robins to come to the conference Valesh was organizing for her new trade union group. It seems likely that after years of dismissing the W.T.U.L., Gompers realized that the strike had made them a dangerous potential rival labor organization, and he was trying to outflank them. See Minutes of the New York Women's Trade Union League, Jan. 28, 1910, PWTUL; Faue, *Writing the Wrongs*, 175–80.

49. MDR to MED, Feb. 12, 1910, MDRP.

50. Schneiderman and Goldthwaite, *All for One*, 95–96.

51. Basch, "Shirtwaist Strike," 47–48. On the history of the I.L.G.W.U., see Orleck, *Common Sense*; Levine, *Women's Garment Workers*; Joshua B.

Freedman, *Working-Class New York: Life and Labor since World War II* (New York: New Press, 2000); Richard A. Greenwald, *The Triangle Fire, the Protocols of Peace, and Industrial Democracy in the Progressive Era* (Ithaca, N.Y.: Cornell University Press, 2005).

52. Schneiderman and Goldthwaite, *All for One*, 100–1.
53. W.T.U.L., *Annual Report 1911–1912*, 7.

14 • Hard Fists, Short Fuses on the City Rails

Epigraph: T. P. Shonts to August Belmont, Aug. 7, 1916, ABP, Box 4, Correspondence, Jan.–Aug. 1916.

1. "The Weather," *New York Times*, Oct. 26, 1916.
2. "Bomb Set by Strikers Wrecks New York Subway," *Los Angeles Times*, Oct. 26, 1916; "Put Extra Guards on Dynamite Caches," *New York Times*, Oct. 26, 1916; "Bomb Explodes in Subway Station," *Hartford Courant*, Oct. 26, 1916; "Five Men Sought in Subway Blast," *New-York Tribune*, Oct. 26, 1916.
3. "Effrontery. Move to Parole John J. M'Namara," *Los Angeles Times*, Oct. 26, 1916.
4. Ibid. In any case, the rumors were untrue: McNamara did not file. See "Dynamiter McNamara Fails to Ask for Parole," *San Francisco Chronicle*, Oct. 29, 1916.
5. "Strikers to Be Taught They Are Not above Law," *Los Angeles Times*, Sept. 15, 1912; Andrews, *Killing for Coal*; "Bomb Kills Six, Injures Scores in Defense Parade," *New York Times*, July 23, 1916; Frost, *The Mooney Case*.
6. "Dynamite Law Sure to Pass," *Los Angeles Times*, Feb. 8, 1911.
7. "Bomb Explosions Damage New Plant of Iron Company," *Chicago Daily Tribune*, Feb. 25, 1911.
8. "Bomb Endangers 75 Nonunionists," *Chicago Daily Tribune*, Mar. 24, 1911.
9. "Mine Superintendent Blown from His Bed by Dynamite," *Los Angeles Times*, March 31, 1911.
10. "Bomb Near Strikebreakers," *New York Times*, Apr. 16, 1911.
11. "Conduit Bombs Laid to Unions," *Chicago Daily Tribune*, June 19, 1911; "Another Dynamite Bomb Exploded in Chicago's Lighting Company War," *Los Angeles Times*, July 3, 1911.
12. "Death and Riots Mark Strike Day," *Chicago Daily Tribune*, Oct. 5, 1911.
13. "Strikers Fire on Policemen," *Los Angeles Times*, Feb. 27, 1912; "American Smelting Strike," *Wall Street Journal*, May 20, 1912; "Dynamite on Tracks of Boston Trolleys," *New York Times*, June 12, 1912.

14. "Coal Mine Is Set on Fire," *Washington Post*, Jan. 10, 1913; "Dynamite Explosion Shakes Buffalo City," *Los Angeles Times*, Apr. 9, 1913.

15. "Rioters at Butte Resort to Dynamite," *New York Times*, June 15, 1914.

16. "J. P. Morgan Is Shot by University Professor," *Washington Post*, July 4, 1915; "Plot to Dynamite Andrew Carnegie's Home," *New York Times*, June 24, 1915; "Dynamite Bomb for J. D. Archbold," *New York Times*, Nov. 22, 1915.

17. See, for example, "Labor's Preaching and Practice," *New York Times*, Nov. 18, 1912; "The Violence of American Trade Unions," *Living Age*, series 7, 58, no. 276 (Feb. 1, 1913): 311–13.

18. This was the case even in conflicts between rich and poor that ultimately produced more spectacular forms of violence. See, for example, Bernstein, *The New York City Draft Riots*; Avrich, *Haymarket Tragedy*; Krause, *Battle for Homestead*; Frost, *The Mooney Case*; Andrews, *Killing for Coal*; Green, *Death in the Haymarket*; Gage, *The Day Wall Street Exploded*.

19. The only two devoted scholarly treatments of the strike are Samuel Waitzman, "The New York City Transit Strike of 1916" (M.A. thesis, Columbia University, 1952); and "The General Strike Fiasco," the final chapter in Dubofsky, *When Workers Organize*, 126–47. Other briefer accounts appear in Emerson P. Schmidt, *Industrial Relations in Urban Transportation* (Minneapolis: University of Minnesota Press, 1937), 185–86; James Joseph McGinley, *Labor Relations in the New York Rapid Transit Systems, 1904–1944* (New York: King's Crown Press, 1949), 260–61; Levinson, *I Break Strikes!*, 172–81; and Joshua B. Freeman, *In Transit: The Transport Workers Union in New York City, 1933–1966* (New York: Oxford University Press, 1989), 17.

20. See, for example, "Sabotage at Work," *Los Angeles Times*, May 3, 1990; Martin Sprouse, ed., *Sabotage in the American Workplace: Anecdotes of Dissatisfaction, Mischief, and Revenge* (Oakland, Calif.: AK Press, 1992); Michael D. Crino, "Employee Sabotage: A Random or Preventable Phenomenon?" *Journal of Managerial Issues* 6, no. 3 (1994): 311–30; Joerg Dietz et al., "The Impact of Community Violence and an Organization's Procedural Justice Climate on Workplace Aggression," *Academy of Management Review* 24, no. 3 (1999): 317–26; Christine A. Henle, "Predicting Workplace Deviance from the Interaction between Organizational Justice and Personality," *Journal of Managerial Issues* 17, no. 2 (2005): 247–63.

21. "T. P. Shonts Dies at His Home Here," *New York Times*, Sept. 21, 1919.

22. Dubofsky, *When Workers Organize*, 128.

23. "T. P. Shonts Dies at His Home Here," *New York Times*, Sep. 21, 1919.

24. "Obituary: General Francis M. Drake," *New-York Tribune*, Nov. 21, 1903.

25. "T. P. Shonts Dies at His Home Here," *New York Times*, Sep. 21, 1919.

26. "Theodore P. Shonts," *Railroad Gazette*, Dec. 13, 1907, 709.

27. Ibid.; "General Railroad News," *Railroad Gazette*, Jan. 10, 1902, 34.

28. Dubofsky, *When Workers Organize*, 128; "Progress of Panama Canal Work Revealed by Theodore P. Shonts," *Chicago Daily Tribune*, Nov. 10, 1905. Shonts referred to the critics as "Hired Ananiases."

29. "Progress of Panama Canal Work Revealed by Theodore P. Shonts," *Chicago Daily Tribune*, Nov. 10, 1905.

30. Dubofsky, *When Workers Organize*, 129–30.

31. Ibid., 127.

32. Ibid.

33. Theodore P. Shonts, "The Development of Individualism the Duty of the Schools" (Des Moines, Iowa: Drake University, 1912), 8–12.

34. Hood, *722 Miles*, 73.

35. Theodore P. Shonts, "The Railroad Men at Panama," *North American Review* 199, no. 699 (1914), 229; "I'll Do as I Please: So Says Mr. Hedley of the Subway," *New-York Tribune*, Feb. 1, 1910.

36. "Fred. W. Whitridge, Railway Head, Dies," *New York Times*, Dec. 31, 1916.

37. Schmidt, *Industrial Relations*, 121–55; Victor John Di Santo, "The Streetcar Workers of Albany, 1900–1921: The Union Era" (Ph.D. diss., State University of New York at Binghamton, 1994); Waitzman, "New York City Transit Strike," 28. Schmidt's conclusion—that "[i]nstead of radicalism . . . the Amalgamated . . . has concerned itself largely with battles on the 'economic front'"—misses the radical implications in struggles for job control within the union, implications taken up by Montgomery in both *Workers' Control in America*, and *Fall of the House of Labor*.

38. Waitzman, "New York City Transit Strike," 7, 28; Dubofsky, *When Workers Organize*, 127–28.

39. "Fitzgerald Pleads for Socialist Help," *New York Times*, Sep. 18, 1916; "'Mother' Jones Says She Approves Riot," *New York Times*, Oct. 7, 1916.

40. For instance, despite the fact that the I.R.T. and N.Y. Railways shared a board of directors, the two companies' workers were organized by separate locals of the Amalgamated, Local 731 and Local 722, respectively. The leadership of these locals proved to have significant differences on devising strategy. See Interborough Rapid Transit Company, *The Effort to Tie Up the Street Railroad Systems of New York City* (New York: Interborough Rapid Transit Company, 1916), 16–17.

41. Waitzman, "New York City Transit Strike," 44.

42. On the historical evolution of balance between private and public interest in the corporate form, see William G. Roy, *Socializing Capital: The Rise of the Large Industrial Corporation in America* (Princeton, N.J.: Princeton University Press, 1997).

43. See Hood, *722 Miles*; Derrick, *Tunneling to the Future*; James Blaine Walker, *Fifty Years of Rapid Transit, 1864–1917* (New York: Law Printing Company, 1918).

44. "Public May Pay Car Lines' Loss," *New York Times*, Aug. 9, 1916.

45. Freeman, *In Transit*, 5.

46. In fact, because the strike diverted so many riders from streetcar lines to the relatively less affected subways and elevateds, the I.R.T. *improved* revenues once the city payments under the dual system kicked in. See Dubofsky, *When Workers Organize*, 127.

47. Shonts earned $100,000 per year from the I.R.T.; see "Morgan Scored by Fitzgerald," *New-York Tribune*, Sep. 12, 1916. On the urgency of greater and more systematic expansion, see Hood, *722 Miles*. On the near bankruptcy and loan arrangements, see "$3,300,000 Averts I.R.T. Receivership," *New-York Tribune*, Jan. 1, 1920; "I.R.T. Paid Bankers over $18,000,000," *New York Times*, Feb. 4, 1920.

48. For an argument that the dual system was ultimately successful in producing the needed expansion, see Derrick, *Tunneling to the Future*.

49. "5,000 Laborers Strike in Subway," *New-York Tribune*, Apr. 4, 1916. On working conditions, see Waitzman, "New York City Transit Strike," 29; for descriptions of transit work, see McGinley, *Labor Relations*, 125–256.

50. "3,500 May Join Subway Strike," *New-York Tribune*, Apr. 5, 1916.

51. Ibid.

52. "Subway Employers Break Negotiations," *New York Times*, Apr. 9, 1916.

53. Ibid.

54. Ibid.

55. Ibid.; "New Strike Ties Up All New Subways," *New York Times*, Apr. 8, 1916.

56. Dubofsky, *When Workers Organize*, 127; Hood, *722 Miles*.

57. See Hood, *722 Miles*, esp. 135–61.

58. Waitzman, "New York City Transit Strike," 14–22; Levinson, *I Break Strikes!*, 172–81.

59. "Strike Paralyzes Yonkers Car Lines," *New York Times*, July 23, 1916.

60. Ibid.

61. "Stones Hurled in Car Strike," *New-York Tribune*, July 26, 1916. The story does not specify that the motorman and conductor were strikers, but it seems likely they were; otherwise, they would probably have been attacked themselves.

62. "Bronx Thousands Walk," *New-York Tribune*, July 27, 1916.

63. Ibid.

64. "Strike Leaders to Meet Shonts and Mayor Today," *New York Times*, Aug. 3, 1916. For more on working conditions, see Dubofsky, *When Workers Organize*; McGinley, *Labor Relations*.

65. "Bronx Thousands Walk," *New-York Tribune*, July 27, 1916.

66. Ibid.

67. "Strike Crisis on Third Av. 'L' and Subways," *New-York Tribune*, July 31, 1916.

68. Ibid.

69. See, for example, N.Y. Railways Company poster, "$200 Reward," and I.R.T. circular of Sept. 12, 1916, both in ABP, Box 4, Correspondence, Sept.–Oct. 1916.

70. "Strike Paralyzes Yonkers Car Lines," *New York Times*, July 23, 1916.

71. Dubofsky, *When Workers Organize*, 127–28.

72. Ibid., 148.

73. "Strike Crisis on Third Av. 'L' and Subways," *New-York Tribune*, July 31, 1916.

74. Ibid.

75. Dubofsky, *When Workers Organize*, 148.

76. Managers also believed it—Shonts referred to the Amalgamated in a private telegram to Belmont as "these group [*sic*] of alien agitators." See T. P. Shonts to August Belmont, Aug. 7, 1916, ABP, Box 4, Correspondence, Jan.–Aug. 1916.

77. "Interboro Gets Loyalty Pledge from Trainmen," *New York Times*, Aug. 4, 1916.

78. "Madison Avenue First Hit," *New York Times*, Aug. 5, 1916.

79. "800 Green Car Men Go Out on Strike," *New-York Tribune*, Aug. 5, 1916.

80. "Madison Avenue First Hit," *New York Times*, Aug. 5, 1916.

81. Ibid.; "800 Green Car Men Go Out on Strike," *New-York Tribune*, Aug. 5, 1916.

82. "Sporadic Rioting in New York Street Car Strike," *Los Angeles Times*, Aug. 6, 1916.

83. Ibid.

84. Ibid.
85. "The Traction Strike," *New York Times*, Aug. 6, 1916.
86. T. P. Shonts to August Belmont, Aug. 7, 1916, ABP, Box 4, Correspondence, Jan.–Aug. 1916.
87. Ibid.

15 • Making the World Safe for Inequality

Epigraph: Interborough Rapid Transit Company, *Interborough Rapid Transit* 3, Apr. 6, 1917, NYHS.

1. "Public May Pay Car Lines' Loss," *New York Times*, Aug. 9, 1916. Six days later, the *Wall Street Journal* put the operating losses at $63,000. See "Subway and Elevated Earnings Helped by Strike," *Wall Street Journal*, Aug. 15, 1916.
2. Ibid.
3. Roland Marchand, *Creating the Corporate Soul: The Rise of Public Relations and Corporate Imagery in American Big Business* (Berkeley: University of California Press, 1998), 7–9.
4. Ibid.; Shirley Harrison, *Public Relations: An Introduction*, 2nd ed. (London: Thomson Learning, 2000), 18–19.
5. Strouse, *Morgan*, xi–xii.
6. Waitzman, "The New York City Transit Strike of 1916," 3.
7. See publicity materials contained in ABP, Box 4, Correspondence, Sep.– Oct. 1916; Interborough, *The Effort to Tie Up the Street Railroad*.
8. Ibid.; Waitzman, "The New York City Transit Strike of 1916," 20–24.
9. "The Traction Strike," *New York Times*, Aug. 6, 1916; Public Service Commission, "Case No. 2126" ["Report Relative to the Strike on the Surface Car Lines of New York, and the Action Taken by the Committee"] (New York State, 1916).
10. "Demands Ready for Interborough," *New York Times*, Aug. 6, 1916; "New Locals Formed by Car Men's Union," *New York Times*, Aug. 10, 1916.
11. For a still-valid explanation of why this is so, see John R. Commons, *Industrial Government* (New York: Macmillan, 1921), 406–7.
12. "Interborough, *The Effort to Tie Up the Street Railroad*, 31.
13. "New Locals Formed by Car Men's Union," *New York Times*, Aug. 10, 1916; Minutes, *New York Strike 1916: Conference between Management and Employees* (Aug. 30, 1916), 21.

14. Minutes, *New York Strike 1916* (Aug. 18, 1916), 6–9; "Carmen Charge Discrimination," *New-York Tribune*, Aug. 12, 1916.

15. "Car Men Vote to Strike if Parleys Fail," *New-York Tribune*, Aug. 17, 1916.

16. Minutes, *New York Strike 1916* (Aug.–Sep., 1916).

17. Minutes, *New York Strike 1916* (Aug. 17, 1916), vi–xvi.

18. "Men to Avoid Hasty Action on Car Strike," *New-York Tribune*, Aug. 18, 1916. Hedley was probably stalling intentionally because voting for the Brotherhood was taking place simultaneously under I.R.T. supervision. See Interborough, *The Effort to Tie Up the Street Railroad*, 30.

19. Minutes, *New York Strike 1916* (Aug. 17, 1916), ix. The "Four Hundred" was shorthand for New York Society's elite.

20. Minutes, *New York Strike 1916* (Aug. 18, 1916).

21. "Mayor Averts Car Strike as Shonts Yields," *New-York Tribune*, Aug. 22, 1916.

22. "Demands of Subway and Elevated Employees Not Expected to Lead to a Strike," *Wall Street Journal*, Aug. 26, 1916.

23. Minutes, *New York Strike 1916* (Aug. 31, 1916), 53.

24. Ibid., 54.

25. Ibid., 57.

26. Interborough Men Threaten to Strike," *New York Times*, Sept. 2, 1916: "Union Will Press Interboro Demand," *New York Times*, Sept. 4, 1916.

27. "To the Employees of the Interborough Rapid Transit Company," Sep. 5, 1916, ABP, Box 4, Correspondence, Sep.–Oct. 1916.

28. "Interboro Men to Vote Again before Striking," *New York Times*, Sep. 5, 1916.

29. Ibid.; "Five Thousand on Way to Break Car Strike," *Los Angeles Times*, Sept. 7, 1916; Levinson, *I Break Strikes!*, 172–81.

30. Interborough, *The Effort to Tie Up the Street Railroad*.

31. "Interboro Men to Vote Again before Striking," *New York Times*, Sep. 5, 1916.

32. "Substance or Shadow?" *New York Times*, Sep. 6, 1916; "Interboro Rejects Demands of Union; Prepares for Subway-Elevated Strike; Mayor Asked to Give Police Protection," *New York Times*, Sep. 5, 1916; "Tube and Elevated Strike Now Expected in New York," *Chicago Daily Tribune*, Sep. 5, 1916; "Interboro Men to Vote Again before Striking," *New York Times*, Sep. 5, 1916.

33. "New York Faces General Tie-Up," *Boston Daily Globe*, Sep. 7, 1916.

34. "Interboro Men to Vote Again before Striking," *New York Times*, Sep. 5, 1916.

35. "New York Faces General Tie-Up," *Boston Daily Globe*, Sep. 7, 1916.

36. "Third Ave. Men Vote Today," *New York Times*, Sep. 7, 1916.

37. "Car Service Crippled," *New York Times*, Sep. 7, 1916.

38. "New York Faces General Tie-Up," *Boston Daily Globe*, Sep. 7, 1916.

39. "Car Service Crippled," *New York Times*, Sep. 7, 1916.

40. Ibid.

41. "Substance or Shadow?" *New York Times*, Sep. 6, 1916; " 'Leaders' Who Don't Lead," *New-York Tribune*, Sep. 9, 1916.

42. Public Service Commission, "Minutes of Hearing" (Sept. 7, 1916), 585, ABP, Box 6, I.R.T. Miscellaneous Papers.

43. "Strike Disorders Checked by Police," *New York Times*, Sep. 8, 1916.

44. "Street Jam Grows as Strike Holds On," *New York Times*, Sep. 9, 1916.

45. "May Join Car Strike," *Washington Post*, Sep. 11, 1916; "Would Tie Up All New York," *Boston Daily Globe*, Sep. 11, 1916; " 'War to a Finish,' Traffic Head Says," *New York Times*, Sep. 11, 1916.

46. "Mob Smashes Car with Police Aboard," *New York Times*, Sep. 12, 1916.

47. "Morgan Scored by Fitzgerald," *New-York Tribune*, Sep. 12, 1916.

48. "Fitzgerald Pleads for Socialist Help," *New York Times*, Sep. 18, 1916. For more on the general strike debacle, see Dubofsky, *When Workers Organize*.

49. "Rioters Beat Men on Cars," *Boston Daily Globe*, Sep. 20, 1916; "Strikers Storm Car Barns; Several Employees Beaten," *Hartford Courant*, Sep. 20, 1916.

50. Ibid.

51. Ibid.

52. "Passengers Hurt in Night Attacks on Transit Lines," *New York Times*, Sep. 20, 1916.

53. "Dynamiter Is Balked," *Los Angeles Times*, Sep. 21, 1916; "More Rioting in New York," *Boston Daily Globe*, Sep. 20, 1916; "Police Battle with Rioters in New York," *San Francisco Chronicle*, Sep. 20, 1916.

54. "Civil War in New York," *The Evening Sun* [New York], Sep. 21, 1916.

55. "Mayor to Call Troops if Disorder Spreads," *New-York Tribune*, Sep. 22, 1916; "Straus Upholds Mitchel," *New York Times*, Sep. 22, 1916.

56. See Dubofsky, *When Workers Organize*, 126–47.

57. "Car Strike Mobs Fight the Police in Westchester," *New York Times*, Oct. 2, 1916.

58. Ibid.

59. "Mobs Again Attack Westchester Cars," *New York Times*, Oct. 3, 1916.

60. "Car Riot Started by 'Mother Jones,' " *New York Times*, Oct. 6, 1916.

61. Ibid.
62. "'Mother' Jones Says She Approves Riot," *New York Times*, Oct. 7, 1916.
63. Ibid.
64. Gage, *Day Wall Street Exploded*, 79–82.
65. Commission on Industrial Relations, *Final Report of the Commission on Industrial Relations* (Washington, D.C.: Government Printing Office, 1916), 30. This quote appears differently in "Guggenheim Wants State to Hire Idle," *New-York Tribune*, Jan. 22, 1915, as "Were it not for philanthropic work there would be a revolution here."
66. "Investigate Car Service," *New York Times*, Oct. 14, 1916.
67. "Take Police from Subway," *New York Times*, Oct. 15, 1916.
68. Ibid.
69. "Five Men Sought in Subway Blast," *New-York Tribune*, Oct. 26, 1916.
70. "Tenderness for Dynamiters," *New York Times*, Oct. 27, 1916.
71. "Put Extra Guards on Dynamite Caches," *New York Times*, Oct. 26, 1916.
72. These men either confessed or were convicted. At least three others were initially implicated, and one was indicted, but prosecution proved unsuccessful for any but these four. See "Trial of Union Man Begins in Subway Dynamiting Case," *New-York Tribune*, Mar. 8, 1917; "Says Violence Was Urged," *New York Times*, Mar. 9, 1917; "To Cell Instead of Altar," *Washington Post*, Mar. 14, 1917; "Dynamiters Plead Guilty," *Christian Science Monitor*, Mar. 15, 1917; "Explosion Was Strikers," *Boston Daily Globe*, Mar. 16, 1917; "Herlihy Confesses Dynamiting Subway," *New York Times*, Mar. 16, 1917; "Subway Dynamiter Tells of Plot to Blow Up Station," *New-York Tribune*, Mar. 16, 1917; "Dynamiters Are Sentenced," *Washington Post*, Mar. 20, 1917; "McGuire Pleads Guilty," *New-York Tribune*, Mar. 23, 1917.
73. "Six Men, Trapped, Confess Dynamite Plots," *New York Times*, Nov. 4, 1916.
74. For Murnagh, see Draft Card for James J. Murnagh, Ancestry.com, *World War I Selective Service System Draft Registration Cards, 1917–1918* (Provo, Utah: Ancestry.com Operations, 2008). Original data: United States Selective Service System (Washington, D.C.: National Archives and Records Administration). For McGuire, see Bureau of the Census, *Fourteenth Census of the United States: 1920—Population*, New York County, New York, Manhattan Borough, Ward 7, Series T625, Roll 1197, 4A and "McGuire Pleads Guilty," *New-York Tribune*, Mar. 23, 1917; for Herlihy, see Bureau of the Census, *Fourteenth Census of the United States: 1920—Population*, Ossining County, New York, Ossining, Series T625,

Roll 1276, 5A; for Molsky and his various aliases ("William McChord," "William McCord," or "James McCord," none of which the papers could decide on as his real name) see "2 Subway Plotters Guilty," *New-York Tribune*, Mar. 3, 1917; and "Jail for Subway Plotters," *New York Times*, Mar. 20, 1917.

75. "Six Men, Trapped, Confess Dynamite Plots," *New York Times*, Nov. 4, 1916.

76. "Dynamiters Plead Guilty," *Christian Science Monitor*, Mar. 15, 1917.

77. "Herlihy Confesses Dynamiting Subway," *New York Times*, Mar. 16, 1917.

78. "Freed in Dynamiting Case," *New-York Tribune*, Mar. 17, 1917.

79. "McGuire Pleads Guilty," *New-York Tribune*, Mar. 23, 1917.

80. Gage, *Day Wall Street Exploded*, 90–91.

81. Minutes, *New York Strike 1916* (Sep. 5, 1916), 1; Minutes, *New York Strike 1916* (Sep. 6, 1916), 1–2.

82. "Six Men, Trapped, Confess Dynamite Plots," *New York Times*, Nov. 4, 1916.

83. Ibid.

84. Ibid.

85. "Explosion Was Strikers," *Boston Daily Globe*, Mar. 16, 1917.

86. Gage, *Day Wall Street Exploded*, 90–91.

87. "Bomb Set by Strikers Wrecks New York Subway," *Los Angeles Times*, Oct. 26, 1916.

88. For numbers in the strike, see Freeman, *In Transit*, 17.

89. Waitzman, "The New York City Transit Strike of 1916," 75–76.

90. Freeman, *In Transit*, 17; Waitzman, "The New York City Transit Strike of 1916," 82.

91. "We Ask Your Help and The Public's Response," *Interborough Rapid Transit*, Apr. 7, 1917, NYHS.

92. *Interborough Rapid Transit*, Dec. 28, 1917, NYHS.

93. See Marchand, *Creating the Corporate Soul*.

94. Karl Marx, *Capital*, vol. 1, trans. Ben Fowkes (New York: Penguin Classic, 2004); Max Weber, *The Protestant Ethic and the Spirit of Capitalism*, trans. Talcott Parsons (1930; repr., London: Routledge, 1992). For a more succinct evaluation of capitalism's compulsion to compete, see Ellen Meiksins Wood, "Modernity, Postmodernity, or Capitalism?" *Review of International Political Economy* 4, no. 3 (1997): 539–560; and Wood, *Origin of Capitalism*.

95. Shays's Rebellion and Thomas Skidmore's Working Men's Party offer prime examples. On Skidmore, see Wilentz, *Chants Democratic*. On Shays,

see Leonard L. Richards, *Shays's Rebellion: The American Revolution's Final Battle* (Philadelphia: University of Pennsylvania Press, 2002).

96. See, for example, the analysis of Samuel Adams's repression of Shays's Rebellion in William Pencak, "Samuel Adams and Shays's Rebellion," *New England Quarterly* 62, no. 1 (1989): 63–74. At first glance, Shays's Rebellion is a sticky example to use when discussing the improvement of property; as Richards shows in *Shays's Rebellion*, the greatest motivating pressure on the rebels came from tax collectors, not private creditors. The distinction is ultimately irrelevant as far as conflictual class relations are concerned, as the heavy tax burden resulted from the efforts of a wealthy elite to pay down debt on Revolutionary War bonds (owned by speculators with whom that same elite socialized and did business) at the expense of struggling farmers. The property being improved, as Samuel Adams understood, was the United States itself—a long-term investment of enormous capital significance.

97. Wood, "Modernity, Postmodernity, or Capitalism?" 548; *Democracy against Capitalism: Renewing Historical Materialism* (Cambridge: Cambridge University Press, 1995).

98. This view is commonly (and, for the most part, correctly) attributed to the social and economic legacy of the post–World War II and Cold War moments in America and Europe. The major forefathers of its intellectual genealogy include F. A. Hayek, *The Road to Serfdom* (1944; repr., Chicago: University of Chicago Press, 1994); Karl Popper, *The Open Society and Its Enemies* (London: G. Routledge & Sons, 1945); Kenneth J. Arrow, *Social Choice and Individual Values* (New York: Wiley, 1951); Milton Friedman and Rose D. Friedman, *Capitalism and Freedom* (Chicago: University of Chicago Press, 1962). For exceptional, recent, and far more detailed overviews of how this intellectual defense of liberal capitalism evolved in the mid-twentieth century, see S. M. Amadae, *Rationalizing Capitalist Democracy: The Cold War Origins of Rational Choice Liberalism* (Chicago: University of Chicago Press, 2003), and Angus Robinson Burgin, "The Return of Laissez-Faire" (Ph.D. diss., Harvard University, 2009).

99. John Maynard Keynes, *The General Theory of Employment, Interest, and Money* (New York: Harcourt, Brace, 1936); John Kenneth Galbraith, *The Affluent Society* (Boston: Houghton Mifflin, 1958). Keynes and Galbraith were both skeptical of capitalism's operations, but their recommendations for adjustment suggested that their overriding concern was the regulation and assurance of reasonable consumption.

100. A small international sampling, from the industrial revolution to the present, of representative "eruption and suppression" both large and small: the Chartist movement; the Working Men's Party in New York; 1848 European uprisings; the Paris Commune; the Great Strike of 1877; the Populist movement; the Ludlow Massacre; the Russian Revolution; C.I.O. sit-down strikes of the 1930s; the Cuban revolution; the C.I.A.'s overthrow of Mohammad Mossadegh in Iran, Jacobo Arbenz in Guatemala, and its assistance of the coup against Salvador Allende in Chile; 2011 popular protests against austerity measures in Greece; 2013 protests against the neoliberal authoritarianism of Recep Tayyip Erdoğan in Turkey.

101. Lenin's famous dictum, "A democratic republic is the best possible political shell for capitalism," offers a view, generally supported by history, that capitalism may have the advantage in this fight. Characteristically, Lenin underestimates democracy. See V. I. Lenin, *The State and Revolution: The Marxist Theory of the State and the Tasks of the Proletariat in the Revolution* (1918; repr., Lenin Internet Archive: marxists.org, 1999), www.marxists.org /archive/lenin/works/1917/staterev/. A more thoughtful and tempered exploration of the tensions between democracy and capitalism (and between liberalism and socialism) can be found in Perry Anderson's critique of Norberto Bobbio; see Anderson, *A Zone of Engagement* (New York: Verso, 1992), 87–129.

102. For a history of the strike wave of which the 1916 transit strikes were a part, see Priscilla Murolo and A. B. Chitty, *From the Folks Who Brought You the Weekend: A Short, Illustrated History of Labor in the United States*, illust. Joe Sacco (New York: New Press, 2001). On radicalism, see Avrich, *Haymarket Tragedy*, and *Sacco and Vanzetti*; Goldman, *Living My Life*; Melvyn Dubofsky, *"Big Bill" Haywood* (Manchester: Manchester University Press, 1987), and *We Shall Be All: A History of the Industrial Workers of the World* (Chicago: Quadrangle Press, 1969). On the domestic front before America's entry into World War I, see Justus D. Doenecke, *Nothing Less Than War: A New History of America's Entry into World War I* (Lexington: University of Kentucky Press, 2011).

103. "T. P. Shonts' 'Friend'," *Chicago Daily Tribune*, Nov. 11, 1919; Shonts, "Development of Individualism," 8; "Sued as Vamp," *Chicago Daily Tribune*, Jan. 22, 1920.

104. "Sued as Vamp," *Chicago Daily Tribune*, Jan. 22, 1920.

105. "Mrs. Shonts Scores in Court," *Washington Post*, Feb. 10, 1920; "Amanda Thomas Wins Tilt with Mrs. T. P. Shonts," *Chicago Daily Tribune*, Feb. 11, 1921.

106. "I.R.T. Paid Bankers over $18,000,000," *New York Times*, Feb. 4, 1920.

107. Ibid.

108. "'Reds' Slain by Bomb They Were Making," *New-York Tribune*, July 5, 1914; "Bombs in Cathedral and at St. Alphonsus Where I.W.W. Rioted," *New-York Tribune*, Oct. 14, 1914; "Bombs Exploded in St. Patrick's and at a Church," *New York Times*, Oct. 14, 1914.

109. "Slavers' Bombs Rock Bronx Court," *New York Times*, Nov. 12, 1914; "Bronx Court Bomb Reds' Calling Card," *New-York Tribune*, Nov. 13, 1914; "Lighted Bomb Put in Tombs Court," *New York Times*, Nov. 15, 1914.

110. "Dynamite Hall of Bronx Borough," *New York Times*, May 4, 1915; "Slavers' Bomb Shakes Bronx Borough Hall, *New-York Tribune*, May 4, 1915.

111. "Bombs in Cathedral and at St. Alphonsus Where I.W.W. Rioted," *New-York Tribune*, Oct. 14, 1914; "What Must Be Done with the Bomb Throwers," *New-York Tribune*, Nov. 29, 1914.

112. "What Must Be Done with the Bomb Throwers," *New-York Tribune*, Nov. 29, 1914.

113. "Let the Anarchists Parade," *New-York Tribune*, July 9, 1914.

114. "5,000 at Memorial to Anarchist Dead," *New York Times*, July 12, 1914; Gage, *The Day Wall Street Exploded*, 102.

115. See, for example, "German Rocks C.P.R. Bridge with Dynamite," *New-York Tribune*, Feb. 3, 1915; James Davenport Whelpley, "The German War in America," *Fortnightly Review* 98, no. 585 (Sep. 1915): 454–64; "German Leaders, in Dynamite Plot, Held in New York," *Atlanta Constitution*, Oct. 25, 1915; "Uncovering a Great Conspiracy," *New-York Tribune*, Nov. 16, 1915; "Von Papen Paid Money to Persons Charged with Using Dynamite," *Atlanta Constitution*, Jan. 15, 1916; "Dynamite Plots Bared in Detail by Von der Goltz," *New York Times*, Apr. 21, 1916; "Many Explosions since War Began," *New York Times*, July 31, 1916.

116. "First Explosion Terrific," *New York Times*, July 31, 1916; "Three Die, Scores Hurt, $25,000,000 Loss in Big Munitions Explosions," *Washington Post*, July 31, 1916;

117. On anarchist bravado, see Gage, *The Day Wall Street Exploded*, 96–110, esp. her treatment of Alexander Berkman.

118. Ibid., 108–11.

119. Ibid., 110–19.

120. Ibid., 119.

121. "Two Deported Anarchists," *New-York Tribune*, Nov. 28, 1919.

122. "Starting the Exodus," *New-York Tribune*, Dec. 6, 1919.

123. Joseph A. McCartin, *Labor's Great War: The Struggle for Industrial Democracy and the Origins of Modern American Labor Relations, 1912–1920*, 88–91.

124. Gage, *The Day Wall Street Exploded*, 113–14.

125. Ibid., 233–34; McCartin, *Labor's Great War*, 173–83, 208–20.

126. Beverly Gage, "Radical Solutions to Economic Inequality," Feb. 15, 2012, *Slate*, www.slate.com/articles/news_and_politics/history/2012/02/income_inequality_the_government_had_better_ideas_for_fixing_it_100_years_ago.html.

127. This bargain would be tested vigorously in the early years, especially in the labor uprisings of the 1920s and 1930s; see, for instance, James Green's forthcoming book from Pantheon Books on the West Virginia Mine Wars.

Epilogue

Epigraph: Herman Melville, "Bartleby, the Scrivener: A Story of Wall Street," *The Norton Anthology of American Literature*, vol. 1, 5th ed. (New York: W. W. Norton, 1998), 2353.

1. Terry Eagleton, *Sweet Violence: The Idea of the Tragic* (Malden, Mass.: Blackwell, 2003).

2. Eagleton, *Sweet Violence*, 290.

3. Arthur Miller, *Death of a Salesman: Certain Private Conversations in Two Acts and a Requiem* (New York: Viking Press, 1949).

4. Thompson, *Making of the English Working Class* (New York: Vintage, 1966), 12–13.

5. This refers to the financial collapse of 2008 and its aftermath.

6. Sheila Post-Lauria, "Canonical Texts and Context: The Example of Herman Melville's 'Bartleby, the Scrivener: A Story of Wall Street,'" *College Literature* 20, no. 2 (1993): 196–205.

7. Herman Melville, "Bartleby, the Scrivener: A Story of Wall Street," *The Norton Anthology of American Literature*, vol. 1, 5th ed. (New York: W. W. Norton, 1998), 2330.

8. David Kuebrich, "Melville's Doctrine of Assumptions: The Hidden Ideology of Capitalist Production in 'Bartleby,'" *New England Quarterly* 69, no. 3 (1996): 381–405.

9. Melville, "Bartleby," 2343–47.

10. Ibid., 2353.

11. Ibid., 2349.

12. Basil Maxwell Maly, Commission on Industrial Relations, *Final Report of the Commission on Industrial Relations* (Washington, D.C.: Government Printing Office, 1916), 30.

13. As quoted in Paul Krugman, "Galt, Gold and God," *New York Times*, Aug. 24, 2012, A25.

14. To their credit, some Occupiers have grappled with this elision, in part because it has unavoidably generated heated debates within the movement regarding the lines of race, class, and gender that divide its ranks. See, for example, Kai Wright, "Here's to Occupying Wall Street! (If Only That Were Actually Happening)," *Colorlines*, Oct. 3, 2011, http://colorlines.com /archives/2011/10/heres_to_occupying_wall_street_if_only_that_were _actually_happening.html; Kenyon Farrow, "Occupy Wall Street's Race Problem," *American Prospect*, Oct. 24, 2011; Karen McVeigh, "Occupy Wall Street's Women Struggle to Make Their Voices Heard," *The Guardian*, Nov. 30, 2011; Rebecca Burns, "As Occupy the Hood National Gathering Concludes, Questions about Race and Occupy Persist," *In These Times*, July 27, 2012, www.inthesetimes.com/uprising/entry/13586/as_occupy_the _hood_national_gathering_concludes_questions_about_race_and_oc/.

Acknowledgments

The Unions at Yale, and in particular the Graduate Employees and Students Organization (GESO), are inextricably entwined in this book. Thanks to my organizers—Jay Driskell, Carlos Aramayo, Anita Seth, Ariana Paulson, and Susan Valentine—and my comrades, especially Jeffrey Boyd, Brenda Carter, Annemarie Strassel, Michael Mullins, Melissa Mason, Mandi Jackson, Sarah Haley, Sarah Egan, Stephanie Greenlea, Lisa and Chris Covert, Adam Patten, Marcy Kaufman, Zane Curtis-Olsen, Robin Scheffler, Antoine Lentacker, Kate Irving, Ted Fertik, Max Fraser, and Gabe Winant. One day longer, friends.

Throughout my years at Yale, David W. Blight provided a model as a teacher, mentor, and scholar. His faith in this project never flagged. Beverly Gage's generosity has been nothing short of astounding; she is a confidante, ally, and the wise older sister I never had. In addition to his insightful readings and regular encouragement, Matthew Frye Jacobson ultimately gave me perhaps the best advice of all: to do as I was told by my editor, the brilliant and inimitable Joyce Seltzer. Thanks to Joyce, and to Brian Distelberg, for shepherding this book to publication. Thanks also to the outside readers on the manuscript who offered astute suggestions for revision, and to Vickie West and Edward Wade for their swift and expert copyediting.

I have received invaluable support in the form of fellowships from Yale University, the Gilder Lehrman Institute for American History, the Mrs. Giles Whiting Foundation, the Tobin Project, the New-York Historical Society, and the New School. Nina Nazionale, Ted O'Reilly, Tammy Kiter, Joseph Ditta, Henry Raine, and everyone else at the N-YHS helped transform my manuscript into a book, as did my fellow balcony reprobates, Matthew Dziennik, Jordan Stein, and Courtney Fullilove. The librarians at the New York Public Library went out of their way to help me, as did Cheryl Beredo at Cornell's Kheel Center Archives, and the superb personnel in the Columbia Rare Book and Manuscript Library, Harvard's Schlesinger and Baker libraries, and Yale's Sterling Memorial and Beinecke libraries. Colleagues at both the New School and Wesleyan offered crucial help and encouragement at various stages; thanks to Louise Walker, Cyp Stephenson, Jeremy Varon, Oz Frankel, Julia Ott, Elaine Abelson, Dael Norwood, Catherine McNeur, Rachel Sherman, Courtney Fullilove, Lori Flannigan, Ann Tanasi, Ann Wightman, Demetrius Eudell, and Ron Schatz.

Of my cohort in graduate school and beyond, Caitlin Casey, Ariana Paulson, Julia Irwin, Steve Prince, Sam Schaffer, Jason Ward, Sarah Haley, Grace Leslie, Brenda Santos, Alison Greene, Mike Amezcua, Sarah Levine-Gronningsater, John Logan Nichols, and Kirsten Weld have at various times read my writing, commented on my ideas, and provided consistent intellectual and personal support. Kirsten is also among friends to whom I owe a special debt because they periodically let me use their homes as my office. Kirsten and Carlos, Susie Jakes and Jeff Prescott, Brenda Carter and Adam Solomon, Lily Sheehan and Chris Nichols: thank you for providing me with such well-appointed and book-stocked work environments when I needed them.

This book exists because of my family's love. My parents-in-law, Bob and Geramy Noone, continue to babysit their grandson at a moment's notice, surely speeding me along in my work as much as, if not more than, anything else. John Handrik, Jessica Handrik, and Rob Noone have likewise been pillars of support in countless ways. My mother, Nina Bernstein, has consistently improved my prose through careful editing; she also taught me, by both word and example, that without empathy even the greatest writers are hucksters. My father, Andreas Huyssen, has expanded horizons for generations of readers and students the world over, myself included, but his greatest gift—unconditional fatherly love—has remained the exclusive province of only two people, my brother and me. Daniel (to whom I owe thanks of a different order) and I count ourselves the luckiest sons we know. Let's hope we pass that luck on to our respective children, June and Benjamin. Two people also deserve special mention as surrogate family and consistent backers of my research and writing: Aaron Jakes and Kate Burch, whose true friendship, intellectual inspiration, and generosity have buoyed me since childhood.

Finally, I thank my incomparable wife, Mary Reynolds, whose passion and ability in her vocation have motivated and informed me in my own, and to whom this work is dedicated. During the years I was formulating, researching, and writing this book, Mary's tenacious struggle helped to empower thousands of working people: clerical staff and graduate employees in New Haven, housekeepers in Fresno, public-school cafeteria workers in Philadelphia, cocktail servers in Las Vegas, bellmen in Toronto, stadium concession operators in Vancouver, and not least of all, us. She is the most courageous, principled, and determined person I know, while also managing to be a fantastic mother to our son and a tirelessly loving partner to me.

I began these acknowledgments by thanking GESO, so it is only appropriate that I conclude by thanking Mary, who led the very first meeting of the union's History organizing committee I attended, just shy of ten years ago. I cannot recall the substance of that meeting, but I remember quite clearly thinking to myself as Mary began to run through the agenda, "I wish I were sitting closer to her."

That inclination has never subsided.

Index

Shaw, Anna Howard, 181, 195–196, 199

Shaw, Elizabeth, 73–74, 76, 78–79, 88, 312n82

Shaw, George Bernard, 177–178

Shays's Rebellion, 356n96

shirtwaist industry, New York: strikes in, 149, 153–154, 156, 160, 167–179, 181–187; Hippodrome meeting and, 192–200; Colony Club tea and, 203–212; Carnegie Hall meeting and, 213–223; Triangle fire and, 223–225

Shonts, Millie (Mrs. T. P.), 232, 265–266

Shonts, Theodore Perry "T. P.": transit strikes and, 227, 241–244, 247–253, 255, 350n76; background of, 231–236, 349n47; public relations strategy of, 245–247, 253, 262–263, 268, 270–271; scandals and, 265–266

Simkhovitch, Mary, 177

slum tourism, 142

Smyth, Frederick, 86–87

social Darwinism, 5, 15, 329–330n27

Socialist Party, 181, 199, 205, 208, 214, 216, 255

socialists, 55, 125, 200, 203, 209–212; individuals as, 148, 160, 194–195, 203–204, 205; Carnegie Hall meeting and, 214–216, 220–223, 345n38; violence and, 235, 255, 267–269

social justice, 109, 126–129

Society for the Prevention of Cruelty to Children (S.P.C.C.), 73

Society for the Prevention of Pauperism (S.P.P.), 68, 72

Society for the Relief of Poor Widows with Small Children (S.R.P.W.), 68

Solomon & Leffler, 168

Spencer, Edmund, 69

Stokes, J.G. Phelps, 194–195, 339n61

Stokes, Rose Pastor. See Pastor, Rose

Straus, Oscar S., 238–239, 243, 248, 253, 256

strikebreakers, 153, 228–230, 270; garment industry strikes and, 165, 167–170, 174, 176–178, 219; transit strikes and, 238, 240, 247, 252–253, 255, 259, 262. See also private detectives

strikes: shirtwaist industry general (1909–1910), 149, 153–154, 156, 160, 167–179, 181–187, 223–225; neckwear industry general (1909), 165–174; Hippodrome meeting and, 192–200, 211; Colony Club tea and, 203–212; Carnegie Hall meeting and, 213–223; contextualizing transit, 230–231; Shonts, management and, 231–237; subway construction (Spring 1916), 237–239; surface lines (July–August, 1916), 239–244; New York transit (September 1916), 252–263. See also Uprising of the Twenty Thousand

subcontracting: landlords and, 51; New York transit and, 158; garment industry and, 162, 223. See also sweatshops

Subway Constructors' Union, 237

suffrage: property and, 5, 286n13. See also women's suffrage

suffragettes, 170–171, 190–191, 220. See also women's suffrage

Sumner, William Graham, 4–5

sweatshops, 138–139, 142, 162

Sweeney, C. E., 119–120

Taft, William Howard, 139

Tammany, 23, 67, 307n16

Tarbell, Ida, 177

Taylor, Frederick, 215

temperance, Salvation Army and, 91. See also Church Temperance Society (C.T.S.)

tenants (of tenements): cross-examination of, 5, 21–25; prescriptive attitudes toward, 25–29, 61; endangered lives of, 40, 49–52, 60, 62; eviction of, 47–48, 53–54; Wald's view of, 136–137